THE POLITICS OF HOMOSEXUALITY

THE POLITICS OF

Homosexuality

Toby Marotta

Boston

HOUGHTON MIFFLIN COMPANY

1981

Library of Congress Cataloging in Publication Data

Marotta, Toby.
The politics of homosexuality.

A revision of Marotta's thesis, Harvard.
Includes bibliographical references and index.
1. Gay liberation movement—United States.
I. Title.
HQ76.8.U5M37   1981   306.7′2′0973   80-29418
ISBN 0-395-29477-0
ISBN 0-395-31338-4 pbk.

Printed in the United States of America

P 10 9 8 7 6 5 4 3 2 1

The author is grateful for permission to quote from the following sources:

The Gay Mystique, by Peter Fisher. Copyright © 1972 by Peter Fisher.
Reprinted with permission of Stein and Day Publishers.
The Greening of America, by Charles A. Reich. Copyright © 1970 by
Charles A. Reich. Reprinted by permission of Random House.
SDS, by Kirkpatrick Sale. Copyright © 1973 by Kirkpatrick Sale. Reprinted
by permission of Random House.

For Rusty

CONTENTS

FOREWORD

WHEN THE HISTORY of twentieth-century America is written, the 1970s will be recorded as the decade in which gay life won legitimacy. People with homosexual feelings more easily, openly, and enthusiastically engaged in homosexual behavior, defined themselves as lesbian and gay, participated in the lesbian and gay male subcultures, and insisted that their ways of expressing themselves sexually be respected by the people around them and by society at large. There was a proliferation of bars, discos, restaurants, galleries, resorts, travel agencies, publishing companies, bookstores, bathhouses, sex shops, escort services, and other businesses catering to the gay community. Openly gay people joined together in every variety of ad hoc group, organized community centers, founded professional associations, formed political clubs, settled neighborhoods, mobilized voters, consulted with business and civic leaders and public officials, won coverage in the established communications media, and pressed successfully for laws banning discrimination on the basis of sexual orientation. Gays were courted by political candidates, they won elections, and they were appointed to major positions in the Democratic and Republican parties. They were even invited to the White House.

The emergence of gay people as a force in modern America can be traced to gay political activity, particularly as it evolved in New York City. Though important events took place in Los Angeles, San Francisco, Boston, and Washington, D.C., breakthroughs in New York were especially important because they were publicized extensively and well analyzed by the participants. To understand the history of gay political activity generally, it is necessary to know how the politics of homosexuality found direction and meaning in New York City.

In the fall of 1973, as a Harvard graduate student trained to see voluntary associations as the prime movers in politics, even in "movement" politics, I set out to uncover this history. From leaders in Manhattan, I learned that the initiatives then current (such as the National Gay Task Force's push to have the American Psychiatric Association remove homosexuality from its list of mental disorders) were the legacy of three distinct waves of gay political activity, each spearheaded by a different pair of Manhattan-based organizations. The first wave originated in California at the beginning of the 1950s and was dubbed the *homophile movement* when New York chapters of the Mattachine Society (MSNY) and the Daughters of Bilitis (DOB–New York) joined forces with Mattachine groups in Philadelphia and Washington, D.C., in the 1960s. The second wave, called the *gay liberation movement,* began in June 1969 with the riots that erupted when the police closed down the Stonewall Inn, a gay bar in Greenwich Village; it was promoted during the following year by the Gay Liberation Front (GLF) and the Gay Activists Alliance (GAA). The third wave, which came to be known as the *lesbian feminist movement,* emerged during the spring and summer of 1970 when lesbian gay and women's liberationists banded together in Radicalesbians (RL). With the disintegration of RL, the institutional focus of the lesbian feminist movement shifted, first to DOB–New York and then to GAA's Lesbian Liberation Committee, which seceded from GAA in 1973 to become Lesbian Feminist Liberation, Inc. (LFL).

To illustrate that there were basic patterns in the evolution of gay political activity, and to show that contemporary gay attitudes and beliefs were both extensions and syntheses of older ideologies, I conceptualized the basic ideas that guided historic gay leaders as distinctive political outlooks—specifically, as homophile, gay liberationist, and lesbian feminist, and as subcategories of each of these. In the following pages, I illustrate that homophile leaders adapted to the case of homosexuals ideas popularized by the civil rights movement, and that many gay liberationists and lesbian feminists derived their viewpoints from perspectives popularized by the New Left, the women's liberation movement, and ultimately the counterculture. I show that the activities of New York City's pioneering homophile, gay liberation, and lesbian feminist groups were inspired not only by political philosophies but by organizational considerations that reinforced or constrained ideological ambition. My analysis is general enough to throw light not only on the histories of gay groups other than the ones I discuss, but on the ideas and organizational concerns responsible for the course of the civil rights movement, the New Left, and the women's movement and on the values and assumptions that characterize the counterculture.

What follows, then, is as much a story of organizational dynamics and political and social movements in modern America as an analysis of gay political activity in New York City. Part I explains how liberal American ideals gave rise to the ambitions of civil rights leaders and how the homophile politics born of these ideals and ambitions guided the leaders of early homosexual rights groups. Part II explains how people disillusioned with the liberal aspirations of civil rights leaders, particularly members of the counterculture, evolved the very different approaches to political activity characteristic of the New Left, and how ideas popularized by "the Movement" gave rise to the first gay liberation groups. Part III explains how the civil rights movement and the New Left engendered different strains of thinking in the women's movement, and how the liberationist strain encouraged the establishment of lesbian feminist groups to bridge the gay and women's liberation movements. Part IV shows how liberationist politics encouraged the disintegration of large gay organizations, the proliferation of specialized gay groups, and the spread of identifiably gay and lesbian life styles, businesses, and neighborhoods.

To develop my argument that basic political outlooks and organizational considerations have shaped gay political history, I have had to limit the attention I give other influential factors: the psyches, feelings, personalities, backgrounds, and personal ambitions of particular leaders; the situations, circumstances, and events they encountered; and the social, cultural, political, and economic systems in which they operated. Fortunately, these factors have been the focus of other studies, most of which are referred to in the text. This analysis is intended mainly to help people think more clearly about the ideological and organizational roots of the contemporary explosion of things gay.

ACKNOWLEDGMENTS

THIS BOOK is a revision of my Harvard doctoral dissertation, which was supervised by Professor Nathan Glazer. For help in shaping and submitting that thesis, I am grateful to Professor Larry Brown, currently at the Brookings Institution, and to Rob Straus.

Both thesis and book are based primarily on material gathered from gay political leaders. Unfortunately, those who spent so many hours telling me stories and answering my questions are too numerous to name. For giving me access to personal and organizational files of notes and documents, I am indebted to Michael Lavery, Rich Wandel, Randy Wicker, Craig Rodwell, Donn Teal, Arthur Bell, Arnie Kantrowitz, Pete Fisher, Marc Rubin, Morty Manford, Marty Nixon, Deni Covello, Arlene Kisner, Sidney Abbott, Barbara Love, Jean O'Leary, Karol Lightner, Susan James, Joan Nestle, Debbie Edel, and Jonathan Katz.

In the task of rewriting and expanding my thesis, I was aided loyally and tirelessly by Toby Johnson, who in the process, with his example as well as his ideas, helped me appreciate the meaning of mythology and religion in the counterculture. For critical readings of the manuscript at various stages and helpful editorial suggestions I am grateful to Tony Segura, Pete Wilson, Pete Fisher, Marc Rubin, and John D'Emilio. For helping me see the book through to publication I want to thank John Brockman, Dick Ferguson, Bill Ament, Jonathan Galassi, John Russell, Rusty Miller, and Howard Grant.

I could not have persisted with this project for seven years were it not for the support of old friends and my family, who endured my long years of political and professional preoccupation without becoming resentful. I am particularly grateful to my mother, Ruth Payne Marotta, who unfailingly stood by me as I wrestled to discover my homosexuality and its politics. I am most indebted to Rusty Kothavala, who joined me in taking the personal and political step of committing myself professionally to the study of gay life and was for many years the major source of the emotional and financial resources that permitted me to persist with my mission.

PART I

THE HOMOPHILE INITIATIVE

1

The Beginnings of
Gay Political Activity

BEFORE THE CHALLENGING CRITIQUES of the 1960s there was widespread belief that America was a place where people of all kinds could live peacefully side by side. At the root of this belief was the idea that the United States was a "melting pot" into which successive waves of immigrants with widely different backgrounds had been successfully assimilated. The Protestant Germans, because they were so much like the Anglo-Saxons who had colonized America, had been absorbed first. The Catholic Irish, Poles, and Italians had been next.

As America approached the midpoint of the twentieth century, socially conscious liberals were concerned not about the quality of life in the melting pot but about how to extend its reach to still-excluded minorities. To further what they most often termed integration, the liberals directed their attention both at those within the melting pot and at members of minorities felt to be denied the equal opportunity that would permit them to enter the mainstream. Wanting those in the mainstream to welcome the outsiders, the liberals called for an end to prejudice (opinions without adequate basis in fact), stereotyping (the portrayal of all members of a minority after a few, generally uncomplimentary, images), discrimination (unwarranted difference in treatment), and segregation (the deliberate separation of one group from others). All of these practices were, and are, referred to simply as discrimination. Wanting victims of discrimination to measure up in ways that would permit them to take advantage of guaranteed opportunities and to fit into the mainstream, the liberals called for acculturation and encouraged members of minorities to adopt the life styles and values of the majority.

Those who formed and ran civil rights groups like the National Association for the Advancement of Colored People (NAACP) and the Urban League had liberal outlooks. To prepare society at large for racial integration, they worked to eliminate discrimination by sponsoring research, education, and public relations intended to show that most blacks were as competent and moral as whites and by lobbying and litigating for an end to discriminatory policies (laws, regulations, and official practices). To prepare needy blacks for assimilation, they worked to provide them with jobs, income, food, housing, schooling, and counseling and to get them to look, dress, act, and talk like whites.

·   ·   ·

The ideas of liberals and the efforts of black civil rights leaders impressed members of many American minorities, but none more deeply than the handful of homosexuals who were beginning to think that they too might belong to an unjustly treated group. One of these homosexuals was "Donald Webster Cory."*

Like many adolescent boys, Donald Webster Cory had had sex with a slightly older male friend without knowing that such behavior was called homosexual. Not until he was a senior in high school did he learn—from one of his teachers—that there were people who actually preferred to have sex with members of their own sex, people referred to as "inverts." Aware that he was attracted to other males, Cory set out to learn more. Almost twenty-five years later, he wrote of his efforts in the preface to his pioneering book on homosexuality, *The Homosexual in America:* "In the years of later adolescence and early manhood, I studied myself and others like me, delved into every volume of literature which might shed light, sought to understand why I could not be like others. I was deeply ashamed of being abnormal and was aware of the heavy price that must be paid if anyone were to discover my secret."[1]

*Throughout this book, gay leaders are referred to by the names they chose to use in gay political activity. Pseudonyms appear in quotation marks the first time they appear in the text.

Partly because he was so sensitive to societal disapproval (in addition to being homosexual, he was short, hunchbacked, and Jewish), Cory's exploration of his homosexuality was painful. According to *The Homosexual in America,* only after "revolting against the struggle" to quell his sexual impulses did he seek friends in homosexual circles and "the permanence of love" with another man. Then, after a series of short and disillusioning affairs, he resolved to give up "the gay world" and marry. When his "urge for gratification with men" persisted after marriage, he went into psychoanalysis to rid himself of it.

Much to Cory's surprise, analysis helped him overcome not his homosexual drives but his feelings of guilt and remorse. With the help of his analyst, he worked to integrate his life as a homosexual with his life as a husband and father. *The Homosexual in America* proclaimed his success: "Today, after many years of a successful marriage, with a happy home and with children, and with a firm bond of friendship that has developed with a man who has been an inspiring person in my life, I sit down to relate what it means to be a homosexual. This is not the thinking of a bitter and unhappy person. It is the accumulated experience and outlook of one who has been through the struggle with himself and with society."[2]

Even more than in his prefatory autobiographical comments, Cory's acceptance of homosexuality radiated throughout the text of *The Homosexual in America.* The book argued that few homosexuals could change and that only conventional prejudice inclined so many to try. It suggested that most homosexuals were in most respects like everyone else; that their problems stemmed from societal disapproval rather than from homosexuality itself; and that being forced to deal with prejudice and injustice gave homosexuals valuable resiliency, sensitivity, and social conscience.

> In most respects the inhabitants of the world of Sodom are not more like each other than they are like those in the other hostile world . . . Nevertheless, all live a life that has certain features in common. They face the same humiliations and rebuffs, have similar qualms and self-doubts, wonder in like manner as to the origins of their personality traits. So great an experience in common has brought forward similarity of reaction. From the hearts and minds of many people, there has come a determination to struggle, sympathy for the lot of others unjustly vilified, compassion for fellowmen in all plights and circumstances.[3]

Cory spoke from personal experience, for his problems had led him from an early age to empathize with others who were disadvantaged, particularly the blacks he encountered in his native Brooklyn. During the 1940s he attended meetings of the NAACP in New York City, and in 1944, the year it was published, he read and reread Gunnar Myrdal's landmark study of race relations, *The American Dilemma.*

Although he had dropped out of college, Cory was unusually intelligent, and the similarities he saw between the problems of blacks and the problems of homosexuals fascinated him. Myrdal's analysis, particularly the Swedish sociologist's thesis that the root of the "Negro problem" was discrimination on the part of whites, helped Cory clarify his ideas. He was particularly impressed by the appendix, in which Myrdal likened the position of blacks to that of women and children. The more Cory thought about it, the more he became convinced that the parallels between the way society deprived blacks of rights and status and the way it treated homosexuals were even greater.

Stimulated by the publicity given the problems of minority groups in the wake of Myrdal's study, and stirred by The Kinsey Report's revelations about the large percentage of males who had had homosexual experiences, Cory decided to write a book applying civil rights ideas to the case of homosexuals. The result was *The Homosexual in America,* published in 1951 by Greenberg, the only house Cory could find that was willing to handle such controversial material. Chapter One introduced Cory's thesis that homosexuals were a minority deprived of rights and status by a prejudiced society: "As I shall demonstrate in these pages, our minority status is similar, in a variety of respects, to that of national, religious, and other ethnic groups: in the denial of civil liberties; in the legal, extra-legal, and quasi-legal discrimination; in the assignment of an inferior social position; in the exclusion from the mainstreams of life and culture; in the development of the protection and security of intragroup association; in the development of a special language and literature and a set of moral tenets within our group."[4] Later in the book, Cory indirectly acknowledged his intellectual debt to Myrdal: "A sociologist writing on racial minorities—and again the parallel is inescapable—has stated that there are no minority problems. There are only majority problems. There is no Negro problem except that created by whites; no Jewish problem except that created by Gentiles. To which I add: and no homosexual problem except that created by the heterosexual society."[5]

Besides arguing that homosexuals shared the "caste-like status" of America's national, religious, and racial minorities, *The Homosexual in America* maintained that the homosexual minority was worse off than others because it was "without a spokesman, without a leader, without a publication, without a philosophy of life, without an accepted justification for its own existence."

As a minority, we homosexuals are therefore caught in a particularly vicious circle. On the one hand, the shame of belonging and the social punishment of acknowledgement are so great that pretense is almost universal; on the other hand, only a leadership that would acknowledge would be able to break down the barriers of shame and resultant discrimination. Until the world is able to accept us on an equal basis as human beings entitled to the full rights of life, we are unlikely to have any great numbers willing to become martyrs by carrying the burden of the cross. But until we are willing to speak out openly and frankly in defense of our activities, and to identify ourselves with the millions pursuing these activities, we are unlikely to find the attitudes of the world undergoing any significant change.[6]

Cory presented his book as a first step toward breaking the vicious circle that kept the homosexual minority from securing rights and status. But the fact that he felt compelled to hide his own identity by using a pseudonym—and that his publisher was, in the wake of an obscenity trial, ordered by the courts to cease publishing books with homosexual themes—made it clear that the road ahead was to be a long one.

· · ·

While Donald Webster Cory was writing his call for justice in New York, out in Los Angeles Henry Hay was trying to form an organization that would seek this justice. Hay's first homosexual experience had been with someone who had known a member of the Society for Human Rights, the short-lived Chicago group modeled and named after the largest of the organizations created to secure rights and status for homosexuals in post–World War I Germany. Although

Hay made the Communist Party the focus of his political activity from the mid-1930s onward, he did not forget that homosexuals could organize, and he was prompted to draw up a prospectus for a homosexual group after he and some homosexuals he met at a party in the summer of 1948 bantered about forming a contingent called Bachelors For Wallace to help with Henry Wallace's Progressive presidential campaign. Although the others later dismissed the prospect of organizing homosexuals as unrealistic, Hay remained enthusiastic and began to look for others willing to help.[7]

Like other Marxists, Hay believed that political organization was the key to self-protection and social change. This belief grew stronger when the souring of relations between the United States and the Soviet Union resulted in an upsurge of domestic anti-Communism and when public officials, linking leftism and homosexuality, began to suggest that "moral perverts" were security risks. In the summer of 1949, the fear that growing native fascism might doom homosexuals in America to the fate they had suffered in Nazi Germany led Hay to replace his original prospectus for a homosexual group with a proposal for a secret society consisting of largely autonomous guilds. This mode of organization was similar to that he had found in the American Communist Party and among the European Freemasons he taught about in his course on music history at the Southern California Labor School. By the summer of 1950, when he enlisted another leftist as his first recruit, Hay was calling his proposed organization the "International Bachelors Fraternal Orders for Peace and Social Dignity, sometimes referred to as Bachelors Anonymous." He described it as "a service and welfare organization devoted to the protection and improvement of Society's Androgynous Minority."[8]

The Korean War broke out several days before Hay enlisted his first follower, and for the next few months, at beaches frequented by homosexuals in Los Angeles and Santa Monica, the two circulated copies of "America's Peace Poll," an antiwar petition prepared by the Communist Party. Though they broached the subject of Bachelors Anonymous with a number of those they asked for signatures, they failed to attract additional recruits until Hay slipped a copy of his proposal to a man in one of his classes whom he suspected would be receptive. With the support of this man and two of his friends, Hay and his original recruit began to hold semipublic discussion groups on the nature and significance of homosexuality. When attendance at these informal meetings began to swell, the founding five proceeded to organize discussion groups into secret guilds. Borrowing the name of a secret fraternity of unmarried French townsmen who in the Middle Ages conducted dances and rituals at festivals, they called their association of groups and guilds the Mattachine Society.[9]

In April 1951, some months before *The Homosexual in America* appeared, Hay and his friends prepared "a statement of missions and purposes" for the fledgling Mattachine Society. They proposed first "to unify" homosexuals "isolated from their own kind and unable to adjust to the dominant culture" by providing "a consensus of principle around which all of our people can rally and from which they can derive a feeling of 'belonging.' " They promised next "to educate" homosexuals, to develop an "ethical homosexual culture . . . paralleling the emerging cultures of our fellow-minorities—the Negro, Mexican, and Jewish Peoples." Asserting that it was necessary for "more farseeing and socially conscious homosexuals [to] provide leadership to the whole mass of social deviants," who constitute "one of the largest minorities in America today," they proposed third "to lead" homosexuals. Their statement concluded that "once unification and education have progressed, it becomes imperative . . . to push forward into the realm of political action to erase from our law books the discriminatory and oppressive legislation presently directed against the homosexual minority."[10]

The emphasis on self-education, minority-group distinctiveness, and community organizing evident in the statement of missions and purposes prepared by the founders of the Mattachine Society stood in marked contrast to the ideas aired by Donald Webster Cory in *The Homosexual in America.* Cory argued that prejudice was responsible for negative stereotyping and discrimination, and he maintained that the public had to be taught that homosexuals were in important respects like heterosexuals and were therefore worthy of equal opportunity and a place in the mainstream. These ideas bespoke the world view of liberals and civil rights leaders who believed that America was an admirable melting pot and that progressives should be concerned with acculturating and integrating members of excluded minority groups. But Hay and his followers held the Marxist view that capitalism required the oppression of minorities. They believed that homosexuals had to organize so that they could explore their sexuality, become aware of how it equipped them to contribute to a more humane society, and prepare to join with other organized minorities in the struggle to replace capitalism with socialism.

Believing that they had to pursue revolutionary goals cautiously, Hay and his followers supplemented their society of secret groups and guilds with a legally incorporated Mattachine Foundation. The plan was to have the private discussion groups explore how homosexuals could contribute to a new order while the Foundation provided a legal front and worked to make homosexual life as it was safer and more pleasant.

While Hay and his associates concentrated on activities in Los Angeles, several members of one of their discussion groups decided to publish a monthly journal that could be circulated nationally. One man whose views were characteristic of this group was Dorr Legg, who had been active in Knights of the Clock, a group formed in Los Angeles in 1950 to promote understanding among black and white homosexuals, and whose ambitions were liberal rather than leftist. Legg and his friends called their organization ONE, Incorporated. Their commitment to civil rights premises was aired in the statement of purposes printed in nearly every issue of their journal, *One* magazine:

> ONE . . . does not claim that homosexuals are better or worse than anyone else, that they are special in any but one sense. And in that one sense ONE claims positively that homosexuals do not have the civil rights assured all other citizens. ONE is devoted to correcting this.
>
> ONE . . . means to stimulate thought, criticism, research, literary and artistic production in an effort to bring the public to understand deviants and deviants to understand themselves as the two sides are brought together as one.[11]

The founders of *One* decided to publish their magazine under independent auspices, partly because they knew that rank-and-file Mattachine members, whose numbers had grown as discussion groups and guilds had formed in Long Beach and the San Francisco Bay area, were beginning to have reservations about their society's operations. Although Hay and his circle were quiet about their Marxist convictions, rumors spread about the leftist leanings of those at the top, and because the members of one group and guild knew nothing about the others, such fears were hard to dispel. A statement asserting that the Mattachine "has never been, is not now and must never be identified with any ism" was circulated by the Foundation in February 1953.[12] What little reassurance this provided was lost when Fred M. Snider, the Foundation's legal adviser, was described as an unfriendly witness before the House Un-American Activities Committee in a column on the "strange new pressure group" professing "to represent the homosexual voters of Los Angeles" that appeared in the *Los Angeles Mirror* in March 1953.[13] Hay was so pleased with the publicity that he duplicated the column and sent it to those on the Mattachine's mailing list, not realizing that members fearful about being associated with Communism were bound to focus on the news about Snider rather than the publicity given their organization. At a statewide convention held in April 1953, these members took the lead in transforming the Mattachine Society into a public, democratic membership organization committed to liberal ideals.

In an interview published in Jonathan Katz's *Gay American History,* Hay portrays the 1953 convention as a struggle between, on the one hand, leftists out to preserve both the Foundation and the secret guilds and discussion groups and, on the other hand, "middle class," "status quo types" fearful that upcoming congressional investigations into the links between private foundations and Communist subversion would taint the Mattachine's reputation and tarnish the respectability of homosexuals.[14] By dismissing his opponents as "status quo types," Hay failed to acknowledge that they had ideas about gay political activity that differed from his own. They had, in fact, what is here called the basic homophile outlook—the belief that prejudice, stereotyping, and discrimination were the source of the homosexual's problems and that education, policy reform, and help for individual homosexuals would bring about the recognition of basic similarity, equality of treatment, and integration that were tantamount to social progress.*

---

*During the 1950s, the term *homophile* was used as a euphemism for *homosexual* by those who wanted to combat the stereotype that homosexuals were obsessed with sex. The suffix *-phile* was supposed to suggest that homosexuality was more an emotional than a sexual attraction and that homosexuals, like respectable heterosexuals, were interested in love more than sex. Early in the 1960s, Mattachine leaders in the east suggested that the word *homophile*

Although Hay and his supporters distrusted the motives of their challengers, they saw that it was impossible to continue on their original course. Midway through the convention, Hay announced that the Foundation would dissolve and cede the name Mattachine to those who wanted to convert the semisecret, amorphous society into a legitimate, national membership organization. The leaders of this group soon had the Mattachine Society incorporated as an educational and research group in the state of California and drew up a constitution that spelled out requirements for membership and established procedures for creating chapters and area councils in different parts of the country. The brochure prepared to introduce this new incarnation of the Mattachine made clear that its orientation toward gay political activity was homophile by explaining that the society's "educational aim is directed toward the public at large, with a view to spreading accurate information about the nature and conditions of variation, and in this way eliminate discrimination, derision, prejudice and bigotry" and also "toward the members of the variant minority, emphasizing the need for the definition and adoption of a personal behavior code which will . . . eliminate most —if not all—[of] the barriers to integration."[15]

. . .

While homophile leaders in California were working to reorient the Mattachine Society, homosexuals in New York City dared meet only in an informal discussion group called The League, the residuum of a gay social club known as the Veterans' Benevolent Association that had flourished after World War II. Familiar with *The Homosexual in America* and *One* magazine, many in The League spoke of the need for a local group that would work to eliminate discrimination, but not until the summer of 1955, after rumors of a police investigation put an end to attendance at League meetings, did Sam Morford and Tony Segura decide to establish a New York chapter of the Mattachine Society (MSNY). Morford, in his fifties, was an industrial psychologist who had learned about the Mattachine's activities in California from Dr. Evelyn Hooker. (Dr. Hooker was one of the

be used to refer to their movement to secure rights and status for homosexuals. The term is used here both to identify the ideas about gay political activity that predominated before the gay liberation movement and to characterize the groups, leaders, and activities that were guided by these ideas.

first psychologists to produce research suggesting that homosexuals were as mentally healthy as heterosexuals; Morford met her at the first seminar on homosexuality held at an American Psychological Association convention.) Segura, thirty-five, was a research chemist who had joined The League after being stirred by *The Homosexual in America* and by copies of *One* and of the journals from European gay groups, which he discovered at the Cory Book Service, a mail-order house started by Donald Webster Cory to make publications on homosexuality more accessible.

Morford and Segura found the homophile orientation of the national Mattachine to their liking. In fact, Segura was eager to form a chapter that would translate, write, and edit articles for the national organization's new magazine, the *Mattachine Review*. Both men had been frustrated by the flimsiness and vulnerability of The League. In the national Mattachine's clear statement of purpose, legal incorporation, and democratic constitution, they saw established group identity and legitimacy that would help guarantee that the new organizational focus of their energies survived.

Morford and Segura's views were shared by the varied half-dozen friends who in December 1955 gathered at Sam Morford's Greenwich Village apartment to form an editorial and writing chapter of the Mattachine. George Kochevitsky was a Russian pianist who had been exiled to Siberia because of his homosexuality before he escaped to America. Malcolm Thurburn, an emigrant from Scotland, was a writer and painter in his seventies. Joe McCarthy, a recent graduate of Fordham University, was working to start his own machinery export business. "Sven Nivens," a Swedish linguist, worked as a translator for an international business firm. Also present were Ross Puryear, recently released from prison, whom Segura had befriended at the request of novelist "James Barr," and "Mary Dorn," the widow of a playwright, whom Segura had been urged to look up by the members of ONE with whom he corresponded.

After receiving the names and addresses of those on the *Mattachine Review*'s mailing list for New York state, Segura sent out notices that the Mattachine Society of New York's first public meeting would be held at the Diplomat Hotel on the evening of January 10, 1956. Thirty or so showed up. Morford welcomed them, explained why MSNY was being formed, and collected twenty-dollar dues from those who wanted to join. Half the money and a request for official chapter status were forwarded to the national Mattachine's board of directors. On February 25, the board approved the application and appointed Tony Segura resident agent. By the time the third annual Mattachine convention ratified the board's action, in April, the New York chapter had fourteen members.

In recognition of his status and seniority, Morford was elected chairman, but from the beginning Segura took responsibility for running the chapter. When Morford moved to San Francisco in the fall of 1956, Segura's stature was unrivaled: the views and the organizational concerns he shared with Joe McCarthy, Curtis Dewees, "Al de Dion," and others he brought into leadership positions made MSNY the small but vital club that it remained until the beginning of the 1960s.

All of MSNY's early leaders admired the NAACP. Although they believed that education was necessary to eliminate discrimination, they would have liked to supplement their research, journalistic, and public relations activities with NAACP-like lawsuits and lobbying efforts aimed at eliminating policies that made life unpleasant and unfair for homosexuals. Instead, because they feared that official sponsorship of anything resembling political activity would endanger the Mattachine's charter and give rise to local investigations that might frighten away members and supporters, they pursued their interest in policy reform indirectly, by providing information to public officials found to be sympathetic, and covertly, by privately encouraging friends in civic groups to push for reforms. Midway through MSNY's first year, in a letter to a resident of Washington, D.C., who wanted to organize a Mattachine chapter that would work for the repeal of laws inimical to homosexuals, Segura spoke of the fears that led him to avoid activities that might seem political:

And now we come to the real important matters—"the repeal of unjust laws." As I said in my previous letter, the Mattachine Society was incorporated as a research and educational organization. As individuals, we fervently look forward to the day when all unjust laws, and particularly those relating to the homosexual, are repealed. The organization, however, must abide by its charter and restrict itself to research and education—although these two terms may be interpreted quite liberally . . . To act otherwise would lead to utter chaos and the destruction of the organization.[16]

Hal Call, the national Mattachine's director of publications, who lived in San Francisco, wrote after seeing Segura's letter that he shared the New Yorker's perspective:

> Tony's statement that Mattachine cannot pursue any path but the educational and research one in accomplishing Mattachine goals is absolutely correct. Our charter is placed in jeopardy whenever we try to influence legislation through any other means publicly. Discretion here is certainly the better part of valor—we will last longer and win more ground by educational effort, including, as the situation demands and/or permits, subtle publicity when someone votes against a good law or for a bad one. We can endorse the action of other agencies working in this field, and "ride on their shirttails," so to speak, with relative safety. But we cannot lobby on our own, and must be careful how we recommend changes of law so that our charter and the right to solicit funds through the mail is not in danger.[17]

This preoccupation with protecting the Mattachine Society's legitimacy was partly a product of the times. These were days when few people dared acknowledge that they were even interested in homosexuality. Homosexual behavior was a felony punishable in New York state by as much as twenty years in jail. People could be arrested simply for talking suggestively about homosexual sex, and plainclothesmen were dispatched to entrap homosexuals by initiating such conversations. Bars and steam baths that attracted homosexuals were periodically raided. The memory of the antihomosexual furor fueled by Senator Joseph McCarthy in the early 1950s was fresh. The danger of being exposed, fired from one's job, or blackmailed because of one's homosexuality was real. Many homosexuals complained that groups established to make life better for them did more harm than good because they attracted attention to behavior that was safest when it went unnoticed.[18] The fact that the Mattachine adopted an obscure name, defined itself as a group committed to increasing knowledge about "sexual variation," and specified that its membership was open to individuals "without regard for sexual orientation" did little to alleviate anxiety. The main concern of those in charge of MSNY was to make sure that their organization survived.

The obsession with organizational survival was even stronger among the organizers of the New York chapter of the Daughters of Bilitis (DOB–New York), which was formed in the fall of 1958. Where the first eastern chapter of the Mattachine Society had been a product of local initiative, the first eastern offspring of the Daughters was established under the direction of Del Martin and Phyllis Lyon, a San Francisco couple who in 1956, after learning about the Mattachine Society and ONE, had transformed their lesbian social club into "a women's organization for the purposes of promoting the integration of the homosexual into society by . . . education of the variant" and "of the public at large." DOB's constitution provided for the establishment of chapters in other parts of the country. Its journal, the *Ladder,* periodically invited lesbians interested in forming local chapters to write to the national officers. In the fall of 1958, before traveling to Manhattan to attend the Mattachine's fifth annual national convention, Martin and Lyon wrote letters inviting the local women they had heard from to meet with them in MSNY's offices. One who received a letter was Lorraine Hansberry, whose first play, *A Raisin in the Sun,* was to open on Broadway six months later.

Although she met with and encouraged Martin and Lyon, Hansberry left the founding of DOB–New York to Barbara Gittings, who, after receiving her letter from the San Franciscans, had persuaded her friend "Meredith Grey" to join her in welcoming the national DOB leaders when they arrived in New York City. After spending an evening with Martin and Lyon, Gittings agreed to be responsible for DOB–New York. In the October issue of MSNY's newsletter she reported: "The Daughters of Bilitis, a San Francisco women's homophile organization similar in purpose to Mattachine, now has a chapter in the New York area. The first meeting, with nine present, was held Saturday evening, September 20th, at the Mattachine offices. Mary Dorn, long an active Mattachine member in New York, was elected treasurer, and two Philadelphia women, Barbara Gittings and Jody Shotwell [pseud.], were voted president and secretary, respectively."[19]

Gittings, then twenty-six, was no stranger to Martin and Lyon, for she had impressed them with her interest in the problems of lesbians when she sat in on one of DOB's first meetings while vacationing in San Francisco during the summer of 1956. Several years before, after becoming aware of her homosexual feelings while a freshman at Northwestern, Gittings had spent hours in local libraries trying to find information that would explain them. Not until she dropped out of school and returned home did she discover Radclyffe Hall's novel about lesbian relationships, *The Well of Loneliness.* Yet even when she moved to Philadelphia, she was unable to locate other homosexuals. Toward the middle of the 1950s, Gittings began to spend weekends in New York City, going to lesbian bars and combing secondhand bookstores for the lesbian novels she found listed in the bibliography at the back of *The Homosexual in America.* It was when she met with Donald Webster Cory to discuss lesbian literature that she learned about the existence of ONE and the Mattachine Society; the Mattachine leaders she looked up when she traveled to San Francisco referred her to DOB.

To make sure that their group would escape the notice of a hostile environment, Martin and Lyon had given it an obscure name and chartered it under the laws of California as a "women's social group."* Though they trusted Gittings to run the New York chapter, they were determined to protect their national organization by exercising tight control over DOB–New York's activities. Partly because Martin and Lyon kept their reins on the New York chapter so taut, and partly because Gittings herself felt it important to protect her group's legitimacy, official statements stressed that DOB–New York was committed to research and education, though most of its activities were kaffeeklatsches and outings intended to give support to local lesbians. Gittings recalls that although many of DOB–New York's endeavors were social, they were described as "service" or "fund-raising" activities so that the group would not look like "an agency for social introductions" and be vulnerable to charges that it was in the business of "procuring" or "arranging for immoral contacts."[21] (Tony Segura, Joe McCarthy, and others active in MSNY in its early years remember that they regulated, curbed

---

*In their heavily autobiographical *Lesbian/Woman,* Martin and Lyon write that the name Bilitis came from Pierre Louÿs's narrative poem *Song of Bilitis,* which depicts Bilitis as a lesbian poetess who lived on the isle of Lesbos at the time of Sappho. They recall that this choice of name was influenced by their anxiety about organizational survival: "We thought that 'Daughters of Bilitis' would sound like any other women's lodge—you know, like the Daughters of the Nile or the DAR . . . If anyone asked us, we could always say we belonged to a poetry club."[20]

mention of, and avoided publicizing social activities for the same reason.)

Yet for all the steps taken to assure that MSNY and DOB–New York would be perceived as legitimate, the first homophile leaders in New York City were unable to overcome the fears and inhibitions that kept their followers few and unassertive. And at the turn of the decade, when well-adjusted and well-educated enthusiasts like Segura turned their attention elsewhere, less self-confident and professional leaders like Al de Dion, Curtis Dewees, and Meredith Grey (who in the early sixties became an officer of MSNY as well as DOB) tried to bolster the status and size of their groups by reemphasizing the serious research and educational roles of these organizations and by trying to involve scholars and professionals interested in mental health and social welfare. To give their groups an aura of studious detachment, the leaders refrained from asserting that homosexuals were as mentally well-adjusted and as ethical as heterosexuals. To accommodate the views and the interests of involved professionals —most of whom made their livelihoods studying the "deviant," ministering to the misguided, and counseling the disturbed—they questioned the attractiveness of traditional homosexual styles and the morality of the gay subculture. Homosexuals who looked and acted "straight" (heterosexual), preferred monogamous couplings, and confined their sexual activity to the bedroom were said to deserve rights and status; those who enjoyed promiscuity, pornography, sex role deviation, and cross dressing were said to have problems; and those who pursued sex in public places, intimacy with minors, and fetishistic sexual activity were alternately pitied and denounced. As Barbara Gittings explains:

At first we were so grateful just to have [professional] people—anybody —pay attention to us that we listened to and accepted everything they said, no matter how bad it was . . . We invited people who were willing to come to our meetings; obviously, it turned out to be those who had vested interest in having us as penitents, clients, or patients . . .

When somebody with professional credentials came to address your meetings, that legitimized the existence of your organization. And then when you went out and approached other people, you could say that Dr. So and So or the Rev. So and So had addressed you; that made you less pariahlike to these other people whom you needed.[22]

The desire to make their groups respectably professional also led those who took charge of MSNY and DOB–New York in the early 1960s to adopt a certain style of behavior. When involved in official business, they dressed in business attire, avoided overly effeminate or ultramasculine behavior, spoke of love rather than sex, and disparaged socializing for its lack of seriousness. They spent their time writing polite letters, planning scholarly publications, arranging for professional consultations, and inviting experts to talk about the origins and nature of "sexual variation" before serious audiences assembled in reputable lecture halls.

In many ways, the reorientation of MSNY and DOB–New York that took place at the beginning of the 1960s paralleled the personal evolution of the man whose initial elaboration of homophile ideas had led to the groups' formation. In 1952 and 1953, after publishing *The Homosexual in America* and starting the Cory Book Service, Donald Webster Cory had served as an editor of *One* and toyed briefly with the thought of making his mail-order house an eastern branch of ONE. But by 1954, when Tony Segura got to know him, Cory had sold the book service and let it be known that he wanted nothing to do with groups intent on persuading people that homosexuals were as well-adjusted and respectable as heterosexuals. In the preface he prepared for a second edition of *The Homosexual in America,* issued in 1960, Cory explained how his thinking had changed:

I too, believe in the rights of the homosexual, and I hope that in some measure I have aided in furthering those rights. But the fact that people should not be persecuted, should not be treated with cruelty and scorn, does not mean that their way of life is a desirable or a mentally healthy one . . .

I feel that homosexuals and their friends have made a grave mistake in seeking to deny the psychological disturbances in order to fight the social cruelties . . .

Ten years after I wrote this book, I find myself completely in agreement with everything stated herein on the wrongs committed against the homosexual, on the rights properly demanded by him, but I find insufficient emphasis on the wrongs he commits against himself, on his inner conflict, on the limitations of homosexuality as a way of life, regardless of any changes in social attitudes or legal sanctions . . .

Once it is recognized that one can accept the homosexual as a human being, and demand the rights that belong to him, without denying that his behavior (or desire for such behavior) is a symptom of an emotional maladjustment, then the need for reorientation is complemented by the psychological foundation that may make it possible. Change toward acceptance of the heterosexual life . . . is aided by freedom from guilt and fear, and hence it becomes far less difficult than I had anticipated in the original text. Inasmuch as this is a subjective study, I am happy to say that I found such a change not only possible, but personally rewarding.[23]

Cory remained uninvolved in gay political activity until 1961. Then, after the national Mattachine's board of directors severed legal ties with its local chapters, Al de Dion and Curtis Dewees sought to boost the status of MSNY, newly incorporated as an educational organization in New York state, by inviting the man they called "the father of the homophile movement" to participate in its activities. In the fall of 1961, Cory moderated a panel of psychologists, ministers, and criminologists at a Mattachine conference on the theme "Current Research Trends." In the spring of 1962, he agreed to join MSNY if de Dion and Dewees would give him space in the newsletter to outline the organizational aims he favored. Playing down his misgivings about homosexual behavior and the gay subculture, Cory wrote:

That it is to the best interests of the homosexual to have a strong, active organization, with level-headed leadership, is self-evident. Certainly it will become increasingly evident in the years ahead that such an organization can play a beneficial role for society at large: by integrating the homosexual into society, by inculcating in him a sense of responsibility, by educating him in self-understanding, by aiding him in his adjustments, by diminishing the hostility against him, by promoting scientific research into the causes of sexual difficulties, by furthering the liberalization of attitudes toward all nonconformist behavior that is not antisocial in character, and by removing from the image of society one more set of stereotypes and scapegoats.[24]

The emphasis in Cory's letter on the importance of helping homosexuals become adjusted, acculturated, and assimilated was very different from the defense of the homosexual's health and worth and the emphasis on the importance of eliminating unwarranted prejudice, stereotyping, and discrimination that had made *The Homosex-*

ual in America so inspiring. Yet both emphases reflected the liberal assumptions and the civil rights premises that kept the activities of MSNY and DOB–New York homophile in character until the beginnings of the gay liberation movement.

2

Mattachine Militancy

IN MARCH 1961, while Al de Dion and Curtis Dewees were working to establish the Mattachine Society, Inc., of New York as an independent educational and research organization, Franklin Kameny wrote and asked them to help him set up a Mattachine chapter in Washington, D.C. De Dion and Dewees replied that the national Mattachine had ceased to charter chapters but that they would help Kameny form his own group by supplying him with the names of homosexuals in the Washington area and by telling him about their own experiences. Little did de Dion and Dewees suspect that Kameny would emerge as the most articulate proponent of ideas destined to transform MSNY in the very ways they feared would destroy it.

Had the two paid more attention to the Washington leader's background, they might have guessed how his thinking would evolve. Born in New York City, Frank Kameny had attended Queens College, served on the front lines in World War II, and completed the course requirements for a Harvard Ph.D. in astronomy before having his first homosexual experience, at the age of twenty-nine. In 1956, after receiving his doctorate and teaching at George Washington University, he took a job with the Army Map Service. In 1957, after being told that the government knew he was homosexual, he was dismissed from his army post. When his fight to have his dismissal reversed through the regular administrative appeal process was unsuccessful, Kameny found a lawyer willing to help him take his case to the federal courts. After losing appeals in two courts, leaving only the Supreme Court for redress, the lawyer gave up, but Kameny did not. Late in 1960 he wrote a brief that argued that "the Civil Service Commission's policy on homosexuality is improperly discriminatory, in that it discriminates against an entire group, not considered as individuals, in a manner in which other similar groups are not discriminated against, and in that this discrimination has no basis in reason . . ."[1] It was on the day after the Supreme Court denied his petition for a hearing that Kameny wrote to de Dion and Dewees.

Kameny's letter told of his disappointment at the Supreme Court's rebuff and of his resolve to challenge the government's discriminatory employment practices. The group he formed with the help of the New Yorkers, called the Mattachine Society of Washington (MSW), became the instrument of his determination to challenge the government. MSW's statement of purpose dedicated it "to *act* by any lawful means . . . to secure for homosexuals basic rights and liberties guaranteed to all Americans." The group's first major project was to send every public official in Washington a news release that called for an end to provisions excluding homosexuals from employment in the civil and military services and for a revision of the regulations governing security clearances. Sympathetic responses from Congressman William Ryan of Manhattan's West Side and Congressman Robert Nix of Philadelphia led Kameny to visit their offices. Conferences with Pentagon and Selective Service officials followed.

Though his visits with federal officials were newsworthy firsts, Kameny's big publicity break came in 1963, when Congressman John Dowdy of Texas, chairman of the congressional subcommittee that dealt with the District of Columbia, introduced legislation intended to deny MSW a license to solicit funds. When the subcommittee held hearings, Kameny testified. The ensuing public controversy gave him his first taste of battle—and a hunger for more.

Kameny described his historic initiatives and the philosophy responsible for them in a speech to the New York Mattachine's one hundredth public lecture in July 1964. He began by maintaining that homophile groups could have one of three distinct emphases: the focus on individual-centered social services that he saw in DOB; the interest in "information-education" that he associated with MSNY; and the involvement in "civil liberties–social action" that he had given MSW. He proceeded to argue that while helping troubled individuals was necessary, information-education and civil liberties–social action were the approaches that would eliminate the discrimination at the root of the homosexual's problems.

Kameny contended that the information-education approach was useful as long as homophile leaders educated the heterosexual public rather than their own members and took unequivocal stands on controversial matters. Attaching particular importance to the issue of homosexuality as illness, he asserted that "the entire homophile movement, in terms of any accomplishments beyond merely ministering to the needy, is going to stand or fall upon the question of whether or not homosexuality is a sickness, and upon our taking a firm stand on it." Kameny's own convictions were clear:

There seems to be no valid evidence to show that homosexuality, *per se,* is a sickness. In view of the absence of such valid evidence, the simple fact that the suggestion of sickness has been made is no reason for entertaining it seriously, or for abandoning the view that homosexuality is not a sickness, but merely a liking or preference similar to and fully on a par with heterosexuality. Accordingly, I take the position unequivocally that, until and unless valid, positive evidence shows otherwise, homosexuality, *per se,* is neither a sickness, a defect, a disturbance, a neurosis, a psychosis, nor a malfunction of any sort.

Kameny criticized his colleagues for their "lightly veiled feeling that homosexuality really is inferior to heterosexuality but that, since we have to live with it, it must be made the best of." He chided those who were interested in what caused homosexuality and how it could be cured:

I do not see the NAACP and CORE worrying about which chromosome and gene produces [a] black skin or about the possibility of bleaching the Negro. I do not see any great interest on the part of the B'nai B'rith Anti-Defamation League in the possibility of solving problems of anti-semitism by converting Jews to Christianity.

In all of these minority groups, we are interested in obtaining rights for our respective minorities *as* Negroes, *as* Jews, and *as* homosexuals. Why we are Negroes, Jews, or homosexuals is totally irrelevant, and whether we can be changed to whites, Christians, or heterosexuals is equally irrelevant.

Kameny's references to blacks and Jews were deliberate and repeated. During the course of his speech, he cited the characteristics that made homosexuals a similar minority, likened the role he recommended for the homophile group to that of the civil rights organization, and argued that it was necessary to build a homophile movement analogous to the civil rights movement. Citing studies of prejudice and integration showing that the communication of facts did little to eliminate bigotry, he contended that steps taken by government officials did more than information and education to affect public opinion. Vigorous action aimed at changing laws and policies was the most effective way to get government officials to act, he postulated, noting "the case of the Negro," who had "tried for ninety years to achieve his purposes by a program of information and education. His achievements in those ninety years, while by no means nil, were nothing compared to those of the past ten years, when he tried a vigorous civil liberties, social action approach and gained his goals thereby."[2]

Kameny left no doubt that his views were shaped by the ideas of militant civil rights leaders, especially Martin Luther King, Jr. Moderate civil rights leaders maintained that "the Negro problem" consisted both of popular prejudice, stereotyping, discrimination, and segregation and of the "pathology" that this engendered in black communities. They argued that progress called for long-term education to change the attitudes of whites, lawsuits and lobbying that would eliminate the barriers to integration, and social services to prepare individual blacks for assimilation. Militant civil rights leaders, on the other hand, portrayed the problems facing blacks as simply societal and the means to progress as basically political. Militants wanted to make racial discrimination into a political issue by pressing for dramatic legislative reforms, portraying their demands as moral imperatives, staging publicity-generating marches and demonstrations, and stirring whites to join blacks in a mass civil rights movement.

In arguing that discrimination was squarely to blame for the homosexual's problems and that boldly challenging discriminatory policies was the most effective way to make progress, Kameny advocated a militant homophile approach to gay political activity. In response, Mattachine veterans whose homophile outlook had been shaped by the ideas of civil rights moderates insisted that one had to change popular attitudes before one could change laws and that it was important to improve life for homosexuals in the meantime.

But some of the younger members of MSNY were inclined to share Kameny's views, and the Washington leader's expostulation encouraged them to step up their efforts to make the New York Mattachine militant.

. . .

Probably the first person to advocate that MSNY assume a bold political course was Charlie Hayden. Though raised by his devout Roman Catholic grandmother in Florida, Hayden was never made to feel that his homosexuality was wrong; growing up, he was repeatedly surprised by the lack of negative reaction he encountered when he told people that he was gay. By the mid-1950s, in college in Virginia, Hayden was an avid reader of *One* and the *Mattachine Review.* When he learned that a chapter of the Mattachine Society had been formed in New York City, he arranged to spend the next summer in Manhattan.

In the summer of 1958, when Hayden showed up at MSNY's headquarters, he was told that he was welcome to participate but too young to become a member. Within a month the brash twenty-year-old raised the hackles of his mentors by distributing flyers to advertise one of the Mattachine's public lectures and attracting, in addition to a large crowd, a visit by curious police. That fall, when he transferred to the University of Texas for his junior year, Hayden started a line of homosexual greeting cards, sent letters to seventy-five religious publications asking for the enlightened treatment of homosexuals, and prepared a questionnaire about homosexuality to circulate among his classmates in the name of Wicker Research Studies, a group that used DOB's statement of purpose for its credo. In 1959, after a campus political career that included participation in a sit-in held to protest housing segregation, Hayden ran unsuccessfully for student body president. During the campaign, afraid that one of his opponents was trying to find out whether he was active in the Mattachine in order to expose him as a homosexual, he wrote to the New Yorkers and asked that they refer to him henceforth as "Randolfe Wicker."

Wicker joined MSNY when he returned to live in New York City in 1961, but he chafed at de Dion and Dewees's efforts to establish the group as a respectable research organization and resolved to do public relations work for homosexuals on his own. In the summer of 1962, billing himself as the public relations director of a group called the Homosexual League, he persuaded the listener-supported radio station WBAI to tape and air a program in which seven homosexuals talked about their sexuality. When *New York Journal-American* columnist Jack O'Brian criticized WBAI for bowing to the wishes of an "arrogant card-carrying swish" and suggested that it change its call letters to WSICK, Wicker used the clipping to get publicity for his program in *Newsweek,* the *New York Herald Tribune,* and the *New York Times.* A full transcript of the radio program was published in the *Realist,* an avant-garde journal.

Elated at his success, Wicker assembled copies of the transcript and press coverage into information packets, which he advertised for sale in the *Village Voice* and sent to writers he hoped to interest in "field trips into the homosexual sub-culture" led by a "real homosexual." By the end of 1963, Wicker had helped with the preparation of William Helmer's story, "New York's 'Middle-Class' Homosexuals," which appeared in *Harper's;* Stephanie Gervis's pair of articles on homosexuals in the *Village Voice;* the first major piece on homosexuality to appear in the *New York Times;* two articles in the *New York Post's* six-part series on sex and the law; and Dan Wakefield's account of Wicker's own activities, called "The Gay Crusader."

Whenever he could, Wicker argued that homosexuals had to become more political. On WBAI he stated that his goal was "making homosexuality a legitimate political and social issue in our day."[3] Through Helmer he reported that his objective was "to bring the subject of homosexuality into the open."[4] With Gervis he discussed his belief in the possibility of organizing a homosexual voting bloc in Greenwich Village. The *New York Post* reported that Wicker had visited several members of Congress during his trips to Washington. Wakefield likened Wicker's role to that of Martin Luther King, Jr., and other speakers for embattled minority groups.

In 1963, Wicker began doing public relations work for the New York Mattachine. As MSNY's representative he broke ground by securing advertisements for homophile events in the *Village Voice* and the *New York Times,* by speaking as an acknowledged homosexual at an official college forum, and by appearing on a local television program, "The Les Crane Show." For MSNY's monthly newsletter, Wicker wrote a column surveying legal and political matters involving homosexuals.

Whenever MSNY refused to sponsor projects he proposed, Wicker acted in the name of his other organizational affiliations—the Homosexual League, the League for Sexual Freedom, the *Marijuana Newsletter*. In the summer of 1964, he tried to persuade those in charge of the Mattachine to support the range of causes championed by the League for Sexual Freedom. After being rebuffed, he helped the League stage picket lines on behalf of issues such as the legalization of prostitution, the right to abortion, and the dispensation of birth control devices. On September 19, 1964, the League for Sexual Freedom and the Homosexual League sponsored a ten-member picket line at the Whitehall Street Induction Center to protest the army's policies of not guarding the confidentiality of draft records mentioning homosexuality and of giving dishonorable discharges to persons found engaging in homosexual behavior. In mid-October, Frank Kameny had to dissuade Wicker and his cohorts from picketing the FBI to protest the arrest of presidential assistant Walter Jenkins in a public toilet. In December, Wicker and three others picketed a lecture at the Cooper Union Forum entitled "Homosexuality, a Disease."

The man who prepared the signs for these first picket lines was Craig Rodwell, for many years the only person at MSNY who shared Wicker's enthusiasm for bold political activity. Like Wicker, Rodwell was young, comfortable with his homosexuality, and stirred by the civil rights movement. Like Wicker, Rodwell had begun to work at the Mattachine before he was old enough to join, and tried almost from the beginning to persuade those in charge to be more militant.

While welcoming Rodwell's contributions, de Dion and Dewees made sure that his arguments for political activism fell on deaf ears by cultivating as leaders people who shared their belief that the Mattachine should be a serious educational and research organization. For MSNY's board of directors they recruited professionals like the Reverend Robert W. Wood, Dr. Richard Robertiello, and Donald Webster Cory. As officers they enlisted people of age, profession, and means. "Gregory Desmannes," aide to a vice-president of IT&T, was appointed editor of the newsletter; Jack Weedon, heir to the Wall Street investment banking firm owned by his family, was elected treasurer; Paul Speier, the publisher of a small specialty magazine, succeeded Dewees as president; Julian Hodges, a member of the liberal Democratic family from North Carolina that also produced John Kennedy's secretary of commerce, Luther Hodges, succeeded Speier. All these men shared de Dion and Dewees's vision of the Mattachine, but Weedon, Speier, and Hodges felt less strongly about the need to avoid political activity and were progressively more open to the views expressed by Kameny, Wicker, and Rodwell.

Julian Hodges became the militants' most important convert. In the fall of 1962, when he first became active in MSNY, Hodges chaired a committee that studied the feasibility of a writers' bureau, an abstract service, and a scholarly journal, all enterprises intended to facilitate the publication of serious articles about homosexuality. De Dion and Dewees were so impressed that they asked him to join them in representing MSNY at ECHO (East Coast Homophile Organizations), a regional association formed in the spring of 1963 to sponsor a conference on homosexuality. By the beginning of 1964, as president-elect of the New York Mattachine, Hodges was ready to support Kameny's proposal to build the 1964 ECHO conference around the theme "Civil Liberties and Social Rights." During the summer of 1964, it was he who selected Kameny to address MSNY's one hundredth public lecture. In the winter of 1965, as president, Hodges helped transform MSNY from a group concerned with education and research on "sexual variation" to an organization committed to the bold political pursuit of rights for homosexuals.

In some ways, Hodges was a reluctant victim of the militant tide. Like his moderate associates, he was inclined to believe that policy reform was best pursued by making information available to policymakers in mailings and consultations, by enlisting prestigious professionals to talk and write about rational courses of action, by working behind the scenes to line up official support, and by playing down the fact that particular reforms were of interest to homosexuals. He revealed his preferences in the fall of 1964, when the chairman of a commission appointed by Governor Nelson Rockefeller to recommend revisions in New York state's penal law and criminal code announced that, because of opposition in the State Assembly, he intended to drop proposed provisions for decriminalizing sodomy. Hodges's response was to invite everyone on the Mattachine's mailing list to dispatch a form letter requesting reinstatement of the decriminalization provisions, a letter that neither mentioned homosexuality nor used the Mattachine's name. (In a letter to a friend, Hodges complained about the militant critics of this low-key approach: "Unfortunately, there are a great many who seem to feel that the homophile movement should get as much 'PR' value out of championing law reform as possible.")[5]

In many cases, Hodges endorsed projects proposed by the militants because they were so eager to work for the organization. One of the most enthusiastic militants was Dick Leitsch, who had been led to MSNY early in 1964 by his boyfriend, Craig Rodwell. A twenty-nine-year-old native of Louisville, Kentucky, who maintained that Kameny's 1964 speech had made him political for the first time in his life, Leitsch spent so many hours at Mattachine headquarters that Hodges asked him to be his assistant. In this capacity, Leitsch wrote dozens of letters asking politicians and public officials to explain their stands on policy matters affecting homosexuals and to speak at Mattachine public lectures. As editor of the MSNY newsletter, he filled it with coverage of legal, governmental, and political events relevant to homosexuals and wrote enthusiastically about the activities of the civil rights movement. During the fall of 1964, he persuaded the leaders of the Washington Mattachine to let him combine the MSNY and MSW newsletters into a journal that could be sold on the newsstands, as the *Eastern Mattachine Magazine,* and arranged for the full text of Kameny's July speech to be printed in the first issue.

By accommodating the militants, Hodges hoped to make MSNY a larger and more versatile organization. But as the militants came to the fore, others who had reservations about them tried to check their ascendance—especially after a committee that Hodges appointed to revise MSNY's constitution recommended that presidents be permitted to serve more than one term and Hodges let it be known that he planned to run for reelection. When it became apparent that his slate was going to include several leading militants, Al de Dion rallied a group of moderates to oppose the constitutional amendments and to field a slate of opposition candidates. To run against Frank Kameny and Dr. Hendrick Ruitenbeek for positions on the board of directors, the moderates drafted Curtis Dewees and the Reverend C. Edward Egan; to oppose Julian Hodges, they nominated "David Goldberg," a founder of the West Side Discussion

Group (the lone survivor of a series of neighborhood discussion groups begun by MSNY in 1959); to run against Dick Leitsch for the post of president-elect (equivalent to vice-president), they selected Donald Webster Cory.

Although the activities of those on the opposing slates themselves reflected the differences between moderates and militants, the candidates outlined their positions in campaign statements mailed to the Mattachine membership. Hodges concluded his statement by trying to distinguish the militant stance of the Kameny-Ruitenbeek-Hodges-Leitsch slate from the moderate stance of the Dewees-Egan-Goldberg-Cory slate:

> There is a dissonant note in the elections this year which I feel it is my duty to point out to you. There is a strong possibility, indeed a probability, that this election may produce a Board of Directors that will be split down the middle on such vital issues as to whether or not homosexuality is an illness, whether or not the Society should be primarily a "civil rights" organization, and whether the Society should aim its program to the homosexual community, in general, or to the individual homosexual.

Leitsch's campaign statement, written by Craig Rodwell, played up the positions the militants believed set them apart most dramatically from the moderates. The statement promised that Leitsch would "work actively for the end of police entrapment procedures, for the elimination of discrimination against the homosexual by the government and other agencies, public and private, and the end of prejudice and discrimination against homosexuals." It emphasized that the root of the homosexual's problem was the "view . . . propagated by such people as Drs. Bieber, Ellis, Bergler, and Haddon . . . that homosexuality, per se, is an illness, perversion, or some other kind of negative persuasion." It pledged that, if Leitsch was elected, his "first order of business will be to introduce to the membership the following statement of policy for the membership's approval: The Mattachine Society Inc. of New York takes the position that in the absence of valid evidence to the contrary, homosexuality is *not* a sickness, disturbance, or other pathology in any sense, but is merely a preference, orientation or propensity on [a] par with and not different in kind from heterosexuality." To contrast this view with Donald

Webster Cory's, Rodwell quoted from the introduction that Cory had recently written for Dr. Albert Ellis's *Homosexuality: Its Causes and Cures:*

> Over a period of years, I have found myself more and more in agreement with Dr. Ellis's basic position . . . Homosexuals in this society, if they are exclusive or near exclusive in their erotic interests in their own sex, are disturbed individuals, and the state of being a confirmed homosexual is hence a disturbance . . . they are compulsive, neurotic . . . tend to be goofers, to be self-destructive, to make poor relationships with fellow human beings, and in fact, they are frequently borderline psychotics.[6]

After the sizable election victories of Hodges, Leitsch, and Kameny—and of Randy Wicker, who ran for secretary independently—the militants redoubled their efforts. On Easter Sunday 1965, Hodges, Leitsch, Wicker, and Rodwell led about twenty-five Mattachine members in a picket line at the United Nations to protest the news that the Castro government intended to round up Cuban homosexuals and put them into work camps. During the next few months, MSNY joined with the Washington Mattachine to demonstrate in front of the White House, at Independence Hall, and at federal agencies notorious for excluding homosexuals from jobs—the Civil Service Commission, the State Department, the Pentagon. The excitement this picketing engendered, as well as the homophile objectives that shaped militant efforts, were evident in an editorial in the *Eastern Mattachine Magazine* entitled "We're on the Move Now"— a line taken from Martin Luther King's talk to the Selma-to-Montgomery marchers: "The most hated and despised of minority groups has shown its face to the crowds, and it is plain for all to see that they are not horrible monsters. They are ordinary-looking, well-dressed human beings."[7]

·   ·   ·

Although Rodwell and Leitsch were pleased with the out-of-town initiatives, which generated a few minor news stories and won Kameny more meetings with federal officials, they wanted to find local issues that would permit MSNY to buttress its activist reputation. For several reasons, Leitsch thought police entrapment was the issue to develop. He belonged to a Manhattan-based coalition then fighting for a civilian complaint review board for the police. Others in the coalition considered the entrapment of homosexuals a serious problem. The professionals who at MSNY's behest had lobbied for the decriminalization of sodomy reported that entrapment was the issue that made the biggest impression on state legislators. Officials of the New York Civil Liberties Union indicated that entrapment was the only realm in which they were willing to fight court cases on behalf of homosexuals. Late in the summer of 1965, when a reporter from the *New York Post* asked Mattachine officials for help with a series of articles on abuses perpetuated by the new state penal code, the opportunity to develop entrapment into a public issue seemed at hand.

In Leitsch's eyes, the first imperative was to make people understand what entrapment was and why it was unfair. The point he wanted to stress was that it permitted a just law to be enforced in an unjust way. Section 722 of the New York Code held that "any person who with the intent to provoke a breach of the peace, or whereby a breach of the peace may be occasioned, commits any of the following acts, shall be deemed to have committed the offense of disorderly conduct." Its Subsection 8 specified as disorderly anyone who "frequents or loiters about any public place soliciting men for the purpose of committing a crime against nature or other lewdness." The courts had held that criminal solicitation required both an intent to breach the peace and an actual breach by one of the designated acts. The Mattachine's complaint was that local police chose to enforce the law against disorderly conduct through entrapment, a practice that victimized persons who had no intention of soliciting or being disorderly.

According to Mattachine officials, members of the Police Department's vice squad eager to impress superiors, fill arrest quotas, or set the stage for securing bribes went to public parks and toilets in civilian dress and used ploys ranging from verbal invitations to fondling their genitals to lure people into making advances. Worse, plainclothesmen selected for their sexual attractiveness were dispatched to entrap those who showed interest in them in bars and baths known to cater to homosexuals. Since the State Liquor Authority (SLA) could then revoke the licenses of such premises on grounds of "disorderliness," the threat of license suspension was used to obtain payoffs. It was not unknown for the police to refer entrapped homosexuals to lawyers who guaranteed to get them released if they would pay appropriate fees to appropriate officials.

Mattachine officials believed that the incidence of entrapment varied not only with the morals and greediness of police officers, SLA authorities, bar owners, lawyers, and judicial officials, but also with local politics. The number of entrapments seemed always to increase before local elections or when top police officers were being criticized. Elected officials needing the support of newspapers, civic groups, and voters got it by vowing "cleanups," and police officials under fire for poor performance or corruption staged them to show themselves active and upright. Or so Mattachine leaders inferred.

Although many who were entrapped called MSNY for legal advice, few were willing to give their names or to let their cases be used in legal challenges that might end the practice. Those entrapped in parks and public toilets were often men with families and careers seeking quick, impersonal homosexual encounters. Many considered themselves heterosexual. Most were anxious to conceal their homosexual interests, and few were concerned about crusading for homosexual rights. None wanted anything to do with the official records and the publicity necessary for any effort to document and eliminate abuses.[8] While those entrapped in bars and baths tended to be more comfortable with their involvement in the gay subculture, they were just as unwilling to risk exposure and embarrassment in a battle with authorities that seemed unlikely to succeed, and which, if it did, would benefit just as much those who had not taken any risks.

Under the circumstances, Leitsch believed he had to persuade the public both that entrapment occurred and that it was objectionable. In the summer of 1965, when *Post* reporter Joseph Kahn first came to MSNY looking for information, there were only one or two affidavits to show him. To obtain more documentation, Leitsch asked the lawyers to whom he referred anxious callers to collect affidavits. When Kahn insisted on firsthand evidence, Leitsch invited him to come to MSNY and listen in on telephone calls from victims. Often there were several a day.

Helping Kahn prepare an article describing the abusive practices of the police was only the first step in Leitsch's strategy to make entrapment a public issue. In response to the *Post* article, which appeared in December 1965, first deputy commissioner John F.

Walsh stated that the Police Department would not tolerate the use of entrapment. When the continued flow of telephone calls to MSNY proved otherwise, a delegation including a member of the Mattachine's Board of Psychiatric Advisers, Dr. Clarence Tripp, and one of his patients who had been entrapped visited *Post* editor James Wechsler and urged him to keep the campaign against entrapment alive by publicizing continued abuses. In March 1966, Wechsler responded by running an editorial on "Entrapment Inc.":

> Despite some expressions of official distaste for the activity, New York City police are still engaged in medieval harassment of real and alleged homosexuals.
>
> At a moment when the city cries out for protection against crimes of violence, a squad of grown robust police officers dedicates itself to the pursuit and entrapment of men suspected of preferring men to women.
>
> At the same time scores of officers are assigned to full-time surveillance of restaurants and bars where raids have occurred. Their presence is peculiarly pointless because the taverns under fire lose most of their patrons as soon as a "These Premises Have Been Raided" sign goes up . . .
>
> In this city of enlightenment, a primitive darkness still envelops the status of homosexuals. As they are driven from taverns, their refuge becomes the streets. Is that a form of social progress?[9]

The support they received from the *Post* encouraged Mattachine officials to look for other ways to publicize their grievances. In the spring of 1966, shortly after John Lindsay was inaugurated as mayor, the police began a cleanup of the Times Square and Greenwich Village areas. In response to the negative public reaction this "Operation New Broom" elicited, city officials scheduled a series of public meetings. In the Village, a seven-member Mattachine delegation attended a public meeting at the Judson Memorial Church, where Randy Wicker and Craig Rodwell drew parallels between the current wave of entrapments and gay-bar closings and a period of harassment in 1959 and 1960. An account of their efforts, and of the support they received from New York Civil Liberties Union executive director Aryeh Neier, appeared in the MSNY newsletter:

> After speeches by the panelists, the floor was opened to discussion . . . The first speaker from the floor was our own Randolfe Wicker, who

pointed out that until a few years ago gay bars were allowed to operate openly and freely. Homosexuals had a place to go and everyone was content. The bars were owned by private individuals and the situation was under control. Then the police "cracked down" on the bars and left the homosexual with no form of social outlet. This opened the door for underworld elements to gain a strangle hold on bars and restaurants catering to homosexuals. Now the city is attempting to repeat this action in the Village, and is forcing the closing of not only gay bars, but coffee houses, restaurants, and other places catering to teenagers. The result will be the same: dissatisfied citizens with no social outlet, forced to use streets and other areas as meeting places, forced to find other means of social outlet not always as harmless to the community as the present ones.

[Police] Chief Inspector [Sanford] Garelik responded by saying that gay bars are illegal . . . and that they are closed by the police because of "illicit activities." Mr. Wicker pointed out that these "illicit activities" were alleged solicitations, to which Garelik agreed, and that most of the solicitations were initiated by plainclothes policemen, which Garelik denied. Aryeh Neier took the podium to correct Garelik's misconceptions. He said that Garelik showed "a certain naivete" in stating that entrapment does not go on, and said, "It's alarming to think that the Chief Inspector doesn't know that a large number of police spend their duty hours dressed in tight pants, sneakers, and polo sweaters . . . to bring about solicitations." A loud ovation and shouts of "Bravo!" followed his statement.

Another Mattachine representative questioned Garelik as to his opinion of the effectiveness of using uniformed police as a deterrent force, as opposed to using plainclothesmen to elicit criminal acts of solicitation. Garelik agreed that uniformed officers are more efficient in most areas, but that plainclothesmen are necessary to arrest homosexuals at the request of neighborhood people concerned by the possibility of their children being molested. His statement was answered with jeers.[10]

Only hours after Garelik assured the Judson Church assembly that the police did not engage in entrapment, two homosexuals were arrested for solicitation a short distance away—at Julius, a Village bar long favored by homosexuals. Mattachine officials made sure that the press learned about the irony of the situation. The *New York Times* ran adjacent reports of Garelik's remarks and the almost simultaneous arrests. The next day Garelik gave an interview condemning the use of entrapment and urging individuals to report any instances of it. The front page of the next day's *Times* quoted this response from Mattachine officials: "The last thing homosexuals are going to do is complain about something; they'll just sit there like a possum, they're so afraid of their families finding out or losing their jobs."[11] More attuned to the circumstances cited by Mattachine leaders, the *Post* published an editorial welcoming Garelik's statement but pointing out that it was "his responsibility, not the public's, to get the word to the plainclothesmen and to review the 'quota' system under which the cops felt obliged to make arrests."[12]

Since one of those entrapped at Julius was an Anglican priest, a number of clergymen joined the fight. The most prominent was John Lassoe, legislative strategist for the Episcopal Diocese of New York and director of its Department for Christian Social Relations. Lassoe had won the hearts of Mattachine officials a year and a half before, when he testified in favor of decriminalizing sodomy at the State Assembly's hearings on criminal code revision. Subsequently, he had addressed a Mattachine public meeting and agreed to be of help when he could. Once entrapment was in the news, those in charge of MSNY prevailed upon Lassoe and other civic and professional leaders to call, write, and meet with city officials.

The campaign against entrapment seemed on the brink of success when Dick Leitsch, who succeeded Julian Hodges as MSNY president at the end of 1965, was invited to participate in an evaluation of Operation New Broom with Mayor Lindsay, police commissioner Howard Leary, and representatives of the Greenwich Village political, civic, and artistic establishments: Village district leader Ed Koch, Aryeh Neier, Village Gate owner Art D'Lugoff, and poet Allen Ginsberg. The Reverend Howard Moody of the Judson Memorial Church opened the meeting by recounting how not long before, Inspector Garelik had barely finished assuring a similar gathering that the police did not use entrapment when it was learned that two men had just been entrapped and arrested. Leitsch and Neier took this cue to describe how entrapment worked. Commissioner Leary responded that he opposed the practice, would limit solicitation arrests to those stemming from citizen complaints, and would take action against police officers who violated this policy. Lindsay promised to cooperate by appointing one of his assistants as a liaison between the mayor's office and the artists, businesses, and civic groups in the Village. Leitsch reported that Lindsay called their meeting one of the most exciting discussions he had engaged in since becoming mayor.

.   .   .

Heady with the success of their first militant campaign, Leitsch and his associates turned their attention to a related problem, the harassment and closing of gay bars. To learn how New York state's Alcoholic Beverage Law affected homosexuals—and subsequently to help make a public issue of the problems they had—Leitsch retained Frank Patton, a partner in the law firm of Ellis, Stringfellow, and Patton. Patton advised that despite widespread belief to the contrary, there was no clear law prohibiting gay bars. What he found was that the State Liquor Authority often revoked the licenses of bars frequented by homosexuals on the grounds that their proprietors permitted "unsavory conduct" or presided over "disorderly premises." The determination of "unsavory" behavior and "disorderliness" was usually made on the basis of incidents in which bar patrons indicated sexual interest in disguised vice squad officers. The courts had backed such license suspensions with rulings suggesting that bars that permitted homosexuals to congregate were by definition "unsavory" and "disorderly."

Those in charge of the Mattachine were convinced that the situation Patton described encouraged corruption and forced gay bars into the hands of criminal elements. They were willing to believe that most bar owners had to bribe SLA authorities in order to get and keep their liquor licenses. But they maintained that anyone who wanted to run a bar catering to homosexuals had to pay doubly because the plainclothesmen sent to encourage solicitations in gay bars would threaten to inform SLA officials that a bar was "unsavory" or "disorderly" unless its proprietors offered payoffs large enough to be divided between them and liquor officials. Thus bars frequented by homosexuals were forced into the hands of underworld figures adept at procuring unrecorded sums of money, paying bribes, and making a profit by developing monopolies, charging high prices, keeping shabby premises, and occasionally blackmailing well-known figures who patronized gay establishments.[13]

Leitsch and his colleagues decided that it was important to establish that bars could legally serve homosexuals. And since the State Liquor Authority refused to answer letters asking about its policy toward gay bars, they devised a plan to force it to reveal its stance. The plan was to have several respectable-looking men walk into a bar, announce that they were homosexual, and ask to be served. Leitsch and the others expected that the men would be refused service, and they planned to publicize this refusal so that the SLA would be forced to reveal its policies and, if they were discriminatory, provide grounds for a legal test case.

Despite the careful calculations, MSNY's "sip-in" failed to unfold as expected. Late in April 1966, when Leitsch, Rodwell, John Timmons, and five members of the press arrived at the Ukrainian-American Village Bar, which advertised its biases with a prominently displayed sign, instructing patrons "If You Are Gay, Please Stay Away," they found that the bar was closed. At a reporter's suggestion, the party moved to a Howard Johnson's, where the Mattachine trio sat down, asked to see the manager, and presented him with this written statement:

We, the undersigned, are homosexuals. We believe that a place of public accommodation has an obligation to serve an orderly person, and that we are entitled to service as long as we are orderly. We therefore ask to be served on your premises. Should you refuse to serve us, we will be obligated to file a complaint against you with the State Liquor Authority.

The manager laughed, declared that he could not tell the three were homosexual, and offered them a drink.[14]

Frustrated, the Mattachine entourage proceeded to Julius, where the management revealed its wariness with a sign reading "Patrons Must Face the Bar While Drinking." When Leitsch announced that he and his friends were homosexual, the bartender refused to serve them. Leitsch threatened to file a complaint with the State Liquor Authority, and the bartender replied that Julius was already suing to prevent the SLA from revoking its license because there had been two recent incidents of entrapment on its premises. Leitsch confessed that he knew about these and was willing to help the managers of Julius with their court battle, but said he had no choice but to file his own complaint.

The consequences of the sip-in were almost as unanticipated as the course of its execution. As planned, even before Leitsch prepared his formal complaint against Julius, reporters called to question SLA chairman Donald S. Hostetter. Articles in the *New York Times* and the *New York Post* quoted Hostetter as saying that the SLA never told bar licensees not to serve homosexuals, but took no action against owners or bartenders who refused to. Perhaps, Hostetter suggested publicly, New York City's Human Rights Commission (HRC) would take action.[15]

When William Booth, newly appointed HRC chairman, was questioned, he told reporters that his commission would investigate if a complaint was filed. For that matter, according to the *Times* story, Booth said that he had already agreed to help MSNY put an end to entrapment and that he believed the HRC's jurisdiction over discrimination based on sex also entitled it to deal with discrimination based on sexual orientation.

This course of events produced mixed feelings in Rodwell and other militants who wanted the sip-in to precipitate an issue that would stimulate public interest. It was more pleasing to Leitsch and others who were genuinely interested in improving the quality of life for local homosexuals. Yet if the results of the sip-in were a tribute to the skill with which Mattachine masterminds like Leitsch employed militant tactics, they also shifted the focus of the campaign into areas where militancy was of limited utility. For by announcing that the SLA did nothing to prevent its licensees from serving homosexuals, Hostetter enabled the SLA and the State Alcoholic Beverage Law to elude challenge, leaving MSNY with the much more subtle task of dealing with specific cases of discrimination and corruption —situations likely to lack the breadth and substance necessary for a militant crusade. Moreover, the prospect of making an issue of the absence of civil rights protection disappeared with Booth's assertion that the Human Rights Commission probably had jurisdiction over cases of discrimination based on sexual orientation.

· · ·

One of the first things that made Dick Leitsch realize that the opportunities for militant action were limited was the difficulty of finding problems that could be developed into public issues. To generate militant crusades, it was necessary to find instances of abuse; to persuade members of the press, civic leaders, and sizable segments of the public that these abuses were significant; and to convince public officials that aroused citizens insisted on reform. This was the strategy that had been used successfully in the spring of 1966 to pressure the Lindsay administration to end entrapment.

In order to gain maximum support, Mattachine leaders had billed the drive against entrapment as a campaign to protect individual civil liberties (specifically, the right to assemble in public without being lured into committing a crime) rather than as a crusade to protect a disadvantaged minority from injustice. Yet those in charge of MSNY viewed individual liberties and minority-group rights as opposite sides of the same coin. Both were favorite concerns of the liberal press; both were expected to strike a responsive chord in civic leaders and sophisticated segments of the public. What Mattachine leaders tried next, then, was to demonstrate that serious discrimination existed against homosexuals as a group.

The SLA's response to the sip-in had defused the discrimination issue in its most visible form: the harassment and closing of gay bars. And the immediacy of the bar issue had disappeared when, after it was announced that the SLA had no policy of denying licenses to bars that served homosexuals, incidents of police harassment and license suspension ceased and William Booth made his statement for the Human Rights Commission.

Both in his statements to reporters and in a letter to Leitsch, Booth suggested that the HRC's jurisdiction over discrimination based on sex permitted it to deal with discrimination based on sexual orientation. By the fall of 1966, when the commissioner admitted at a Mattachine public lecture that the HRC's authority over cases involving sexual orientation was ambiguous, the militants had lost their momentum. Nevertheless, when Booth tried to sweeten his news by promising to urge Mayor Lindsay to issue a proclamation banning discrimination against homosexuals in city jobs and by offering to help MSNY amend the local human rights ordinance, Leitsch jumped to rekindle enthusiasm. The next day, he issued a glowing memo to the Mattachine board of directors:

This is, of course, the most revolutionary breakthrough the Society has made yet. Under Booth's leadership, the HRC has become the most advanced and effective agency of its kind in America today. The pattern it is setting will certainly be emulated by other groups throughout the

country. It is imperative that we follow through on this offer of cooperation, and do it quickly . . .

Both John Lassoe, of the Episcopal Diocese, and several representatives of the New York Civil Liberties Union have expressed interest in
the amendment idea. Neither of them can pledge support at this early
date, of course, but the future does look bright.

Two months later, in another memo to the board, Leitsch was less
sanguine:

Unfortunately, we have found it difficult to get the rights cases to send
to [Booth] (most employment discrimination seems based on a prior
arrest, rather than on homosexuality, *per se,* and these are entirely different matters). The study done two years ago by the Society is inadequate,
in my opinion, to be of much help. I am at a loss for what to use as an
"opening" to begin a campaign against employment discrimination, and
I'd like your suggestions and advice on Friday. I keep getting secondhand
reports that Booth is getting impatient waiting for us to bring him
something to work with.

It had first become apparent that documenting discrimination
would be difficult in the spring of 1965 when, upon undertaking the
"study" Leitsch mentioned, the militants had written to fifty local
corporations asking whether they employed known or rumored
homosexuals. There had been only thirteen vague replies. As Leitsch
suggested, the difficulty with making employment discrimination
against homosexuals a public issue was that it was hard to prove that
there was such a thing. Employment discrimination was a more
subtle matter than entrapment and gay-bar harassment. Although
governments and businesses did have regulations prohibiting the
employment of homosexuals, and could discriminate discreetly even
if they did not, the incidence of actual discrimination against homosexuals seemed to be relatively small. People open about their homosexuality tended to cluster in professions like fashion and the arts,
where homosexual preferences were inconsequential, or even advan-
tageous. Those in more conventional jobs found that as long as they
were careful not to be arrested for soliciting sex or for being in a gay
bar or bathhouse, they could avoid difficulties. Because so many
homosexuals found it easy to pass as heterosexuals, the real problem
seemed to be less the actual discrimination experienced by the few

homosexuals who were obvious or exposed than the threat of discrimination that kept so many homosexuals fearful, inhibited, neurotic, and subject to arbitrary fortune. Moreover, since "passing" made one safe, homosexuals who were discovered and discriminated against in one instance were reluctant to supply any documentation or to endure any publicity that might identify them as homosexual elsewhere. As a result, although Leitsch and his colleagues asked every homosexual they came in contact with to report incidents of discrimination, and even set up sidewalk tables in Greenwich Village for that purpose, they found few who could give concrete examples of discriminatory treatment and even fewer who would do so for the record.

The situation was such that in early 1967, when the acting chairman of New York City's Civil Service Commission announced that the city had been hiring homosexuals for all but a few positions, Mattachine officials had to stretch to take credit for the reform. An announcement in MSNY's newsletter was candid:

> We were sitting calmly at home on January 6, watching a late news program, when all of a sudden the announcer reported that the City of New York has, for the past year, quietly been hiring homosexuals, unwed mothers, and parolees, which had all been against city policy previously. The next day the story was in all of New York's newspapers. When we asked President Dick Leitsch about this, after his initial, "I didn't do it all," he admitted that this was as much news to him as to anyone else in the Society. Not that we haven't been trying for years to accomplish something like this: Mayor Lindsay has been on our mailing list for a very long time (at *least* since he voted, along with a very few others, in Congress against Dowdy, who was trying to illegalize the Washington Mattachine), and William Booth, New York's Commissioner of Human Rights, has been extremely sympathetic to our work and spoke to us last October. And of course we write letters to everyone we can think of about employment, so we can take credit for agitating, if not directly bringing the change about.[16]

In fact, Leitsch had long been looking elsewhere for problems that could be turned into public issues. At the board meeting that followed his memo on the difficulty of documenting job discrimination, he reported that meetings he had held with housing and license commission officials to discover if their regulations were discriminatory had been unproductive and then asked for suggestions about what to do next. Because no one had any other ideas, most of the talk focused on campaigning to repeal the sodomy laws. (Although the Commission on Revision of the Penal Law and Criminal Code appointed by Nelson Rockefeller had recommended decriminalization, the legislature had voted in 1964 to keep sodomy a crime but to make it a misdemeanor rather than a felony and to reduce the maximum penalty from twenty years to three months.) Members of the board spoke not only about persuading important legislators to sponsor bills but about circulating petitions and picketing the opening day of the 1967 legislative session.

Despite all the talk of action, a subsequent "bulletin to all homophile organizations" announced only that Mattachine representatives were visiting newly elected state legislators to seek support for sodomy-law reform. Although the circular also mentioned a concurrent campaign to persuade the state constitutional convention scheduled to meet in the spring of 1967 to add sexual orientation to the categories of discrimination proscribed by the state constitution, its concluding paragraph seemed a weary epitaph to MSNY's efforts to make civil rights protection the focus of a militant crusade: "Though it is unlikely that New York's Constitutional Convention will accept the proposal of MSNY, public discussion of the need for laws prohibiting discrimination against homosexuals cannot help but create a climate in which such discrimination will be attacked."

Even as he dispatched the bulletin, Leitsch knew that the nature of the proposed initiatives precluded new militant campaigns. Writing to a friend shortly after the board directed him to look into sodomy-law reform, he confessed: "I wish they hadn't voted this until we had the advice and counsel of John Lassoe and some of our other legislature-watchers . . . I'll confess ignorance of lobbying techniques, legislative processes, etc., but I guess there's no better way to learn than to do it."[17] As it was, ignorance forced Leitsch to rely on Lassoe, MSNY legal adviser Irwin Strauss, and other Mattachine veterans with moderate homophile outlooks. These counselors admonished him to proceed slowly, to work behind the scenes, to cultivate influential civic, professional, and religious leaders, and to accommodate the concerns of those who would lose support if it became known that they were viewing the problems of homosexuals sympathetically.

If the turn to long-term, low-key negotiations was one sign of a retreat from militancy, the growing emphasis on legal initiatives was another. Lawyers "Irwin Tuck" and "Austin Wade," insisting that legal endeavors were a legitimate extension of research and education, had talked from the New York chapter's inception about helping MSNY challenge discriminatory laws and policies in the courts. Yet partly because those eager to make MSNY a professional educational association were skeptical about the appropriateness of legal initiatives, and partly because the two lawyers were reluctant to go public, MSNY had initiated no legal test cases before Leitsch took charge. During 1967, as the Mattachine executive became progressively more pessimistic about developing new public issues, he spent more and more time working with legal associates and officials of the Civil Liberties Union on court cases involving entrapment, solicitation, disorderly conduct, cross dressing, and the deportation of homosexual aliens.

To perpetuate the impression that MSNY was politically powerful even as circumstances deprived it of issues around which to mobilize support, Leitsch frequently mentioned litigation. In the fall of 1966, when talking about ending employment discrimination, he spoke of "crusading for reform." But in the fall of 1967, spurred to turn his attention to the problem by the city's reluctance to extend its policy of nondiscriminatory hiring to the jobs of hospital-care investigators, welfare workers, and children's counselors, he took a distinctly moderate line. Late in 1967 he reported in MSNY's newsletter:

> MSNY is currently bombarding the City government with letters, memoranda, and professional opinions in the hope of changing their minds about these traces of discrimination. If negotiations are not successful, there are at least two possible test-cases on the horizon, and we may be compelled to support suits against the City . . .[18]

Whether engaging in legal initiatives or consultations, as long as Leitsch kept MSNY concerned primarily with reforming official policies, he preserved the keystone of its militant orientation. The ultimate triumph of moderation came when he began to speak less of changing laws and more of working with public officials to solve problems of common interest; less of mounting political crusades and more of educating important professionals; less of eliminating injustices endured by the homosexual minority and more of making tangible improvements in individual lives.

Limited resources joined circumstances in dictating this return to moderate aims and tactics. In 1965 and 1966, working to make the Mattachine militant, Leitsch and his supporters had argued that new recruits and financial contributions would be attracted if people saw that MSNY had been transformed into an ambitious civil rights group. Their strategy had not been without success: in 1965, MSNY's membership jumped from 125 to 300. But most of the new members thrilled at the daring of militant initiatives without feeling that they could contribute personally. MSNY leaders were enthusiastic about sponsoring picket lines in Philadelphia and Washington, D.C., partly because most of the two dozen or so marchers they could muster were reluctant to be publicly political in Manhattan. Only three had "sipped-in," partly because so few Mattachine members were willing to have their photographs printed in the local newspapers. (By 1966, Kameny had quarreled with Leitsch and was devoting most of his energy to drawing homophile groups into coalitions; Wicker, having made money producing and selling gay rights buttons, had withdrawn from gay political activity to enter the button business; and the militant reorientation of MSNY had frightened away most of the closeted homosexual professionals whom de Dion and Dewees had enlisted in 1962 and 1963.)

The truth is that for all of the publicity generated by its season of militancy, toward the end of the 1960s MSNY could boast fewer than a dozen members willing to participate in activities that required them both to reveal that they were homosexuals and to endure the attendant embarrassment, risks, and costs. Craig Rodwell's committee, Mattachine Young Adults, created to attract idealistic new recruits in the summer of 1965, had petered out soon after it was started. So had the Community Alert Program, which brought members of MSNY to the sidewalks of Greenwich Village for the same purpose in the summer of 1966. Most of those willing to work for the Mattachine wanted to meet other homosexuals, to help peers in distress, to enjoy the camaraderie. Few were caught up by the militant vision of a political crusade to secure rights and status for the homosexual minority.

It was partly this lack of support that forced Leitsch to invest more and more time in educational and negotiating ventures which he could pursue by himself or with the help of a few discreet professional associates. And soon he began to think as well as to act like a moderate. He came increasingly to believe that the issues raised by homosexuality were complicated. He contended that long-term efforts to gather and disseminate information, to win the support of mental health and social welfare professionals, and to help troubled individuals were more important than dramatic crusades to reform policies. And he maintained that consultations and court tests that resulted in concrete improvements were more important than bold public initiatives that made headlines but alienated influential supporters.

By the end of the 1960s, Leitsch's views were not unlike those of the half-dozen homosexuals Sam Morford and Tony Segura had assembled into a New York chapter of the Mattachine Society in 1955. The difference was that MSNY's mid-sixties militancy had so established the group as a homosexual rights organization that Leitsch was able to do what his predecessors had only dreamed of doing.

3

The Failure of Coalition

TOWARD THE MIDDLE of the 1960s, when Franklin Kameny and other militant homophile leaders resolved to build a homosexual rights movement modeled after the black civil rights movement, they tried to draw homophile groups into coalition. During the first half of 1963, at Kameny's initiative, the Washington Mattachine, the Janus Society of Philadelphia, and MSNY and DOB–New York joined in a regional federation, East Coast Homophile Organizations. After 1965, ECHO was succeeded by a series of larger and more ambitious Eastern Regional Coalitions of Homophile Organizations, dubbed ERC, ERCH, and ERCHO. After attending ECHO's third annual conference, leaders of important homophile groups in other parts of the country created a National Planning Conference of Homophile Organizations, later renamed the North American Conference of Homophile Organizations and nicknamed NACHO. Each of these efforts at interorganizational cooperation was undercut by ideological differences and organizational rivalries. DOB–New York became alienated from its homophile neighbors first. MSNY disavowed coalition later but remained aloof longer.

. . .

Frank Kameny saw ECHO as a vehicle for making other homophile groups militant. In the fall of 1963, at the first ECHO conference, he won admirers by describing MSW's first contacts with federal officials. To the next year's conference, built around the theme "Homosexuality: Civil Liberties and Social Rights," he invited lawyers and civic leaders to discuss discrimination. At the same session, to highlight the differences between those who favored civil liberties–social action and those satisfied with information-education, Kameny engaged in a formal debate with a proponent of moderate homophile tactics.

In an article called "Act or Teach," reporting on that debate for the *Ladder,* Barbara Gittings and "Kay Tobin" sharpened the issues at stake by presenting the opponents' views as "the case for legislation" and "the case for education." Although these captions were slightly misleading, they captured the drift of debate between the militant and moderate camps in late 1964 and early 1965. By that time, both groups were willing to concede that homophile efforts should be concerned with reforming discriminatory policies. But they differed, as before, on how official reforms should be pursued —with actions boldly political or through education. As 1965 progressed, these differences came to a head over the matter of staging demonstrations.

The first picket lines held by MSNY and MSW produced a sharp division among DOB–New York's leaders. As Gittings and Tobin assumed responsibility for editing the *Ladder* and became less involved in day-to-day operations of the New York chapter, they applauded the homophile picket lines and urged the Daughters to join. Left in charge of DOB–New York, Meredith Grey and Shirley Willer remained convinced that picketing was extremist. In May 1965, when Kameny proposed that ECHO sponsor monthly demonstrations in Washington during the summer, Willer and Grey objected. In June, the two submitted a resolution asking that the coalition "not engage in any activity contrary to the policy or welfare of any participating organization."[1] When the resolution was voted down, the Daughters withdrew from ECHO.

DOB–New York was officially absent, but some of its members marched in ECHO's demonstrations. One was "Ernestine Eckstein," a young black woman who had been active in the NAACP while an undergraduate at the University of Indiana in the early 1960s. Others were Gittings, Tobin, and lesbian members of the Mattachine chapters in Washington, Philadelphia, and New York, many of whom had joined DOB–New York to get the *Ladder* and were enrolled in DOB–New York because it was the Daughters' only eastern chapter.

During the summer of 1965, Eckstein and her out-of-town friends worked to make DOB–New York militant. When they succeeded in persuading a majority of the dozen who gathered for the group's July business meeting to approve a resolution asking the national governing board to support ECHO's program of demonstrations, Grey challenged the eligibility of one of their supporters and Willer called for a new vote in August. Eckstein and the others were able to marshal support for an even more elaborate proposal:

> Resolved, that the New York chapter of Daughters of Bilitis requests that the Governing Board revise its present nonparticipatory policy and adopt a full scale progressive program of direct action to push the drive for full equality for the homosexual citizen. That Daughters of Bilitis not only endorse by giving its name to such action, support with monetary contributions and use of its facilities, but cooperate by helping to plan the direct action program of the several East Coast Homophile Organizations . . .[2]

Although the governing board declined to cooperate, and although Willer and Grey remained disapproving, Eckstein redoubled her efforts. In the fall of 1965, hoping to politicize members and to attract more socially conscious "sisters," she scheduled discussions about civil rights and publicized them in the *Village Voice*. Her election to the chapter vice-presidency that winter she saw as a sign of a subtle shift towards activism.

But the subtlety was lost—and the trend reversed—when Deni Covello came down from the Bronx. Only two years out of high school, where she had been active in a student civil rights group and had helped plan demonstrations against civil defense drills in the public schools, Covello was told that she was too young to become a member of DOB but was welcome to attend its programs. Almost immediately, the young Bob Dylan fan began to urge participation in civil rights protests and antiwar demonstrations, expressing sentiments about life style, culture, and politics that would later be characterized as countercultural and New Left. Covello hoped to persuade her lesbian sisters that a variety of related causes called for political activism, but she succeeded in doing just the opposite. Her arguments disrupted DOB events, scared members who had begun to think about politics, and regenerated support for moderates who insisted that DOB–New York's mission remain research, education, and counseling.

In April 1966, Willer and Grey persuaded a frightened DOB majority to endorse a new program of action: establishing a speakers' bureau, collecting and distributing information about homosexuality, forming a committee to investigate legal issues, and obtaining the services of a psychiatrist for individual and group counseling. The moderate homophile outlook responsible for this program prevailed as well in the platform that, in the summer, brought Willer the national DOB presidency and Grey the post of national secretary. Addressing the second National Planning Conference of Homophile Organizations shortly thereafter, Willer first asserted that the approaches of homophile groups should be "as diverse as imagination will allow" and then made clear that she considered picketing beyond imagination:

> Demonstrations which define the homosexual as a unique minority defeat the very cause for which the homosexual strives—*to be an integral part of society.* The homosexual must show that he is, in fact, *not* a unique "social problem." That concept is too widely held to require endorsement from homophile organizations.[3]

In correspondence with the author, Willer and Grey responded to a query about DOB–New York's abstention from ECHO's militant initiatives by saying that they had always favored picketing but were prevented from leading their chapter onto the lines by the objections of the national governing board and by the reservations of the local rank and file. Their recall of their past positions is faulty, but their recollection of organizational constraints emphasizes something significant: that maintenance of the group was as important a factor as political convictions in determining chapter policy.

The need to defer to the governing board mentioned by Willer and Grey was the most immediate organizational consideration behind DOB–New York's withdrawal from ECHO. When Willer and Grey called Del Martin and Phyllis Lyon, who dominated the board, and reported that ECHO was determined to sponsor demonstrations, Martin and Lyon instructed them to withdraw from the coalition. The two San Franciscans may well have been recalling the incident when they wrote in *Lesbian/Woman* that "DOB felt a responsibility to temper the more rash or 'far out' tactics of male organizations."[4]

Willer and Grey followed Martin and Lyons's instructions not only because of their personal reservations about rash tactics but also because they felt responsible for safeguarding their chapter's identity, legitimacy, and resources. To protect these mainstays of their organization, they wanted to keep their chapter under the official umbrella of the national DOB and to avoid activities that might compromise its official commitment to education and research or diminish its appeal to lesbians seeking psychological and social support. As Grey explained in a letter describing DOB–New York's activities:

> The best-attended activities were gab 'n java [talk and coffee] sessions, uninhibited in-group discussions of problems, and the perennial favorite topics selected by the participants give a fair idea of the type of problem the average young lesbian considered important.
>   1. Butch and Femme (role playing, its use and abuse)
>   2. Shall I tell them I'm gay? (Parents, friends, associates)
>   3. Children in a gay family (including many childless gay girls who wanted to adopt children)
> On the whole, the questions were matters of private concern. These women were not social-conscious oriented. The organization was geared to this type of person and it was with greatest difficulty that the officers suggested to unheeding members there might be greater issues worthy of their attention. The one thing the average member wanted was personal privacy and the suggestion that the member give up her privacy for a greater good was not well received.[5]

. . .

When Shirley Willer addressed the second National Planning Conference of Homophile Organizations in the summer of 1966, she made some observations that throw additional light on why she, Grey, and other lesbians went unstirred by the crusades of the homophile militants. In that speech, although she failed to acknowledge that the paucity of lesbian bars, the virtual absence of public sexual activity among gay women, and the characteristic patterns of the lesbian subculture were in large part responsible, Willer argued that "police harassment, unequal law enforcement, legal proscription of sexual practices and . . . disproportionate penalties for acts of questionable taste such as evolve from solicitations, washroom sex acts and transsexual attire" were not problems for female homosexuals. She further contended that lesbians were mainly concerned about "job security, career advancement, and family relationships," in which their problems usually stemmed more from their gender than from their sexual orientation, and which were the concern more of the "women's civil rights movement" than the "homosexual civil liberties movement."[6] In short, Willer suggested that the issues championed by militant homophile leaders had little potential for politicizing female homosexuals because they had little bearing on lesbian lives and because they ignored what was most responsible for the lesbian's problems—discrimination based on sex.

Though Willer wanted DOB to develop what she called "the women's angle," she was not inclined to lead the Daughters out of the homophile movement. Indeed, she believed that DOB should participate in homophile coalitions, not least so that it could teach male homosexuals about the special problems lesbians had because they were women, but she felt it should not surrender the autonomy that would permit it to devote its resources to the distinctive concerns of lesbians. Thus Willer wanted homophile coalitions to be loosely structured conferences where ideas could be exchanged, not tightly knit federations where policies would be developed and carried out. Foster Gunnison, chairman of the National Planning Conference's credentials committee, described her views this way: "Basically, she's in favor of a very loose federation without any rules, organization, policy, etc.—just a sort of UN-type forum for ideas."[7]

Gunnison was also known to remark, "A conference is not truly a conference unless . . . Shirley Willer breaks down in tears over DOB getting left out in the cold."[8] This was taken as proof that few male homophile leaders understood the feminist concerns that led DOB's leaders to be so jealous about their organization's autonomy. The perceived obtuseness provoked Martin, Lyon, and other western leaders of the Daughters of Bilitis to charge that homosexual men were as insensitive to women's concerns as heterosexual men.

In an editorial, "The Lesbian's Majority Status," she wrote for the June 1967 issue of the *Ladder,* Del Martin went so far as to suggest that because their lives were so different from those of gay men, lesbians should think of themselves more as women than as homosexuals and associate more with women's organizations than with homophile groups. "The Lesbian, after all, is first of all a *woman*—an individual who must earn her own livelihood . . . much more concerned with problems of inequality in job and educational opportunities," Martin argued, urging her readers to involve themselves in organizations like the newly formed National Organization for Women (NOW), the League of Women Voters, and the Business and Professional Women's Club, rather than in groups dominated by homosexual men. She did not urge lesbians to withdraw from all homophile organizations, mentioning the San Francisco–based Council on Religion and the Homosexual, a pioneering coalition of gay leaders and clergymen, and the Tavern Guild, an organization of gay-bar owners, as groups in which women had found it possible to work side by side with men. But the National Planning Conference of Homophile Organizations and its regional coalitions she dismissed as "time-consuming and costly" associations that lesbians would do better to avoid.[9]

For Martin to let feminist sentiments carry her to these extremes jolted Willer and Grey, who believed it important to work side by side with male homosexuals, and who feared that heterosexual women and women's organizations would be less receptive to lesbians and their concerns than male homosexuals and homophile groups. Grey wrote a letter to the *Ladder* saying that it was "obvious lesbians should participate in the fight for improved civil rights for women" but that Martin's suggestion that lesbians had more in common with heterosexual women than with homosexual men went too far. "I am not sure which offends me more," she wrote, "the banal, supine sex of the soapsuds ads, to which I am constantly exposed, or the tea room scenes, which I can avoid." As for the question of whom DOB and its members should affiliate with politically, Grey argued that male homophile groups approved of "the lesbian's preference for a member of her own sex as a love object . . . at least in principle" and that "before sending my $5.00 to Miss Friedan's group, I would require some token of good faith that they would accept my sisters as happily as they would accept my money." She concluded by defending the operations of the credentials committee of the National Planning Conference: "Why has the majority failed its call to greatness? Mostly because girls have not learned to do, but only to applaud . . . or whine . . . Nowhere in our society have women played a more prominent role than on the credentials committee of the National Planning Conference of Homophile Organizations."[10]

Although Martin recanted some of her words in a letter printed in the *Ladder* even before Grey's challenge appeared ("I am very happy to eat my words—The editorial was written prior to the regional meetings which . . . were all highly successful"),[11] the drift of her sentiments was clear. In 1968, she and Lyon became the first openly lesbian couple to join the National Organization for Women. Shortly thereafter, identifying herself as Dorothy L. Martin, secretary of the San Francisco chapter of the National Organization for Women, she wrote an article for the *Ladder* called "The Lesbian's Other Identity." Meanwhile, the presidency of DOB and the editorship of the *Ladder* passed into the hands of Rita LaPorte and "Gene Damon," who made little secret of their belief that DOB belonged in the women's movement rather than the homophile movement.

Fighting with male leaders to keep DOB from becoming too deeply embroiled in homophile affairs, Willer and Grey were inclined to raise their feminist banner; fighting with western leaders to keep DOB from forsaking the homophile movement for the women's movement, they were inclined to lower it. The New York chapter followed their lead. From the summer of 1966 until the summer of 1967—a year in which *Pageant* magazine quoted Shirley Willer as saying that "women are sociologically an oppressed minority who seldom question the ruling group's right to keep them down and exploit them,"[12]—DOB–New York's newsletter carried such items of feminist concern as an announcement that NOW had been formed and a review of an article on men in *Look* that Grey described as "in keeping with the prevailing fiction of male supremacy."[13] Yet the newsletter never stopped reporting on the homophile movement. And after the exchange between Martin and Grey, articles focusing on women in general were rare. For that matter, in May 1967, DOB–New York took the initiative of convening the first Eastern Regional Conference of Homophile Organizations held since ECHO's collapse at the end of 1965. DOB–New York's leaders told those invited that ERC's "meetings will focus on those important issues and interests that give some promise of keeping such an alliance together" and "that participants . . . will be committed to take only such actions as the participating group itself deems necessary, regardless of the preponderance of sentiment at the meeting."[14]

To some extent, Willer and Grey's loyalty to the homophile movement reflected that, personally and politically, they identified more strongly with homosexuals than with women; to some extent, it reflected their responsiveness to rank-and-file chapter members. Although, in Willer and Grey's perceptions, the lesbians drawn to DOB–New York strongly identified as women and felt that they suffered discrimination more as females than as homosexuals, few of them felt very close to heterosexual women or took much interest in women's political organizations. The prejudice, defensiveness, and rejection these lesbians encountered from heterosexual women paralleled what their homosexual brethren experienced from heterosexual men. The reason the women came to DOB was to be with other lesbians. And those aware that the work of women's organizations would benefit lesbians as well as other women were convinced that the overt involvement of lesbians in feminist efforts would only impede progress.

Initially the couple who replaced Willer and Grey at the helm of DOB–New York saw things much as everyone else in the group did. Late in 1967, when "Jeanne Perry" and "Eleanor Krane" assumed control, they said their goal was to make DOB–New York a "safe haven" for lesbians. Only after attending a session of ERCH, which had evolved out of the coalition meetings DOB–New York had sponsored the spring before, did Krane inform the membership that she had come to see the importance of the "outer-directed activities" advocated by militant homophile leaders. Although Perry and Krane were also concerned about women's rights, they believed that DOB–New York's priorities were very different from those of local feminist groups. In the summer of 1968, when Ti-Grace Atkinson, the newly elected president of the New York chapter of the National Organization for Women, offered to address DOB–New York, Perry and Krane told her an appearance would be inappropriate.

By the end of the 1960s, the leaders of ERCHO, ERCH's successor, were regularly urging the leaders of DOB–New York to make their group a more integral part of the homophile movement. Yet even though Perry and Krane supported the efforts of the militants, participated in their coalitions and conferences, and lent DOB–New York's name to demonstrations and negotiations, they respected the reluctance of rank-and-file members to get further involved.

In the fall of 1968, "Martha Shelley" became president of the New York chapter. In a letter to the membership, she summed up circumstances that from the beginning had kept DOB–New York distant from its gay political neighbors:

DOB is an organization with two major functions: It assists the Lesbian, and it attempts to make changes in straight society. We have been doing a good job in taking care of our own . . . Our socials, discussions, counseling and referral services have been a tremendous help to many people.

We have not been so successful in making changes in society. Many girls do not feel this as a strong need, and prefer to settle down with a mate, go out in gay society once in a while, and forget about the outside world.

It is true that the problem posed by straight society is less urgent for women than for men. Very few women get in trouble with the law. But most of us want to function freely in society, without fear, and this requires that we educate the public.

In order to fight for change, we need to band together with the men in the homophile movement. We must not lose our autonomy as DOB, or we will lose our ability to serve the Lesbian through an organization "just for girls." But we must also take action outside our own home.[15]

Shelley worked to politicize her sisters, but not until two years later, when she had left her militant homophile views far behind and become an ardent lesbian feminist, was she successful in steering DOB–New York from its nonpolitical course.

. . .

To the militants who wanted to build a strong and coherent homophile movement, the aloofness of the New York Mattachine was even more frustrating than that of DOB–New York—not least because Dick Leitsch had once been militant himself. As editor of MSNY's publications and office manager, then as president-elect, Leitsch had been as loud as Kameny, Rodwell, and Gittings in calling for coalition. Late in the summer of 1965, writing to persuade Kameny's successor as head of the Washington Mattachine to support an ECHO strong enough to fashion a unified homosexual rights crusade, he spoke passionately of his own commitment:

. . . as for myself, I freely admit that the movement and the ends for which we are all working are a hell of a lot more important to me than any single organization . . . I ran for my office on the ground that I am interested in the *movement,* and the aims of that movement. I publicly stated that

I considered the Mattachine Society Inc. of New York less important
than the movement . . .

We must work together and not worry [about] who gets credit, or
whether ECHO or MSNY or MSW gets credit for an action. The important thing is the action—and with pooled resources, pooled power,
pooled efforts, the action will be swifter and more effective.[16]

As his emphasis on action implied, Leitsch saw militant campaigns less as vehicles for rallying popular support and edifying the
public than as instruments for securing official reforms. This was
where he and Rodwell parted company. When Rodwell spoke of
action, he envisioned demonstrations and other public relations
initiatives that would make people aware of the grievances of homosexuals and would motivate them to join the movement to eliminate
discrimination. Leitsch was more inclined to stress getting reforms.
And he grew to believe that reforms were more important for the
improvements they made in the lives of individual homosexuals than
for the edifying example they provided for the populace.

Leitsch's preoccupation with tangible results marked him as a
militant with moderate leanings; and the more willingly he settled for
quietly negotiated changes that benefited individuals, instead of reforms that produced publicity and set an official example, the more
moderate he became. It was his desire for concrete accomplishments
that led Leitsch to turn to consultations with officials and court tests
as he found that militant campaigns were unfeasible. And it was this
same desire that prompted him to change his mind about the importance of coalition.

The fall of 1965 was full of quarreling between MSW and MSNY.
MSW refused to pay what MSNY maintained was its fair share of
the costs of the 1965 ECHO conference. MSNY insisted that MSW's
contribution to production of the *Eastern Mattachine Magazine* was
insufficient. In December, Leitsch wrote Kameny that these and
other experiences had soured him on future cooperation:

It is because of this sort of thing that MSNY is going to become more
and more a New York operation, and to hell with the rest of the country.
We'll cooperate when we can, but every step towards cooperation will
be pragmatically considered and suspiciously examined . . .

I'm sorry for the invective, but I'm damn mad. I've spent the last year fighting with the WSDG [the West Side Discussion Group], the DOB, and MSW. I'm sick to death of it, and I want to fight City Hall. Perhaps by ignoring other organizations I can find the time to do it.[17]

During 1966, Leitsch avoided dealings with other homophile groups, ignored the first two meetings of the National Planning Conference, and gave his full attention to MSNY's militant agenda —the fight against entrapment, the legitimization of gay bars, civil rights protection. He defended his determination to keep MSNY out of cooperative endeavors by arguing that homophile groups should spend their time bettering life for homosexuals and that those that worked to become powerful in their own bailiwicks would be the most successful at this.

Not until Leitsch had a series of clashes with his former allies did he recognize that his ideas about gay political activity had evolved in a way that set him apart from the militants. The first of these clashes came in May 1968, when the Mattachine president was asked to join Barbara Gittings and Clark Polak, of Philadelphia's Law Reform Society, in a meeting with staff representatives of the United Church of Christ. The joint endeavor got off to a bad start when, ignoring Leitsch's objections, Gittings and Polak invited Kameny to join them. Tensions came to a head when Leitsch repeatedly disagreed with the views expressed by the others.

In an account of the church conference prepared for (but not printed in) MSNY's newsletter, Leitsch reported fundamental differences in what he and "the big three" regarded as major obstacles to justice for the homosexual. According to Leitsch's account, when asked to name the single most important problem facing American homosexuals, Kameny had cited "the inability to work for the Federal Government, which underwrites all other forms of employment discrimination." Gittings and Polak had concurred. Leitsch contended "that most homosexuals find jobs in which they can be happy, despite the admitted prejudice against us in some."[18] He pointed instead to the attitudes about homosexuality that made homosexuals feel inferior and to the fears and abuses that prevented them from having satisfying social lives. In retrospect, these positions are easily identified: the focus on official policy was the keystone of the militant homophile outlook, the focus on popular prejudice and real deprivations that of the moderate homophile outlook.

Instead of writing about these differences in basic political philosophy, Leitsch focused on how Kameny, Gittings, and Polak behaved. He complained that they ignored questions and comments. He charged that they shouted about bias and evil when the views of experts were mentioned, insisting that they, as homosexuals, were better equipped to talk about homosexuality. What Leitsch failed to recognize was that homophile leaders eager to rouse support for a militant crusade believed their goals best served by the fervent portrayal of issues as simple and moral, just as those who wanted to establish good working relationships with influential professionals believed theirs served by courtesy, reason, and tact.

. . .

In an exchange of letters after the conference, Leitsch and Kameny explored their disagreements more fully. The exchange helped not only the two principals but many of their followers to become clearer about the differences between moderate and militant views on the nature of sexual orientation, the appropriateness of discouraging and hiding homosexual preferences, and the advisability of labeling and emphasizing the differences between "gays" and "straights." This clarification of views strengthened Leitsch's resolve to keep MSNY out of militant-dominated coalitions. MSNY avoided the National Planning Conferences, sent only an observer to the New York Cooperation Committee created by ERCH in the summer of 1968, and boycotted ERCHO's meetings and demonstrations until 1969, when the emergence of gay liberation groups prompted Mattachine officials to reassess the independence Leitsch insisted on.

At the United Church of Christ conference, Kameny had provoked Leitsch by challenging the notion that most people, during the course of their lives, have a mixture of homosexual and heterosexual feelings and experiences. According to Leitsch, when some of the ministers cited Kinsey statistics maintaining that a relatively small number of people engaged exclusively or nearly exclusively in homosexual behavior while a much larger number engaged, simultaneously or at different stages in their lives, in both homosexual and heterosexual activity, Kameny insisted that "homosexuality and heterosexuality are not really a continuum," that "people are always either one or the other," and that "those who engage in sexual acts with men and women both are simply 'closet queens' who use their heterosexual acts as a facade to hide their homosexual behavior."[19]

In his first letter to Kameny, Leitsch accused him of "spieling hogwash" by "twisting . . . the Kinsey data to make a point which Dr. Pomeroy and Dr. Kinsey would not agree with." Citing his own sexual history, his dealings with those who sought help from MSNY, and his talks with Drs. Wardell Pomeroy, C. A. Tripp, and other mental health professionals associated with the Mattachine, Leitsch maintained that most people were bisexual and that MSNY's activities were premised on this:

> We operate under the theory that what can be called the homosexual comprises only a small handful of all those who can and do have problems with homosexuality. Just read through the briefs in the cases involving homosexuality and you'll notice that the preponderance of them involve people with only sporadic homosexual behavior . . . nearly all of the entrapment cases we have on file here, and 90% of the people who get arrested in subway toilets, are only occasionally homosexually active. Similarly, those who want psychiatric, religious or other counselling are seldom the committed homosexuals, who participate freely and openly in the homosexual community, but the ones who now and again participate in homosexual acts in addition to their regular heterosexual acts— which they find fully satisfactory.
>
> MSNY wants to reach these people and help them come to grips with themselves. We're not interested in "bringing them out" and encouraging them to give up their heterosexual activities and commit themselves as homosexuals. We (or at least I) encourage them to swing both ways and enjoy themselves, and try to help them avoid trouble.[20]

Leitsch's emphasis on helping people "come to grips with themselves" reflected his moderate homophile disposition to make tangible and immediate improvements in the lives of troubled individuals while engaging in the long, slow process of changing attitudes. This same disposition underlay his belief that it was appropriate to support individuals who wanted to stop being homosexual or to pass as heterosexual:

> I still think you have balls to say that a guy shouldn't try to change what he doesn't like or accept in himself. If big noses are out of style, why not

have a nose job? If you're unhappy being a faggot, why not try to change to something else? . . . If someone would rather pass or try to change, rather than change the world, it's his right, and you have no business telling him to suffer for your sake.[21]

In reply to Leitsch, Kameny expressed reservations about devoting attention to intellectual debate instead of political activism, pointing out that Leitsch's own views on the matter had changed. "I have not at all altered my basic position in regard to research vis-à-vis the homophile movement, as indicated [in] my July, 1964, speech to MSNY . . . (the speech which you have claimed so changed your own personal directions)." Turning to the substance of Leitsch's letter, Kameny noted that he had expressed concern in his 1964 speech about homophile leaders who were ambivalent about the healthiness and worth of homosexuality, that this concern persisted, and that Leitsch's opinions pointed to a persisting problem that demanded attention. He elaborated:

Now, I take credit for a good many of the worthwhile ideas floating around in this movement, and for the phrasing of them. One which was *not* initially mine came from several sources, but I subscribe to it fully. It came from SIR,* for one, and from the Negro movement, for another . . .

This is the point, that we must instill in the homosexual community a sense of the worth of the individual homosexual. A sense of high self-esteem. We must counteract the inferiority which ALL society inculcates into him in regard to his homosexuality.

SIR overdoes it with its homosexual ghettoes, to which I do NOT subscribe. The Negro militants overdo it, with their renewed separatism. But the basic idea is there.

The other day, on television, I saw Stokely Carmichael before a group of Negroes chanting: "Black is Beautiful." To a Negro, living in a society in which "white," "snow," "purity," and "good" are all equated together, and "black," "evil," "darkness," "dirt," and "ugliness" are all equated together, Carmichael's tactic is understandable—and necessary, and desirable.

Within our somewhat different framework, we need the same kind of thing.

*SIR, the Society for Individual Rights, was a gay group formed in San Francisco in 1964.

Again—please don't get me wrong—I'm not preaching homosexual superiority, or any of that stupidity. But I do not grant one single whit of inferiority.

Our people need to have their self-esteem bolstered—singly, and as a community.

The very idea of changing to heterosexuality . . . is a tacit acknowledgment of inferiority . . .

You can cloak this with all the verbal sophistries that you want, but that is the way it WILL come across.

People who are TRULY equal, and TRULY not inferior, do NOT seriously consider acquiescing to the majority and changing themselves. Ask a Protestant in Southern Ireland, or a Catholic in Northern Ireland, or a Jew in Russia whether he would change his religion, even though it would make his life FAR easier, or whether he ought not to advise his youngsters to become Catholics, or Protestants, or atheists . . . and see the response.

To submit to the pressure of immoral societal prejudice is immoral. Self-respecting people do not so submit. Self-respect is what *I* am trying to inculcate into my people, even if you are not.

When you acquiesce to "therapy" and "change" in the manner which you do, you simply confirm (on a "gut" basis) all of the feelings of inferiority, wrongness, and self-contempt with which society has inculcated the individual homosexual. You harm the homosexual, and you harm the movement . . .

The ONLY people in this entire country—in the entire world—that I know of, who are standing up and telling the homosexual person that he IS equal, and that his homosexuality is NOT a badge of inferiority, etc., and who are doing it without reservation, without excuse, not as a "crumb of pity from the table, for those poor psychologically maimed people who can't help themselves," who is saying NOT merely grudgingly, "Homosexuality is a valid way of life for some people," but, in parallel to Carmichael, "Homosexuality is GOOD"—positively and without reservation—the ONLY people in all the world who are doing this are the pitifully small handful of us in the homophile movement. And our people are very sensitive to any squeamishness and half-heartedness on our part.

There are times when leadership requires the taking of total positions.[22]

Kameny's stress on the need to instill pride in homosexuals was new. Four years earlier, in 1964, his major contention had been that crusades for official reforms were more effective than research and education for convincing heterosexuals that homosexuals were as well-adjusted and respectable as they were. Though such crusades were said to require a political movement of homosexuals and concerned heterosexuals—a homophile movement—most of the militants made policy change their major concern. Only for a few, like Craig Rodwell, was the priority building a movement.

But when breakthroughs in communications with the media, civic and professional leaders, and public officials failed to increase the size and strength of the homophile movement appreciably, Kameny and his allies began to reexamine their priorities. Though they remained preoccupied with policy reform, they devoted more attention to building coalitions that would provide the infrastructure for a political movement. They continued to seek heterosexual support, but began to think more about attracting homosexuals into the movement. This need to attract homosexuals was what alerted Kameny to the significance of Stokely Carmichael's "Black Is Beautiful" slogan. The "Homosexuality Is Good" analogue he expounded in his letter to Leitsch was the precursor of the "Gay Is Good" motto he persuaded the North American Conference of Homophile Organizations to adopt in the summer of 1968.

But Leitsch argued that the militant drive to get people to identify themselves according to their sexual orientation betrayed basic homophile ideals. And he objected to what he saw as militant polarizing efforts not only because he believed in integration but because he had developed a moderate homophile belief in the efficacy of education. On the one hand, the MSNY executive wrote that he was sanguine about the strategy of enlisting professionals to speak in behalf of homosexuals. "There are articulate, responsible, and eminently sensible professionals who are ready and willing to work with us." On the other hand, he maintained that he was optimistic about the potential for grassroots education:

We have the built-in advantage of automatic integration: homosexuals can be born into any family, work at any job, have any background whatsoever, and even succeed in any field. Further, everyone has traces of homosexual urges in his personality, unlike Negritude, which is distinct and unique to a few. Rather than separating homosexuals only to fight for integration, we should exploit the integration facilities that exist and work from there.

This means an abandonment of the old ploy of preying on paranoia. Give up this crap about how sad it is that we all have to wear masks, and that we're going to be kicked around. Those are self-fulfilling prophecies . . . Discourage self-pity and feelings of uniqueness and difference, and emphasize likeness and universality.[23]

Leitsch perceived that the movement-building ambitions of the militants partly accounted for their wanting to have homosexuals think of themselves as a breed apart. He objected not only because he thought the militants were unrealistic about the nature of sexual preference and unfaithful to homophile ambitions, but also because he considered the model for their new strategic tack inappropriate:

The history of the Negro is quite different from that of the homosexual. I think it is a mistake to try to put the homosexual where the Negro was a century ago, just so we can go through the same stages . . .

[Militants] can't understand that Negroes usually have identifying characteristics, come from Negro families, frequent particular parts of town, and are quite different in every way from homosexuals, who are born integrated.

We should be aiming to retain the integration we have, and build more, thanking god or whatever that we never had to suffer the segregation period. We should not be copying a model that is really not applicable . . .[24]

Leitsch accused Kameny of forsaking homophile ideals in order to ape the proponents of black power, but there is little evidence that Kameny went that far—especially in comparison to Craig Rodwell. Rodwell had resigned as vice-president of MSNY in the spring of 1967 when Leitsch showed no enthusiasm for his plan to mobilize homosexuals by establishing a storefront Mattachine office. Later that year, he initiated political activity that was gay liberationist rather than homophile in character by opening the Oscar Wilde Memorial Bookshop in Greenwich Village and by starting a newsletter committed to "bringing Gay Power to New York." The first issue of that newsletter, called the *Hymnal* to suggest its crusading character, explained: "We will make no pretense of speaking to the heterosexual in trying to persuade him to 'accept' homosexuals. *Hymnal* is solely concerned with what the gay person thinks of himself. The community has the economic, political, and social potential to shape its own future. This potential only needs to be encouraged and channeled."*[25]

In this regard, Kameny's long letter to Leitsch is significant not only for its testimony to the model that Kameny found in Stokely Carmichael's efforts to build black pride, but for its evidence that Kameny took a cue from Carmichael without compromising either his homophile aspirations or his liberal assumptions. The belief that acculturation and integration were desirable led Kameny to praise Carmichael's "Black Is Beautiful" slogan when writing about the need to instill homosexuals with pride but to emphasize his objections to "renewed [black] separatism" and to "homosexual ghettoes." The conviction that members of minorities were, could be, and should be like members of the majority moved him to specify that eliminating the homosexual's feeling of inferiority did not mean "preaching homosexual superiority, or any of that stupidity."

Kameny's letter stressed the importance of "telling the homosexual person that he *is* equal," and because his homophile outlook and his liberalism led him to equate equality with similarity, he saw this as assuring the homosexual not only "that his homosexuality is NOT a badge of inferiority" but that he is successful and respectable *in the same ways* as heterosexuals—that he has the same competencies, the

---

*Almost from the time he joined MSNY, at the beginning of the 1960s, Rodwell distinguished himself from other homophile leaders by stressing how important it was to make homosexuals proud of their lives and to get them involved in the efforts that were being made to better their lot. Early issues of the *Hymnal* pointed to some of the political influences on his thinking. The third issue carried an obituary for Martin Luther King that noted that "like the Negro, we are beginning to assert our dignity and self-respect."[26] The sixth issue reported, "In adopting the slogan 'Gay is Good,' the NACHO took a cue from our black brothers' slogan 'Black is Beautiful'."[27] Periodic reports on the community centers, economic boycotts, and electoral involvement sponsored by gay groups in San Francisco and Los Angeles noted that the westerners were following the lead of the proponents of black pride and black power.

Rodwell's precocious belief that homosexuals needed to develop pride, community, and power was clearly stimulated by the ideas about community organizing popularized by the founders of the New Left. But the roots of his gay liberationist orientation lay in the Christian Science training that he had received at boarding school and in the daily reading and reflection he continued to do. Christian Science principles about the dignity of all things human and the importance of making things true by believing them so inspired Rodwell to work at encouraging homosexuals to think of themselves positively. Following the Christian Science example, he did this by reaching out into the community, by conversing with fellow homosexuals, and by making available literature with positive messages about homosexuality. The Oscar Wilde Memorial Bookshop, the first bookstore devoted to building the gay movement, was modeled after the Christian Science reading room. Craig Rodwell, the first eastern homophile leader to act like a gay liberationist, was an unintended offspring of Mary Baker Eddy!

same values, the same modes of achievement, fulfillment, and reward. The overriding importance Kameny attached to persuading people, homosexual as well as heterosexual, that homosexuals are just like heterosexuals showed even in his extensive essay on the theme "Gay Is Good," which he prepared in the fall of 1968 for Ralph Weltge's anthology, *The Same Sex*. In that essay, before urging "homosexuals who may read this . . . to live your homosexuality fully, joyously, openly, and proudly," Kameny addressed the "larger heterosexual community" in order to stress how similar homosexuals are to heterosexuals:

> To the heterosexual community, I say that we are full human beings—children of God, no less than you—with the same feelings, needs, sensitivities, desires, and aspirations. We are not the monsters that so many of you have been led to believe we are. We differ not at all from you except in our choice of those whom we love and with whom we relate intimately—in those ways, in their narrowest sense, but in no other ways.*[28]

Of course, the methods for eliminating prejudice, stereotyping, and discrimination popularized by the liberals and civil rights leaders who spoke and wrote about minority problems reinforced the insistence of Kameny and other homophile leaders that in important respects homosexuals were like heterosexuals. Because the absence of prejudice and stereotyping was commonly portrayed as inattention to characteristics like skin color or religious preference, which "made no difference," homophile leaders were encouraged to argue that a person's homosexuality should be ignored because sexual preference "made no difference." Because nondiscrimination was commonly presented as treatment based solely on significant personal and professional characteristics—not those, like skin color or religious preference, that were "irrelevant"—homophile leaders were encouraged to advocate that homosexuals be assessed and

---

*Kameny's homophile outlook was so deeply rooted that, much to the chagrin of DOB's leaders, he also insisted that lesbians were no different from male homosexuals. This was dramatically demonstrated in the summer of 1969, when he wrote a letter to the *Ladder* to take issue with a previously published letter that had criticized an article on homosexuality because it "ignored the Lesbian as usual." Retorted Kameny: "The article most certainly does NOT ignore the Lesbian. You seem to forget that the Lesbian IS, after all, a homosexual, first and foremost—subject to *all*—yes all—of the problems of the male homosexual and with *no* special problems as a Lesbian."[29]

treated on the basis of their personal and professional attributes rather than their sexuality, which was "irrelevant."*

Paradoxically, the preoccupation with assuring people that in important respects homosexuals resembled heterosexuals, because it encouraged homosexuals to think their sexuality insignificant and made them all the more reluctant to risk ostracism, was precisely what kept homophile leaders from rousing large numbers of people with homosexual feelings to identify themselves as gay and to support homophile efforts to secure rights and status for homosexuals. This situation persisted until homosexuals began to abandon conventional views and values and to reject liberal assumptions as the basis for their gay political thinking. These homosexuals were countercultural. The assumptions that shaped their political perspectives were those of the New Left. And their gay political outlooks were not homophile, but liberationist.

*Of course, despite the official positions of homophile groups and the public pronouncements of their leaders, there had long been private discussions—particulary in groups held solely for the benefit of homosexuals—about the extent to which homosexuals were and were not like heterosexuals. A program note in MSNY's March 1962 newsletter described one such occasion:

Is there such a thing as a homosexual culture? Or, perhaps more properly, a homosexual sub-culture? On Wednesday, 21 March, a Mattachine panel will debate this tantalizing question under the title "Homosexual or Gay?—A Semantic Approach." A panel of men *and* women will present the respective ways of life, often so different from one another, that each of these concepts evokes.

The word "gay" implies the gay bar, colorful clothes, avant-garde and "campy" slang, the determined pursuit of frivolity, etc. Many persons foster a gay society and go out of their way to proclaim their participation in it. On the other hand, we all know homosexuals who feel that they are integrated citizens of their country and the world at large. Such persons attempt to mold their personalities along general, i.e. heterosexual, patterns.

Which is the *real* homosexual?[30]

PART II

THE GAY LIBERATION MOVEMENT

4

The Stonewall Riots
and the Gay Liberation Front

LATE IN THE EVENING of Friday, June 27, 1969, deputy
inspector Seymour Pine and seven other officers from the Public
Morals Section of the First Division of the New York City Police
Department set out to close the Stonewall Inn, a gay bar near the
corner of Christopher Street and Seventh Avenue in Greenwich
Village, just across from Sheridan Square. Arriving shortly after
midnight, the police presented the Stonewall's manager with a warrant charging that liquor was being sold without a license, announced that employees would be arrested, and stood at the door to
check patrons as they were ushered out one by one. Following routine practice, the authorities released customers who could produce
identification and asked those who could not, plus suspected cross
dressers, to step aside to be taken to the station for questioning.

The Stonewall was a dimly lit dance bar that welcomed homosexuals with countercultural life styles. Many of those present on the
night of the raid were "dope-smokers," "acid-heads," or "speed
freaks." Some wore their hair long and dressed in unconventional
garb. Some were raggedly flamboyant homosexual cross dressers
known as "street queens."

Partly because the extreme unconventionality of their lives gave
them little status and security to lose, most of those dismissed from
the Stonewall chose not to run to safety but to gather across the street
to wait for their friends. Laughing and joking, stoned on drugs and

high in spirits, they applauded each time someone they recognized appeared in the doorway. Their applause encouraged brassy individuals passing through the hands of the police to make clever remarks and effeminate gestures. In the words of reporter Lucian Truscott IV, who had come to watch from the offices of the *Village Voice* just fifty yards away:

> Cheers would go up as favorites would emerge from the door, strike a pose, and swish by the detective with a "Hello there, fella." The stars were in their element. Wrists were limp, hair was primped, and reactions to the applause were classic. "I gave them the gay power bit, and they loved it, girls."

The mood of the crowd soured when a police van arrived to take suspects to precinct headquarters, and a melee soon followed. Truscott explained:

> Suddenly the paddywagon arrived and the mood of the crowd changed. Three of the more blatant queens—in full drag—were loaded inside, along with the bartender and doorman, to a chorus of catcalls and boos from the crowd. A cry went up to push the paddywagon over, but it drove away before anything could happen. With its exit, the action waned momentarily. The next person to come out was a dyke, and she put up a struggle—from car to door to car again. It was at that moment that the scene became explosive. Limp wrists were forgotten. Beer cans and bottles were heaved at the windows, and a rain of coins descended on the cops. At the height of the action, a bearded figure was plucked from the crowd and dragged inside . . .
>
> Three cops were necessary to get [him] away from the crowd and into the Stonewall. The exit left no cops on the street, and almost by signal the crowd erupted into cobblestone and bottle heaving. The reaction was solid: they were pissed. The trashcan I was standing on was nearly yanked out from under me as a kid tried to grab it for use in the windowsmashing melee. From nowhere came an uprooted parking meter —used as a battering ram on the Stonewall door. I heard several cries of "Let's get some gas," but the blaze of flame which soon appeared in the window of the Stonewall was still a shock. As the wood barrier behind the glass was beaten open, the cops inside turned a firehose on the crowd. Several kids took the opportunity to cavort in the spray, and their momentary glee served to stave off what was rapidly becoming a full-scale attack. By the time the fags were able to regroup forces and

come up with another assault, several carloads of police reinforcements had arrived, and in minutes the streets were clear.[1]

Truscott's story, published the following Wednesday on the front page of the *Village Voice,* was the source of what most people learned about the rioting on Christopher Street. An eyewitness account by one of the rioters for the underground paper *Rat* offered a somewhat different perspective:

The crowd grew larger and more agitated as the squad car drove off and a wagon pulled up. People began beating the wagon, booing, trying to see who was being hauled out and off. Several pigs were on guard and periodically threatened the crowd unless they moved back. Impossible to do. "Nobody's going to fuck around with me. I ain't going to take this shit," a guy in a dark red tee-shirt shouted, dancing in and out of the crowd . . .

A couple more were thrown into the van. We joined in with some who wanted to storm the van, free those inside, then turn over the van. But nobody was yet prepared for that kind of action. Then a scuffle at the door. One guy refused to be put into the van. 5 or 6 cops guarding the van tried to subdue him with little success . . .

Several others tried rescuing the guy held by the cops, but the latter escaped into the Stonewall. Soon the van pulled out leaving the street unguarded. A few pigs outside had to flee for their lives inside and barricade themselves in. It was too good to be true. The crowd took the offensive. The cat in the tee-shirt began by hurling a container of something at the door. Then a can or stone cracked a window. Soon pandemonium broke loose. Cans, bottles, rocks, trashcans, finally a parking meter crashed the windows and door. Cheers went up. A sort of wooden wall blocking out the front plate glass window was forced down. Then with the parking meter a ram, in went the door. The cops inside were scared shitless, dodging projectiles and flying glass. The orgy was taking place. Vengeance vented against the source of repression—gay bars, busts, kids victimized and exploited by the mafia and cops. Strangely, no one spoke to the crowd or tried to direct the insurrection. Everyone's heads were in the same place. Some chanted "occupy—take over, take over," "Fag power," but kids were really scared about going too far as they saw the cops pulling guns from inside, pointed directly at the crowd . . .

The pigs carried futility to the extreme and turned the firehose on the mob through the door. Jeers, derision. Someone shouted "grab it, grab his cock." Some then lit a trashcan full of paper afire and stuffed it through the window. Flames leaped up. Then "Riot pigs" somebody was shouting. Sirens approached and kids started spilling over the fences of Sheridan Square to flee the scene. On each side together there must have been around 1500–2000 people by this time milling about, being pushed back by about 30 or more riot cops . . .

People hung around till 4 am talking in little groups. People were excited and angry. In talking to a number of kids who had been inside, it was evident most understood at least rudimentarily what was happening to them. What was and should have always been theirs, what should have been the free control of the people, was dramatized, shown up for what it really was, an instrument of power and exploitation. It was theatre, totally spontaneous. There was no bullshit.[2]

As both the *Voice* and the *Rat* narratives make clear, the disturbance in front of the Stonewall resulted from several specific circumstances: the closing of a gay bar populated by a particularly unconventional group of homosexuals; the procedures the police used to deal with the patrons; mockery of the police by brazen individuals egged on by a high-spirited, rebellious crowd; and the agitation of that crowd by a few who saw the raid on the Stonewall as an unjustified intrusion that called for resistance. But where Truscott recounted events with the perspective of an astonished outsider, *Rat*'s reporter wrote as one convinced that he was participating in an "insurrection" against "the source of repression—gay bars, busts, kids victimized and exploited by the mafia and cops."[11]

Rat's writer acknowledged at the end of his article that the political convictions of his cohorts were by no means as clear as his were. Others who were present agree that for most of the rioters, the impulse to protest came not from gay political perspectives but from feelings of resentment about official interference. Craig Rodwell, for instance, remembers stumbling upon the crowd in front of the Stonewall, seeing that there had been a raid, starting to chant "gay power," and being surprised that almost no one joined in.

Rodwell's chanting was no sudden burst of inspiration. For the first issue of the *Hymnal* he had written an article complaining that "Mafia (or 'The Syndicate') control of New York City's gay bars [made it] virtually impossible for a legitimate businessman to open a gay bar with a healthy social atmosphere." Moreover, Rodwell reported that *Hymnal* investigators had encountered nothing but evasion from the New York City Health Department and the State Liquor Authority when they tried to investigate charges that the Stonewall Inn, one of the best known of the Mafia-controlled bars, was responsible for an epidemic of hepatitis because it rarely washed its glasses. Rodwell's article concluded that "the Community cannot rely on governmental agencies to break the Mafia control of gay bars until the day comes that pay-offs and collusion between the Syndicate and governmental agencies are ended" and that homosexuals should "stop patronizing bars run by concealed Mafia interests" as a first demonstration of "gay power."[3]

It was almost a year and a half later that Rodwell tried to stir the rambunctious crowd in front of the raided Stonewall to chant "gay power." The next day, he prepared a leaflet for distribution on Christopher Street repeating the themes of his article in the *Hymnal.* Headlined "Get the Mafia and the Cops Out of Gay Bars," the leaflet demanded that "homosexual men and women boycott places like the Stonewall" and that "gay businessmen step forward and open gay bars that will be run legally with competitive pricing and a healthy social atmosphere."*

Although Rodwell worked to politicize homosexuals after the raid on the Stonewall, the pattern of the first disturbance on Christopher Street was repeated the next night. As Truscott's report in the *Voice* suggested, even though political slogans were more evident during the second round of disorders, activities remained self-assertively defiant rather than self-consciously political:

> Friday night's crowd had returned and was being led in "gay power" cheers by a group of gay cheerleaders. "We are the Stonewall girls/We wear our hair in curls/We have no underwear/We show our pubic hairs!" . . . Hand-holding, kissing, and posing accented each of the cheers with a homosexual liberation that had appeared only fleetingly on the street before.[4]

A reporter writing for the *East Village Other, Rat*'s rival among the local underground papers, scolded the second night's demonstrators for failing to be political:

*Quoted here is the first of dozens of photocopied leaflets, position papers, and brochures that have been collected or reproduced from the files of gay and lesbian liberationists and their groups. Quotations from documents of this sort, which can be found in numerous personal files and organizational archives, are not footnoted.

Saturday night was very poor. Too many people showed up looking for a carnival rather than a sincere protest. Queens were posing for pictures, slogans were being spouted out, but nothing really sincere happened in the way of protest. On Monday night, July 2, everything became more than serious . . .

But the word is out. Christopher Street shall be liberated. The fags have had it with oppression. Revolution is being heard on Christopher Street, only instead of guttural MC-5 voices, we hear it coming from sopranos and altos.[5]

The crowds responsible for the street disorders that took place on several successive nights on Christopher Street—disorders which soon came to be referred to as "the Stonewall Riots"—consisted largely of gay and straight hippies, Village residents, and tourists. But they also included partisans of the New Left (like the reporters for *Rat* and the *East Village Other*) who saw an opportunity to stir homosexuals to join the Movement, and homosexuals with counter-cultural views and values who had begun to think about their sexuality in the light of political perspectives popularized by the New Left.

In the wake of the Stonewall Riots, several of these homosexuals turned to the established gay groups in the city. Those who went to MSNY and DOB–New York found that their budding ideas about gay political activity were very different from the homophile outlooks of the leaders in charge. Those who looked in on the Oscar Wilde, which was enlisting recruits for HYMN, the Homophile Youth Movement in Neighborhoods, saw that Rodwell's need to keep his bookstore legal and self-sustaining put a limit on the types of operations its new crusading arm could undertake. In the end, the visits made to already established gay groups were significant because they helped newly aware homosexuals develop the distinctive political and organizational perspectives that guided the formation of gay liberation groups and shaped the burgeoning gay liberation movement.

.   .   .

The established homophile leaders in New York City were not oblivious to the Stonewall Riots. After the first two days of disturbances on Christopher Street, members of MSNY were down in the West Village handing out fliers hailing "the Christopher Street Riots" as

"The Hairpin Drop Heard around the World."* This circulation of leaflets was only the first of several steps MSNY took to capitalize on the events precipitated by the Stonewall raid, and Mattachine veterans often cite these steps to contend that MSNY fathered the gay liberation movement. In fact, Mattachine leaders did a good deal to encourage the emergence of the gay liberation movement, but less by promoting liberationist activity than by letting homosexuals partial to New Left political perspectives know that they would have to pursue liberationist aims on their own.

One of these New Left–oriented homosexuals was Michael Brown, who was thrilled by the openly gay behavior he saw on Christopher Street the day after the raid on the Stonewall. Although Brown, twenty-eight, had enjoyed traditional gay male pastimes since his days as a teenager in Hollywood, he was disgusted with the secrecy and sordidness he found in existing gay life and stirred by the possibilities for change he detected in the ferment in the Village. In the crowds that clustered around Christopher Street Brown recognized a force that could be harnessed to further new openness. From the reports in *Rat* and the *East Village Other* he sensed that the time was right for politicized homosexuals to join with blacks, antiwar activists, and others who professed a determination to transform American society. Although he had been a staff member in Hubert Humphrey's 1968 presidential campaign and worked in an interior decorating firm on Wall Street, Brown considered himself countercultural and socialist. He believed that America under Nixon was falling apart.

After seeing MSNY's flier, Brown called the Mattachine and made an appointment to see Dick Leitsch. When he shared his views with Leitsch, he was told to be realistic and lectured about the need for groups eager to help homosexuals to protect their good relations with the authorities. When Brown insisted that some active form of Mattachine response to the Stonewall Riots was essential, Leitsch agreed to accommodate him and other newly politicized homosexuals by creating an Action Committee and by sponsoring a "community meeting" at Freedom House, the midtown Manhattan site of MSNY's monthly public lectures. Brown agreed to head the Action

*In the argot of the gay subculture, "dropping hairpins" meant dropping clues that one was homosexual.

Committee, drew up a flier advertising the community meeting, and distributed it in the Village.

Several days later almost a hundred people gathered at Freedom House to talk about the Stonewall Riots. Most favored staging some sort of demonstration to protest police harassment. Brown considered the suggestions timid and pressed the gathering to move closer to its roots by holding a second meeting in Greenwich Village, which he called "the heart of the gay community."

In the interim, Brown worked to persuade kindred spirits to join the Action Committee. One of the first he enlisted was Bill Weaver, whom he worked with on the Fifth Avenue Peace Parade Committee. Another was Earl Galvin. And these three were joined by Martha Shelley, who, partly at the urging of her friend Bob Martin, had left her post as president of DOB–New York early in 1969 to explore radical politics. (Martin, brought into MSNY by Julian Hodges, had in the fall of 1966 formed Columbia University's Student Homophile League [SHL], the first officially recognized gay group on a college campus; he had become acquainted with New Left politics during the disturbances at Columbia in 1968; and he was busy organizing a youth caucus to radicalize NACHO in the summer of 1969.)

When Dick Leitsch adamantly maintained that MSNY could not afford to sponsor ventures that might offend authorities or alienate supporters, Brown and his followers began to talk about acting independently. While posting notices for the community meeting to be held in Greenwich Village, they saw leaflets announcing a demonstration in support of members of the Black Panther Party jailed in the Women's House of Detention, the prison that occupied the triangle at the intersection of Greenwich Street and Sixth Avenue in the Village. They decided that they could show that newly politicized homosexuals were ready to join with other oppressed minorities in the struggle for a new society by attending the demonstration scheduled at "the House of D." So that no one would associate the initiative with MSNY, the Action Committee decided to say that their attendance was being sponsored by the Gay Liberation Front, a name Martha Shelley suggested.

At the second community meeting, Brown and his associates handed out fliers announcing that a rally would be held on July 19 at the Women's House of Detention: "The newly formed Gay Liberation Front urges all homosexuals to join in this demonstration with

Yippies and Panthers to show our concern for unharassed life styles." During that meeting, when Leitsch ignored the pamphleteers and tried to limit discussion to plans for a vigil in Washington Square to protest police harassment, newcomer Jim Fouratt and others challenged him to "join the revolution." Subsequent clashes between homophile leaders and gay liberationists were dramatically depicted in an article, "The New Homosexual," which journalist Tom Burke wrote for *Esquire:*

> Dick Leitsch, in a staid brown suit, strides to the front . . . With professional aplomb, he reopens the meeting. Police brutality and heterosexual indifference must be protested, he asserts; at the same time, the gay world must retain the favor of the Establishment, especially those who make and change laws. Homosexual acceptance will come slowly, by educating the straight community, with grace and good humor and . . .
>
> A tense boy with leonine hair is suddenly on his feet. "We don't want acceptance, goddam it! We want respect! Demand it! We're through hiding in dark bars behind Mafia doormen. We're going to go where straights go and do anything with each other they do and if they don't like it, well, *fuck them!* . . ."
>
> "Well, now I think," says Mrs. Cervantes (Mattachine assistant), "that what we ought to have is a gay vigil, in a park. Carry candles, perhaps . . . I think we should be firm, but just as amicable and sweet as . . ."
>
> "Sweet!" The new speaker resembles Billy the Kid. He is James Fouratt, New Left celebrity, seminarian *manqué,* the radical who burned the real money on the floor of the New York Stock Exchange as a war protest.
>
> "Sweet! *Bullshit!* There's the stereotype homo again, man! . . . Bullshit! That's the role society has been forcing these queens to play, and they just sit and accept it. We have got to radicalize, man! . . . Be proud of what you are, man! And if it takes riots or even guns to show them what we are, well, that's the only language the pigs understand!"
>
> Wild applause . . .
>
> Dick Leitsch tries to reply, but Fouratt shouts him down.
>
> "All the oppressed have to unite! The system keeps us all weak by keeping us separate . . . We've got to work together with *all* the New Left."[6]

. . .

Unaware of these events, at just about the same time, Bill Katzenberg asked Charles Pitts if he was interested in helping homosexuals organize. A member of Students for a Democratic Society (SDS), Katzenberg believed that minorities had to be mobilized around their own causes in order to create an "alliance of the oppressed" powerful enough to overthrow the capitalist system. As a homosexual, he felt that he could contribute to the revolution by organizing homosexuals, and he wanted to talk to Pitts because he admired the programs about homosexuality that Pitts had produced for radio station WBAI.

Pitts had moved to Manhattan in the mid-sixties because he had heard of a psychotherapist there who considered homosexuality a difference rather than an illness. This therapist was Mattachine adviser C. A. Tripp, already at work on the study of sexual behavior he was to publish as *The Homosexual Matrix*. After meeting with Tripp and joining a therapy group of gay males led by Kinsey associate Wardell Pomeroy, who was also on the Mattachine's Board of Psychiatric Advisers, Pitts developed a strong and positive gay identity and a deep anger at the cultural standards that for so long had kept him guilty and unhappy. Attracted by the more affirming mores he found in the counterculture, he moved to the lower East Village and found a job at WBAI, where he used his air time to explore the lyrics of rock and folk-rock songs. Pitts provoked many of his listeners when he suggested that songs like Donovan's "Try for the Sun" had subtle gay themes. And he created a sensation at the station in June 1968 by discussing homosexuality on WBAI's late-night talk show and acknowledging on the air that he was gay.

That fall, Pitts coproduced a series of programs on homosexuality for WBAI called "The New Symposium" (a play on the title of Plato's dialogue about love and sex). During the spring of 1969, for "The New Symposium II," Pitts arranged a series of panel discussions with Barbara Gittings and Pete Wilson, who, when he had been Randy Wicker's lover, belonged to the League for Sexual Freedom and participated in most of the first homophile picket lines. Aware of Wilson's interest in radical theories of sex, society, and politics, Pitts invited him to attend the meeting with Katzenberg.

Even before Wilson arrived, Pitts, Katzenberg, and one of Katzenberg's revolutionary friends had drawn up a flier with a lead that punned, "Do You Think Homosexuals Are Revolting?" It answered, "You Bet Your Sweet Ass We Are." The cleverness was Pitts's; the sentiments were shared. In smaller print the flier promised, "We're

going to make a place for ourselves in the revolutionary movement."
A note at the bottom announced that a meeting would be held July
24 at Alternate University, the center for radical education housed
in a loft at the corner of Sixth Avenue and West 14th Street in lower
Manhattan.

Although Katzenberg, Pitts, and Wilson did not know it, they had
set up their meeting at "Alternate U" through its nineteen-year-old
director of programming, Susan Silverman. Silverman had begun to
think about issues important to women in the fall of 1967, when she
was active in the Queens College chapter of SDS. In the spring of
1968, she had attended meetings of the women's group formed at
Columbia University's Free School and been befriended by Robin
Morgan. Encouraged by Morgan, Silverman joined New York Radical Women, the first radical feminist group organized in New York
City, and participated in events important in the early history of the
women's liberation movement, such as the demonstration held at the
1968 Miss America Pageant and the creation of WITCH—the
Women's International Terrorist Conspiracy from Hell. This exposure to the beginnings of radical feminism had heightened Silverman's feminist awareness without helping her come to terms with
her secret lesbian longings. And it was partly because she felt isolated
among her radical feminist friends that in the winter of 1969 she left
WITCH and began to work at the newly opened Alternate University. For Alternate U's second term, Silverman ran a feminist workshop, there for the first time meeting a woman willing to talk about
being a lesbian, a follower of Meher Baba named Lois Hart.

The July 24 meeting scheduled at Alternate U by Katzenberg,
Pitts, and Wilson drew not only Hart and Silverman, still identifying
herself as a straight feminist, but Brown, Weaver, Galvin, and Shelley, now, with the exception of Shelley, ex-members of the Mattachine's Action Committee. Also attending were Fouratt, Jerry
Hoose, and Leo Martello, who had been recruited after the clashes
with Leitsch at the Mattachine's second community meeting. Wilson
remembers that most of the forty or so who met at Alternate U were
so overwhelmed to find so many others who felt that being homosexual had something to do with being radical that they were moved,
one by one, to tell about their backgrounds and to explain why they
wanted to meet again. The flier drawn up to announce a second
meeting on July 31 summed up prevailing sentiment with more of

Pitts's punning: "Homosexuals Are Coming Together at Last."

On Sunday, July 27, several from the Alternate U assembly carried the new fliers to the vigil in Washington Square that MSNY and DOB–New York were sponsoring. The vigil was being run by Marty Robinson, who had taken charge of the Mattachine's Action Committee after Michael Brown moved on, and by Martha Shelley, the only lesbian the leaders of DOB–New York could enlist to speak publicly. Three hundred or so assembled in Washington Square, listened to Robinson and Shelley, and then marched, wearing lavender armbands and singing "We Shall Overcome," to the front of the Stonewall Inn. There Robinson encouraged the crowd to disband, infuriating members of the contingent from Alternate U, who wanted the marchers to continue on to the nearby headquarters of the Police Department's Sixth Precinct.

Although Robinson feared that the Alternate U people simply wanted to use homosexuals for the Movement's revolutionary aims, he went to their July 31 meeting, witnessed their vote to call themselves the Gay Liberation Front (GLF), and joined in the ensuing debate. Some wanted GLF to become involved in the full range of Movement activities immediately, and others wanted it to begin by concentrating on gay issues. When those in favor of postponing involvement in Movement activities seemed to be in the majority, several of their opponents shouted objections and threatened to walk out. They got their way when Robinson and others left instead. Jerry Hoose, later active in developing a reform-oriented approach to gay liberation, recalls that the victory of the radicals was sealed when the responsibility for preparing a statement for *Rat* announcing GLF's birth was delegated to Michael Brown, Lois Hart, and Ron Ballard, a black who was enthusiastic about having GLF support the Panthers.

Although Brown, Hart, and Ballard took steps to identify GLF with all the major concerns of the Movement, they made concessions to win the support of activists eager to deal first with gay issues. And although Robinson, Shelley, and others continued doing political work in the name of MSNY and DOB–New York during August, they also attended meetings of GLF. At the beginning of August, Robinson, Shelley, and others working under the auspices of the Mattachine's Action Committee spent two weekends distributing leaflets and demonstrating at Kew Gardens in Queens, where neighborhood vigilantes had cut down trees in an effort to drive out male homosexuals using the park for "cruising," i.e., searching for sexual partners. Later in the month, the Action Committee sponsored a "protest hangout" on Christopher Street, a third community meeting, and a picket line at the United Nations to celebrate West Germany's decriminalization of sodomy. Not until the end of August did Robinson, Shelley, and their followers become convinced that their ideas about gay political activity were more in line with the Gay Liberation Front than with MSNY or DOB. Only when the loyalties of these leaders became clear was the demarcation between homophile leaders and gay liberationists complete.

·   ·   ·

Brown, Hart, and others who took the lead in organizing the Gay Liberation Front spoke of their views as both countercultural and New Left. Since many with countercultural views and values considered themselves part of the Movement and many in the Movement had countercultural outlooks, the counterculture and the New Left had come to be equated. But to appreciate the variety of ways in which countercultural thinking was manifested in political perspectives, it is important to recognize that the grassroots growth of interest in fuller and freer self-expression and in supportive community that gave rise to the counterculture and the organized political effort known as the New Left were actually different movements that overlapped increasingly during the second half of the 1960s.

The New Left was a political movement started in the early 1960s by the Student Nonviolent Coordinating Committee (SNCC) and the Students for a Democratic Society (SDS). The leaders of SNCC abandoned the liberal assumptions of the civil rights movement when they decided to concentrate on helping rural southern blacks acquire political and economic power by building "alternative institutions" and strong black communities. This interest in extending participatory democracy and economic redistribution was shared by the early leaders of SDS, who adopted and popularized SNCC's community organizing strategy. Although several early SDS theorists argued that political and economic reforms were necessary to eliminate "dehumanization," they were mainly concerned with altering the political and economic institutions that alienated the poor and the working class, and they portrayed the exercise of political and economic power as the key to personal fulfillment and community development.

Early New Left activism had little to do with the quest for more self-expressive and humane ways of life that gave rise to the counterculture. In *The Greening of America,* Charles Reich identified this quest as the central dimension of a new consciousness, Consciousness III, which germinated before the beginnings of the New Left and then flourished alongside it:

> The earliest sources were among those exceptional individuals who are found at any time in any society: the artistic, the highly sensitive, the tormented . . . A subculture of "beats" grew up, and a beatnik world flourished briefly, but for most people it represented only another dead end . . .
>
> Unquestionably the blacks made a substantial contribution to the origins of the new consciousness. They were left out of the Corporate State, and thus they had to have a culture and life-style in opposition to the State. Their music, with its "guts," contrasted with the insipid white music. Their way of life seemed more earthy, more sensual than that of whites. They were the first openly to scorn the Establishment and its values . . .
>
> The great change took place when Consciousness III began to appear among young people who had endured no special emotional conditions, but were simply bright, sensitive children of the affluent middle class. It is hard to be precise about the time when this happened. One chronology is based on the college class of 1969, which entered as freshmen in the fall of 1965. Another important date is the summer of 1967, when the full force of the cultural revolution was first visible.[7]

Perhaps the most striking thing about Reich's analysis is that it says nothing about why so many of those who began to explore alternative life styles came to identify themselves in the late 1960s as members of the New Left. This marriage of social and political movements was of enormous consequence for the shape of modern American political and social currents, but few have appreciated its significance. Analysts of the New Left have tended to equate the counterculture with the bohemian modes of thinking, looking, and behaving evinced by latter-day Movement activists. Reich compounds the confusion by equating the grassroots growth of interest in enhanced self-realization and more validating social interaction responsible for the counterculture with the way this interest was manifested only in members of the counterculture politicized by New Left leaders.

Of course, many New Left leaders did come to embrace the counterculture. In his comprehensive history of SDS, Kirkpatrick Sale suggests that veteran SDSers, always rather bohemian, found countercultural life styles increasingly attractive after being exposed to the attitudes and behavior of the students they began to recruit in the middle of the 1960s.[8] In his broader history of the New Left, Edward Bacciocco says nothing about Movement leaders converting to countercultural outlooks, but he does describe how certain of them presented themselves as converts in order to politicize those they called hippies, freaks, and flower children:

> Despite the esoteric, apolitical character of the hippies, their complete estrangement from the norms of "straight" society placed them in total opposition to that society, a point clearly perceived by some of the politically militant radicals. Mario Savio had discerned their political potential in 1966 and called for a "coalition between student politicos and hippies," but to no avail. Jerry Rubin, veteran of the Free Speech Movement and the Vietnam Day Committee, also noticed the possibility of a new constituency at the Pentagon march in November 1967 as "flower children" planted daisies in the gun barrels of some of the troops guarding federal buildings.
>
> In February 1968, Rubin, Abbie Hoffman, Paul Krassner, and Ed Sanders announced the formation of the Youth International Party (Yippies) as a merger between the free-wheeling hippies and the politically motivated revolutionaries. They planned to hold a "life festival" at the Democratic National Convention in August at Chicago. Rubin, among other political activists, knew that more and more young people were drifting into the hippie scene, and he wanted to capitalize on its potential. By "borrowing" the clothes, style, and attitudes of the hippies to promote a new political party, they were assured of publicity and followers, but they also blurred beyond recognition the hippie vision of a society populated with individuals kindly disposed toward one another.[9]

To persuade members of the counterculture to participate in political activity, particularly demonstrations, New Left leaders argued that imperialistic capitalism had to be eliminated before individual freedom and humanistic community could flourish. To dramatize their arguments, they raised issues and contrived confrontations to show that government officials were as insensitive about individuals and as intolerant of diversity as the military-industrial complex they served.

Aided by the course of events—riots in the ghettos, assassinations, escalated American involvement in Vietnam—the New Left leaders succeeded in politicizing many in the counterculture. Some of those politicized, aspiring to transform the system without abandoning their pursuit of personal growth and social harmony, developed the concept of cultural revolution. They maintained that by embracing a new "consciousness"—new ways of looking at the world from which new ways of behaving would follow—individuals could generate a new culture that slowly but surely would replace traditional mores, undermine the "system," and ultimately transform society. The essence of what is here called the cultural radical outlook is what Charles Reich had in mind when he wrote of "the revolution of the new generation" that "will originate with the individual and with culture, and it will change the political structure only as its final act."[10]

Reich described the essence of "new consciousness" as the "liberation . . . [that] comes into being the moment the individual frees himself from automatic acceptance of the imperatives of society." He specified that this meant "the individual is free to build his own philosophy and values, his own life-style, and his own culture" and that the pursuit of liberation would thus lead different individuals in different directions at different times.[11] Yet he repeatedly illustrated "new consciousness" by describing views about society, politics, and life style specific to cultural radicals. For example, although Reich's depiction of "new consciousness" suggests otherwise, nothing in the decision to chart one's own course requires one to believe that one should engage in political activity or participate in political demonstrations. In retrospect, it is clear that such beliefs characterized only those politicized members of the counterculture identified here as cultural radicals, or simply as radicals.

By the end of the 1960s, the ranks of the New Left were filled with radicals. And the most prominent of their peers in the Movement were not those still bent on redistributing political and economic power through community organizing, but those whose pessimism about reforming capitalist institutions led them to Marxist solutions.

Although the Movement contained activists with a variety of Marxist and socialist perspectives, for the purposes of this analysis all are classified as political-economic revolutionaries, or simply as revolutionaries. Of course, there were Movement members with every variation and combination of radical and revolutionary views as well as large numbers with countercultural views and values who participated in Movement activities but lacked radical political outlooks.

The countercultural imperative to express oneself in ways that felt natural and right led growing numbers of homosexuals in the Greenwich Village area to be more openly gay following the raid on the Stonewall Inn. But it was radical conviction that exploring homosexuality was political that led to the formation of the Gay Liberation Front.*

Some of the founders of GLF, particularly those involved in the Movement, had begun to think about their sexuality in radical terms even before Stonewall. Jim Fouratt, one of the original Yippies, began to challenge his New Left associates to deal with their "uptightness" about homosexuality when Jerry Rubin and Abbie Hoffman seemed awkward in personal situations with him and uncomfortable when his lover was present. Lois Hart, who had spent time at the Millbrook, New York, estate of Timothy Leary and Richard Alpert before turning her attention to Indian mysticism, feminism, and anarchism at Alternate U, spoke of the importance of exploring relationships between lesbianism, feminism, and "life style politics" when she told Susan Silverman about her homosexuality. Charles Pitts's determination to be open about his sexuality grew as his contact with radicals at WBAI bolstered his belief that individuals could revolutionize society by thinking and acting in new ways. Pete Wilson was persuaded of the importance of challenging conventional sexual constraints through open enthusiasm about one's own sexuality in the League for Sexual Freedom—whose leader, Jefferson Poland, set an example by adopting Fuck for a middle name. Wilson was also influenced by Michael Itkin, who from the early 1950s had

---

*In his *Homosexual Oppression and Liberation* (New York: Avon, 1971) Dennis Altman traces the rise of the gay liberation movement to the counterculture without making the distinction between countercultural and cultural radical outlooks that is needed to explain why only a few of the many countercultural homosexuals affected by the Stonewall Riots were moved to form or join gay liberation groups.

riled homophile leaders on both coasts with talk about radicalism, religion, and the importance of expressing homosexual feelings openly; and by the lives and writings of three scholars who fathered the radical strain in Movement thinking—Norman O. Brown, Paul Goodman, and Herbert Marcuse.

The statement that Michael Brown, Lois Hart, and Ron Ballard prepared for *Rat* on the night of the Gay Liberation Front's christening elaborated the radicalism that guided most of its founders. In response to an imaginary questioner asking why GLF was radical, the trio of authors expressed the New Left conviction that the American system was economically unjust, racist, and dehumanizing —"a money-making machine." To a question about how the system oppressed homosexuals specifically, they explained that society attempted "to impose sexual roles and definitions of our nature" and "through a system of taboos and institutionalized repressions . . . controlled and manipulated . . . [and] denied . . . sexual expression."*

Radical thinking was apparent not only in what Brown, Hart, and Ballard called problems but also in what they said about social transformation. The GLFers advocated the overthrow of "this rotten, dirty, vile, fucked-up capitalist conspiracy" and said they planned to work for change in concert with "all the oppressed: the Vietnamese struggle, the third world, the blacks, the workers." But thereafter, they mentioned neither the overthrow of capitalism and imperialism championed by revolutionary-minded Movement members nor the abolition of racism demanded by those concerned primarily with nonwhite minorities. Instead, they discussed the elimination of "existing social institutions" and the revamping of norms governing personal behavior. These were the changes important to those interested in freer self-expression and more fulfilling social relations.

The statement also displayed radical biases in its suggestions about how these changes could be affected. For where members of the New Left concerned with material equality stressed working-class mobili-

---

*The radicals were able to reconcile their concern about conventional mores with the revolutionary preoccupation with political and economic arrangements by reasoning that the capitalist system of production required norms and roles that limited sexual and emotional interaction in order to maximize production (a Marcusian line of analysis). Still, what little attention was given matters of political economy in the *Rat* presentation can be traced largely to the fact that Ron Ballard, an avid Marxist, helped Brown and Hart prepare it.

zation, and those primarily interested in eliminating racism emphasized the need to build pride and power in nonwhite communities, the GLFers expressed hope "that masses of homosexuals will be open about their sexuality, and will challenge the bags the system puts people in." They suggested that by "stepping outside . . . roles and simplistic myths" and by "be[ing] who we are," "liberated" homosexuals could embody ways of thinking and acting that would lead others to forsake conventional values and traditional paths and create an "alternate culture."[12] They implied that supplanting established mores was the way to undermine existing economic and political institutions.

Although the views elaborated in GLF's credo were radical, from the beginning the founders of GLF were joined by a few whose outlooks were revolutionary. Ron Ballard, Bill Katzenberg, John O'Brien, and others differed from the radicals both in what they considered basic problems and in what they thought were effective ways of pursuing change. The revolutionaries were most concerned about eliminating the material inequities they believed perpetuated by capitalism. They were convinced that minorities aware that their oppression had common economic roots would band together and press for a new economic order. They believed that political and economic transformation had to precede cultural and social transformation.

Radical rather than revolutionary homosexuals took the lead in forming and defining GLF because revolutionaries, lacking the radical eagerness to explore the personal in the name of the political, were little inclined to think of sexuality in political terms. The few revolutionaries who did join in founding GLF were attracted by the idea of associating politically with their own kind and by the prospect of developing homosexuals as a new category of recruits for the fight against capitalism. (John O'Brien wanted to lead a gay phalanx into the socialist vanguard even though the Young Socialist Alliance had ousted him when he disclosed that he was homosexual.)

As one might expect, the few revolutionary GLFers who did not rapidly convert to radicalism never ceased to deplore the attention their cohorts gave to personal, social, and cultural issues at the expense of economic and political issues. Bill Katzenberg dropped out of GLF before the end of the summer because he thought the radicals spent a ridiculous amount of time criticizing him because he was not open about his homosexuality when working in SDS. Bob Fontanella, John Lauritsen, and the handful of other revolutionaries who remained resolute soon withdrew into an informal clique and then formed, in rapid succession, a Marxist study group, an independent cell, and an autonomous gay socialist group called the Red Butterfly.

GLFers with radical and revolutionary outlooks came to view their differences as fundamental, but these differences were far from clear during the first few months of GLF's existence. At the outset, gay liberationists were so busy extending and applying general Movement perspectives to the case of homosexuality that they had neither the time nor the inclination to differentiate between their views. Moreover, there were marked variations within the basic radical and revolutionary outlooks. And the views of most GLFers were constantly evolving—a situation that made (and makes) it difficult to specify that any single individual was consistently or permanently radical or revolutionary.

Indeed, what most impressed rank-and-file GLFers at the beginning were the similarities between the views of the radicals and the revolutionaries. Despite their differences, both held capitalism responsible for bureaucratic organizations, boring and mundane jobs, materialism, status hierarchies, compartmentalized lives, rigid roles, and standards and assumptions that stifled sexual and emotional expressiveness and kept individuals from pursuing personal growth and enjoying interpersonal intimacy. Moreover, although the radicals championed anarchy while the revolutionaries looked forward to socialism, most radicals said that the new living arrangements they envisaged would be "communal," just as most revolutionaries maintained that socialism would lead to new, humanistic living and working arrangements.* Radicals and revolutionaries shared the convictions that since every dimension of the existing system was bankrupt, a total transformation of society was desirable, and that

---

*Later, when radicals and revolutionaries began to focus on the differences in their perspectives, radicals argued that socialistic political and economic institutions produced the same evils as capitalistic ones, that dehumanization stemmed not from capitalism per se but from industrialization, bureaucracy, and the centralization of power and restrictive mores that technological development required.

to effect such change, it was necessary to unite all oppressed minorities into a broad-based movement.

The themes common to radical and revolutionary thinking produced a shared jargon. For a long time this, plus the feeling that all GLFers interested in any revolution had to "hang together" so that they would not be overshadowed by reformers, kept the two breeds of gay liberationists most prominent at GLF's creation from recognizing that their ideological differences would prevent their ever working together effectively.

. . .

In the heady days of August 1969, the radical founders of GLF insisted that their group was not an organization, but the visible tip of a burgeoning movement. For them, the term *organization* conjured up visions of the New York Mattachine, with its staid and professional board of directors, its all-powerful officers and absent members, its preoccupation with perpetuating itself by doing everything it could to please the authorities and keep the support of the Establishment. Yet the imperatives of organization have to be dealt with, and although the first radical gay liberationists vowed to avoid traditional modes, they nonetheless acted to provide GLF with identity, legitimacy, and resources.

Simply by settling on a name, the radicals who met at Alternate U acknowledged that any persisting collectivity had to have an identity. Gay Liberation Front—each word in that name was selected with organizational as well as political considerations in mind. Unlike *homosexual,* the clinical term bestowed by heterosexuals, and *homophile,* the euphemism coined by cautious political forerunners, *gay,* which homosexuals called each other, was thought to be the word that would most appeal to homosexuals who were thirsting to be known as they knew themselves. Hence also *liberation,* intended to suggest freedom from constraint. *Front* implied a militant vanguard or coalition; it suggested that GLF was the crest of a swelling wave destined to force people to recognize and respect the openly gay population.

The name Gay Liberation Front was also favored because it had the same ring as National Liberation Front, the alliance formed by the Viet Cong. Radicals and revolutionaries thought that this would help attract others with leftist perspectives and establish GLF's place in the Movement.

By the summer of 1969, among radical members of the Movement, it was an article of faith that groups striving to build a new society had an obligation to embody the principles of participatory democracy and humane community which they advocated. From the start, Movement veterans like Hart and Fouratt worked to give a radical cast not only to GLF's name and credo but also to its operation. In their view, radical ideals required "structurelessness." In GLF, this meant having a different moderator for each meeting instead of officers; organizing ad hoc project groups instead of formal committees; basing decisions on consensus reached through discussion rather than on the vote of the majority; and permitting access to all comers rather than establishing requirements for admittance and membership. In the second issue of GLF's newspaper, *Come Out!,* Lois Hart explained how these forms and procedures served radical ideals:

> The big news with GLF is that its radical approach to structure (some of us call it organic, others call it structure-less structure) is not only happening, which is probably its greatest validity, but that it gives good indication that it works. The many mentalities, dispositions, and persuasions of GLF activists and dissenters are finding expression in small groups structured after the needs, goals and philosophies of the participants . . .
>
> In the knowledge that growth and change occur within individuals and that individuals develop only through active involvement in projects and goals of their own choosing, GLFers chose the rocky road of fluid cellular organization rather than perpetuate older, oppressive structures of Follow the Leader and passive participation by voting.[13]

Like exploring "structure-less structure," participating in Movement activities was thought necessary to show that GLF belonged in the vanguard of the New Left. And just a week after the Gay Liberation Front was named, several who were already active in antiwar groups set out to introduce GLF to the Movement by carrying a gay liberationist banner to a march and rally in Central Park marking the last day of Hiroshima-Nagasaki Week. Much to their surprise, some in the crowd at the rally tried to topple their banner, and members of a Women's Strike for Peace contingent then berated the GLFers for creating the disturbance.

Early members of the Gay Liberation Front endured the hostility they encountered at antiwar marches and pro-Panther demonstrations not only because they thought their attendance would help certify that GLF belonged in the Movement, but also because they hoped to draw like-minded contemporaries to their side. The radicals believed gay liberation had something to offer all who were seeking "human liberation," whatever their sexual preference, and their desire to attract followers and enlist allies buttressed the idealism that led them to proclaim that GLF welcomed "all the people."

.   .   .

Those who responded to this welcome tended to be not members of the Movement interested in exploring their homosexuality but devotees of traditional gay pastimes whose countercultural views led them to believe that they had a right to enjoy the unconventional activities that pleased them. Typical was Jerry Hoose, who, although he lived in Queens with his parents and three younger brothers, participated enthusiastically in the outdoor sex scene in Greenwich Village, particularly the anonymous sex that took place in the backs of trucks parked near the West Village piers. The police had chased homosexuals out of the trucks just a few weeks before they raided the Stonewall Inn, and Hoose's resentment over what he perceived as "an unwarranted intrusion into a subcultural scene that hurt no one"[14] prompted him to join the angry crowd he found rioting in front of the Stonewall Inn on June 28.

In 1964, when he was nineteen, Hoose had seen Randy Wicker on television, and Wicker's enthusiastic talk about gay life had encouraged him to be open about his sexuality with his family, friends, and employers. Finding that he was happier than most of the secretive homosexuals he met, Hoose felt that most homosexuals would be happier if they "came out." In the riotous crowd on Christopher Street he saw energy that could be used to protect those who were freely homosexual from harassment. He viewed GLF as a vehicle for using this energy both to defend the homosexual's right to enjoy subcultural pleasures and to reach guilty and closeted homosexuals with the message that there was support for those who wanted to be

open. Hoose had never identified himself as a member of the Movement or the counterculture, but personal experience and the do-your-
own-thing *Zeitgeist* filled him with the same desire to organize and
influence homosexuals that radical thinking had stimulated in the
leading organizers of GLF.

The phrase "do your own thing" has a ring that trivializes the
interest in fuller and freer self-expression at the root of the counterculture, but it emphasizes that the guiding ethos was fundamentally
libertarian, directing individuals to express themselves in ways they
enjoyed and to respect others who did likewise. Endorsed as a goal
of political activism by the Movement, and applied to the case of
homosexuality by the first gay liberationists, this ethos led all
GLFers to vow that they were fighting for the homosexual's right to
self-expression. Yet GLFers had different understandings of which
aspects of the homosexual's life deserved political attention and of
how best to make these aspects legitimate and respectable. Jerry
Hoose was just one whose political interests were limited to the
homosexual dimensions of self-expression and who had no moral
reservations about the traditional gay subculture or about conventional social, professional, and political involvements. Exposure to
the very different views of the radicals helped transform Hoose and
others like him into a pioneering breed of reform-oriented gay liberationists.

The GLFers who developed reformist outlooks shared the basic
understandings that distinguished gay liberationists from homophile
leaders. They blamed the homosexual's problems on sexually repressive mores rather than on simple prejudices about homosexuals and
on policies that enshrined these prejudices. They wanted to persuade
people that for many, homosexual behavior was a valid way of
self-expression, rather than to stress that homosexuals were in important respects like heterosexuals and that homosexual preferences
mattered little. They considered it more strategic to bring pride and
power to homosexuals than to try to edify heterosexuals.

The reformers differed from the radicals and the revolutionaries
both in the scope of the changes they wanted to make and in the
nature of the steps they thought it necessary to take. Where the
radicals and revolutionaries called for a complete reconstruction of
America's cultural, social, economic, and political systems, the reformers wanted openly gay people to be a respected presence in

existing institutions. Where the radicals and revolutionaries wanted
to stir all of the oppressed to think about their lives in totally new
ways and to support a wide range of political causes, the reformers
aspired only to stir homosexuals to be open about their sexuality and
to support specifically gay causes.

Just as there were cultural radicals and political-economic revolutionaries, there came to be cultural and political reformers. But
unlike the radicals and revolutionaries, the two strains of reformers
differed from one another less in their views of the cause of the
homosexual's problems and of the nature of desirable change than
in their strategies for effecting that change. Influenced by the radical
belief that social change followed from changing consciousness, the
cultural reformers wanted to encourage homosexuals to define themselves as gay, to be proud and open about their homosexuality in
their social, family, and professional lives, and to join together in
explicitly gay institutions and a self-aware gay community. They
believed that as heterosexuals became impressed with the gay people
they were exposed to, they would welcome openly gay people into
existing institutions. Political reformers, by contrast, argued that
political influence was necessary to protect the activities advocated
by the cultural reformers. Influenced by revolutionary warnings
about the need for power to prevent repression by the state, the
political reformers wanted to develop influence in the political system: they wanted to make homosexuals aware that they had political
interests, to lead them into political activities, to organize them into
a political bloc, and to force politicians and public officials to acknowledge that "gays" were a legitimate political minority. Political reformers, in short, believed that power was the only thing
that would pave the way for gays to participate in existing institutions.

The prototypical political reformer in GLF was Marty Robinson.
The son of a Jewish doctor, Robinson attended public and private
school and majored in biology for three years at Brooklyn College
before discovering, in his early twenties, that he was homosexual.
After fighting with his parents over his desire to be "who he really
was," he dropped out of college, moved to Greenwich Village, and
began to support himself by doing carpentry. The second night of
disturbances after the Stonewall raid stirred Robinson to join
MSNY, where he succeeded Michael Brown as head of the Action

Committee. The nascent political reformism that slowly but surely led him out of MSNY and into GLF showed in the leaflet Robinson prepared to advertise the vigil he ran in Washington Square. Among other things, it promised, "We will vote as a bloc for the politicians who support our rights." In his speech at the vigil, Robinson suggested that local homosexuals could exercise gay power by burning their Bloomingdale's charge cards.

The radical and revolutionary gay liberationists at the vigil found Robinson's suggestions silly, but his recommendations reflected ideas popularized by the very groups responsible for the emergence of the movement they considered their own. The Student Nonviolent Coordinating Committee inaugurated the New Left in the early 1960s when it abandoned the civil rights movement's strategy of mobilizing white support and turned instead to organizing black communities. This effort began with voter registration and evolved into the creation of alternative institutions and constellations of economic and political power that would give blacks influence in local institutions. SNCC's efforts stirred SDSers like Tom Hayden and Carl Wittman to think about community organizing. In the summer of 1963, these SDS members met with SNCC field workers, including Stokely Carmichael, who argued that blacks could do the job for blacks in the south and that whites ought to organize whites in the north. In 1966 SNCC formally committed itself to the policy of blacks organizing blacks and asked whites to go elsewhere. The notion that minorities could best organize their own communities became popular thereafter.

SNCC's ouster of whites was prompted not only by the assessment that black field workers could achieve greater rapport with the rural blacks they hoped to organize, but also by the recognition that there were fundamental differences in the ways blacks and whites expressed themselves and that distinctively black patterns were enjoyable and attractive. SNCC's embrace of black power was at least partially motivated by the desire to cultivate styles and customs believed characteristically black. This is why the growth of attention to black power was accompanied by a growth of interest in black pride. The complementary drives for black power and black pride helped popularize two ideas: first, that people had a right to styles of self-expression and social interaction that were unappreciated by the majority; and second, that minority communities had to organize, both to secure rights and benefits and to command recognition and respect for their own subcultures.

Among blacks, the drive for black pride and black power produced radicals and revolutionaries as well as reformers. The growing belief that American society was racist—that it was dominated by whites who ascribed traits they considered alien and inferior to all those with colored skin—pushed blacks with radical and revolutionary outlooks to argue that blacks were indeed different, that they shared a superior cultural heritage with Africans and other Third World peoples. Radical and revolutionary black leaders contended that domestic black communities were psychologically castrated and politically and economically exploited "colonies." They asserted that by making blacks aware of their cultural heritage and by organizing them politically, they could foment a revolution that would transform American society. These were arguments that led many in the New Left to see the Black Panthers as the leaders of the Movement in the late 1960s.

SNCC itself became progressively more revolutionary, attempted to merge with the Panthers during the spring and summer of 1968, and then faded from the scene. But its early views on community organizing—and the understanding of black pride and black power passed on to most blacks—produced reformers concerned primarily with developing and defending black cultural, social, economic, and political community and with using community power both to secure representation for blacks in existing institutions and to command recognition and respect for distinctively black cultural styles.[15] The efforts of reform-oriented blacks were the inspiration and the model for reform-oriented gay liberationists who set out to develop gay pride and gay power.

Marty Robinson was stirred by the Stonewall Riots to discover how gays could emulate the efforts of reform-oriented blacks effectively. But not knowing how and why the proponents of black power had abandoned liberal assumptions, he was slow to recognize the fundamental ways in which his approach to gay political activity differed from the homophile approach of Mattachine officials. Products of ideological confusion heightened by organizational loyalty, the statements that Robinson issued in the name of MSNY's Action Committee were alternately fired with reformist gay liberationist sentiment about the need to secure the right to be openly homosexual and tempered with moderate homophile assurances that the lives of homosexuals had improved. His leaflet advertising the vigil in Washington Square maintained:

> Homosexuals have never had it so good in New York. Within the last three years, gay bars have opened and police entrapment has all but ceased. The homosexual living in other areas of the country, however, still must fear plain-clothes entrapment, raids on gay bars, or exposure on the job. Imagine having to sneak into a bar instead of having the right to walk into one as a free citizen. Homosexuals have been beaten, blackmailed, ridiculed, lynched, imprisoned, fired from their jobs, forced to live dual lives, disgraced, labeled as sinners and psychopaths, and victimized by society's guilt feelings about sex.

All in all, probably the most significant result of Robinson's early activities was the excitement they produced in Jim Owles, who had come to New York from Chicago just a few months before Stonewall. Owles went to the Washington Square vigil after seeing advertisements for it posted in the Village. He found that he was both sexually attracted to Robinson and stirred by his ideas. At the July 31 meeting where GLF was named, the two met and discovered their personal and political compatibility. Robinson asked his new friend to help him manage the Mattachine's Action Committee. There and at GLF meetings, the two formulated the political reformist approach to gay liberation.

Although the radical founders of GLF were wary about the appearance at their meetings of homosexuals who wanted to protect and even promote traditional gay styles and to make a place for openly gay people in existing institutions, they welcomed individuals like Jerry Hoose and Leo Martello from the beginning and they applauded Robinson and Owles's decision early in September to commit themselves to GLF. The radicals included the reformers partly because they recognized that they needed all the help they could get, partly because they believed that anyone thirsting to be openly gay and aspiring to build community pride and power was on the road to liberation, and partly because they believed that they could educate—"raise the consciousness" of—those unfamiliar with the logic of revolution through consciousness change.

For the radicals, GLF existed primarily to raise consciousness—

their own as well as that of their associates, of the homosexuals they intended to mobilize, and of the Movement members they expected to enlist as allies. Indeed, the story of GLF is largely the story of how radical consciousness-raising efforts enlightened and then alienated political and cultural reformers, frightened and offended homophile leaders, antagonized revolutionaries, divided radical women from radical men, and resulted finally in almost all radicals separating themselves from the Movement responsible for their gay political involvement in the first place.

5

The Consequences of
Radical Consciousness-Raising

The liberal . . . is always engaged in "fighting someone else's battle" . . .

The liberal does not speak comfortably of "freedom" or "liberation," but rather of justice and social amelioration. He does not sense himself to be unfree . . .

Liberal consciousness is conscience translated into action for others . . .

Radical or revolutionary consciousness . . . is the perception of *oneself* as unfree, as oppressed—and finally it is the discovery of oneself as *one of the oppressed* who must unite to transform the objective conditions of their existence . . . Revolutionary consciousness leads to *the struggle for one's own freedom in unity with others who share the burden of oppression.*

It may have seemed a very ordinary perception, this distinction between liberal and radical, but it was not. It was a sharp pinpointing of where the Movement, and SDS, had come to—"the struggle for one's own freedom"—as a result of having been told by Black Power to consider their *own* problems, having been led by student syndicalism to a concern with the student's *own* power, and having finally seen in draft resistance the potential of young men acting out of their *own* oppression. It was also a profound realization of where the Movement and SDS were heading —a "unity with others who share the burden of oppression"—in the move to create a community of identity beyond selfishness, a sense of mutual need, a "revolutionary consciousness."[1]

In these paragraphs from his study of SDS, Kirkpatrick Sale identifies the shift from liberal to radical consciousness as a watershed in the history of the New Left. What he nowhere points out is that the urge to explore their own oppression gradually led homosexuals in the Movement to turn to gay liberation. Yet the realization that they were not free to express their homosexual feelings was what led radicals like Hart and Fouratt to help organize the Gay Liberation Front in the summer of 1969. And their Movement-bred radicalism gave shape to consciousness-raising efforts that served not only to mold and antagonize activists with other gay political outlooks, but also to lead most of the radicals themselves to conclude that they had to leave the Movement, and even GLF, in order to find the freedom they sought.

• • •

All the statements issued by the fledgling Gay Liberation Front bore evidence of the radical consciousness-raising impulse. The flier that brought together the front's organizers declared, "Homosexuals are coming together . . . to examine how we are oppressed and how we oppress ourselves." The interview announcing GLF's birth in *Rat* promised "a program that allows homosexuals and sexually liberated persons to confront themselves and society through encounter groups, demonstrations, dances, a newspaper, and by just being ourselves on the street."[2] But no better synopsis of the educational objectives championed by the founders of GLF appeared than the one printed in the first issue of *Come Out!:*

> Because our oppression is based on sex and the sex roles which oppress us from infancy, we must explore these roles and their meanings . . . Does society make a place for us . . . as a man? A woman? A homosexual or lesbian? How does the family structure affect us? What is sex, and what does it mean?
>
> What is love? As homosexuals, we are in a unique position to examine these questions from a fresh point of view. You'd better believe we are going to do so—that we are going to transform society at large through the open realization of our own consciousness.[3]

In the early days, Lois Hart did more than anyone to explain how the radicals expected "to transform society at large through the open realization of our own consciousness." Essentially, she argued that as homosexuals learned how to express themselves fully and freely, they would become more integrated psychologically and more capable of relating to others successfully. This personal integration and interpersonal sophistication in turn would give them a charisma that would inspire others to follow their lead.* As more and more people refused to let convention inhibit their sexual and emotional expression, Hart concluded, there would be a grassroots flowering of mores that would undermine inhibiting roles and standards and slowly but surely transform society.

To those unacquainted with the logic of revolution through consciousness change, Hart's line of argument was difficult to comprehend. Many attracted to GLF found it hard to understand why she and other radicals insisted that activities they themselves considered personal, therapeutic, or social were, in fact, political. To demonstrate that the personal could be political, Hart organized an encounter group. Because she was particularly eager to impress GLFers whose political perspectives differed dramatically from hers, she invited revolutionaries like John O'Brien and political reformers like Robinson and Owles to join. Hart was willing to work with skeptics not only because she thought it possible to convert them but also because she saw that they could help identify the conventions that kept homosexuals inhibited and unhappy.

In *The Greening of America,* Charles Reich depicts the radical quest for consciousness as a search for self-awareness that "begins with an effort to shake off the 'false consciousness' imposed by society" and proceeds to efforts "to restore sensitivity."[5] Describing her goals in the first issue of *Come Out!,* Hart explained that she considered encounter groups a vehicle for identifying and dispensing with "false consciousness" and envisioned a host of additional enterprises to "restore sensitivity":

---

*In the first issue of *Come Out!,* replying to a letter from a man who asked what the benefits of being open about his homosexuality might be, Hart told of the personal experience that reinforced her political convictions:

There is no question that you will feel more whole and happier when you can be who you are all of the time. This is no easy thing, I know. It took me until age 32 to finally give in to myself and though it felt at the time that I was losing everything (the good opinion and sanction of this society from my family right on up to any career dreams I have had), I have in truth gained the whole world. I feel at a loss to convey to you right now what that means. I can just say that I have never felt better in my life. I know now in retrospect that I only began to be really alive when I was able to take that step.[4]

At first it seemed that I was mainly aware of what I didn't want. Leo has said it well—to no longer consent to be the victims—to throw off every piece of shit that has held me down until now. Shit like "dyke," "sick," "degenerate," "non-woman," "queer," "corrupter of children," "unnatural," "sinful," "damned." In our groups we trace the outlines of our pain; we delineate the scaffolding of a society that has arranged our crucifixion . . .

What do I want to do? It has something to do with sharing, with caring for myself and others, with working to transform my immediate environment so that it fosters our growing humanity . . .

We need a place, my friends and I, we who call ourselves G.L.F. We need space to be together—to meet, to rap, to eat, to dance, to dig each other and plan our work. It would be a place for our paper, communal dinners, meetings and dances—space where we can begin to break down our fragmentation—to create a communal environment closer to our needs and purposes.[6]

Leo Martello, whom Hart mentioned, wrote an article for the first issue of *Come Out!* describing in greater depth the insights gained in early encounter group sessions. He began by explaining the cultural oppression Hart referred to as "the scaffolding of a society that has arranged our crucifixion":

The homosexual, whether born or bred (and the psychiatric argument is still raging), has been conditioned into thinking of himself as "sick," an outcast, a "sinner," unworthy, something to be despised. The minute he discovers that he's "different" he avidly reads anything he can on the subject. And what does he find? More ammunition for his self-contempt. He's told by psychiatric "authorities" that he's "sick." So he begins to tell himself NOT that "The psychiatrists say I'm sick" BUT "I am sick." He programs himself into perpetual feelings of unworthiness.

Like his account of the dynamics of cultural oppression, Martello's explanation of how cultural conditioning denied the homosexual personal and social fulfillment reflected the countercultural premium placed on expressing oneself naturally, freely, and fully:

Homosexuals handle their societally induced problem in many ways. They passively accept everything said about them as true and then proceed to act out and live down to what others say they are. Or they live a double life, conventionally proper and respectable and in the most intimate area of their lives furtively acting like fugitives from justice. Or some resent, rebel, and flaunt their homosexuality in defiance of the guilts and self-contempt fostered in them by society. These are all overcompensations. They do not help the homosexual into a sense of his own worthiness.

Martello then argued that in order to achieve liberation, homosexuals had to become aware of how they were affected by conventional standards and assumptions:

> The greatest battle of the homosexual in an oppressive society is with himself, more precisely the image of himself forced on him by non-homosexuals . . .
> He must CHALLENGE every single feeling of worthlessness that he has about himself. He must make sure that he is not accepting an UNEARNED GUILT. Deep in his gut he must ask if the deepest, secret, unconscious, inner picture that he has of himself is really of himself . . . or is it one fostered in him by parents, society, religion, psychiatry, and the heterosexual majority?[7]

When Martello argued that liberation required homosexuals to discover unwarranted guilt and inferiority and to learn to feel good about themselves, he was expressing sentiments shared by all the early gay liberationists. But Martello carefully equated liberation with the elimination of negative feelings about homosexuality and portrayed voyages of homosexual self-discovery as open-ended and diverse. With subtlety, he urged homosexuals to reject cultural conditioning and to be true to their own selves without suggesting that this would result in specific conclusions or choices.

Determining what it meant for homosexuals to be liberated was one of the first things that alienated GLFers with reformist inclinations from their radical associates. For as the weeks passed, Martello, Hoose, Robinson, Owles, and others who came to be leading reformers contended that becoming a liberated homosexual meant learning how to express one's sexual feelings as one wished. But Hart and other radicals, specifying that expressing such feelings was simply one aspect of a multifaceted phenomenon known as self-actualization, insisted that liberation meant learning how to lead one's entire life so as to contribute to the construction of a humane new society.

In fact, as the radicals withdrew into the collective formed to produce *Come Out!* and then organized what they called the Come Out Cell (later the 28th of June Cell), they began to equate liberation with adherence to a sweeping new credo. Its most prominent tenets were: first, transient, anonymous, and purely erotic sex was bad, but committed, personalized, and emotion-filled sexual relations good; second, role-playing was obsolete, but role violations desirable; third, seeking conventional professional recognition, social status, and material reward was harmful, but seeking unconventional emotional, sensual, spiritual, artistic, and interpersonal experience was salutary; and fourth, cerebral, controlled, manipulative, aggressive, and competitive behavior was detrimental, but intuitive, expressive, genuine, gentle, and cooperative behavior was beneficial.

As one might expect, the new standards reflected the experiences of those who worked to develop and apply them. The standards pertaining to sexuality were typical. When they discussed what it was like to be gay, radical male GLFers rapidly agreed that they found gay life unpleasant and unsatisfying. This led them to conclude that male homosexuals who wanted to be fulfilled sexually had to abandon traditional styles of promiscuity and to avoid subcultural institutions like bars, bathhouses, and pornographic bookstores. What they neglected to consider was that some homosexuals found participation in the gay male subculture genuinely fulfilling. Instead of arguing "each to his own," the radical males tended to generalize their personal preferences and to condemn traditional gay male patterns as "unliberated."

It is not surprising that except for a few GLFers like Charles Pitts and Pete Wilson, self-taught radicals with strong libertarian biases and little experience in the organized Movement, most radical males involved in the beginnings of GLF did not have strong gay identities —that is, a strong and positive sense of identification with the gay subculture. Bill Weaver, for example, had experienced but a single homosexual relationship and had never been to a gay bar before joining GLF. Jim Fouratt spoke for many of his friends when he wrote that he found the word *homosexual* "hard to relate to because it puts me in a category which limits my potential. It also prescribes a whole system of behavior to which I'm supposed to conform, which has nothing to do with the reality of my day-to-day living."[8] Though Fouratt's objection to labeling seemed a humanistic proposition, it ignored the reality that many considered their homosexuality central to their identities and felt strengthened when they presented themselves and were acknowledged by others as gay.

One can only speculate about the mix of personal experience and political philosophy responsible for the weak gay identities of so many of the first radical men in GLF. Clearly, however, radical understanding of the relationship between personal experience and political imperative reinforced this situation. It was inevitable that the radical pursuit of unfettered self-actualization would give rise to the feeling among GLFers ignorant about or dissatisfied with the gay subculture that they were "human beings with homosexual feelings," just as it would strengthen the sense that they were "gays" in those who enjoyed traditional gay pastimes. This is why most of the relatively few early GLFers with strong gay identities evolved reformist rather than radical political outlooks.

That so many of GLF's founders developed radical outlooks in the Movement helps explain why they equated liberation with the rejection of conventionally cherished behavior of every sort. Radical thinking evolved as New Left leaders politicized members of the counterculture by arguing that the American system was a dehumanizing machine that had to be destroyed before people would be free to be themselves. Inevitably, the first radicals equated freedom with an abandonment of traditional patterns.*

The criteria the radicals developed to define liberation were heavily influenced by lesbian GLFers, whom Lois Hart gathered into all-lesbian encounter groups with radical orientations in the fall of 1969. The lesbian consensus was that their path to fulfillment lay in the emotional and interpersonal dimensions of their lives, a predilection said to reflect the greater interest in relationships that had

*In *The Greening of America,* Charles Reich pointed out that the countercultural quest for liberated life styles would lead different individuals in different directions. He stressed that the nature of particular paths was less important than their being chosen to express self rather than to conform to societally enshrined or externally imposed values, and that the hope for countercultural community was that those who opted for self-actualization would develop the integration and awareness that would permit them to deal genuinely and respectfully with those whose self-actualization involved very different paths. But Reich contradicted these basic premises when he suggested (1) that living a self-directed life required creating new patterns and structures rather than developing self-actualizing attitudes and approaches towards existing patterns and structures; (2) that expressing one's "self" meant expressing oneself innovatively, emotionally, sensually, spiritually, artistically, and interpersonally, but not traditionally, analytically, formally, professionally, institutionally, and materially; and (3) that a traditionally distinguished lesbians from gay men. (Not until the spring, when there was more awareness of radical feminist thinking, was this predilection attributed more to the lesbian's womanhood than to her homosexuality.) The lesbian subculture lacked most of the sex-related pastimes and institutions characteristic of the gay male subculture, and most of the radical lesbians, though rarely involved in monogamous relationships themselves, were appalled by the bald pursuit of sex many of their male associates relished. The lesbian stand reinforced the feeling among radical males that liberation required abandoning traditional gay male patterns.

The radical lesbians agreed that the bane of their own traditional patterns was excessive role-playing. As one might expect, few of them were comfortable with the "butch" and "femme" roles adopted by many older lesbians, just as few of the radical males who welcomed their reservations about role-playing were comfortable with transvestites in the drag queen subculture or with male homosexuals who enjoyed the macho "leather" and "biker" subcultures.

As with other radical ideas about the nature of liberation, sentiments about role-playing crept imperceptibly into talk about how conventional standards and assumptions kept homosexuals from expressing themselves genuinely and from dealing with one another naturally. The nature of this process, and the pain it caused those who enjoyed traditional styles, was poignantly described in the first issue of *Come Out!* by Marty Stephan, a lesbian who enjoyed being butch:

> After a GLF meeting, five people sit in a pad, four of them rapping about the dreams of the beautiful life styles they want for themselves. I sit there

humanistic community would be composed only of expressive, spontaneous, gentle, peaceful, sensitive, straightforward, and altruistic people and not of cold, controlled, aggressive, angry, imperceptive, calculating, and self-contained people. Like most of the first radicals, Reich found it hard to accept the relativism inherent in the countercultural call. Such relativism implied (1) that the choice to be traditional, professional, cognitive, etc., as long as it was made to fulfill self rather than to meet external expectation, was as true to the countercultural ideal of self-actualization as the choice to be unconventional, nonprofessional, affective, etc.; (2) that opting for a self-determined, personally expressive life style required one to be self-involved and feeling-focused only to the extent that it required one to be aware enough of one's feelings to make choices guided by personal predilection rather than external dictate; and (3) that all the countercultural ideal of community required of existing society was that as much genuine recognition, respect, and support be accorded to modes of self-expression that were unconventional, nonprofessional, affective, etc., as to modes that were traditional, professional, cognitive, etc.

wishing them well, hoping they make it. Then a leading GLF political theorist routinely says of two good people not present, "They're old line homosexuals." Not, "They're in GLF and they do good work and their heads are into costume/transvestism/drag or whatever you want to call it." Three people nod in common understanding—a stereotype has been added to the GLF lexicon; by implication I'm an old line lesbian, and I don't bother to argue.

Although every GLF member does not dig the term at this time, you can damn well bet that as encounter groups evolve into life style and political action groups the term will progress from being a stereotype to a cliche to a shrug, which always precludes both potentiality and argument and requires a whole new civil rights organization to fight it—like maybe the Drag Queen and Drag Butch Anti-Defamation and Liberation League. Knowing that the Gay use of "old line homosexual" zaps your life style, defines you as having a rigid immutable mind and destroys your validity and worth as a person (see COME OUT editorial and disregard if you are in drag) you might yearn for the simpler "drag queen," which only meant cross-dressing and carrying on in public, but the "drag queen" label is a straight put down; Gay radicals try to eliminate straight thinking wherever they find it. Apparently the Aquarian Age and doing your own thing doesn't protect you from either your liberators or your oppressors . . .

Sure I know I have to decide what my life style really is and what is merely reaction to straight thinking, but those decisions require some hard work and thought, so while I and other drag types are thinking or maybe not thinking, just enjoying our lives and so what?—stop shitting on our life style—we're not shitting on yours.[9]

As Stephan's final comments testified, it was difficult to specify what it meant for homosexuals to express themselves naturally, if only because it was impossible to know just what it meant to be homosexual and whether traditional gay styles of self-expression were externally dictated, happily embraced, or the result of a combination of conditioning and choice. Leo Martello showed his awareness of these complexities by arguing not for the elimination of traditional gay patterns but for investigation of the negative feelings many homosexuals had about them. But the modesty and subtlety of what Martello recommended had little appeal to radicals searching for answers that would permit them to lead others to "correct consciousness." And when the reformers in GLF objected to the denigration of traditional gay ways, the radicals became not more open-minded but ever more challenging.

. . .

For GLFers with strong gay identities and reformist outlooks, most of them men, Martello's argument that "you can't go any higher than your own thoughts" was a call not to condemn the old and invent the new, but to enjoy their gay subculture with a new spirit of pride, sharing, and openness and to encourage other homosexuals to do likewise. These, in fact, were Martello's ambitions, and this is why he was excited about the appearance of *Gay Power* and *Gay,* the first professionally published local newspapers aimed at homosexuals. When radicals complained that the new publications were pornographic and exploitative, Martello charged that the critics were motivated by "hatred of ability, fear of competition, and power lust."

Martello had agreed to write for *Gay* and to some extent his words were a response to radical criticism of this decision. Yet in defending himself, Martello took another step away from GLFers who opposed all conventional pursuits, countering that gainful employment was essential for liberation:

> How high can any homosexual's "consciousness" be if he is preoccupied with the bare necessities of life? Just how "giving" can any gay be who hasn't got for himself? . . .
> How much self-esteem and self-respect can any homosexual have if he has to live on handouts? GAY POWER . . . means earning and paying one's own way . . . PAY POWER . . . the best way to fight Establishment-engendered oppression.[10]

Although his remarks dealt with the economic basis of liberationist visions, Martello recognized that the issue at stake for most radicals was not whether liberation required individuals to be financially responsible for themselves but whether the capitalist system could provide the masses with the occupational opportunities it afforded the advantaged. This Martello considered a complicated side issue. In fact, in the eyes of Martello and others who became reformers, the problem with both radicals and revolutionaries was that they were concerned not only with each facet of each homosexual's self-expression but with each dimension of each human being's liberation.

Fearing that the breadth of radical and revolutionary concerns would inevitably force a slighting of the issues raised by homosexuality itself, the reformers wanted to devote their attention solely to the homosexual's freedom to express homosexual feelings. They felt that gay liberationists could most appropriately make society more humane by helping homosexuals be openly gay, by developing and protecting gay-identified enterprises, by claiming areas frequented by homosexuals as "gay turf," by eliminating obstacles to the efflorescence of identifiably gay communities, and by helping homosexuals and heterosexuals alike appreciate the meaning of sexual liberation.

As the radicals became ever more dogmatic about their own ideas about sexual liberation, the reformers began to call their sexual philosophy libertarian. Yet the reformers had countercultural biases that made them very different from traditional libertarians. The traditional libertarian position on homosexual activity was that an individual who wanted to engage in it had a right to do so and that others had an obligation not to interfere if it did them no harm. Reform-minded gay liberationists believed further that individuals with homosexual feelings were better off if they expressed them fully and freely and that others had an obligation to recognize and respect homosexual paths to personal fulfillment. In their view, a "liberated" homosexual was one who was comfortable with his sexuality and his subculture and successful at integrating his homosexuality into his life instead of denying, concealing, or compartmentalizing it. A "liberated" heterosexual was one who felt free to explore homosexual as well as heterosexual feelings, was comfortable with homosexuals, and saw gay life as valid, even if it was personally unappealing.

Martello, a Ph.D. and the author of several books on witchcraft, was a thinker, and his reformist views were crystallized through intellectual exchange with radical colleagues. Jerry Hoose shared Martello's countercultural biases, but organizational concerns more than ideological debate prompted him to clarify and articulate reformist positions. Among other things, Hoose argued that it was necessary to welcome homosexuals who enjoyed subcultural pursuits and lived conventionally so that GLF would have the numbers it needed to stage effective demonstrations.

Although Hoose objected to the puritanism, dogmatism, and self-righteousness he saw in the radicals, he let their ideas on tactics and strategy influence his. When he first enlisted in GLF, Hoose had assumed that demonstrations were the essence of political activity and that self-help, social, community-service, and public-relations activities were only vehicles for organizational aggrandizement. Early in August 1969, he arranged to speak on Alex Bennett's late-night radio show to promote GLF as a political alternative to local homophile groups, which, he said, were preoccupied with social events, services, and education. Later that month, he helped run a GLF dance—not, like the radicals, because he believed that having a privately run, open gay dance was community-building, convention-challenging, and hence political, but because he felt it would attract new recruits, raise money for a bail fund, and thus permit more GLFers to participate in militant demonstrations. Yet, as he worked with the radicals, Hoose began to accept their argument that GLF-sponsored self-help, social, community-service, and public-relations activities were political because they helped homosexuals express themselves more freely and relate to one another more naturally. Indeed, in mid-October, he, Bob Kohler, Mike Lavery, and others eager to build gay community by sponsoring dances and communal dinners formed a cell named, with countercultural aptness, Aquarius. Like other Aquarians, Hoose was led by his interest in organizational maintenance and his attention to radical arguments to pioneer cultural reformist approaches to gay liberation.*

One of the tactics the cultural reformers began to adapt for their own purposes was demonstrating. Radical and revolutionary GLFers saw demonstrations as vehicles for spreading political consciousness among homosexuals while teaching Movement members that homosexuals were an oppressed minority. Their reform-oriented associates saw that protest activity could be used to encourage homosexuals to become proud, open, and political in ways that would force the public to acknowledge the validity of gay life.

The budding reformist perspective on protest activity accounted for a picket line in front of the offices of the *Village Voice* in Septem-

---

*Though the cultural reformist Aquarians saw their efforts as a key to gay liberation, they were slow to follow the radical lead in characterizing self-help, social, community-service, and public-relations activities as political. Like their peers with political reformist outlooks, they tended to describe their efforts as consciousness-raising activities and to reserve the term "political" for enterprises pertaining specifically to political institutions.

ber 1969—the first GLF demonstration staged over an issue important to homosexuals alone. The *Voice* had decided to drop the heads in two classified advertisements submitted by GLFers: the head "Gay Community Dance" from an ad for the first GLF dance, and the heading "Gay Power to Gay People" from a solicitation for material to be published in *Come Out!* The day after the second ad had been submitted, an official from the *Voice* telephoned the GLFers responsible and explained that the newspaper had a policy of keeping obscene words out of classified ads. Reported *Come Out!:*

> When questioned why anyone would consider such a word obscene, the *Voice* said that the staff had decided that "Gay" was equatable with "fuck" and other four-letter words, and that either the ad would have to be changed or the ad could not be printed. Since "homosexual" was also not acceptable, and since GLF wanted the ad for the dance placed, we accepted their only admissable substitute, "homophile" (which is a genteel bastard word not included in most dictionaries).[11]

For the radicals, the biases exhibited in the *Voice* simply underscored the need for journals that would foster "alternate consciousness." But in Jerry Hoose, Marty Robinson, and other reformers eager to make a place for gays in the existing system, the *Voice*'s stance sparked desire to make institutions in the Village responsive to the real if invisible homosexual community at their feet. After *Voice* publisher Ed Fancher refused to meet with them, the reformers decided to picket.

Late in the afternoon of the protest, shortly after a GLFer cheered his cohorts by submitting a classified advertisement saying "The Gay Liberation Front sends love to all Gay men and women in the homosexual community," representatives of the picketers were invited to discuss their concerns with Fancher. Though the publisher refused to interfere with derogatory references to homosexuals made by his columnists, he agreed to permit the words *homosexual* and *gay* in classified ads. A flier prepared to promote a hastily scheduled victory dance exulted: " 'Gay' is no longer a four-letter word, even at the *Village Voice.* Friday . . . members of the homosexual community demonstrated the reality of gay power . . . GLF hopes that all members of the community will take note of this, and that they will take appropriate action to bring about the day when the

Voice may become truly representative of the people of the Village."

During the next few months, as GLF reformers inclined to take more overtly political actions experimented with demonstrations involving politicians, the first cultural reformers joined not only in confronting political candidates but also in staging antiwar and pro-Panther demonstrations with radical and revolutionary comrades: in demonstrations of every kind they found an occasion for the types of public appearances they thought would embolden homosexuals. Yet the cultural reformers felt that neither candidate confrontations nor Movement demonstrations highlighted the particular messages they wanted to communicate: that modern society through its psychiatric, ecclesiastical, and media establishments perpetuated standards and assumptions that kept individuals from freely expressing their homosexual feelings, and that these conventions would be undermined if homosexuals were openly enthusiastic about their interests. Only at the end of October, when *Time* magazine published a seven-page cover story on "The Homosexual: Newly Visible, Newly Understood," did the cultural reformers see an opportunity for a demonstration that would speak directly to their concerns.

Although homophile stalwarts were delighted with the unprecedented attention *Time* gave homosexuality (Dick Leitsch and Frank Kameny were quoted as spokesmen for homosexuals), GLFers were offended because the article quoted experts who pronounced homosexuality a condition of dubious mental health and questionable morality. The radicals felt that *Time*'s effort was all that could be expected from an institution with a stake in perpetuating mores that buttressed capitalistic profit-making; the cultural reformers were less willing to dismiss the opportunity to challenge so important a culture-shaping institution. Hoose remembers calling members of the Aquarius Cell to Bob Kohler's house to make plans: "We went over, for about four hours, the different alternatives. It turned out that we decided we were going to ask for equal space, reparations—figures ranged from half a million dollars up, but I think we finally agreed on something like $10,000. We agreed that it was going to be a mass demonstration in front of Time and Life. Thousands of people were going to get out."

The dreams of the Aquarians came nowhere near realization. Receptionists in the Time-Life Building prevented GLFers from reaching important offices. Snow kept the number of demonstrators

below thirty. A construction crew across the street pelted the protest-
ers with eggs. Yet ABC-TV's local affiliate included coverage of the
demonstration in its evening news, and the publicity helped clarify
the understanding that demonstrations, by attracting the attention of
the news media, could convey important messages to homosexuals
even if they did not affect target institutions directly. Hoose noted
as much in remarking on the results of the demonstration: "I think
it raised the consciousness of a lot of people who saw that the few
of us there were fair prey, game for anything. We were on television,
we were exposed, and that helped other people to come out the next
time."[12]

While the cultural reformers tried to devise demonstrations that
would stir homosexuals while alerting opinion leaders to the role
they played in oppressing them, Marty Robinson and Jim Owles
worked to generate publicity by confronting political candidates. In
their eyes, demonstrations directed at politicians were desirable because they would most effectively give homosexuals the political
awareness and the influence with public officials that would serve to
secure their rights. This ambition to make gays influential in the
political system was what aroused the revolutionary suspicion and
the radical antagonism that later in the fall led Robinson and Owles
to leave GLF and organize the Gay Activists Alliance (GAA).

Although GLF's Aquarians also wanted to influence established
institutions, they drew less wrath from radicals and revolutionaries
because they found few opportunities to pursue these ambitions.
Time's cover story was a clear instance of the type of portrayal of
homosexuals that concerned the cultural reformers, and it provided
a dramatic occasion to use militant tactics. But most opinion-shaping
activity was less institutionalized (thousands of clergymen and psychiatrists daily spread negative attitudes about homosexuality) and
more subtle (the media's reluctance to deal with homosexuality regularly was as much a problem as the dubious and sensationalistic
nature of its occasional coverage). As much as anything else, it was
their inability to figure out how to challenge culture-shaping institutions that pushed cultural reformers toward the radical view that
mores were transformed most effectively through seemingly nonpolitical consciousness-raising activities.

Circumstances impelled the first cultural reformers to devote most
of their time to self-help, social, and service activities and to be

content with using incidents of police harassment as occasions for demonstrations to convey messages about life style, community, and culture. Since demonstrations against the police suited the radical and revolutionary aim of undermining the system by challenging its authorities, most of the cultural reformers felt they could best pursue the consciousness-raising activities they thought important by working with the radicals. Few of them followed Robinson and Owles to GAA.

But as the radicals became ever more dogmatic, the cultural reformers were forced to spend more and more time defending their view that enjoying the gay male subculture was perfectly compatible with being liberated. What remained of their energy went into running dances. Few incidents other than police raids on gay bars provided opportunities for protest. Neither time nor opportunity permitted the design of demonstrations that highlighted cultural reformist concerns. By the summer of 1970, most cultural reformers had been driven from GLF; not until the next year, in GAA, was the cultural reformist approach to gay liberation institutionalized and elaborated.

.   .   .

Early in November 1969, at the urging of Columbia Student Homophile League stalwart Bob Martin, and under the sponsorship of Craig Rodwell, whose Homophile Youth Movement in Neighborhoods belonged to the Eastern Regional Coalition of Homophile Organizations, a delegation of radical GLFers traveled to Philadelphia to attend the sixth biannual ERCHO convention. Upon arrival, they asserted their presence by expressing outrage that Madolin Cervantes, the avowedly heterosexual treasurer of MSNY, was being permitted to participate in a conclave that was supposed to represent homosexuals.

Ironically, the homophile militants in attendance viewed Cervantes's presence as a cause for celebration. Those active in the national and regional homophile planning conferences had been trying to persuade MSNY to participate in Movement-strengthening coalitions since 1966. At the urging of MSNY lawyer Austin Wade, who had joined the North American Conference of Homophile Organizations as an individual and become chairman of its Legal Committee, the Mattachine board of directors had agreed to let Wade and

Cervantes represent MSNY at the fifth annual NACHO conference in the spring of 1969. Their presence at the ERCHO meeting signified a historic breakthrough in MSNY's longstanding reluctance to cooperate with its eastern homophile neighbors.

It was a measure of the difference in the political outlooks of the homophile militants and the gay liberationists that what Kameny and his associates viewed as a victory, the disgruntled GLFers dismissed as a vestige of obsolete liberalism. Among other things, this difference ensured that the first regional conference in years to draw representatives from all of the important gay groups in the east would also be the last, for the consciousness-raising efforts of the radicals exacerbated the divisions between moderate and militant homophile leaders and alienated both from the gay liberationists.

After their experiences at the conference, Wade and Cervantes prepared a ten-page letter reconfirming the distance between homophile moderates and homophile militants by arguing that the militants had more in common with the radicals:

> The ERCHO conference disclosed an amazing affinity between the Kamenyites and the revolutionists, led by the GLF, which tried to take over the meeting and very nearly succeeded. The Kamenyites, of course, are not radicals or revolutionaries. They are too old and set in their ways, and they lack the necessary youthful resiliency and volatility to make good radicals. But they do find themselves in agreement with the revolutionaries on a surprising number of issues. When the leader of the GLF contingent . . . menacingly strode up to Mrs. Madolin Cervantes, one of the MSNY delegates and a heterosexual, with fire in his eyes and threats in his voice and gestures, and told her to leave the meeting forthwith because she was a heterosexual—which information had been obligingly supplied to him by the proprietor of the Oscar Wilde Bookstore—the leader of the Kamenyites [Frank Kameny], who was the conference chairman, sat by in utter silence and never once exercised his prerogative as presiding officer to have the ruffian expelled, or to offer an apology to the lady for the outrage. On the contrary, at a private gathering at the conclusion of the conference, this same chairman had the unparalleled effrontery to add insult to injury by declaring, in Mrs. Cervantes's presence, that there may be heterosexuals who are authorities on homosexuality, but *he* had never heard of any.[13]

The moderates from MSNY may have been convinced that their militant associates had much in common with the GLFers, but the militants themselves saw little kinship. Foster Gunnison, who made his Hartford home an archive for homophile movement papers and who was close to Kameny, Gittings, and others, responded to the ERCHO affair with a scathing critique of the GLF contingent. When Bob Kohler saw the letter and complained that it generalized about all GLFers on the basis of a few radicals, Gunnison detailed his objectives in a second circular. The first point he raised was GLF's attack on Cervantes:

> What upset me most at the ERCHO conference were two episodes set off by the group from GLF who were down there who we assumed were representing GLF, and were things that I thought were extremely crude and unnecessary and, to me, indicative of what went on in the minds of these people. One was the shocking manner in which they attacked Madolin Cervantes of MSNY because she was a heterosexual voting on homosexual matters. Certainly one is entitled to have his views on such a matter, but to express them [in] as crude a way as was done down there and embarrass a good person like that right on the floor in front of everyone I thought—and will always feel—was crudeness to the point of soliciting violence.[14]

Gunnison's distress about the Cervantes incident was all the greater because he, Kameny, and Gittings received much the same treatment at a GLF meeting just a few weeks after the conference. There, too, Jim Fouratt took the lead in charging that the homophile leaders were "lackeys of the Establishment" whose very presence compromised GLF's commitment to a radical new consciousness. Although GLF's general assembly eventually voted to let the homophile delegation remain, they spent more than an hour and a half discussing whether "pigs" should be permitted to participate in a collectivity that was trying to embody a humane new society.

Though that experience was disconcerting, it helped the homophile militants to clarify how their political perspectives differed from those of the radical gay liberationists. In his letter to Kohler, Gunnison identified the major differences as the "concern with other minority group and political/social/economic issues" and the "resentment against authority and structure and systematic administration and procedure."

While Gunnison and his associates gauged that the differences between homophile and liberationist approaches were evidenced in GLF's penchant for social incivility, unstructured activity, and manifold political interests, the radicals concluded that the lack of appreciation for conciousness-raising expressiveness, innovative procedure, and systemwide concerns attested to an unbridgeable gulf between "uptight closet queens" and avant-garde liberationists. Lois Hart summed it up simply in a report for *Come Out!:* "The mentality was largely conservative, parliamentary, 'please oh please straight world accept me,' and generally out of touch with the morality and consciousness of the evolutionary changes that are so loudly demanding realization these days."[15]

Although they disavowed traditional ways, a number of the radicals, believing that they could further their aims by manipulating conventional institutions, had learned parliamentary procedure. At the ERCHO meeting, they used their parliamentary skills to pass resolutions that, first, established June 28 "as a national holiday for the celebration of the Liberation of Homosexuals"; second, censured *Gay Power* "for exploiting and pandering to oppressive homosexual stereotypes"; and third, asserted that "dominion over one's own body," "freedom from society's attempts to define and limit human sexuality," and "freedom from political and social persecution for all minority groups" were "inalienable rights . . . above and beyond legislation."[16] Some radicals thought that the enactment of these resolutions would help unite gay groups in the east around a liberationist consensus, but Hart, in *Come Out!,* was suspicious: " . . . Words are only words and do not constitute real change. It was questionable whether some who voted 'aye' understood the implications of the statements."[17]

As Hart anticipated, within six weeks, MSNY, DOB–New York, and most other homophile affiliates officially asked to be disassociated from the resolutions rushed through ERCHO by the radicals. And during the spring, to elude a second radical onslaught, the officers of ERCHO voted to suspend the coalition's administrative structure and to run only a loosely structured annual conference. In a letter to *Playboy* magazine published in May 1970, Bob Martin boasted that ERCHO had become "the first association of homophile organizations to take a stand as homosexuals on nonhomosexual issues, thus breaching a wall that homophile liberals had successfully maintained for years."[18] Eager to dispel any impression that the radicals had made converts of homophile militants, Gunnison wrote a rejoinder that appeared in the August *Playboy:*

> Lest the letter from my good friend Bob Martin . . . leave your readers with the impression that the homophile movement has been captured by the New Left, I should point out that some of us take a dim view of this noisy intrusion by long-haired, wild-eyed street urchins. It is common knowledge that the Commie-pinko-anarchist fringe tries to take over any minority cause it can latch onto; and for us, it had to come sooner or later. But Martin gives a false picture of the young radical contingent bulldozing its platform through the Eastern Regional Conference of Homophile Organizations, leaving the elderly liberals in total defeat. The fact is that, immediately afterward, E.R.C.H.O. voted to suspend itself for one year—a curious move, akin to shooting yourself in the head before the next guy does it for you. In this way, however, we prevented a takeover of our organization by the extremists.[19]

.   .   .

During the spring of 1970, the course of radical consciousness-raising changed dramatically because of ideas absorbed by lesbian GLFers from members of radical feminist groups such as Redstockings and The Feminists and from disenchanted lesbians from the National Organization for Women. Radical feminist ideas encouraged radical lesbians to believe that attitudes and values perpetuated by men were what oppressed lesbians and that lesbian liberation required an escape from conventional assumptions about sex roles and the sexes.*

But radical lesbian leaders were not content to argue that liberation beckoned them to ignore common notions about what women could and should do and to express themselves as they wished. Instead, they began to equate liberation with the rejection of behav-

---

*Hart had begun to think seriously about feminism in the spring of 1969 while attending the women's workshop that Susan Silverman ran at Alternate U. Martha Shelley's interest in feminism had been stimulated by her association with the leaders of DOB. But not until Rita Mae Brown left the New York chapter of the National Organization for Women and, in February 1970, invited lesbians from GLF to join lesbians from the women's movement in a consciousness-raising group did most of the lesbians in GLF begin to think about liberation in terms of feminism. The talk of stifling sex roles in some of the early statements issued in GLF's name was the result of Hart's precocious appreciation of radical feminist thinking.

ior assumed to be male and the embrace of behavior assumed to be female. Thus the traits that dogmatic radicals condemned and praised in the name of liberation came to be linked with gender. Fast, anonymous, promiscuous sex was characterized as intrinsically male or "male-identified," while sex in the context of sustained emotional and personal sharing was said to be female or "woman-identified." Aspirations for professional, social, and material status were called male-identified, while ambitions for intimacy, interpersonal skill, and communal sharing were declared woman-identified. Traits like rationality, calculation, control, aggressiveness, insensitivity, intolerance, and invidiousness were said to be generically male; those like intuition, guilelessness, expressiveness, gentleness, sensitivity, acceptance, and altruism were described as inherently female.

As radical lesbians withdrew into all-lesbian groups to develop liberated (now called "woman-identified") life styles, radical males scheduled their own consciousness-raising groups. Though billed as sessions to help male homosexuals learn how to escape inhibiting sex roles and how to express themselves and interact naturally, they were dominated by men persuaded by radical lesbians and feminists that liberation required the total abandonment of male-identified ways of thinking and acting. Indeed, male ways were said not only to lead heterosexual men to oppress women, but also to lead male homosexuals to contribute to the oppression both of women and of themselves.

GLFer Steve Dansky was one of the first to think about how radical lesbian and radical feminist ideas applied to the behavior of male homosexuals. He shared some of his conclusions in an article titled "Hey Man" in the fourth issue of *Come Out!:*

> Every man growing up in this culture is programmed to systematically oppress, dehumanize, objectify and rape women . . . Every expression of manhood is a reassertion of this cock privilege. All men are male supremacists. Gay men are no exception . . .
>
> Homosexuality is a manifestation of the breaking down of male roles. This "unacceptable" affront to conventional manhood forces male straight society up against the wall; so much so that they must suppress, repress and oppress all signs of a life-giving homosexuality and force it into their warped death-dealing definitions. Their task, then, becomes a bludgeoning of homosexuality into parodistic expressions within this culture. Gay men are violently driven toward a false goal: the mutation

of homosexuality into a male heterosexual persona. This results in the constant struggle of gay men to fit themselves into a heterosexual idealization of manhood . . . We have begun in our struggle for liberation to reject the internalization of this male heterosexual identity. Gay men must examine all forms of their homosexuality and be suspicious of all of them because the ways we express homosexuality have been molded by male supremacy . . .

G.L.F. must demand the complete negation of the use of gay bars, tea rooms, trucks, baths, streets, and other traditional cruising institutions. These are exploitative institutions designed to keep gay men in the roles given to them by a male heterosexual system . . .

In order that we fight our oppressor we must band together in living collectives . . . Within the . . . collective we will reject our parody of male heterosexual society's pairing off. We will instead begin to remold our homosexuality by developing a communistic sexuality of sharing, cooperation, selflessness and total community.[20]

The radical lesbian feminist perspective was powerful because it suggested that lesbians, heterosexual women, and male homosexuals were all kept from self-realization by the same phenomenon: conventional ideas about the nature of and the behavior appropriate for each sex. Some attempted to develop this insight into the arguments, first, that women are oppressed because they are forced into limited and devalued roles, particularly those of sex object and child-rearer; second, that male homosexuals are denigrated and persecuted because they fail to conform to conventional male roles when expressing their sexual feelings and affections; and third, that lesbians suffer both because they are women and because as homosexuals they are denied even the meager rewards accorded females who succeed in roles deemed appropriate for women.

Instead of perceiving that sexism stemmed from culturally based sex and sex-role stereotyping and value judgments and criticizing the ascription of characteristics on the basis of gender and the perpetuation of conventional assumptions about the roles appropriate for men and for women, Dansky adopted the simplistic radical feminist line that American society was dominated by men bent on oppressing women and that sexism was "male" thinking perpetuated by *all* men to enslave *all* women. Thus he concluded that liberation called for all to express themselves in ways that were female rather than male.

During the summer of 1970, several groups of radical GLFers attracted to Dansky's arguments formed living collectives in order to develop nonsexist life styles. In a report prepared for *Come Out!*, a member of the household known as the 95th Street Collective attested to the prominence of the view that nonsexist meant nonmale. He wrote that his male homosexual group had a natural advantage in developing liberated life styles because they were all effeminate:

> In my nine months in GLF I always noticed that the women were more together than the men. By "together" I mean there was less fighting with one another, and the women did not have the need to compete as the men did, therefore feeling more solidarity with their sisters.
>
> The men who make up the 95th Street Collective are mostly femme males. I feel that by virtue of being femme males we have the ability to love one another and have stronger emotional bonds than the "straight" homosexuals. When ideas are in conflict in the collective we do not compete to see whose idea is best, but we collectively search for a solution that meets all of our needs. When a member of the collective is hurt, we are sensitive to the other's personal pain. There is no need to hide our pain as so many men do in order to uphold the masculine image which our society forces on males. We express pain as well as the love and anger which run rampant in us.
>
> As long as we let the femme in us come through, our collective will continue functioning as a whole, not as one "man" competing against another. I feel our collective has much to offer as an example to men who are still handicapped by a masculine image that is slowly dying, and which women and femme men feel is oppressive to us.[21]

In the 95th Street Collective, the radical quest to discover how people with homosexual feelings could express themselves freely and fully produced a group of male homosexuals who condemned all modes of personal expression they did not consider female and who argued that male homosexuals who were in any way "male" were unliberated.* It was a sign of how divisive radical consciousness-raising activity had become that the particular "straight" or mascu-

---

*Eventually, Steve Dansky, John Knoebel of the 95th Street Collective, and Kenneth Pitchford identified themselves as "faggot effeminists" and issued broadsides and journals in the name of a group called The Flaming Faggots. They contended that the aims of the gay liberation movement were antithetical to those of the women's liberation movement and that male homosexuality was by definition counterrevolutionary because male bonding of every type perpetuated the oppression of women. Pitchford was married to radical feminist Robin Morgan, whose arguments shaped Dansky's thinking as well as her husband's.

line homosexuals criticized by members of the 95th Street Collective were working to develop nonsexist life styles in another GLF collective—a commune assembled by Jim Fouratt, the man who had helped initiate the radical quest for liberation in the first place.

.   .   .

Fouratt was particularly rankled by the charges of the 95th Street Collective because he considered his communal enterprise the climax of a long Movement career devoted to ascertaining and making known the meaning of oppression and liberation. Like his political comrades, he believed that radical homosexuals could play a special role in the quest for liberation by discovering how and why the system prevented the expression of homosexual feelings and by helping New Left associates as well as homosexuals to understand this. "Ellen Bedoz" and Allan Warshawsky defended these ambitions in an article on "GLF and the Movement" in the second issue of *Come Out!:* "Some homosexuals denounce the Movement because they feel that it has not sufficiently embraced the homosexual cause. However, in order for our goals to become part of the Movement, we must define our cause and ourselves, thereby creating a radical homosexual consciousness. Then we can begin to educate our radical sisters and brothers to our oppression and our needs."[22]

When revolutionary GLFers talked about extending radical homosexual consciousness, they meant something very different. The revolutionaries, seeing capitalism as the root of all evil, believed that Marxist analysis had to be applied to the case of homosexuals, that fellow Marxists had to be apprised of ideological extensions, and that homosexuals had to be made aware of economic class dynamics. This is what they envisioned doing when they spoke of extending radical homosexual consciousness.

Though the radicals often turned to Marxist arguments to explain why the system stifled individual expressiveness and sustaining community, they mainly wanted to understand how particular standards and attitudes discouraged individuals from expressing homosexual feelings and to challenge these intangible but powerful constraints by being natural and open and by encouraging others to do likewise. Inevitably, the radicals' search for understanding led them to focus on social conventions. Their effort to behave in ways that would undermine existing mores made them preoccupied with feelings, interpersonal relations, and day-to-day living. And they stressed personal experimentation and interpersonal proselytizing over Marxist exegesis and political propagandizing.

Conflict was soon to come, for as the radicals grew ever more convinced that the essence of gay political activity was living in liberated ways, they began to insist that personal behavior said more about political commitment than ideology. As they came to identify "being liberated" with behaving in certain ways, they began to admonish their associates to live "correctly."

After restive reformist GLFers had been driven to coalesce in the Aquarius Cell and to set up the Gay Activists Alliance, the radicals turned their attention to revolutionaries like John O'Brien and John Lauritsen, who refused to believe that developing liberated life styles was the key to political change. By this time O'Brien and Lauritsen had withdrawn into a Marxist study group, the Red Butterfly Cell; they and other Red Butterfly members were criticized for failing to be open about their homosexuality at activities sponsored by socialist groups and for focusing on class and race issues more than sex and sexual orientation when they discussed the homosexual's problems at GLF meetings.

Partly to answer radical critics, the Red Butterfly Cell produced a series of pamphlets elaborating Marxist perspectives on the oppression of homosexuals. The first was a reprint of the "Gay Manifesto" written in San Francisco by Carl Wittman, an SDS activist in the mid-1960s, with a commentary explaining that Wittman's radical outlook raised two matters of concern to gay liberationists with Marxist convictions.

The first matter, called the question of "coming out," was described as "the polarity between personal head-freeing and the need for collective, social action to change institutions . . . two distinct and in some ways opposed actions . . ." Under this rubric, members of the Red Butterfly Cell expressed their reservations about the radical preoccupation with personal behavior: "Emphasis on personal liberation, the experience of feeling free, which is the meaning often given to 'coming out,' can and often does lead to a kind of escapism or . . . detachment from the actual conditions confronting us."

The second matter was "the kind of social and economic viewpoint most conducive to our liberation as gays." At the heart of this

discussion lay a profession of commitment to the pursuit of socialism: "We believe that economic and social democracy are the necessary conditions for liberation. In Marxist language, we assert that a
democratic socialism is the necessary basis for building a classless
society, i.e., communism." The question of social and economic
viewpoint was said to be "basic to our movement, since the answers
we give it will determine the concrete political alignments we make
and, ultimately, the success or failure of our struggle for liberation
—which in the long run is a political struggle."[23]

Although the remarks about social and economic viewpoint called
for discussion, they revealed differences of assumption that would
further divide GLFers. The revolutionaries characterized their concern with transforming institutions as "political" and the radicals'
interest in changing life styles as "personal." Yet the very essence of
the radical argument was that the personal *was* political.

The Red Butterfly's reluctance to grant even that much added
bitterness to disagreement. The radicals charged that the revolutionaries' primary loyalties lay with socialist groups conspiring to
use the gay movement for their own purposes. The revolutionaries
countered that their opponents were self-indulgent "red-baiters."
An editorial written by John O'Brien for the second issue of the
Red Butterfly's newsletter showed that even as they moved to establish an independent gay socialist group in the spring of 1970,
revolutionary leaders refused to countenance the personal-is-politi-
cal argument central to radical thinking: "If people are not interested in politics, then they should leave GLFs, because they were
formed around a political purpose. In fact they should leave this
world because it is made up of economic politics, which everything
is based on."

Although they found it impossible to work with their revolutionary associates, radical GLFers professed continued loyalty to the
Movement. Yet their differences with revolutionary peers prefigured
those that would arise with nongay members of the New Left, especially when the radicals tried to raise consciousness at Movement
conferences and demonstrations.

•   •   •

The Gay Liberation Front was formed by homosexuals with a radical
vision, to serve as a vehicle for social change. We began with a conscious-

ness of ourselves as an oppressed minority within an oppressive society. Through direct action (such as the *Village Voice* protest) we will also try to reach our gay sisters and brothers who have accepted the values of a society in whose embrace they can never rest with both dignity and honesty; in reaching them our numbers and power will grow . . .

Gay Liberation Front's contribution to the Movement must now be dealt with. Our participation in Movement actions (e.g. the Moratorium, Panther rallies) is a beginning. Each time we appear at a Movement function identified as GLF we reinforce the bonds between us.[24]

As suggested by these remarks about "direct action" in Bedoz and Warshawsky's article, "GLF and the Movement," radical GLFers believed that protest activity spread liberated consciousness both by enabling individuals to display their rejection of the system and to revel in the sense of self that came from resistance and assertion in concert with peers, and by inspiring others to do likewise.

As usual, Lois Hart articulated the radical perspective most eloquently, this time in her account of GLF's picket line at the *Village Voice:*

That festival of life, our Zap of the *Village Voice,* was more Nay saying. A beautiful day when we said "NO" to the oppressor. But the capitulation of the *Voice* was not our greatest victory that day. It was that we were there together joyfully, earnestly standing up for ourselves, reaching out to other responding Gays, seeing the respect and affirmation of the Village community, Gay and straight.

So a "yes" has come into it. YES, here I am, goddamit! And as I stand up and take that breath I can feel that being here is no static thing. We are not just existing at a time when an old, unworkable world is dying, but we are living as a new one struggles for birth. I feel my oneness with the struggles and groanings of the entire planet.[25]

Hart made it clear that she and other radicals were saying no not only to society's view of homosexual feelings, but to what society prescribed for life in general. This is why they participated in antiwar and pro-Panther as well as gay liberationist demonstrations. But as those in the New Left revealed their uneasiness with GLF's participation and their reluctance to acknowledge that homosexuality raised important issues,* the radicals began to think less about them-

---

*Even New Left leaders responsible for promoting the cultural radical strain in Movement thinking, those expected to be most sensitive to the issue of sexual self-expression, struck

selves and more about their so-called comrades. Those who traveled to Washington, D.C., for the second antiwar moratorium in November 1969 reported, "The 28th of June Cell went to affirm our solidarity but also to confront the Movement: 'You announce your opposition to oppression but still have not addressed yourself to your own oppressive attitudes, your male, heterosexual chauvinism.' "[28] Hart expressed her concern in a response to Bedoz and Warshawsky's article:

I agree with most of the positions presented but nonetheless it is all pretty abstract. When you break it down into people—the ones walking around in February, 1970, New York USA—what have we got? How do Movement people really feel about all us dykes and faggots popping out of our straight drag and insisting this world belongs to us, too? Gotta know the facts, ma'am. Gotta know just how to relate to all these folks.[29]

Hart was skeptical about how "Movement people" really felt, but this did not keep her from trying to put the concerns of homosexuals onto the New Left's agenda. In fact, like Bedoz, she continued to attend Movement demonstrations and conferences even after the spring of 1970, when she abandoned GLF for Radicalesbians in order to concentrate on lesbian liberation. Yet the more New Left leaders revealed their reluctance to consider sexism as serious a problem as racism and economic exploitation, and something worth working to eliminate from their personal lives, the more aloof from Movement activities the radical lesbians became.

Like the lesbians, radical male GLFers grew dissatisfied with the New Left as they perceived that those in the Movement cared little about the problem of sexism and about working to develop nonsexist life styles. In the fall of 1969, Jim Fouratt had defended Yippies, Panthers, and other leftists by explaining that they used the term

GLFers as prejudiced and hostile. Jerry Rubin revealed his bigotry in *Do It!*, the radical manifesto he published in the spring of 1970: "Look at the criminal record of a political activist. It reads like the record of a sex deviant—public nuisance, loitering, disorderly conduct, trespassing, disturbing the peace."[26] Torn because *Do It!* reeked of the sexism she thought it essential to eliminate, Hart wrote an equivocal review for *Come Out!:* "Ya gotta DO IT—read Jerry Rubin's handbook of social revolution and world change. He is a shitty, fuckhead heterosexual-chauvinist pig supremacist and he hasn't looked around to see the revolution that's nipping at his tail—but it's O.K. cuz it's a dynamite book that delivers the viewpoint and attitude that is going to do all the things we have been talking about doing."[27]

faggot "to describe any castrated male made impotent by society," but he expressed growing impatience in his remarks at a New Haven rally in support of the "Panther 21" on May 1, 1970:

> The homosexual sisters and brothers who are in this crowd have a complaint to make. The very oppression that makes us identify with the Black Panther Party and all oppressed people, which makes us revolutionaries, which makes us work for a society and a vision which is far beyond what we live in today, we find that oppressiveness pervading this so-called liberated zone. It is that very oppressiveness that is stopping us from making a revolution, and we call upon every radical here today to Off the word faggot, to Off the sexism which pervades this place and to begin to deal with his own feelings about the homosexual brothers and sisters.[30]

As Fouratt suggested, for those convinced that learning to be liberated was the essence of radical activity, personal behavior became the index of political conviction. To demonstrate their personal commitment to ending "classism" and racism, radical GLFers worked to eliminate their elitist and racist attitudes in consciousness-raising groups. Expecting similar commitment from nongay radicals, they asked Movement members not just to acknowledge that sexism was a problem but to wrestle with their "own feelings about the homosexual brothers and sisters." One must appreciate the extent of radical expectations to understand why GLFers with strong New Left loyalties grew disillusioned with the Movement even as some of its important leaders welcomed them into it.

Perhaps the most dramatic welcome came in a letter about gay and women's liberation that Huey Newton wrote for the August 1970 issue of the *Black Panther.* Among other things, Newton said that "whatever your personal opinions and your insecurities about homosexuality and the various liberation movements among homosexuals and women . . . we should try to unite with them in revolutionary fashion," and that "when we have revolutionary conferences, rallies, and demonstrations there should be full participation . . ."[31]

Shortly after Newton's letter appeared, GLFers were invited to the Panther-sponsored Revolutionary People's Constitutional Convention. Seeing an unprecedented opportunity to bring radical homosexual consciousness to members of the Movement, in early September 1970 about thirty male GLFers traveled to Philadelphia for the convention's first session. There, with radical homosexuals from other cities, they prepared a list of demands for inclusion in the revolutionary constitution under preparation and staged in-house demonstrations to raise consciousness. An account circulated by members of Fouratt's collective elaborated:

> At the convention floor, we really made people feel the significance of our presence . . . We chanted Gay Powerful chants. We screamed, shouted, stomped, and clapped. About 60 gay male delegates together with others scattered over the audience screamed together louder than anyone there. "Right ons" for everything anti-sexist. We just generally turned on everyone to our pride and defiance for our way of life and solidarity with everyone's own goals. It was beautiful, we were beautiful, and we knew it.[32]

Although the consciousness-raising activities exhilarated those who undertook them, the convention itself produced mixed feelings. The snickers that greeted official mention of a report from the male homosexual workshop were wounding; the applause that erupted at the end of the report was elating. But the elation disappeared when the GLF men learned that their radical lesbian sisters, feeling slighted and antagonized, had walked out. An account written for *Come Out!* described one of the incidents that had alienated the lesbians: "I recognized some of the Gay sisters from New York and went to sit with them. As we were waiting for the speaker, a man sitting a few rows behind us suddenly jumped up and started screaming at the women. Get out of here, you freaks! . . . Get away from here you sex freaks!"[33]

Incidents like this provoked several male GLFers to complain about the sexism they were witnessing. Almost as soon as they expressed their feelings, they were challenged by black members of their own ranks, particularly GLFers who, back in New York, had formed a Third World Caucus to deal with the combination of racism and sexism they felt oppressed them. The blacks said that while they were loyal to the male homosexual workshop, their Third World loyalties had been aroused by the objections to Panther sexism the whites had expressed. They prepared a statement condemning not only sexism on the part of nonhomosexual white and Third World revolutionaries but racism and elitism in white homosexuals, and they insisted that the male homosexual workshop issue a statement acknowledging the Panthers as "the vanguard of the people's revolution in Amerikkka."[34]

Although the white male GLFers agreed to issue such a statement, they felt torn about their commitments. In the wake of the convention, they tried to pursue each of the tasks they thought important: liberating themselves from their own classism, racism, and sexism; persuading other male homosexuals to do likewise; urging lesbian and nonlesbian feminists not to forsake the struggle against classism and racism; and convincing nongay New Left associates that eliminating sexism was as worthwhile a personal and political challenge as the fight against classism and racism. Yet the radical males found living up to their ideals and working with lesbians and feminists progressively more demanding, while their experiences with nonhomosexual New Left associates continued to be disillusioning. Although few white male radical GLFers immediately followed the lead of the radical lesbians, most of them also ended up walking out of the Movement.

A poignant personal account of the evolution that led so many Movement veterans in GLF to become alienated from the New Left appears in the autobiographical sketches that Allen Young wrote for the anthology of gay liberationist writings that he and Karla Jay edited in 1971. Young joined GLF after a career in the New Left that included service at the Liberation News Service, membership in SDS, a stay in Cuba, and a hand in setting up the Venceremos Brigades, which brought shiploads of young Americans to work in the Cuban sugar fields during 1969 and 1970. During all of this Movement work, he felt compelled to hide his homosexuality:

I grew up in a Communist Party household, and I learned at an early age about socialism, about how the workers are unjustly exploited by the bosses, about the beautiful system known as socialism. I also quickly learned that socialism wasn't for fairies, because my parents and their friends would occasionally make jokes about fairies . . .

I joined the staff of Liberation News Service in Washington, D.C., shortly after it was founded in the autumn of 1967. By then I was actively homosexual. I used to sneak away from the LNS office, and from my "comrades" in SDS, to meet other homosexuals . . . Now I know more of what was really happening: at one time, there were no fewer than six male homosexuals associated with LNS in Washington.[35]

Partly because his firsthand experience had been painful, Young had mixed feelings about the eagerness of GLFers to impress their peers with visions of Marxist utopia. He was particularly torn when the subject was Cuba, the focus of his own New Left involvement. In the spring of 1970, Young was jolted into a reexamination of his Marxist convictions by the antagonism many of his radical associates showed toward a group of GLFers who had been part of a Venceremos Brigade:

The returned brigadistas wanted to tell GLF about how wonderful Cuba was, about the accomplishments of the revolution . . . I felt the security blanket of the New Left right-on revolution slipping away from me; I could see that my involvement with gay liberation was going to challenge many of my previous political notions. I got my first chance to react to this new contradiction when I read an article by Martha Shelley about the GLF–Cuba forum, published in the *Liberated Guardian*. I found myself strongly motivated by years of conditioning to defend Cuba above all. One sentence in that article particularly angered me: "Marxist, schmarxist, get off our backs!" Martha had exclaimed to the world. The label "Marxist" was sacred to me, and I blanched. Of course, Marxism provides a valid framework for all of us to fight against economic exploitation. But that is simply not enough. Before long I came to embrace Martha's sentiments. Why should a label be sacred if it is used—as in Cuba—to justify oppression?[36]

After several months, like most who went from Movement groups to GLF, Young was convinced that the elimination of sexism was as essential as the elimination of classism and racism, and that the hope for social transformation lay in having small groups of peers work to eliminate these evils from their own lives. He stopped working for the Liberation News Service, began living in Fouratt's collective, and devoted his journalistic talents to the series of Gay Flames pamphlets published under its auspices. By the fall of 1971, working on his anthology, Young was convinced that few of his former political associates were willing to take the steps he had come to believe necessary for the elimination of sexism:

> Some people seem to think that things have gotten better. In very small ways, maybe they have. Homosexuals do not have to be invisible any more in many movement groups. There has been formalistic recognition of gay liberation by such diverse groups as the Black Panther Party, International Socialists, Peace & Freedom Party, the Young Socialist Alliance, The Yippies and various local collectives and underground papers. This has not, in my opinion, altered the basic pattern of anti-gay oppression within the straight movement . . .
>
> The "pro-gay" segment of the straight movement is telling us, "Now you don't have to hide any more, so everything is OK." We are saying in return, "Everything is not OK. Not hiding is only the beginning. You have to stop holding on to your straight identity. By denying our form of love, by saying it is essentially a private matter, you wish to perpetuate male supremacy and patterns of dominance which are basically sexist and which are in the end anti-homosexual."

Young's observations demonstrated the degree to which he had absorbed the radical conviction that the personal was political. They showed also how he, like other male homosexual veterans of the Movement, had come to define liberation for heterosexual males. Young argued that members of the New Left had to demonstrate their commitment to radical ends by developing nonsexist life styles and that for male heterosexuals, this meant not only changing how they felt and acted towards women, lesbians, and male homosexuals, but also dealing with their own sexual self-expression. Young was not content to ask merely that male heterosexuals examine how conventional assumptions about sex roles shaped their behavior and then work to express themselves sexually and emotionally in fulfilling ways. Rather, he suggested that to be a heterosexual male was to be sexist and that to be a liberated male was to be homosexual, or at least bisexual:

> Straights who are threatened by us like to accuse us of separatism—but our understanding of sexism is premised on the idea that in a free society everyone will be gay. It may be utopian to think that all people who now

define themselves as "straight" will become gay, but it is not utopian to ask people who call themselves revolutionaries to struggle against sexism by working toward establishing a gay identity.[37]

With the demand that male heterosexual members of the Movement demonstrate their commitment to eliminating sexism by becoming homosexual—an analogue to the radical lesbian demand that radical feminists show their commitment to the struggle against sexism by becoming lesbian—Young brought to their logical end the ideas about personal behavior and political commitment that induced most radical male GLFers to part company with the Movement. Where revolutionary gay liberationists sensitive to the problem of sexism asked only that New Left allies list this struggle as a revolutionary concern, radical gay liberationists, believing that the development of nonsexist life styles was the essence of radical activity, demanded that radical brethren *live* in the ways they claimed would eliminate the problems of women and of homosexuals. Radicals reluctant to be dogmatic about the meaning of liberation asked only that male heterosexuals explore departures from conventional male roles in their own lives and recognize and respect others who did not abide by traditional dictates. Their more self-righteous peers equated heterosexual male liberation with male homosexuality, a definition that few men in the Movement were willing to accept— and a condition for coalition that few agreed to meet.

6

The Gay Activists Alliance

OF THE TWELVE FOUNDERS who approved the constitution of
the Gay Activists Alliance in December 1969, two went on to write
books about the gay liberation movement. Arthur Bell was director
of publicity for children's books at Random House when he and his
lover, Arthur Evans, attended meetings of GLF and then turned to
GAA. To early planning sessions Bell invited Donn Teal, who had
written an article on homosexual themes in drama that appeared in
the spring of 1969 under the pseudonym Ronald Forsythe on the
front page of the *New York Times* Sunday arts section. Two years
later, when GAA was the best-known gay political group in the
country, Bell and Teal each wrote books that chronicled its beginnings. What most people understand about the origins of GAA is
based largely on Bell's *Dancing the Gay Lib Blues* and on Teal's *The
Gay Militants.*

Both Bell and Teal portray GAA as the work of gifted individuals
spurred to act by displeasing conditions in GLF. Bell tells that
"weekly character assassinations and havoc" and "differences in
issues" prompted Marty Robinson, Jim Owles, and Arthur Evans to
create an alternative to GLF.[1] (The example he cites is Owles's view
that GLF "sluffed over" the needs of homosexuals because it
"aligned itself with all minority groups.") Teal quotes Jerry Hoose
and Bob Kohler as saying that a GLF vote to support the Black
Panther Party provoked Robinson and Owles to set out on their own.
To corroborate this interpretation, Teal takes the explanation Owles
offered an interviewer from the *New York Times Magazine* in June
1970: "I personally left the group because I felt that many of these

other organizations were viciously anti-homosexual, that many of the leaders they followed had certainly shown no mercy to homosexuals they had taken in."[2]

There is truth in the view that Robinson, Owles, and Evans were induced to form a single-issue gay liberation group because they objected to the breadth of GLF's concerns, but this is only part of the story. For the reservations that Robinson and Owles had about supporting groups like the Panthers only hinted at the gaps between reformist and radical and revolutionary outlooks that became apparent to the two during their days in GLF. And such ideological differences were in many ways less pressing than their misgivings about GLF's viability as an organization. For the full story of GAA's creation, one must look beyond disagreements over particular issues to what they reflected: basic differences in gay political outlook and in ideas about organization.

.   .   .

Bell's and Teal's accounts of GAA's origins are simplistic because they fail to explain the reformist political and organizational views that Robinson and Owles had worked out as they listened to the arguments advanced by homophile leaders, radicals, and revolutionaries and as they thought about the situation of homosexuals in the light of early New Left ideas. Early in July 1969, when Michael Brown proposed to inaugurate gay liberationist activity by demonstrating in support of Black Panthers at the Women's House of Detention, Marty Robinson, believing that the Panthers were against homosexuals* and for violence and that working with controversial extremist groups would alienate many homosexuals, decided not to join those who acted in the name of "the newly formed Gay Liberation Front." Soon afterward, when Brown and others who had demonstrated in support of the Panthers exhorted marchers from MSNY's Washington Square vigil to proceed to the sixth precinct police station, Robinson and Owles began to fear that the founders of GLF were radicals bent on provoking violent confrontations for the sake of general revolution rather than activists concerned primar-

---

*Eldridge Cleaver had publicized his prejudices in *Soul on Ice* with the memorable lines, "I, for one, do not think homosexuality is the latest advance over heterosexuality on the scale of human evolution. Homosexuality is a sickness, just as are baby-rape or wanting to be head of General Motors."[3]

ily with homosexuals. Bell and Teal suggest that GLF's November 1969 decision to support the Panthers solidified Robinson and Owles's feelings about the need to avoid alliances with nonhomosexual groups. In fact, from the time they had opted to lead MSNY's Action Committee instead of enlisting in GLF, the two had believed that groups associated with extraneous issues and violent tactics would be unable to organize the gay community.

In each initiative they undertook under the auspices of the Action Committee, Robinson and Owles experimented with tactics for unifying homosexuals. They intended the demonstrations in Washington Square, Kew Gardens, and Christopher Street to dramatize issues and to produce publicity showing homosexuals that their lives were being intruded upon enough to warrant political mobilization. The third "community meeting" was an attempt to consolidate community power by building bridges between newly politicized gays and the closeted homosexuals who lived and worked in Greenwich Village.

Although none of these initial bloc-building efforts succeeded, the undertakings helped Robinson and Owles recognize that their approach to gay political activity was very different from that of the MSNY leadership. The two liberationists emphasized the need for demonstrations that would stir homosexuals to band together; Mattachine officials stressed the importance of public relations that would help eliminate prejudice, and negotiation and litigation that would bring tangible improvements. Robinson and Owles worked to rally homosexuals by defending subcultural practices like cruising; Mattachine officers warned against attracting attention to habits that might appear less than respectable to heterosexuals. The aspiring political reformers believed that homosexuals needed to participate in organizational decisions in order to gain the awareness and commitment that would motivate them to participate in bold public enterprises; Dick Leitsch chafed at the disorganization produced by overzealous volunteers and mistrusted activities that might alienate professionals, heterosexuals, and "respectable" homosexuals. Slowly but surely, Robinson and Owles saw more potential in GLF, which encouraged independent enterprises, countenanced militancy to build and defend gay community, and had its base in Greenwich Village. (The Mattachine's office was on the Upper West Side and, because Leitsch and his lover lived with Madolin Cervantes, its informal headquarters was Cervantes's nearby apartment.) Early in September 1969, therefore, Robinson and Owles decided to shift their allegiance to GLF.

Just as the quest for issues and publicity that would edify and elicit support from heterosexuals had led homophile militants to play up discriminatory policies, so the search for ways to mobilize homosexuals turned the attention of pioneering political reformers to local politics. The mayoral campaigns of John Lindsay, Mario Procaccino, and John Marchi provided immediate opportunities. In mid-September, Robinson and Owles approached Procaccino in the streets of Queens, inaugurating the strategy of "zapping" politicians that would later become GAA's trademark. The event was immortalized in the first issue of *Come Out!:*

> Mario has taken Jim's hand and is smiling. Jim asks: "Mr. Procaccino, what are you going to do about the oppression of the homosexual?" Mario is no longer smiling, his look is Christian as he says, "Young man, I can see that you're very interested in this problem . . . That is one of the many problems that we face in New York. It is sick rather than criminal, and we must show understanding and compassion for them."[4]

While questioning Procaccino resulted in no useful responses and in little provocative publicity, the "zap" helped Robinson and Owles see the potential of more carefully staged confrontations. Not two weeks later, having gauged that candidates would be particularly vulnerable in closed but public forums, they disarmed John Marchi at a meeting of the Gotham Young Republican Club by asking the same question put to Procaccino. Subsequently, at a candidates' night sponsored by the League of Women Voters at Temple Torah in Queens, GLFers scattered in the audience periodically rose to ask if Procaccino and Marchi favored rights for "the gay community." Robinson and Owles had learned that homosexuals could infiltrate political gatherings and make themselves heard through sheer brashness.

The Temple Torah affair resulted in an item on NBC's televised local news and a story in the *New York Post*. Encouraged, the self-styled "gay commandos" informed members of the press as well as candidates that they expected potential leaders of the city to address the concerns of their "gay constituents" at the Greenwich Village

Association's candidates' night on October 7. Although the candidates each sent a representative instead of appearing in person, all of the representatives responded more or less favorably to questions posed by the "commandos." Robinson and Owles's sense that their new tactics were destined for success was enhanced when they learned that the reporters present included a journalist from *Time* working on a cover story on homosexuality (the story their cultural reformist colleagues later used to develop their own distinctive genre of "zapping").

Not surprisingly, perfection of the technique of zapping politicians served not only to confirm the political reformers' ideas about strategy but also to highlight the differences in political outlook that distinguished reformers from radicals and revolutionaries. Cultural reformers like Jerry Hoose applauded the candidate zaps for producing publicity that inspired homosexuals to be open about their sexuality. But both revolutionary and radical GLFers expressed reservations about the involvement in the system represented by dealings with politicians.

The revolutionaries complained that Robinson and Owles viewed their questioning of candidates not as a tool to politicize homosexuals but as a step toward securing reforms that would only make homosexuals complacent about the system. Indeed, the revolutionaries charged that it was this interest in reform that kept the commandos from challenging Lindsay with the questions they had put to Marchi and Procaccino.

Robinson and Owles responded to revolutionary criticism by admitting that they *were* interested in protecting Lindsay. At MSNY they had learned that the mayor was responsible for eliminating the harassment, entrapment, and discrimination that had been rampant during the previous regime of Robert Wagner. Additional reforms, they argued, would provide protections and produce publicity that would encourage homosexuals to participate in gay political activity. As Owles explained several months later in his interview with the editor of the Sunday *Times Magazine:*

I felt that, in terms of organizing the homosexual community, I was interested in reaching *them* by working to bring about changes, such as the fair employment law; whereas the revolutionaries at GLF said, "I hope Procaccino gets in, I hope things become so conscious to the gays

that they see no alternative but to join up with us and pick up a gun."
They *wanted* the police to shut down the bars so it would completely
antagonize and alienate the homosexuals and drive them into the radicals' hands.[5]

In contrast to the revolutionaries, the radicals complained that
conventional political involvement would inhibit the spread of liberated consciousness. They feared that the pursuit of traditional political recognition and reward would undermine commitment to countercultural values. They contended that jockeying for the attention
of the established news media bred ambition, "ego-tripping," and
invidiousness at the expense of modesty, selflessness, and community. Few radicals maintained that the way to mobilize homosexuals
was to make their lives worse so that they would grow disillusioned
with the system. But most maintained that the only feasible way to
raise consciousness was to communicate through leaflets, person-to-
person contact, and untainted alternate newspapers, if only because
relying on the established news media belied the message that new
ways of proceeding were both possible and desirable.

Of course Robinson and Owles were eager to engender political
awareness in homosexuals with countercultural as well as traditional
values, and they wanted the news of their zaps to travel in the
avant-garde as well as the established media. With this in mind, they
encouraged Ralph Hall, who had followed them to GLF from the
Action Committee, to take a job reporting on GLF's activities for
Gay Power (the journal started by Joel Fabricant, publisher of the
East Village Other, in the fall of 1969). They also wrote lengthy
accounts of their first forays into conventional politics for the inaugu-
ral issue of *Come Out!* Ironically, given radical objections that they
were too ambitious for the spotlight of the established news media,
it was the reformers' interest in *Come Out!* that led to the problems
that provoked Robinson and Owles to think about creating an alternative to GLF.

Robinson and Owles had their first shock when they discovered
that the radicals who produced *Come Out!* had juxtaposed their
accounts of the zapping of Marchi and Procaccino with a letter
from Ron Ballard and Bob Fontanella expressing reservations
about gays participating in the electoral process: "In posing ourselves the question, 'Does Mayor Lindsay deserve the homosexual

vote?,' we misplace our priorities. The real question should be, 'Do any of the candidates deserve support of the people?' More explicitly, does the power structure, which capitalist politicians maintain, deserve even to exist?"[6] Just as upsetting was a lead article dismissing *Gay Power* as "an enterprise designed to make money" and castigating Joel Fabricant for trying "to cash in on the new interest in homosexuality" by producing a publication that "endorsed Mafia-run bars, included borderline pornography, and started a personal column in which people advertised for sex à la 'Kiss' and 'EVO.' "[7]

Robinson and Owles objected not only to the publication of views they considered personally biased and strategically detrimental, but to the fact that the *Come Out!* collective had printed the critique of *Gay Power* despite the consensus that it should not, reached at an open meeting held to review material slated for the paper. This reversal they saw as evidence that GLF had no means of controlling the various subgroups that acted in its name. And their distress increased when, after members at another general meeting resolved to postpone financing a second issue of *Come Out!* in order to save money for a gay community center, Lois Hart announced that the publishing collective intended to leave GLF, raise money by selling copies of its first issue, and thereafter publish on its own.

Although Robinson and Owles objected to MSNY's centralized authority and hierarchical structure because they felt it stifled individual initiative and discouraged membership participation, they had feared from the beginning that GLF went too far in the other direction. Various incidents had confirmed these fears. At the end of July, a few radical and revolutionary firebrands had disrupted GLF's initial assembly when it appeared that the majority wanted the group to spend its first few months concentrating on gay issues. In August, GLF's near-complete absence of operating procedures brought Robinson and Owles to loggerheads with Hart over the virtues of structurelessness. In September, when members of the *Come Out!* collective announced that they intended to call themselves a cell, the two reformers argued that the proliferation of autonomous units would splinter the organization. By the time Robinson and Owles saw that successful zaps required delegating responsibility and disciplining the ranks, they were convinced that GLF's *modus operandi* permitted individual freedom and self-determination at the price of the authority and control that was needed to sustain organization.

The *Come Out!* collective's attempt to secede confirmed their worst fears. Late in August 1969, when GLF's dances began to bring in money, there had been a debate over priorities. The radicals argued that a newspaper to spread the word about liberation deserved first funding, while the reformers and revolutionaries maintained that a bail fund to support those who might be arrested during demonstrations was more important. Partly because of Hart's eloquence, and partly because Hoose and others with traditional views about organizational maintenance had acquiesced in order to preserve harmony, the *Come Out!* collective had been given the funds. But in the fall, when it came time to allocate money for a second issue, the reformers succeeded in persuading the GLF assembly that money for a community center had to be set aside first. It was then that the *Come Out!* collective declared its independence.

Hart described the prospective secession as a natural evolution prompted by human needs and changing circumstances. The reformers responded that this "evolution" was nothing less than an attempt to steal GLF's mouthpiece, which belonged to all because it had been financed with money raised by all. In retrospect, it is impossible to gauge the mix of machination and idealism responsible for the *Come Out!* collective's attempt to secede, but it is clear that none of the reformers believed the idealistically phrased justifications that the radicals offered. The cultural reformers refused to acquiesce a second time. Robinson and Owles, threatening literally to fight fire with fire, vowed to burn the issues of *Come Out!* that were stored in Robinson's Jones Street apartment rather than turn them over to a clique that seemed bent on dismantling GLF if it could not control it.

In response to the reformers' charge that they were engaged in self-serving manipulation, radical leaders defended their need for "humanistic forms" using tactics that were anything but humane: they excoriated Robinson and Owles not only for their political reformist ideas but for their ambitions to be gay political leaders and for their enjoyment of cruising, anonymous sex, and other traditional gay male pastimes the two had talked about in Hart's encounter group.

Many GLFers were charmed by the radicals, who maintained that personal purity and humane procedures were more important than organizational survival and strategic accomplishment. But Robinson and Owles saw nothing in the radicals but personal vindictiveness and political aggrandizement masked in self-righteous radical rhetoric. Ralph Hall, accused of "selling out" because he had agreed to write a biweekly column on GLF for *Gay Power,* spoke for many of the reformers when he used his forum to complain: "Weekly, I listen to those politically articulate dogmatists . . . I watch them shrewdly manipulate and brainwash the membership. Those who do not fall for their bullshit rhetoric are openly criticized and cleverly attacked when they express their disapproval. Persons questioning points of view or dissenting to majority consensus of GLF are openly embarrassed, insulted, and/or humiliated . . ."[8]

Ideological differences and personal hostilities alienated Robinson and Owles from the radicals, but the threat to GLF's survival they saw in the proposals of the *Come Out!* collective and in radical tactics did as much to persuade them that a more structured group was necessary if the goals they thought important were to be achieved. Their feelings were shared by Kay Tobin, the former DOB member, who had been watching GLF's meetings with a mixture of fascination and horror since the summer; and by Arthur Evans and Arthur Bell, who, even though they sympathized with radical and revolutionary sentiments, found GLF's paralyzing inefficiency intolerable. All this happened before the issue of supporting the Black Panthers came up in November, and even that matter raised organizational as well as ideological concerns.

The question of supporting the Panthers was handled in a way that reinforced all of the qualms of those who believed that effective action and strong organization were as essential to gay liberation as individual metamorphoses and mass social movement. When Bob Kohler proposed that GLF contribute money to a bail fund for imprisoned Panther leaders, Robinson and Owles argued that the needs of homosexuals and their groups should take priority over the needs of other minorities and theirs. After GLF's general assembly spent three consecutive meetings trying to arrive at a consensus on the matter of Panther donations, the two political reformers insisted that a vote on the issue be taken so that important matters would no longer be delayed.

Kohler told Donn Teal that the Panther issue provoked Robinson and Owles to leave GLF because the parliamentary procedure they insisted on using led ultimately to the defeat of the position they favored. According to Kohler, when those in attendance at one Sunday night meeting voted to support the Panthers, Robinson and Owles recruited people to vote to repeal that resolution at the next Sunday meeting. But just after the repeal was approved, Kohler rushed outside, met Lois Hart and her friends, and enlisted them to vote to repeal the repeal. In Kohler's words, "That was the silver bullet through Jim Owles's heart. We had suddenly overloaded more than they had loaded it . . ."[9]

But for Robinson and Owles, the problem was less the vote lost than the time and energy spent on intraorganizational wrangling over matters they considered irrelevant to homosexuals. Indeed, they had come to believe that since GLF's "structure-less structure" permitted anyone to introduce any concern at any time, it ensured that no consensus could be protected from the unsettling arguments of newcomers and that nothing could be made binding on any who disagreed with decisions reached. In the end, Robinson, Owles, and others who set out to form a reformist alternative to GLF were motivated almost as much by their desire to have a group that was effectively organized as by their ideas of what its aims should be.

· · ·

Each of the half dozen or so GLFers whom Robinson and Owles interested in their plans for a reform-oriented gay liberation group believed, with them, that GLF was strife-ridden because its members did not share basic principles. To prevent this situation from recurring, the ex-GLFers carefully devised a credo for their new organization. This credo became the preamble to the constitution approved three days before Christmas in 1969 by the founders of the Gay Activists Alliance.

The preamble made the clearest statement yet of reformist gay liberationist ideals. Its introduction strongly asserted the belief of politicized members of the counterculture that they could make society more respectful of unconventional self-expression and social interaction by engaging in political activity: *"We as liberated homosexual activists* demand the freedom for expression of our dignity and value as human beings through confrontation with and disarmament of all mechanisms which unjustly inhibit us." Basic New Left ideas that the roots of problems were systemic and that the hope for social transformation lay with those unjustly treated reappeared in the assessment that "mechanisms . . . economic, social, and political" inhibited homosexual self-expression and that the "lasting procurement" of rights depended on the actions "of oppressed homosexuals themselves." The focus on specifically homosexual issues and the enthusiasm about traditional gay pastimes that separated reformers from radicals and revolutionaries were reflected in the statement that GAA's aim was to end "all oppression of homosexuals" by securing "the right to feel attracted to the beauty of members of our own sex," "the right to make love with anyone, anyway, anytime," "the right to treat and express our bodies as we will," and "the right to express our own individuality." Willingness to work within the system, another distinctly reformist disposition, was evident in the resolve to make GAA "completely and solely dedicated to . . . implementation and maintenance" of "social and political rights which are guaranteed by the Constitution of the United States and the Bill of Rights, enjoined upon all legislative bodies and courts, and grounded in the fact of our common humanity."[10]

Although the themes delineated in the preamble reflected both countercultural values and New Left ideas, the framers were more aware of the experiential than the ideological roots of their views. The declaration that GAA was concerned solely with rights for homosexuals enshrined Robinson and Owles's early judgment that it was unwise to take stands on outside issues if homosexuals with diverse convictions were to be united. The open-ended interpretation given the right to homosexual self-expression reflected conviction that moralism had to be avoided if "traditional" homosexuals were to be enticed into joining those exhilarated by the prospects of liberation. The founders' bad feelings both about the homophile preoccupation with conventional respectability and about the radical tendency to equate liberation with rejection of the gay subculture reinforced this conviction.

The emphases in the preamble stemmed not only from judgments about what would best help organize the gay community but also from assessments of what would best build the organization. The stress on the beauty of being liberated came partly from the desire to attract homosexuals whose countercultural belief in the desirability of being true to themselves would attract them to a group formed to make it safe for homosexuals to be openly gay. The lack of moral judgment about traditional homosexual pastimes reflected awareness that, for many, being openly gay meant being enthusiastic about precisely those pastimes—from cruising, promiscuity, and sex in gay-identified institutions and places ("the right to make love with anyone, anyway, anytime") to experimentation with gender roles ("the right to treat and express our bodies as we will"). The use of words like *rights, demands, actions,* and *confrontation* reflected belief that potential recruits would be stirred by the Movement-popularized line that aggressiveness was necessary to combat a system at war with humanity.* The preamble's disavowal of "violence (except for the right of self-defense)," "ideologies," and "alliance with any other organization except for those whose concrete actions are likewise so specifically dedicated" was designed to ensure GAA's appeal to homosexuals with reformist rather than radical or revolutionary outlooks. After their experiences in GLF, the founders were determined to keep their efforts from being impeded by those interested primarily in ideological debate, nongay causes, or revolution.

To make sure that it would remain efficient and effective, the founders endowed GAA with structures and operating procedures very different from GLF's. Where GLF's structureless structure limited leadership positions to a pair of treasurers and to chairpersons appointed for monthly terms to preside over the weekly Sunday night meetings, and confined "organization" to ad hoc project groups, cells, and free-form discussion sessions, GAA's constitution established the offices of president, vice-president, secretary, treasurer, and delegate-at-large, called for the creation of committees, and mandated the use of Robert's rules of order at general and committee meetings. These arrangements reflected ideals as well as practicality. Through bitter experience, the founders had come to believe that only by allocating authority among officers, committees, and members could they prevent participatory democracy from being subverted by individuals—like members of the *Come Out!* collective— who were skillful at manipulating others. Indeed, because they felt that radical demagogues had been successful in GLF partly because its lack of membership requirements permitted transients to exercise

---

*The Greek letter lambda, now a popular symbol for gay liberation, was selected as GAA's logo because as a symbol for wavelength in quantum physics, it was thought to suggest dynamism. The founders wanted a symbol that would associate GAA with energetic action in the pursuit of gay liberation.

undue influence at meetings, the founders tried to safeguard GAA by devising strict regulations for the admission and ouster of members.

Determined to avoid the benighted structurelessness they saw in GLF, the architects of GAA also sought to escape the autocratic rule and pro forma democracy they associated with MSNY. To prevent their formalized authority and established operating procedure from thwarting participatory democracy, they spelled out the duties of officers, delegated the authority to act in intervals between weekly membership meetings to an executive committee, and gave the membership the power to nominate candidates for office and to initiate votes of no confidence in elected officers.

Like their beliefs about goals and strategy, the views of GAA's founders on participatory democracy and its significance can be traced to ideas popularized by the New Left. In the early 1960s, SDS leaders had been persuaded that their group should embody the participatory democracy it advocated for society at large by the success of SNCC's field workers, who discovered that their efforts to get rural blacks to participate in the political process were most successful when the blacks they were trying to organize participated themselves in doing the organizing. By the end of the 1960s the organizational models pioneered by SNCC and SDS had become so popular that it was assumed that any group advocating a participatory political system would itself permit membership participation.

GAA's founders, most of whom had taken part sporadically in antiwar activity, were aware of contemporary political currents. In setting up their organization, they worked both to abide by ideals they believed in and to win the support of politicized homosexuals. Underlying GAA's limited but liberationist goals, its nonviolent but militant strategy, and its structured but participatory framework was an attempt to reconcile political convictions and organizational considerations so as to appeal to homosexuals ready to become political but wary of extremes.

This effort to tailor GAA to the tastes of the "hip" homosexual mainstream stemmed from a desire to establish the group's legitimacy as well as from ambition to attract support. With a perspective shaped by the Movement, the founders believed that the consent necessary for a group to exist had to come from the community it vowed to serve rather than from the system it intended to reform. The radicals who ran GLF, believing the Movement their community, worked to establish GLF as a homosexual division in the radical vanguard. But the creators of the Gay Activists Alliance, aspiring to make their group the political representative of all homosexuals, structured it with an eye to winning the acceptance of those they considered the leaders of the local gay minority.*

Perhaps the most dramatic evidence that GAA's shape was dictated as much by organizational concerns as by political convictions is the fact that the man most responsible for putting the reformist sentiments of the founders into writing was a revolutionary who thought reform was necessary for organizational as well as strategic purposes. This man was Arthur Evans, who left his post as the head of GLF's radical study group to help construct GAA.

To some extent, Evans's reputation as "the brains behind GAA" was a tribute to his scholarly bent. In the early 1960s, he had majored in philosophy and helped form a Free Thinkers' Society at Brown University. When the sense of isolation he felt as a homosexual in Providence prompted him to move to New York, he completed the requirements for his bachelor's degree at City College and began work on a doctorate in philosophy at Columbia. In GAA, as Evans developed a reputation for being a revolutionary thinker, he attributed his politicization to the disturbances that rocked Columbia during the spring of 1968. But that politicization had no relation to his homosexuality: he had not been involved in Columbia's Student Homophile League and he freely acknowledged that he first went to GLF because he "thought it would be a good place to cruise."[11]

Evans's bluntness about his enjoyment of traditional gay pastimes was indicative of the perspective that distinguished him from most

*Later, when GAA's leaders moved to incorporate their organization under the laws of New York state, they did so primarily for the political reformist purpose of establishing that homosexuals were a legitimate political minority, and therefore entitled to charter political organizations. These political reformist ambitions received an unexpected boost when Secretary of State John Lomenzo refused to charter GAA, giving its leaders an opportunity to mount a series of publicity-generating legal challenges that came to a climax in the spring of 1972, when the Appellate Division of the Third Judicial Department overruled the secretary of state and the Supreme Court of Albany County and held that GAA had a right to incorporate.

of the radicals he met in GLF. Although critical of conventional restraints on sexual expression, he tended to see liberation as the legitimation and spread of traditional gay practices and institutions. While he too called for cultural transformation, he was skeptical that "a revolution in consciousness" could be brought about simply by having individuals develop unconventional life styles that would tempt others to follow their example. In fact, for all of his talk about repressive mores, and for all of his complaints about the obsolescence of Marxism, Evans was most aligned ideologically with GLF's revolutionaries. He maintained that political and economic institutions molded cultural values, that political power was necessary to influence political and economic institutions, and that homosexuals had to have gay groups structured to acquire and exercise power if they hoped to gain rights and status.

During 1971, Evans elaborated these views in a manuscript called "The Oppression of Homosexuals." Here he argued that homosexuals would have to pass through two reformist stages before they would be ready for revolutionary struggle and that a "vehicle" like GAA was necessary for the first stage. In explaining the need for the stage here called political reformism (which he called bread and butter reformism), Evans recapitulated many of the assessments that had guided the construction of GAA:

Long oppressed, most homosexuals try to hide their identity, an attempt which produces a serious political consequence: political thought in general is avoided like the plague, for it brings to mind the painful awareness of one's own political oppression. As a result, the overwhelming number of homosexuals are apolitical. If they do become political they tend to do so in areas other than homosexual liberation.

The vehicle which is created to attain political power for homosexuals must bear in mind the basic apolitical disposition of most homosexuals. If the vehicle goes into a gay ghetto and begins to preach the dialectic of class warfare, the horrors of industrialism and militarism, it will be laughed off the streets . . .

To reach as many homosexuals as possible, the vehicle should begin as a one-issue organization, viz., the issue of homosexual civil rights. It should avoid involvement in any other issue, including the issues of war, racism, and imperialism. As a one-issue organization, the vehicle will have the widest possible appeal. To homosexuals who are apolitical, it will speak to them about the one issue which concerns them: homosexuality. To homosexuals who are already political, it will appeal to all different political types, whether radical, liberal, or conservative.[12]

.   .   .

Arthur Evans did a great deal of talking and writing about gay political activity, and he always spoke about the need to politicize homosexuals without specifying that it was as necessary to provide for gay political "vehicles" as it was to weld homosexuals into a politically aware bloc. To some extent, this was because Evans was more interested in political strategy than in organizational maintenance. To some extent, it was because he believed that goals that sounded public-spirited and altruistic were, or would be perceived as, more worthy than those that appeared useful only to groups. To some extent, it was because he saw that the strategic and organizational efforts he recommended were mutually reinforcing.

Indeed, the beauty of the gay political tack suggested by early New Left ideas was that it eliminated the tension between goals and organizational concerns that had bedeviled homophile leaders. The homophile strategy of trying to persuade people that in important respects homosexuals were like heterosexuals called for downplaying and discouraging distinctively gay patterns in a way that estranged potentially supportive homosexuals. Although the creators of GAA spent little time exploring the contradictions between homophile ambitions and gay organizational success, they were convinced that the homophile approach alienated more homosexuals than it excited and confident that their own strategic and organizational interests coincided in a way that would make it easy for GAA to outshine its predecessors. Indeed, they were sure that their efforts to politicize homosexuals would automatically make GAA New York City's premier gay political group—an organization "hip" and "militant" where MSNY and DOB were "uptight" and "conservative" and where GLF was "freaky" and "revolutionary."

In early GAA strategy sessions, then, the major topic of conversation was how best to go about politicizing homosexuals. The founders believed that homosexuals had to think of themselves as a minority with legitimate political concerns before they could be active enough politically to force politicians and public officials to acknowledge that this was so. What lay in the way, they saw, was that few homosexuals felt the political system could or would do much to affect their gay lives. Most homosexuals encountered little trouble with the law: few were directly affected by the rarely enforced provisions criminalizing sodomy; most avoided arrest for solicitation and disorderly conduct by cruising stealthily and having sex discreetly; only a few had firsthand experience with police raids. Most homosexuals seemed to avoid discrimination by passing as heterosexual. Many who felt inhibited and unhappy blamed themselves, those who looked for the roots of their problems elsewhere focused on prejudice and stereotyping, and few saw much connection between the political system and the freedom to be homosexual. Those who did seemed to believe that the Lindsay administration had brought abuses like entrapment, police harassment, and public-employment discrimination to an end. In fact, with the flowering of gay bars and bathhouses that accompanied Lindsay's hands-off attitude, they felt that things had never been better. These realities convinced GAA strategists that they would have to politicize homosexuals by pursuing goals that would be viewed as political and by eliciting responses from politicians and public officials that would verify that homosexuals had legitimate political grievances and effective ways of dealing with them.

For their debut, the GAAers decided to circulate petitions asking Carol Greitzer, the Village representative on the city council, to sponsor a bill that would outlaw discrimination on the basis of sexual orientation in both public and private employment. The petitions also asked her to "seek the repeal of existing laws prohibiting the solicitation for and participation in homosexual acts between consenting adults" and to work for the elimination of "all discriminatory restrictions to the existence of gay businesses." Petitioning was seen as a way not only to suggest to homosexuals that there were concrete political issues affecting them but also to give notice that there was a new local gay group intending to work boldly but appropriately within the political system.

While GAA's petitioners usually referred to those they were trying to reach as members of "the gay community," they welcomed the signatures of all who offered them, recognizing that it was not always easy to distinguish homosexuals from heterosexuals and that many who engaged in homosexual behavior were reluctant to identify themselves as gay. GAA's first organizational brochure explicitly welcomed heterosexuals as well as homosexuals. It stated, further, that "while believing that . . . public confrontation is the best way for homosexuals to reaffirm their own sense of self-pride, Gay Activists Alliance also recognizes the plight of those who, for whatever reason, are unable to make a public commitment, and welcomes their help behind the scenes."

Recognition that "the gay community" was an entity as elusive as the individuals it comprised also led GAA's strategists to turn their attention to institutions whose roots in Greenwich Village made them seem the property of homosexuals even when the institutions had no explicitly gay character. One such organization was the Village Independent Democrats, commonly called the VID, a political club that became the target of GAA's second political action. The occasion was the candidates' night held at the end of January 1970 in the VID clubhouse at the corner of Seventh Avenue and West 4th Street; the guests were four men seeking the Democratic gubernatorial nomination. The strategy was the one perfected when zapping mayoral candidates under GLF auspices: GAAers scattered themselves in the audience, waited for the question-and-answer session, then stood up, introduced themselves as emissaries from the Gay Activists Alliance, and asked about issues important to "the gay community."

As before, the questions elicited surprised and tentative responses from the candidates and a mixture of consternation, disapproval, and applause from the audience. At the end of the evening, VID president Robert Egan invited the GAAers to attend the next night's meeting of the group's Committee on Human Rights. That appearance led to a vote by the committee to endorse each of the demands on GAA's petition; committee members also advised the GAAers to meet with Carol Greitzer, who had been a leader of the club in the early 1960s. The VID's endorsement pleased GAA's leaders not just because it was an important first acquisition of political support but because, as an acknowledgment of GAA's claim to being the political mouthpiece of local homosexuals, it would encourage others to grant approval and support.

Of course, to elicit such support, it was necessary to reach others. This was the concern underlying GAA's third political initiative. The target was the *New York Post.* During the fall of 1969, *Post* columnists Pete Hamill and Harriet Van Horne had written pieces containing derogatory comments about the GLF contingents that had participated in antiwar demonstrations. Citing these as the basis of their grievances, a group of GAAers went to the *Post* offices and asked for a meeting with publisher Dorothy Schiff. Unable to get past Schiff's secretary, they talked with a reporter in the newsroom until editorial page editor James Wechsler agreed to see them.

In their session with Wechsler, the GAAers castigated the columnists, complained about the lack of coverage given serious homosexual endeavors, and talked about GAA's plans. Wechsler contended that the coverage was slim because there was little to cover. His visitors assured him that this was going to change.

GAA's strategists believed they had to get publicity in papers like the *Post* in order to reach homosexuals who avoided Greenwich Village and kept their distance from local gay bars and baths (almost all of which refused to post gay political notices anyway). They expected to reach less elusive homosexuals by distributing leaflets in heavily homosexual sections of the Village and through coverage in the gay news media that had begun to flourish after the Stonewall Riots. Leo Martello offered to write articles on GAA for the *Advocate,* a gay newspaper published in Los Angeles but working to develop a national readership. Arthur Bell volunteered to compose a column for the biweekly *Gay Power* and was selected to head GAA's Publicity Committee. Bell's work at Random House both made him aware of the need for organizational promotion and gave him the necessary skills. In *Dancing the Gay Lib Blues,* he noted that his Publicity Committee "initiated news releases and discussed future actions to spread the Gay Activists Alliance name."[13]

It was a sign of the importance attached to publicity that two of GAA's original four committees—Bell's Publicity Committee and Marty Robinson's Street Committee—dealt with getting news to the public. The interest in publicity also reinforced enthusiasm for protest activity, for it was clear that public demonstrations were more newsworthy than private meetings and that coverage in newspapers and on television reached more people than leaflets and person-to-person conversations. Both of GAA's communications committees worked closely with Arthur Evans's Political Action Committee to plan demonstrations that would attract attention. And the prospect of prodigious publicity largely accounted for the decision to hold

GAA's first big demonstration at City Hall, the local political arena with the largest resident press corps.

In the middle of March 1970, the Publicity Committee prepared the way for the action at City Hall by notifying reporters and photographers that members of the Gay Activists Alliance planned to ask the mayor personally to put an end to police harassment at the Continental Baths (later to be celebrated as the place where singer Bette Midler launched her career). Two score GAAers showed up and were greeted by police as well as press. When they were told that the doors of City Hall were temporarily closed, and when Jim Owles was prevented from entering, they raised their signs and began to march, posing for photographers and talking to reporters about their grievances as they circled.

Mayoral chief counsel Michael Dontzin soon arrived and said that since Lindsay was out of town, he would meet with representatives of the picketers. Yet the ensuing meeting stirred less excitement than the reports about the picket line broadcast on local radio stations, the film clips shown on evening news programs, the stories printed in the *New York Post* and *Women's Wear Daily,* and the front-page spreads that appeared in the *Advocate, Gay Power,* and *Gay,* the local publication put out by the publishers of *Screw.*

On the heels of this publicity came a round of news items about a young man, arrested during a raid on a gay bar called The Snakepit, who had leaped from the window of the sixth precinct police station and been impaled on its spiked fence. Activists used this incident as an opportunity for another publicity-generating demonstration. By distributing leaflets in gay bars on the East and West sides of Manhattan as well as in the Village, and by asking GLFers to invite nongay supporters from the Movement, they mustered almost five hundred people for a procession from Sheridan Square to the Charles Street precinct headquarters and from there to St. Vincent's Hospital (where, determined to protect GAA's reputation as a one-issue group, Jim Owles ignored pleas that everyone move on to the "House of D.") Thanks to GAA's Publicity Committee, reports on the march appeared in the daily newspapers and a feature on gay political activity ran in the *Village Voice,* the first since the coverage of the Stonewall Riots the summer before. GAA's officers used these articles to persuade the VID to pass a resolution demanding a moratorium on gay-bar raids and Congressman Ed Koch to send a letter of protest to the police commissioner, Howard Leary. The Publicity Committee issued press releases to make sure that these too were publicized.

The behavior of the press confirmed belief that private sessions with low-level administrators and staff assistants produced less that was newsworthy than public statements by important officials. And if one dimension of the strategy of prodding homosexuals to become politically active was to publicize that some of their number were engaging in political activity, another was to force political figures to respond to their efforts publicly. This second ambition was what led to GAA's demand that John Lindsay openly commit himself to protecting the rights of homosexuals. A flier drawn up after the picketing at City Hall aired the more ambitious aim: "Forty G.A.A. members went to City Hall to require that the Mayor provide Gay People the legislative, political, and verbal representation accorded other minority groups. Our planned sit-in to help gain open recognition of the Gay Voting Bloc was thwarted by police, but a nonviolent confrontation led to a meeting with the Mayor's Chief Counsel, Michael Dontzin."

Significantly, instead of a specific issue, such as police harassment, the flier emphasized the general matter of minority-group representation. This was how Robinson, Owles, and Evans hoped to sharpen their message and reach the broadest possible audience. By demanding that Lindsay recognize the "Gay Voting Bloc," they introduced the idea that there was such a bloc. If Lindsay agreed to deal with the grievances of gays, homosexuals would be encouraged to believe that gays were indeed a legitimate political minority. If, on the other hand, he either denied that homosexuals had serious grievances or refused comment, his homosexual and liberal supporters would have cause to doubt the sincerity of the mayor's support: If Lindsay was comfortable with homosexuality, why was he reluctant to mention it publicly? If he favored rights for all, why would he refuse to speak out about rights for homosexuals?

The GAAers who met with chief counsel Dontzin at City Hall insisted that the mayor make a public statement. When neither official response nor private communication followed, they resolved to embarrass Lindsay into speaking out. At a celebration of the one hundredth anniversary of the Metropolitan Museum of Art, shortly after Lindsay had begun an address on the front steps of the museum, Marty Robinson rushed up to him and screamed, "When are you going to speak out on homosexual rights, Mr. Mayor?" Police led Robinson away and Lindsay completed his remarks, but as he strolled among the guests afterwards, individual GAAers made their way up to him, reached to return his handshake, and held tight, hollering about the need for a public statement on gay rights until security guards tore them loose and hustled them out.

Six days later, at a taping of the mayor's weekly Sunday night television show, there was more disruption. This time Sandra Vaughn, a reporter from the *Village Voice,* was enlisted to publicize events. Her account read:

> Mayor Lindsay asked [his guest] Arthur Godfrey, "What kind of audiences do you usually get?" Arthur Evans, a member of the Gay Activists Alliance, responded by rushing to the platform: "What about homosexuals? Homosexuals want an end to job discrimination." . . . Evans was escorted from the room as GAA members clapped, stomped, and chanted: "Answer the homosexual!" . . .
>
> For almost 20 minutes after the Evans interruption, GAA members shouted: "What about the laws against sodomy? We want free speech! Lindsay, you need our votes. Homosexuals account for 10 per cent of the vote . . ."[14]

The chaos in the studio came to an end when Dontzin huddled with GAA's leaders and then scheduled a meeting at City Hall. Deputy mayor Richard Aurelio and chief of patrol Harry Taylor were there when the GAAers arrived for their appointment. Evans told the officials that it was necessary to "work on solutions to the underlying problems of the State Liquor Authority and Police Department corruption," maintaining that "gays are no longer sitting back and accepting police hanky-panky."[15] Aurelio assured the group that Lindsay was willing to deal fairly with homosexual grievances and insisted that public confrontations with the mayor stop. Owles replied that the elimination of objectionable police practices would improve matters but that GAA's drive to establish homosexuals as a political minority required the mayor's explicit acknowledgment: "There's a moral issue and a political issue at stake here. Lindsay owes a political debt to his homosexual constituents. He owes us his support both politically and humanistically. Yet we don't exist as far as the New York public is concerned. We demand public recognition by the mayor. It's absolutely essential."[16]

Three days before the City Hall meeting, representatives of GAA had discussed the need for legislation banning employment discrimination on the basis of sexual orientation with Eleanor Holmes Norton, William Booth's successor as chairman of the city's Commission on Human Rights. Norton had agreed to explore the matter. The GAAers who went to City Hall were pleased to find that Aurelio knew of the commissioner's commitment but were taken aback by his noncommittal observation, "If the problem is proved and the need exists for such legislation, I don't think you will find the Mayor withdrawing from that battle."[17] After Norton's encouraging response—and Aurelio's guarded one—GAA strategists decided to make employment discrimination the focus of their politicizing efforts.

To pave the way for the submission of legislation banning discrimination, Jim Owles carried GAA's petitions to councilwoman Greitzer. When she expressed reservations about becoming involved in the gay rights issue, GAA's strategists planned an appearance at the Village Independent Democrats to force her to change her mind. Their strategy was to challenge Greitzer to speak out in front of an audience that would contain closeted homosexuals and sympathetic liberals who would be alienated by her refusal to comment or by her equivocation. Arthur Bell, then writing under the pseudonym Arthur Irving, described in *Gay Power* how pressure was brought to bear on Greitzer:

Poor Carol . . . walked to the speaker's stand. And she, and all of those V.I.D.'ers and G.A.A.'ers heard Arthur Evans say, "Carol Greitzer refused to accept the petitions. She said she would not sponsor a job discrimination bill . . . If she doesn't relate to the homosexual cause, the Village Independent Club doesn't relate and we are prepared to sit in."

Mrs. Greitzer turned to platform chairman Robert Egan and said, under her breath, "I don't want to make a statement. I don't want to talk. Tell them I have a terrible cold. I didn't refuse those petitions. I told them I couldn't take them home that day. I had too many things to carry. Tell them I have a cold and the mike isn't working . . ."

Egan persists. "You've got to speak." Carol reneges. Her dark eyes flash. She speaks. "If your president had left them there, I'd have taken your petitions home . . . The City Council is not going to be able to move in any way on such petitions." Commotion from the audience.[18]

Though Greitzer was cold and aloof, Bella Abzug warmly welcomed the troupe of GAAers who visited the headquarters of her campaign to unseat Congressman Leonard Farbstein in the end-of-June Democratic primary. The GAAers were so impressed that they invited her to address their group. Late in May 1970, Abzug became the first prominent politician to speak at a membership meeting of the Gay Activists Alliance. A few weeks later, when a delegation from GAA went to candidates' night at the Greenwich Village Association, they greeted her introduction with a standing ovation.

GAA's visit to the Greenwich Village Association resulted in supportive public statements not only from Abzug but from state assemblyman William Passannante, Senate hopeful Paul O'Dwyer, and others. The statements reassured GAA's leaders that they could get responses legitimizing their political status by asking direct questions in public forums, but the lack of publicity reminded them that political breakthroughs had to be publicized if they were to stir masses of homosexuals to identify themselves as members of the "gay voting bloc." Challenging important candidates to speak out about gay rights when reporters were present seemed the most effective way to proceed. Model coverage of a model challenge occurred in Kay Tobin's account of GAA's confrontation with Arthur Goldberg, who became the Democratic gubernatorial nominee in the same primary in which Abzug was nominated for a seat in Congress:

> When Democratic gubernatorial hopeful Arthur J. Goldberg paid a routine campaign visit on June 5 to the huge, busy intersection of 86th and Broadway, he was met by . . . three dozen members of the Gay Activists Alliance . . . completely interspersed with the many members of the public who had assembled in anticipation of his pre-announced visit.
>
> As planned, Mr. Goldberg was approached quietly by GAA members when he first emerged from his white limousine. They shook his hand, smiled, and asked him if he was in favor of fair employment laws for homosexuals, if he favored repeal of the state laws against sodomy, and what could be done to end police harassment of gays in the state.

Goldberg's response was completely unexpected: "I think there are more important things to talk about," he reiterated to each gay questioner. From then on . . . GAA members, who had previously obtained in open confrontation a variety of mildly favorable responses from other Democratic gubernatorial hopefuls, reacted by pressing the same questions in shouts.

A loud chant of "Answer homosexuals, Answer homosexuals," began. Goldberg moved through the crowd and seemed not to know which way to turn next in an effort to avoid grasping the out-stretched hands of GAA members. He finally settled on shaking the hands of children as a safety measure . . .

GAA members switched to the chant of "Gay Power!" as Goldberg headed for his white limousine and climbed inside. "Surround the car, surround the car," a GAA member called out. This accomplished, Goldberg was treated to a final chant: "Crime of Silence, Crime of Silence, Crime of Silence!" . . .

Jim Owles, president of GAA, addressed a member of the Establishment press who was in the crowd. "When Goldberg goes to a Black community he speaks to Black concerns, when he goes to a Jewish community he speaks to Jewish concerns. He's in a homosexual neighborhood right now. Why can't he speak to our concerns?" . . .

GAA's president told [State Assemblyman Al] Blumenthal, "I think we showed Arthur Goldberg that wherever he appears here in this city, he can expect to be asked questions by his homosexual constituents."[19]

GAA's leaders hoped to convince Goldberg that gay liberationists were ready to turn his refusal to speak publicly about their concerns into an issue that would cost him votes not only among Manhattan's large if invisible population of homosexuals but also among liberal Democrats. Primarily to rally the support of these liberals, the GAAers made Governor Nelson Rockefeller and the Republican Party the target of their next demonstration. Few expected that the Republicans would be more forthcoming than the Democrats, but there was faith that pursuing Rockefeller would yield publicity and hope that the governor's failure to lend support would spur Democratic candidates to light on homosexual rights as an issue through which to win homosexual votes and attract liberal support.

In the middle of the Gay Pride Week held to commemorate the first anniversary of the Stonewall Riots, GAA's leaders staged a sit-in at the offices of the Republican State Committee. They demanded that the Republican Platform Committee endorse the requests in

GAA's petition and that Rockefeller air his views about homosexuality. As planned, the loud and colorful picket line staged outside GOP headquarters attracted the attention of reporters and photographers. Those inside vowed not to leave until they were granted a public interview with the Republican state chairman. Five of GAA's leaders stayed until they were arrested, becoming the first gay political activists ever to be arrested in the course of duty. During July and August, the trial of the "Rockefeller Five" became a focus for well-publicized demonstrations aimed at establishing that homosexuals were a minority with legitimate political grievances. (Arthur Bell submitted a story about the "Rockefeller Five" to the *Village Voice,* and its publication marked the beginning of his career as a writer for the *Voice.*)

As the summer progressed, public confrontations with candidates were complemented with more conventional techniques for soliciting political support. Toward the end of July, a delegation from GAA visited the executive committee of the New Democratic Coalition (NDC) and persuaded its members to set up a committee on homosexual rights and to permit GAA to lobby at the upcoming NDC convention. There, GAA negotiators won promises of support from important Democratic candidates like Richard Ottinger, Adam Walinsky, and Arthur Goldberg (who said of his previous encounter with gay activists, "I'm always available to conduct a decent conversation. That was no way to approach me.").[20] Subsequently, an Ad Hoc Elections Committee was created to handle GAA's electoral involvement. During September and October, it dispatched questionnaires to candidates, invited nominees to address membership meetings, fed information about their stands to the gay and straight press, and sponsored a drive to persuade homosexuals to register and vote.*

It was a sign of GAA's growing influence that 25 percent of its questionnaires were returned and that the responses from candidates

---

*Each of these endeavors had been undertaken by MSNY, but not with the thought that politicians could be persuaded that homosexuals were an active political constituency, nor with the conviction that their responses were important less for what they promised than for the impression they made on potential recruits for the gay political minority. MSNY queried candidates on behalf of homosexuals and civil libertarians; GAA urged nominees to respond to their gay constituents and promised to publicize results so that the gay voting bloc would know who to support. MSNY spoke of the need to educate potential officeholders; GAA stressed the importance of giving homosexuals the sense that they were members of an influential political minority.

in Manhattan and Brooklyn were overwhelmingly favorable. Explicit statements of support came not only from Senate hopeful Ottinger and (after the threat of another zap) gubernatorial candidate Goldberg, but also from the incumbent Republican senator Charles Goodell. Marc Rubin, chairman of the Ad Hoc Elections Committee, was so heartened that when Goodell submitted remarks referring only to the rights of minorities generally, he insisted that the senator mention homosexuals specifically—and, citing the positions taken by prominent Democrats, succeeded in persuading Goodell to comply.

The statements favoring gay rights from the nominees for senator and governor were a first in the history of New York electoral politics, and Rubin went to the *New York Times* to make sure that the news was duly reported. Although the reporter he spoke with assured him that the developments had the makings of a front-page story, nothing appeared. Subsequent visits and phone calls led only to a three-paragraph article on an inside page. Persuaded that the established news media were intentionally obstructing their efforts to establish homosexuals as a legitimate political minority, GAA's leaders held a news conference to complain about the "media blackout" and redoubled their efforts to distribute leaflets at the polls. They blamed the straight press for sapping their political surge and resolved to make dealing with the media a postelection priority.*

In truth, the established news media had played a key role in making GAA as successful as it was, for GAA's strategy was to persuade homosexuals to think of themselves as a political minority by behaving in ways that suggested that homosexuals *were* a political minority. Protest activities were crucial to this politicizing strategy because they permitted a relatively small number of politically minded homosexuals to stage dramatic public events that forced politicians and public officials to speak out about gay rights. There was evidence that the straight press had contributed to the success of these politicizing efforts—by publicizing them widely and seriously—both in the number of important political figures who ac-

---

*Marty Robinson demonstrated his concern by resigning as head of the Political Projects Committee to chair an Ad Hoc *New York Times* Committee. After the series of meetings he initiated failed to convince *Times* officials that gay political news was fit for more print, members of the *Times* Committee tried to exert pressure by telephoning and writing letters to those listed in the *Times* directory, by plastering posters complaining of the *Times*'s bias in the New York subways, and by arranging for the publication of a feature on the *Times*'s "media oppression" in the *Village Voice.*[21]

knowledged gays as a political constituency and in the flood of homosexuals who joined in gay political activity. It showed how far GAA had come that its leaders could fault the news media for inadequate coverage of gay political activity when, only a year before, the same media had considered the word *gay* too obscene to print.

7

Conflicts Between Political
and Cultural Leaders

AT FIRST, THE POLITICAL REFORMERS who organized GAA
welcomed recruits with cultural reformist outlooks, believing their
ambitions would be compatible with their own. The preamble to
GAA's constitution acknowledged the validity of cultural reformist
concerns with its vow to eliminate the "social" as well as the "political mechanisms" that inhibited homosexuals. Political reformist
leaders confirmed that there was room in GAA for those eager to
confront inhibiting "social mechanisms" by permitting a Street
Theatre Subcommittee to be formed under the auspices of the Political Action Committee and by letting the fourth of GAA's original
committees be devoted to "Pleasure and Fund-raising." GAA's first
brochure also acknowledged the cultural as well as the political road
to liberation: "Through weekly meetings, militant political action,
and joyous social events, Gay Activists Alliance will build an un-
shakable political and psychological base for the complete liberation
of homosexuals and for the universal recognition of their autonomy
as free men and women."

Organization-building ambitions encouraged Robinson, Owles,
and Evans to accommodate those who believed that activities that
affected life styles, built community, and changed culture were essential to the pursuit of gay liberation. The politicos needed a sizable
number of homosexuals to carry out their projects, and both to
attract recruits and to show GAA was committed to participatory
democracy, they tried to let members do what they wanted. GAAers

with cultural reformist ambitions attempted to reassure political reformist leaders by participating in political activities. The only time they griped was when the politicos called projects proposed by the Street Theatre Subcommittee silly or dismissed the Pleasure and Fund-raising Committee as a group that simply raised money and absorbed the energies of those GAAers not yet ready for political activity.

In truth, the task of establishing homosexuals as a political minority so absorbed GAA's political reformist leaders that they often forgot that some of their associates saw GAA activities primarily as a means to influence life style, community, and culture. Yet culturally oriented GAAers joined in projects like distributing leaflets and zapping candidates less to politicize other homosexuals than to convince them that homosexuality was the basis of a life style characterized by warmth, humor, and humanity—indeed, by the traits suggested by the word *gay*. To them, handing out fliers and joining in demonstrations were ways of "going public." Going public, in turn, was seen as a way both of strengthening one's own sense of being gay and of inspiring others to "come out" (a term the liberationists used to mean not only acknowledging one's homosexuality, becoming familiar with the gay subculture, and presenting oneself as gay to other homosexuals, but also being proud and open about one's homosexuality and identifiably involved in the gay community). Cultural reformers believed that as the numbers of those who were gay, proud, and open increased, and as explicitly gay institutions and communities proliferated, the public would be forced to recognize that gays had something to contribute to society at large and would make room for them in existing social, cultural, political, and economic institutions.

Convinced that the key to survival and social progress for gays lay in stirring masses of homosexuals to be politically active and in forcing politicians and public officials to acknowledge their political status, the politicos considered cultural reformist ideas about strategy naive. In their eyes, the point of encouraging homosexuals to come out was that homosexuals who were "out" would be most inclined to support gay political organizations and to become conscientious members of a gay political bloc. Similarly, the reason for developing gay-identified institutions and promoting gay community was that these would help convince people that homosexuals were a group substantial enough to warrant official acknowledgement and political representation. Instead of working to help individuals come out and trying to raise consciousness through social events and non-political demonstrations, the politicos wanted to concentrate on political activity.

Although the cultural reformers in GAA found activities involving the political system one vehicle for the consciousness-raising they thought important, they were eager to develop their own genre of demonstration, which they called "street theater." For this purpose they banded together in the Street Theatre Subcommittee. Arthur Bell, later to become a leading spokesman for culturally oriented GAAers, wrote of the subcommittee's abortive first initiative: "The committee decided to meet at noon on Easter Sunday at the fountain in front of the Plaza Hotel. Dress optional: suits or khakis or calicoes or jeans. Then we'd join the strollers in a display of homosexual affection for the benefit of photographers and television cameras, as well as for our own sheer enjoyment. Unfortunately it snowed. Torrents. Our Easter Parade action was called off."[1]

In the wake of the storm, members of the Street Theatre Subcommittee waited for the snow to melt and then staged a small "gay-in" at Central Park. Then they set about organizing a more elaborate program of openly gay frolic for the rally after the march being planned to mark the first anniversary of the Stonewall Riots.

.   .   .

Of all the proposals the radicals railroaded through the Eastern Regional Conference of Homophile Organizations in the fall of 1969, the one that had the most far-reaching consequences was the resolution establishing Christopher Street Liberation Day:

RESOLUTION #1: that the Annual Reminder, in order to be more relevant, reach a greater number of people, and encompass the ideas and ideals of the larger struggle in which we are engaged—that of our fundamental human rights—be moved both in time and location.

We propose that a demonstration be held annually on the last Saturday in June in New York City to commemorate the 1969 spontaneous demonstrations on Christopher Street and this demonstration be called CHRISTOPHER STREET LIBERATION DAY. No dress or age regulations shall be made for this demonstration.

We also propose that we contact Homophile organizations throughout the country and suggest that they hold parallel demonstrations on that day. We propose a nationwide show of support.[2]

Although the ERCHO resolutions responsible for Christopher Street Liberation Day were introduced by the head of the Student Homophile League at New York University (an offshoot of the SHL at Columbia), the inspiration came from Craig Rodwell. In 1965, Rodwell had worked with Frank Kameny to plan the first "Annual Reminder," the ECHO-sponsored picket line held on July 4 at Independence Hall in Philadelphia. Thereafter, though he became progressively more disenchanted with Kameny's insistence that the Reminder be used to demonstrate that homosexuals were as respectable as heterosexuals (an insistence that led, among other things, to the requirement that all picketers wear suits and ties or dresses and heels), he led a group to Philadelphia each Independence Day. A week after the raid on the Stonewall Inn, Rodwell followed his custom of taking a busload of appropriately groomed New Yorkers to the July 4 event. But during the picketing, when Kameny peremptorily divided two lesbians who had moved from their assigned positions in the picket line and begun to hold hands, Rodwell exploded. Violating the rule that no one but the leader speak to observers, he interrupted Kameny's interview with a reporter from Reuters and announced that the Stonewall Riots marked the beginning of new militancy on the part of homosexuals. To demonstrate that this was militancy in the name of gay liberation—the freedom to express homosexual feelings—all of the New Yorkers paired up and marched holding hands.*

After his clash with Kameny and the exuberance that accom-

---

*A few days later, in a letter to Rodwell, Kameny made it clear that the New York contingent's insubordination in no way altered his homophile perspective on demonstrations:

I am genuinely sorry about the disagreement which surfaced at the demonstration. "Love-ins"—homosexual and/or heterosexual, both—have their place; so do picketing demonstrations. Neither is likely to be effective, and both are more likely to be ineffective, if they are mixed.

As the elected Chairman of ERCHO, it was my duty and obligation to administer the demonstration in keeping with the spirit of ERCHO as I was best able, in good faith, to interpret it. That spirit has always been in the direction of a somewhat conservative, image-conscious, conventionally dignified demonstration, intended to get a message across by avoidance of needless abrasion of the sensibilities and sensitivities of the large mass of people.[3]

panied the formation of the Gay Liberation Front, Rodwell felt the time had come to replace the Annual Reminder with a demonstration more in keeping with liberationist sentiments. Hoping to avoid opposition from homophile leaders offended by his July 4 apostasy, he arranged for the resolution establishing Christopher Street Liberation Day to be introduced by his friends in N.Y.U.'s Student Homophile League.

Although MSNY's moderate homophile delegates refused to endorse the proposal for a Christopher Street Liberation Day demonstration, homophile militants like "John Marshall," of the Washington Mattachine, and Foster Gunnison agreed to help. Marshall was appointed chairman of ERCHO's Christopher Street Liberation Day Umbrella Committee (CSLDUC). Gunnison agreed to be treasurer, and the two continued to be active on CSLDUC even when ERCHO's executive committee suspended the coalition's by-laws in the spring. What distinguished these homophile participants from their liberationist associates was their perspective on the purposes of the demonstration. As homophile militants, Gunnison and Marshall saw the march as a vehicle for showing the public that homosexuals deserved support for their efforts to eliminate discrimination. As culturally oriented gay liberationists, Rodwell and his allies saw Christopher Street Liberation Day as an occasion for encouraging homosexuals to be proud and supportive of the gay community.

Early in February 1970, Marshall invited each group that had belonged to ERCHO to a planning meeting at Rodwell's Bleecker Street apartment. The delegates who came agreed to keep the structure of CSLDUC to a minimum and to entertain all suggestions about how to commemorate the Stonewall Riots. Those who reassembled for a second meeting favored a street festival the weekend of June 26 and 27. When subsequent investigation revealed that this would require posting a bond of many thousands of dollars, consensus grew in favor of a march. The first impulse was to march from Christopher Street to City Hall, where individual groups could sponsor the festival CSLDUC could not afford to underwrite in the Village. When the planners judged Central Park a more favorable locale for post-march activities, the decision was made to march from Christopher Street to Central Park.

Marshall, Gunnison, and Rodwell worked to involve all of ERCHO's affiliates in planning the march, but they met with scant success. Moderate homophile organizations like MSNY, DOB–New York, and the West Side Discussion Group remained aloof. Gay liberation groups were careless about sending delegates to the monthly meetings. Marshall lived in Washington and Gunnison in Hartford. So the bulk of the responsibility for specific arrangements fell to Rodwell, his lover, and a few others who spent time at the Oscar Wilde Memorial Bookshop, including Michael Brown, who by this time had left GLF, and GLF treasurer Marty Nixon. Not until the beginning of May did GAA's delegates attend faithfully, and only in early June did MSNY, DOB–New York, and WSDG officially agree to support Christopher Street Liberation Day.

The cultural bent of Rodwell's clique was responsible for their resolve to make the first Christopher Street Liberation Day an occasion for affirming liberated gay life styles and celebrating gay community. In the words of CSLDUC's official greeting: "Welcome to the first anniversary celebration of the Gay Liberation movement. We are united today to affirm our pride, our life-style and our commitment to each other. Despite political and social differences we may have, we are united on this common ground: For the first time in history we are together as The Homosexual Community."

The greeting's mention of political and social differences attested to the committee's recognition that different gay groups had different ideas about how best to pursue gay political activity. The differences in strategy favored by political and cultural leaders were particularly marked. Since the band of revolutionaries from the Red Butterfly was small compared to the contingent from the Gay Activists Alliance, the political reformers from GAA were the ones who most challenged the cultural leaders of CSLDUC. Where the leaders of CSLDUC were determined to have their march and gay-in exemplify liberated gay community, the GAAers wanted to make homosexuals aware of the need to exercise political power and to confront politicians and public officials with evidence of the gay voting bloc. Instead of a picnic in the park, they wanted a program of speeches by political leaders and politicians. Where the leaders of CSLDUC balked at letting gay bars enter floats in the march (both because they doubted that bars belonged in a liberated gay community and because they saw them as instruments through which the Mafia exploited homosexuals and prevented community self-determination), the GAAers argued that every institution associated with the gay community should be encouraged to participate and that most of the homosexuals who had to be politicized enjoyed bars. Where the cultural leaders, in the name of movement, community, and humanity, wanted to downplay individual organizations, the GAAers wanted to tout their own group as the political mouthpiece of the local gay minority.

Because Rodwell and his supporters refused to acquiesce to the wishes of the political reformers, GAA was reluctant to contribute enthusiastically to their efforts. Other groups with specific agendas, similarly frustrated, followed suit. Hoping to keep all of the major gay groups involved without giving up their vision of the march and gay-in, the leaders of CSLDUC designated the days preceding the main event as Gay Pride Week, a time when individual organizations could pursue their own projects, political or otherwise.

As it turned out, the heads of GAA found it easier to go along with CSLDUC's plans than moderate homophile leaders did. Those at MSNY, though unperturbed by the well-regulated picket lines sponsored by ERCHO, worried about the Christopher Street Liberation Day march: its proponents seemed so determined to make a spectacle of their gayness, and some of them even talked of fighting if they were attacked. Comparable reservations dominated what Wade and Cervantes had to say about CSLDUC's plans in their report to MSNY's board on the ERCHO conference:

So they voted to a man for new Stonewall riots, the implementation of which was placed in the trustworthy hands of HYMN and its leaders, whose Oscar Wilde Bookstore already serves as general field headquarters for every revolutionary gay in the New York area. The combined votes of the radicals and the Kamenyites proved irresistible. The appeal to youth inherent in the proposal swept along all the college organizations present with the result that MSNY found itself in a minority of one in opposition to the Stonewall proposal.[4]

Some at MSNY wanted to keep their distance from gay liberation groups for ideological reasons; others fretted about organizational competition. Though Dick Leitsch and those involved in the day-to-day operations of MSNY found it easy to dismiss radical and revolutionary gay liberationists, they saw that GAA's single-issue, rights-focused approach threatened MSNY's status as the local gay group with the most political influence. Early in 1970, when GAA began to attract attention with its candidate confrontations, Mattachine officials responded by contrasting the confrontations' lack of concrete results with the success of their own negotiations and lawsuits. ("And barging into meetings and breaking them up by shouting down proceedings, or forcing their way into the offices of public officials to bring about a 'confrontation,' does not constitute political activity in the effective sense of the word.")[5] With the approach of summer, Leitsch moved to protect MSNY's preeminence by emphasizing its distinctiveness as a group comprising homosexuals of every political persuasion, a group more all-encompassing than GLF, GAA, or any of the other groups that had sprung up.

While Leitsch responded to the threat posed by GAA by stressing the range of MSNY's interests, "Michael Kotis" contended that the Mattachine had to demonstrate its versatility by working with gay liberation groups. In April 1970, after being elected president of MSNY, Kotis opened a Mattachine-sponsored conference on inter-organizational unity with a speech proposing that gay groups in New York City join together in a Homosexual Community Council (HCC).

Kotis saw that to effect harmony he had to be a reconciler, dispelling hostility towards Leitsch, Cervantes, and Wade among those in GLF and GAA and reassuring his Mattachine colleagues about the intentions of the liberationists. At Kotis's suggestion, the HCC used its first meeting to discuss the plans for Christopher Street Liberation Day. Once he was assured that violence would at all costs be avoided, he was able to persuade MSNY's board of directors to let him add their name to the list of official sponsors. DOB–New York, which had established closer relations with its moderate homophile cousin following the Stonewall Riots, followed MSNY's lead.

Thanks to these reconciliations, the first Christopher Street Liberation Day was officially sponsored by every major gay political group in New York City. On the morning of June 28, the leaders of GLF, GAA, and MSNY raised colorful banners and urged those who assembled in Sheridan Square to group behind their favorite; the delegates from DOB–New York were content to set up a table to enlist new recruits. Faced with requests to lead the march from transvestites, who boasted that it was they who had started the Stonewall Riots the summer before, and from radical lesbians, who contended that they needed visibility more than the men, Rodwell resolved to preserve what aura of unified community remained by appointing an honor guard of men, women, and transvestites to accompany the Christopher Street Liberation Day banner. The groups, he said, could fall in where they would.

Under the eyes of marshals trained by the Quaker Project on Community Conflict, a line of march was formed around the corner from Sheridan Square in Washington Place. Shortly after two in the afternoon, the several hundred who had lined up spilled out onto the Avenue of the Americas and headed for Central Park. Just forty-five minutes later, the marchers at the front of the column entered Sheep Meadow, climbed to the crest of the hill at its far side, and turned. At the sight of the throngs, swelled now by the two or three thousand who had joined en route, they clapped, they wept, they chanted: "Together! Together! Together!"

Yet even in that euphoria of community, the ideological differences and organizational considerations that perpetuated division crept to the fore. During the afternoon gay-in, they were evident in the distinctive themes pressed by the different group leaders interviewed by Lacey Fosburgh for what was to become a front-page story in the next day's *New York Times.* Michael Brown, in a comment that became the *Times*'s quote of the day, aired the theme most dear to culturally disposed gay liberationists: "We're probably the most harassed, persecuted minority group in history, but we'll never have the freedom and civil rights we deserve as human beings unless we stop hiding in closets and in the shelter of anonymity." Marty Robinson interpreted the march by highlighting political reformist ambitions: "It serves notice on every politician in the state and nation that homosexuals are not going to hide any more." Michael Kotis, striving to paint MSNY in the liberationist colors of its rivals, stressed the need for homosexuals to develop pride in being different: "The gay people have discovered their potential strength and gained a new pride. The main thing we have to understand is that we're different, but we're not inferior."[6] Only the statement of DOB–New York's president, quoted in a summary in the Sunday *Times*'s News of the Week in Review section, indicated the homophile propensity to stress that homosexuals were just like heterosexuals: "We don't belong in the closets any more and people shouldn't be afraid of what we represent. There's just nothing wrong with us, nothing queer or freaky and as soon as everybody in the gay world and the straight world recognizes this everything will be all right."[7]

The different thrusts of the statements made by gay leaders gave only a hint of the organizational rivalry that was to prevent the resurrection of ERCHO, keep organizational participation in the next year's CSLDUC minimal, and reduce the HCC to a superficial forum for communication. The rivalry stemmed partly from the differing political outlooks of gay leaders, partly from their concern to protect the identities and the legitimacy of their groups, and partly from the competition for persistently scarce resources. Differences between GLF's cultural leaders and GAA's political leaders inevitably led to disputes at demonstrations sponsored by gay liberation coalitions. Frictions between GAA and MSNY waxed until 1971, when the Mattachine acquiesced to GAA's political preeminence and settled for being a gay service organization. And dissension among culturally and politically oriented gay liberationists and between gay liberation and homophile groups paled in comparison to the disputes that erupted when lesbian feminist groups took their place alongside the others.

.   .   .

Ironically, the very success GAA's leaders had in promoting their organization led them to worry about preserving its political reformist identity, for the more GAA became known, the more it attracted individuals enthusiastic about consciousness-raising events rather than political involvement, and the more the politicos feared that this new blood would undermine GAA's capacity for political initiatives.

By May 1970, Robinson, Owles, and Evans were concerned enough to oppose several new projects proposed by politically inactive members. In a debate with GAAers who wanted to form a legal committee, for example, Owles argued that involving members in activities that heightened their sense of political commitment and that helped instill other homosexuals with political awareness was strategically important. A legal unit was inappropriate, he maintained, because it would make GAA "more and more an organization that appropriates money or provides a study group . . . an organization of people who *listen* and who vote on paper resolutions."[8] Although the membership went ahead and authorized creation of a Legal Committee, it acknowledged Owles's reservations by restricting the scope of the committee's operations. The limits spelled out in the committee's mandate are especially telling:

> To provide legal *referrals only* for gays who are in trouble with the law . . . Since such cases are not of political importance (they do not result in political gains or set legal precedents), the GAA Legal Committee has no authority to provide any further assistance, either financial or advisory. The GAA Legal Committee cannot act as a legal aid society in *any* but this minimal way. (GAA is a political activists' organization and not a philanthropic service organization.)

Owles's determination to protect GAA's political priorities led him to discourage ventures he deemed misguidedly educational as well as those he considered legal, philanthropic, or social. This attitude generated the first bitter floor fight in GAA's history in the middle of July, when several members asked for authorization to create a committee to educate clergymen. The fight centered on the appropriateness of forming a committee for educating heterosexuals in a group committed to politicizing homosexuals. But it was a minor dispute compared to the brouhaha that erupted the very next week over the notorious "Natasha incident."

In the afterglow of the successful social activities of Gay Pride Week, GAAer Phil Raia had called a meeting of the Pleasure and Fund-raising Committee and Street Theatre Subcommittee to plan a dance, scheduled for July 10. Among those who met to arrange entertainment for the dance were two women new to GAA and a tall black transvestite, "Natasha." According to Arthur Bell, who was also present, Natasha and a white go-go dancer proposed a "happening" in which the dancer, wearing only a black leather jockstrap, would pull a heavy rope into the center of the dance floor with Natasha, dressed in prize drag, bound at its end. Natasha would then loose her bonds, strip off her dress, reveal a naked male body, and fire a gun that popped paper flowers. Bell called it "the ultimate transvestite flower child anti-war trip."[9]

Whatever it was intended to be, the plan upset the two women and stirred others to ask the Executive Committee to ban it. Owles took it upon himself to veto the skit. Nothing was said at the next night's membership meeting and the dance went on without the happening.

The problem came at the following week's meeting, when Natasha and "her" transvestite friends interrupted the proceedings by charging that Owles was uptight, censorious, and dictatorial. Phil Raia and Ron Diamond spoke out in support of the angry transvestites. Owles countered with a sermon on political reformist priorities.

When the outbursts were over, Marty Robinson tried to restore harmony through a resolution "to reaffirm GAA's support and affection for its transvestite members as well as all transvestite members of the gay community, and at the same time to reaffirm our support and affection for Pres. Jim Owles."[10] However, at a subsequent leadership meeting called to discuss differences, the politicos blamed Raia and the "social people" for bringing GAA to the brink of ruin. Robinson complained that GAAers convinced they could "dance their way to liberation" diverted energy and attention from important political enterprises. Owles reiterated his arguments about preserving GAA's reputation as a group committed to political activism. Evans objected to the lack of respect shown parliamentary procedure. Before stalking out of the meeting, the "big three" said that probably GAA would have to divide, with the "political people" keeping GAA's name and constitution and the "social people" forming a group that could hold street theater and social events.

Arnie Kantrowitz, the highest-ranking officer to remain neutral, presided over the confrontation. To prevent the threatened fission, he arranged for the disputants to gather and work out a compromise before the following week's membership meeting. In an early draft of his autobiography, *Under the Rainbow,* Kantrowitz explains, "I was no Henry Clay, but I worked out a mandate for the Pleasure Committee that would satisfy the political people. It said that dances would be given with political themes, so that the people who came would learn about what we were doing."[11]

The truth is that more than by Kantrowitz's redrafting of the Pleasure Committee's mandate, GAA's political and cultural leaders were reconciled by the decentralization of authority that followed the Natasha incident. With characteristic concern about the efficiency of the "vehicle" that he had done so much to design, Arthur Evans focused on the organizational rather than the ideological issues responsible for dissension. At the July 22 membership meeting he distributed a leaflet identifying "the amount of power vested in the president by the constitution" as the root of recent problems. To remedy matters, the leaflet called for constitutional amendments stipulating that meetings be run by a parliamentarian; that the Executive Committee be expanded to include committee chairmen; and that the president's authority to appoint, assign projects to, and evaluate committee chairmen be distributed among president, Executive Committee, committee chairmen, and membership. The membership approved each of these amendments.

According to Evans and others responsible for the constitutional changes, the amendments and committee restructuring that ensued would redistribute authority to divide power among GAAers with competing priorities. Reducing Owles's prerogatives by putting committee chairmen on the Executive Committee would enhance the influence of Raia, Diamond, and others who favored social activities. Establishing different committees for fund-raising and social affairs would acknowledge the validity (apart from purposes of raising money) of activities bearing primarily on life style, community, and culture. Replacing Marty Robinson's Political Affairs Committee with a group mandated only to recommend ad hoc committees for specific political projects would curtail Robinson's sway.

The structural changes were portrayed as the beginning of a new integration, but the way they were implemented belied this promise. Among other things, a man with no ties to members of the original Pleasure Committee was selected to chair the new Social Affairs Committee, and this committee was authorized "to recommend dances and other social events . . . in order to raise the political consciousness of the homosexual community, to promote the unity and morale of GAA members, and to oversee the carrying out of such approved events."[12] Raising "the political consciousness of the homosexual community" was the primary goal of the political reformers. Promoting "the unity and morale of GAA members" was as vital as fund-raising to their aim of building a powerful organization. Clearly, the politicos acquiesced in GAA's sponsorship of social activities not because they wished to accommodate cultural reformers and their ambitions but only because they recognized that they needed the support of members who enjoyed social activities and of newcomers who, attracted by social activities, might then be schooled in political reformist thinking.

Even as the special committee appointed to restructure GAA's committees was at work, conflict between political and cultural leaders flared anew. Several on the Street Theatre Subcommittee had begun to see transvestism as a phenomenon in which the issues central to gay liberation came to a focus. These cultural reformers argued that if liberation meant the freedom to express oneself in ways one found fulfilling, then gays who wanted to cross dress should be encouraged to do so and others who fancied themselves liberated had an obligation to resolve any qualms they had about such behavior. Furthermore, they maintained that since the goal of gay liberation was to produce a culture that accorded respect to people whose sexual self-expression was unconventional, the most effective way to pursue this aim was to champion the type of homosexual who deviated from convention most visibly—the homosexual transvestite. With these arguments in mind, early in August members of the Street Theatre Subcommittee proposed that GAAers "publicly accompany a transvestite held aloft on a litter along Lexington Avenue when it is closed to traffic."[13]

Not surprisingly, this proposal stirred a new round of debate, not only between cultural and political reformers but among cultural reformers themselves. Many cultural reformers believed that encouraging homosexuals to be openly gay in order to gain public respect for gay life styles called for debunking the popular misconception that male homosexuals thought of themselves as women and dressed and acted in stereotypically feminine ways. They argued that this misconception would only be reinforced by a dramatic demonstration that focused on transvestites. Members of the Street Theatre Subcommittee retorted that it was just as important to embolden homosexual transvestites as to give heart to straighter-looking homosexuals, and that liberating homosexuals meant not only making them comfortable with their own sexuality but teaching them to respect those whose sexual self-expression was different. They reminded their associates that the liberationist strategy was not to win societal acceptance by showing that homosexuals were just like heterosexuals but to make the culture more accommodating of diversity by forcing people to acknowledge that human beings expressed themselves in diverse ways.

For the political reformers, the issue was less the substance or target of messages about liberation than the appropriateness of a GAA demonstration that lacked specific political content. When the cultural reformers had been content to pursue their aims in politically oriented demonstrations, whatever their own intentions, they had helped further political reformist objectives; GAA's political strategists had then considered them a boon. But the boon became a threat when the cultural reformers began to insist on the value of social events. And the same considerations that caused the politicos to balk at strictly social activities led them to chafe at expending energy on consciousness-raising street theater. Leading political reformers responded to the Street Theatre Subcommittee's proposal with the argument that GAA's demonstrations should make homosexuals politically aware and that a spectacle involving transvestites would belie the message that serious political activity was necessary, threaten GAA's reputation for militant political activism, and alienate the many homosexuals uncomfortable with transvestites and reluctant even to think of themselves as gay.*

To undercut the faction of cultural reformers who wanted to champion homosexual transvestites, the politicos argued that making the world safe for unconventional self-expression required militant political action and that the problem with the Street Theatre Subcommittee's plan was that it approached this serious matter in a silly way. Reports that the police had begun to arrest transvestites and male prostitutes in the Times Square area illustrated their argument with timeliness. After the Street Theatre Subcommittee's proposal was voted down, the politicos offered a "serious" way to deal with the oppression of especially oppressed minorities within the gay minority: they proposed that "legal observers" be dispatched to verify that street queens and hustlers on 42nd Street were indeed being hassled.

At the next membership meeting, the members of the Street Theatre Subcommittee announced that they had decided to resign. The legal observers then reported that the midtown crackdown seemed to be an attempt to divert attention from charges of corruption that were being leveled at the Police Department. This, the politicos submitted, warranted a protest. To win the support of

---

*Although the politicos cited strategic and organizational considerations when arguing against the Street Theatre Subcommittee's proposal, resentful cultural reformers charged that the politicos themselves were personally uncomfortable with and unsympathetic to transvestism. Yet, before they felt GAA's political reformist priorities threatened, Robinson, Owles, and Evans had supported a demonstration on behalf of Ray "Sylvia" Rivera, a street queen arrested for circulating GAA's petitions on 42nd Street; and Owles had asked the Political Affairs Committee "to promote membership in G.A.A. among types of gays not now adequately represented, e.g. transvestites, prostitutes, leather fetishists, et al."[14]

cultural reformers, the politicos portrayed the 42nd Street harassment as a violation of the homosexual's right to self-expression and as an attempt to intimidate all homosexuals by "coming down" on segments of the gay subculture that were particularly vulnerable. To buttress this contention, they pointed out that the police were also hassling homosexuals who stopped to socialize on Christopher Street, bothering patrons of a bar off Sheridan Square known as The Haven, and arresting individuals for loitering and disorderly conduct at the popular cruising strip on Third Avenue between 53rd and 59th streets.

At the following week's membership meeting there was overwhelming support for a proposal that GAA join GLF in a Saturday night march in Times Square. Yet their agreement to join in the explicitly political protest in no way eliminated the cultural reformers' desire to use demonstrations for consciousness-raising. Arthur Bell, whose identification with the cultural crowd led him to title his book with a paraphrase of Marty Robinson's pejorative characterization of social leaders as people who wanted to "dance their way to liberation," focused in *Dancing the Gay Lib Blues* on the dimensions of the Times Square demonstration important to cultural reformers:

> The march began. We walked from Eighth Avenue to Broadway, crossed Forty-second Street, and marched back to Eighth again. We blew minds! Natasha, with hair teased like never before, carried a placard: "We're the people our parents warned us against." The "Gay Power" signs were there and "Gays Unite" and "We Will Smash Your Heterosexual Culture" and "Hands Off Our Community" . . .[15]

Less cheerful was the rioting that erupted when the demonstrators marched back to the Village and discovered that the police were raiding The Haven.

For the politicos, the dramatic reemergence of the police harassment issue was a mixed blessing, for though it did more than words to persuade the cultural reformers that political militancy was the key to gay liberation, it also made more appealing the argument that militancy meant not only engaging in serious political demonstrations but resorting to violence when forced into self-defense. Radical and revolutionary GLFers made this argument with increasing frequency, and after the riot in the Village the night of the demonstration in Times Square, it was voiced by GAAers who were beginning to echo radical viewpoints.

GAA's leaders believed that any association with violence would hinder their politicizing efforts and hamper their attempt to win support in the political establishment. At the membership meeting that followed the rioting in the Village, Jim Owles noted for the record, "The riot that followed the group's appearance in Greenwich Village was neither sponsored nor supported by GAA, whose policy is to respond neither to provocateurs in the street nor to politicians who would offer empty promises simply to calm the community." General acquiescence was apparent in the defeat of a motion presented by newly politicized cultural reformers "that in the event of further rioting in the gay community, after determination of police aggression, GAA summon legal witnesses, media reporters, and medical help, and bring the GAA banner to the streets to rally or do whatever the people present feel is appropriate in the situation."[16]

To divert attention from the proponents of aggressive self-defense and put newly aroused passions to work for political reformist purposes, GAA's strategists advocated protest activities that would help with politicization while appealing to members mainly interested in building and defending gay community. One such initiative came from the Police Power Committee, which Eben Clark had organized after the riot and for which many of the politicized cultural reformers signed up. The Police Power Committee resolved to demand that Mayor Lindsay officially denounce police harassment and vowed to confront him constantly in public until he did so.

This mission stirred culturally oriented GAAers to political confrontations of unprecedented brashness in the fall of 1970. For the opening of the Metropolitan Opera's new season, Alliance members donned tuxedos and milled in the Lincoln Center lobby. "When the Mayor and his wife entered, they were stopped in their tracks and surrounded by shouting gays, and the lobby (whose staircase was filled with 'dignitaries') boomed with the sound of 'END POLICE HARASSMENT!' and 'GAY POWER!'" About a month later a repeat performance occurred at a Broadway benefit for the New York City Cultural Council. According to Morty Manford, a member of GAA who was an undergraduate in political science at Columbia when he asked Arthur Evans to help him write about the "theater zaps" for a seminar paper on the "Theory and Practice of

Confrontation Tactics in the Gay Liberation Movement," GAAers resorted to abrasive personal confrontations with the mayor because they were convinced that nothing less would force Lindsay to curb the police.[17]

Since GAA's strategists had conceived of political demonstrations as a publicity tool to politicize homosexuals more than as an instrument to secure actual reforms, the stress that Manford and Evans placed on having Lindsay act on complaints was significant. Among other things, it attested to the politicos' need to pursue real reforms in order to keep the support of cultural reformers who had come to believe that certain policy changes would facilitate their efforts to encourage homosexuals to be openly gay and active in the gay community. After the Village riot, the Police Power Committee voted to demand not only that Lindsay "end . . . individual harassment for loitering or for style of dress . . . harassment of all gay bars . . . [and] verbal abuse, physical assault, and illegal arrests," but also "that the Tactical Police Force not be allowed into a gay ghetto," "that police live within the precinct where they work," "that regular patrolmen within a gay ghetto not be allowed to carry clubs," and "that the position of Precinct Captain be an elected position by the people rather than an appointed one."[18] The politicos found themselves having to argue that the latter set of demands was too extreme—that it would alienate the homosexual masses and the politicians and public officials whose support was needed to make homosexuals a legitimate political minority.

. . .

It is one of the paradoxes in the evolution of gay political activity that several of the political reformers who at first believed that GAA's strategic priorities were threatened by cultural reformers ended up both popularizing the idea that working to change contemporary mores was political and developing innovative tactics for dealing with opinion-shapers commonly considered nonpolitical. The stage for this development was set by the news coverage of the rioting in the Village that followed the protest march in Times Square. Pete Fisher, one of several politically oriented newcomers outraged by the way the media ignored and trivialized events gays found deeply disturbing, responded to the reporting he heard on radio station WINS with a letter:

Your coverage of the demonstration at Times Square on the evening of August 29 was misleading in the extreme. You reported it as a Gay Power rally, when actually the issue which had necessitated our action was a great increase in police harassment of homosexuals throughout the city. More than three hundred gay people had been arrested in the Times Square area alone in the preceding three weeks; all charges in these cases were dropped before being brought to court—but the record of arrest remains on the books in each case to jeopardize current and future employment for those arrested, as well as providing an issue for potential blackmail. Your coverage presented the demonstration as some sort of lark.

Following this demonstration against police harassment, the crowd marched down to Greenwich Village, where the police were found raiding The Haven, a local gay bar. This, and the existence of police provocateurs in the crowd, led to the outbreak of rioting which followed, yet you presented the incident as a bunch of homosexuals on a meaningless rampage.

Fisher's letter not only expressed the concerns newcomers were developing with the way the press handled the dramatic events of late August but also pointed up the heightened expectations of the news media spreading among veteran politicos as they won promises of support from politicians and public officials. During GAA's first six months of activity, when the goal had been simply to reach nonpolitical homosexuals, any press coverage of gay political activity was welcomed. But when it became clear that GAA actually could exercise political influence—that it could prevail upon candidates and policymakers to certify through actions and words that homosexuals were a legitimate political minority—the precise sort of news coverage given became important. Deepened sensitivities and heightened expectations led GAA leaders new and old to look at the media more critically. As Fisher explained in his letter:

The repeated examples of an anti-homosexual bias in your news coverage are not merely a sign of poor reporting and lack of responsibility to the New York public, ten percent of which is homosexual, they are political in nature, whether by design or by accident.

At a time when homosexuals in New York are attempting to get candidates for office in the upcoming elections to take a stand on the oppression of homosexuals, your misinformed and biased reporting stirs up public hatred against us and adds to public ignorance about homosexuals and the discrimination they face. Your coverage deters some candidates from speaking out on issues that are vital to us and which must be spoken on if we are to have the opportunity to exercise our voting rights intelligently; it directly undercuts those candidates, such as Bella Abzug, who have spoken out for an end to homosexual oppression and for guaranteeing and protecting homosexual civil rights.[19]

The incident that pushed activists like Fisher to act was the appearance, in the September 1970 *Harper's,* of Joseph Epstein's "The Struggle for Sexual Identity." Promoted with a cover photograph of a muscular torso in a tight red blouse, the article aired Epstein's strong negative feelings about homosexuality and discussed unflattering opinions about homosexuals advanced by contemporary "experts." GAAers were repelled by the sensationalism of the cover and by the photographs of fey male mannequins accompanying the copy. Epstein's portrayal of homosexuals as fitting all the conventional stereotypes offended them, along with the bluntness with which he expressed his personal distaste: "Cursed without clear cause, afflicted without apparent cure, they are an affront to our rationality, living evidence of our despair of ever finding a sensible, an explainable, design to the world . . . There is much my four sons can do in their lives that might cause me to anguish, that might outrage me, that might make me ashamed of them and of myself as their father. But nothing they could ever do would make me sadder than if any of them were to become homosexual."[20]*

Right after the September *Harper's* appeared, the Political Affairs Committee proposed that GAA "sit in at *Harper's* offices to demand that they agree to print an article on the oppression of homosexuals." Pete Fisher was selected to write the piece and to chair an ad hoc committee mandated to compel *Harper's* "to balance its recent antihomosexual article by Joseph Epstein."[21] (One of the members of the so-called Ad Hoc Harper's Committee, an editor at Stein and Day,

---

*Arthur Evans countered those who suggested that Epstein was candidly exploring his personal prejudices by saying: "That's as if someone were to say, 'I look into myself and I discover that I really hate blacks—boy, do I hate blacks! I think they're stupid, they're too sensual, and they eat watermelon!' That's the level of the Epstein article."[21]

Eric Thorndale, contending that Epstein's piece revealed "cultural lag" not uncharacteristic of *Harper's,* turned to the magazine's August 1870 issue and found a diatribe against women's suffrage asserting that women "will sell their vote any day for a yard of ribbon or a tinsel brooch."[22]

was so impressed with Fisher's work that he contracted him to write a book about gay life, published the next year as *The Gay Mystique*.)

Convinced that the communications media exercised enormous political influence, most of GAA's political strategists saw no reason to exercise special restraint in approaching *Harper's*. But Fisher and the culturally oriented GAAers attracted to his committee believed that dealing with publishers was different from dealing with political figures. To make an impression not only on *Harper's* but on the whole literary establishment, and to win the support of homosexuals, liberals, and others sensitive about freedom of the press, Fisher and his associates set out to develop special tactics for dealing with institutions popularly perceived as nonpolitical.

Seeking redress in conventional ways was seen as an important first step. In the middle of September, Fisher wrote *Harper's* editor-in-chief Willie Morris that "The Struggle for Sexual Identity" was "uninformed, biased, and more important, offensive to our organization and to all homosexuals," and that GAA had an "obligation to insist upon an article of rebuttal in a forthcoming issue of *Harper's Magazine.*"[24] Although *Harper's* replied that it would consider publishing an article of rebuttal, its editors rejected several pieces submitted by GAAers, refused to commission an article by someone the Alliance approved of, and finally informed Fisher that they judged the publication of twenty letters provoked by the Epstein article an adequate response. Members of the Ad Hoc Harper's Committee felt that this attitude evidenced a moral insensitivity and political naiveté that called for militant action.

When GAA's leaders tried to force political figures to respond to their demands, all they needed to do was to persuade the targets of their zaps and those whose support they wanted that homosexuals had political grievances; they did not have to convince anyone that rights, protest tactics, and politicians were in and of themselves appropriate focuses for gay political activity. The problem with taking on publishing ventures was that their status depended on their appearing invulnerable to political interests. Editors were reluctant to acknowledge that their works had a political dimension, and the constituencies to which they appealed looked unfavorably upon using protest tactics when dealing with the press. Therefore, Fisher and his committee concluded that they had to persuade people of two things: that editors had moral responsibilities when it came to publishing writings that affected human rights, because of the inevitable political consequences such writings had; and that when they exhibited moral and political irresponsibility it was appropriate to respond politically.

A graduate student in political science at Columbia, Fisher was sensitive to the issues of free speech involved. To edify political peers less willing to accommodate what they saw as the fiction of the free market of ideas, and to muster enthusiasm for his method of handling the media, he wrote a circular elaborating his views:

> We have developed some very effective tactics in dealing with politicians . . . But there are other areas where these tactics are less effective, where we need to develop new tactics. One of these areas is the mass media—television, radio, the press, etc. . . . We must develop effective tactics to force them to give us equal time when they put down gay people. We must show them that this is a political issue and that they can't get away with it.
>
> The situation with the press is somewhat different and it requires different tactics. Under the first amendment, the press has the right to print what it chooses—there is no equal time provision, because it is assumed that opposing views can be printed elsewhere. It doesn't always work that way for gay people, and we must find ways of stopping the kind of slander and prejudice we get in the press, in magazines, and in books. We need tactics that will bring pressure to bear on them. We've learned how to embarrass politicians in public; we've got to learn how to embarrass TV stations, publishing houses, and the like . . .
>
> We're going to embarrass *Harper's* and show them up as phony liberals. We're going to get our equal time in the form of press coverage of *our* side of the story—at *Harper's* expense . . . We want other magazines to think twice before they pull the sort of crap *Harper's* pulled.

The key to the tactics devised to deal with *Harper's* was tone. For those he enlisted to participate, Fisher characterized the ambience he wanted to create as "civilized, intelligent, educational, consciousness-raising, hospitable—no demands, no threats, no damages to office or files." In an on-the-spot interview with Donn Teal, one recruit explained how the forty or so GAAers who trooped to the Park Avenue offices of *Harper's* on the morning of Tuesday, October 27, behaved: "In the reception area one group of us set up a table with coffee and doughnuts, others spread out and leafleted every desk in the company. As people came to work, we walked up to them, offered a handshake, introduced ourselves, saying, 'Good morning, I'm a homosexual. We're here to protest the Epstein article. Would you like some coffee?' "[25]

While rank-and-file GAAers showed office workers and passersby what it was like to break bread with homosexuals, political leaders tried to make editors see why publication of the Epstein piece was both immoral and political. When executive editor Midge Decter insisted that the article was "serious and honest and misread" and that "the question of changing the minds and hearts of men is a complicated one that does not yield to political demands," Arthur Evans stabbed his finger at her and shouted: "You knew that his article would contribute to the suffering of homosexuals. You knew that. And if you didn't know that, you're inexcusably naive . . . We have a right to come here and hold you politically and morally responsible for it. You are a bigot and you are to be held responsible for that moral and political act."[26]

The GAAers who came to breakfast at *Harper's* deliberately used person-to-person consciousness-raising tactics of the type advocated by cultural reformers. This was one of the things that made the *"Harper's* zap" a notable synthesis of political and cultural reformist tactics.

Yet the political leaders who joined in the zap did not use cultural reformist tactics out of any new faith that challenging the attitudes of individuals through eye-opening personal presentations was the best way to alter behavior. Rather, they gauged that consciousness-raising techniques had strategic utility in demonstrations involving institutions commonly perceived as nonpolitical. The tenor of the arguments offered editors reflected the politicos' judgment that publishers and their constituencies would be more receptive to challenges with a flavor of moral education than to intrusions that smacked of political manipulation.* The tone of the activities in the reception area was planned to keep people concerned about freedom of the press from thinking that GAA had resorted to unethical strong-arm tactics.

---

*To buttress their moral claims, GAA's leaders carried a supportive letter from author Merle Miller, formerly a *Harper's* editor: "Dear Willie and Robert and Midge et al: I would certainly be with my friends today if I did not have a previous commitment . . ."[27]

Indeed, the politicos believed that, edifying or not, the consciousness-raising approach would maximize the pressure put on publishing executives. They intended their private venting of rage to convince the editors that they would go to extreme lengths to challenge the publication of articles perpetuating the problems of homosexuals. They designed their front-office caper to make the news and expected the resulting publicity to impress liberal audiences, to raise moral and political questions about institutions whose success depended on their appearing principled but nonpolitical, and to shock other publishers enough so that they would think twice before publishing negative pieces about homosexuality.

So the *Harper's* zap marked the coming of age of a politico-cultural reformist approach to the job of changing culture: the approach of challenging culture-shaping institutions with demonstrations that combined consciousness-raising tactics with politicizing and pressuring tactics. Thereafter, consciousness-raising became more prominent in protests involving political targets, and consciousness-raising, politicizing, and pressure tactics were combined in demonstrations involving publishing houses, television and radio stations, motion picture enterprises, and scholarly and professional associations.

Yet for all that the demonstration at *Harper's* was an innovative reformist hybrid, each group of demonstrators continued to use its own strategic priorities to appraise the effort—the cultural reformers exulting because the zap had furthered the reputation of homosexuals for having cleverness and style, the political reformers congratulating themselves for having found a new way of suggesting that homosexuals had grievances serious enough to warrant militant political activism. Indeed, the *Harper's* zap showed hardcore political reformers that challenging the media was another way to convey politicizing messages, but it did little to convince them that it was essential to include consciousness-raising tactics or to allow for moral niceties when they set out to influence culture-shaping institutions.

The recalcitrance of the hardcore politicos was apparent in the planning for a zap involving television which they undertook while Fisher and his committee were orchestrating their dealings with *Harper's.* As members of GLF, Robinson and Owles had been made aware of the cultural roots of the homosexual's oppression, and though they had devoted most of their attention to politics after organizing GAA, they had called the producer of "The Dick Cavett Show" demanding an opportunity to respond to antihomosexual remarks that comedian Mort Sahl had made on the show in the spring of 1970. After a summer of temporizing responses from Cavett's program director and with renewed interest in relationships among culture, media, and politics provoked by the Epstein article, an Ad Hoc Cavett Action Committee was formed. To force Cavett to comply with GAA's demand for equal time, the politicos on the committee decided to infiltrate his studio audience and threaten to disrupt the taping of his program. The Cavett zap was scheduled for the evening of the *Harper's* zap.

After fifty members of GAA had obtained tickets for the October 27 show, Cavett's staff was notified. Failing to hear from them, GAA's "zap squad" trooped from the offices of *Harper's* to the television studio. Just before the studio audience was to be admitted, a staffer appeared, asked if there were GAAers present, and said that Cavett, who had seen coverage of the *Harper's* demonstration on the evening news, would meet with their representatives. After a short session, Cavett agreed to let two members of GAA appear on one of his programs.

Robinson and Evans were selected to appear on the November 27 show. As coached, they aired both the cultural and the political concerns of reformist gay liberationists. Asked what GAA was seeking, Robinson responded: "Heterosexuals live in this society without any scorn—they live openly, their affection is idealized in movies, theater. Homosexuals want the same thing: to be open in this society, to live a life without fear of reprisal from anybody for being homosexual—to live a life of respect."

Stressing that institutionalized discrimination inhibited the homosexual's freedom of self-expression, Evans pointed out that gays had to choose between personal fulfillment and survival: "We're faced with a kind of cruel alternative: if we deny our emotions, don't show them in public, and appear to be straight, then we can have a career; but if we're open, and show our affections the way heterosexuals do, and lead an open sexual life, then our careers are ended. We feel that it is repressive and unjust that we have to face the alternative. There is no reason why we can't be full people, both economically and in terms of our feelings!"

Questioned about strategy, Evans stressed that homosexuals needed to become aware and active in the political system: "We've a phrase called 'coming out'—gay people, when they first realize that they're gay, have a process of coming out, that is, coming out sexually. We've extended that to the political field. We feel that we *have* to come out politically, as a community which is aware that it is oppressed and which is a political power bloc feared by the government. Until the government is afraid of us—afraid of our power— we will never have our rights."

Robinson emphasized the need for homosexuals to be proud as well as political about their gay identities, taking issue with negative ideas about homosexuality perpetuated by articles like Epstein's: "I can say to Mr. Epstein that my own personal experience as a homosexual is that of a happy human being. That my homosexuality is one of the assets of my life. I like my life style. I love my lover. I'm happy being what I am. I don't see why Epstein should be trying to define how I should grow up. Rather, when his children grow up, he should wish them happiness and fulfillment in life."[28]

Robinson and Evans carefully acknowledged that both cultural and political reforms were necessary for the well-being of homosexuals; both personal and political education were needed, they said, to transform homosexuals into powerful community. Though firm in their political reformist priorities, the two shared the ambitions of their cultural reformist colleagues. If nothing else, they were reminded by the anxiety they felt at identifying themselves on national television as homosexual about how deeply people internalized the idea that admitting to a homosexual life would result in dire personal and professional consequences. Robinson had already told his parents that he was gay and abandoned all conventional professional aspirations. But Evans, still a graduate student at Columbia, was convinced that his television appearance would mean the end of his academic career; only after the taping did he dare call his parents and tell them that they would learn something important about their son if they watched that evening's "Dick Cavett Show."

Sensitive as they were to the power of social conditioning, GAA's political leaders remained pessimistic about changing established mores by dealing with institutions widely viewed as nonpolitical. They asked: How could one challenge the taboos and misconceptions about homosexuality such institutions perpetuated when the same taboos and misconceptions kept most of the institutions from dealing explicitly with homosexuality? How could one persuade people that cultural biases made homosexuals suffer when most of the suffering was hidden, and when part of the suffering was the psychic and emotional cost of having to hide pain? How could one rally those whose sexual self-expression was inhibited by traditional standards when most of them had so internalized these standards that they were unaware of them? How could one convince those who realized that society forced them to curb their sexual self-expression that the prospect of changing something so intangible as beliefs warranted enduring the costs of acknowledging their homosexuality publicly and joining in efforts to change something so sweeping as culture? The politicos admitted that events like the publication of Epstein's article and the broadcast of Mort Sahl's antihomosexual remarks provided openings for dealing directly with cultural problems because they made biases public and provided an occasion for gay activists to challenge them. But they argued that it was only on rare occasions that biases were aired so publicly and that in contexts not clearly political only limited steps could be taken.

If anything, the experience of the *Harper's* and Cavett zaps made the politicos even more convinced that cultural reformist objectives were most effectively pursued through political reformist enterprises.* Talking about gay rights not only suggested that homosexuals had political grievances, but also conveyed the impression that homosexual behavior was natural and prevalent. Spotlighting homosexuals through political demonstrations not only suggested that gays were determined to use political activism to secure political representation, but publicized that there were homosexuals who had developed fulfilling gay life styles and joined together in vital gay institutions. Getting politicians and public officials to announce that they supported gay rights not only developed public issues, attracted support, and established homosexuals as a political minority, but affirmed that homosexuals had a right to express sexual feelings, to

*Paradoxically, the more the cultural reformers were persuaded that it was difficult to deal directly with culture-shaping institutions, the more they believed that self-help and social activities affecting individuals best helped embolden homosexuals and build community. To counter the cultural reformist argument that gay identity-building and community organizing was best done apart from political demonstrations, the politicos quipped that "one good zap is worth ten years of analysis."

develop gay life styles, and to join together in a distinctive gay community.

. . .

During the summer and fall of 1970, the political reformers in charge of GAA worked to politicize their cultural reformist associates and to recast their initiatives so that they served political reformist priorities. Resentful cultural reformers responded by charging that the behavior of the politicos violated the countercultural ethos that individuals "do their own thing" and let others "do their own thing." The politicos retorted that GAA was concerned with this ethos only as it applied to homosexuality and that political activity was necessary to make it safe for homosexuals in society at large to "do their own thing." Disaffected cultural reformers responded with the radical contention that enhancing individual fulfillment and harmonious personal relations mattered more than staging initiatives to make society more humane—indeed, that only by proceeding in humane new ways could society be made more humane.

None of the GAAers who voiced these radical sentiments had the inclination or the intellectual drive to puzzle out what it was that countercultural values demanded of an organization committed to working within the political system and composed of individuals who enjoyed different roles and activities. Some simply dropped out, complaining that the politicos were unliberated. Others became angry and contentious, unaware that in their temper they might be violating the very principles they professed to be defending. In fact, the most disaffected cultural reformers began to assess the behavior of the politicos not open-mindedly, as their countercultural ideas would dictate, but using the criteria developed by radicals eager to equate specific traits and behavior with liberation.

The most vocal such critic was Arthur Bell, then in the throes of a bitter breakup with longtime lover Arthur Evans. During the fall of 1970, Bell's embrace of radical views led him to object to the "elitism" he discovered in the name and the closed meetings of GAA's Executive Committee and to the selfishness he saw in Jim Owles's reluctance to lend GAA's new stereo equipment to STAR, Street Transvestite Action Revolutionaries, a group formed by transvestites disillusioned by the Natasha incident and the controversy over the proposed transvestite demonstration. (Owles maintained that GAA had to protect its property.) As GAA's end-of-the-year elections approached, Bell and other newly radicalized GAAers decided to support Eben Clark rather than Owles or Evans for the office of president, taking the radical line that being liberated meant abandoning conventional ways and that social transformation would come as individuals adopted exemplary new ways of thinking and acting. He elaborated his views in a flier written to support Clark:

> Eben has mastered the art of understanding freedom and the needs that make for freedom. He can therefore free people from what they have been taught to be, and transform them into what they ought and want to be . . .
> We mention this because we feel that Eben Clark is the one person to save GAA from the false rhetoric, from the abstract gibberish, from the bogged-down parliamentary procedure, from the use and destruction of people as political pawns in a game of chess, from the massive ego power trips that pass for the yellow brick road to liberation.*

When Owles was re-elected, Bell and his followers continued their opposition by charging that none of the committee heads Owles appointed believed that "changing the laws mean nothing, if we can't change heads, too." Then the Bell-Clark faction, as their numbers swelled with radicals from the disintegrating GLF, proposed that GAA's constitution be changed so that committee members could select their own leaders. As supporters of the politicos responded with a campaign to preserve the existing arrangements, membership meetings degenerated into heated disputes between factions called "the left wing" and "the right wing." Before the end of February

---

*One gets a sense of how reform-oriented GAAers with countercultural values felt norma-tive radicals violated these values in the explanation Marc Rubin offered Arthur Bell in a personal letter:

> michael morissey asked me if gay liberation doesn't include truth and honesty. yes it does. all liberation includes this. but it also includes the right of an individual to be judged by himself and to weigh himself against the standard of liberation. i don't think it includes the concept of other-directed judgment. again, it was at a g.l.f. meeting that a bible was brought forth, the red book. g.a.a. doesn't have such a convenient bible. robert's rules give you a framework in which to act and think. the red book tells you what to think. the red book is anti-liberation for that reason. gay liberation is building in the work and in our selves that absolute rightness of being ourselves. attacks on other people and self-righteous accusations never liberated anybody.[29]

1971, GAA's political reformist command was faced with a conflict not unlike the one that had begun the breach between "social people" and "political people" the summer before.

This time the resolution took a very different shape. For although Bell, Clark, and others attracted to radical views formed only a small segment of GAA's social people, their agitation forced the politicos to deal with dissatisfaction and to vie for support by paying attention to the demands of members with cultural interests. Pete Fisher, in a seminar paper for one of his political science courses, described how the politicos came to commit GAA to cultural as well as political goals:

> As we continued talking, a general consensus began to evolve. There was almost an aura of conversion in the room. We began to refer more and more often to the "social people" rather than to the "left wing" . . . We began to speak of our "blindness" in denying them social ways in which to contribute to the movement and GAA . . .
>
> Kantrowitz said that the social people, headed by Diamond, had been frequently raising the concept of gay culture. What use, they argued, was the passage of legislation that would enable homosexuals to be openly gay without fear of losing their jobs, if there was no way to be gay outside of the tawdry bar scene? What must be developed in order for political gains to be meaningful was a new life style, an integral gay counterculture which could draw uptight gays out of their closets of secrecy and shame into a new expressive and creative way of life. What was needed, in effect, was the initiation of a grand social experiment, the creation of a new society within the old.[30]

Although Fisher wrote that he and other politicos were "converted" as they came to understand why the social people believed it important to develop "a new expressive and creative way of life," he made no mention of the theory of revolution through consciousness change that accounted for the social people's belief that self-help and social activities were in and of themselves political. Moreover, Fisher admitted that Owles and others may well have agreed to promote cultural as well as political activities simply to make sure that they—and GAA—survived. Arthur Bell expressed his doubts about ideological conversions on the part of the politicos in the flier he circulated before withdrawing from GAA to write *Dancing the*

Gay Lib Blues: "The patriarchal group, since the latest break-up threat . . . has claimed that they see the light . . . I hope that they are sincere, that this is more than just another political concession to save the organization . . ."

For whatever mix of organizational maneuvering and true intellectual awakening, the politicos demonstrated their commitment to cultural reformist thinking by creating an Ad Hoc Gay Culture Study Committee "to make recommendations to GAA for new committees whose purposes will be to foster the development of an indigenously gay culture and to create a sense of community among gays who are now culturally isolated from each other, and to make detailed recommendations for a voluntary program of consciousness-raising sessions."[31] To compensate for their hubris in the summer, they struck the directive to "raise political consciousness" from the mandate of the Social Affairs Committee and appended a statement specifying that "profits are not the primary purpose of such social affairs."

The challenge of developing "an indigenously gay culture" instilled cultural reformers with elaborate new ambitions. Beyond building pride and community by encouraging homosexuals to be free and open about their sexual feelings and enthusiastic about the gay subculture, they set out to discover and develop distinctively gay traits and behaviors. As in GLF, most of the cultural reformers were male homosexuals who thought of gay male life when they spoke of things gay. In the first issue of the *Gay Activist,* a GAA newsletter started to enhance unity through better communication, a leader of the Ad Hoc Gay Culture Study Committee left no doubt that his perspectives were male:

> Is there a specific gay culture? We know there's a specific type of subculture among gays. Like all other ghettoized minorities, gays have grouped together and developed their own slang and sensibility. *Camp,* for instance, and words like *cruising, humpy, trick,* and *poppers.* But is there a specific world view among gays? Some people said yes, some no. What we decided to do was find out by providing committees and workshops as forums in which gays could for the first time get together and create —openly, out of the closet—anything they wanted to do in a cultural context. We figured that if a gay culture exists, or could be created, it will emerge out of these workshops . . .

The Culture Committee decided to recommend committees and projects which celebrated, analyzed, or propagated gay liberation. By *celebrate,* we meant creatively, as in plays, art, music. By *analyze,* we meant looking inside ourselves, as in talk groups or through theater, documentaries, and even simply reading books. And by *propagate,* we meant telling people about it—gays and straights—through a speaker's bureau, films and television.

By *gay liberation,* we meant everything we do in GAA—the act of becoming ourselves without the guilt and neurosis society, our parents, and we ourselves put upon us.[32]

GAA's leaders had long talked about setting up a group headquarters, and the ambitiousness of the Culture Committee's program convinced them finally to act. In April 1971, when GAA had nineteen committees (additions recommended by the Culture Committee bolstered the number) and more than three hundred members, the Executive Committee voted to lease an abandoned firehouse near the intersection of Wooster and Spring streets in Soho, south of Greenwich Village.

GAA's Firehouse, as it continued to be known, rapidly became the base for gay cultural enterprises of unprecedented scope and variety. New committees explored gay themes in literature, theater, film, art, and music. Prominent figures like author Merle Miller and artist John Button gave talks about how their homosexuality affected their work. Dances were scheduled weekly and advertised widely. "Talk groups" were formed to help people come out.

Stigmatized as illicit, immoral, and unhealthy, nonpolitical enterprises associated with homosexuality had till now remained relatively modest and clandestine. By institutionalizing the cultural reformist approach to gay liberation, GAA took a giant step in the direction of legitimizing homosexual interests and promoting the idea that enjoying traditional gay pastimes was not only moral and salutary, but political. As more and more homosexuals, often without appreciating the political outlook most responsible for legitimizing and encouraging their activities, followed the lead of the first cultural reformers, there was a surfacing of the gay subculture and a proliferation of identifiably gay bars, discos, restaurants, bathhouses, bookstores, sex shops, artistic enterprises, publishing ventures, hotels, community centers, and neighborhoods. Directly and dramatically, the leaders of GAA paved the way for an explosion of gay life.

. . .

Although the politicos agreed to accommodate the cultural reformers by institutionalizing and promoting gay activity of every kind, they continued to believe that making homosexuals a politically influential minority was the key to gay liberation. Consequently, they pushed ahead with their efforts to politicize homosexuals. To minimize confusion about terminology, they insisted on identifying matters pertaining to life style, community, and culture as *cultural* and on reserving the term *political* for matters explicitly involving the political system. Readers of the first issue of the *Gay Activist* were subtly informed of the preferred usage:

> . . . newer members coming into GAA were frequently more interested in the so-called "cultural" aspects of gay liberation than they were in GAA's political zaps and legislative efforts. How to ensure coordination so that the political groups and the culture groups worked to support each other and the common goal of gay liberation? Clearly part of the answer was to gather everybody under one roof and have a little of what biologists call "cross fertilization" take place.[33]

Like the care taken to distinguish between endeavors cultural and political, the mention of cross fertilization attested not only to the politicos' continuing skepticism about the strategy of social and political change advocated by cultural reformers, but also to their persisting determination to use cultural activities for political ends. To politicize gays attracted to cultural events, they papered the Firehouse with literature advertising GAA's legislative, electoral, and protest initiatives; decorated it with a mural intended (in the socialist realist tradition) to show that gays were marching in the streets to protest injustice; played videotapes of dramatic demonstrations during dances; and mandated talk groups to "promote . . . awareness of the unity of personal and political liberation."

Continued reluctance to let cultural reformist ideas about what was political supplant their own was perhaps reflected most in the politicos' plans for educational outreach. In July 1971, after a year and a half of objecting that such efforts were "Mattachine," GAA's political leaders agreed to support the efforts of some who wanted to operate a speakers' bureau and to prepare materials on homosexuality for distribution in the schools. Those who proposed this educational outreach were persuaded to call themselves the Agitation-Propaganda Committee; at the urging of the politicos, their mandate specified that "our primary purpose is to politicize high school students who are gay, and to motivate them to assert their rights and dignity by coming out and joining the struggle for liberation."[34]

GAA's political leaders, in short, used every means they could to impart the message that being a liberated homosexual meant not only enjoying traditional gay pastimes freely and openly but also participating in gay political activity. As a result, their historic institutionalization of gay community-building activity was also an unprecedented program of gay politicization. The results of this were most visible in the growing size and scope of the demonstrations the Gay Activists Alliance sponsored to secure gay rights legislation.

8

The Drive for
Gay Rights Legislation

IN THE SPRING of 1970, when GAA's reformist leaders first looked for ways to politicize homosexuals, they decided that the issue of discrimination on the basis of sexual orientation was strategic. Not only would it concern a broad cross-section of homosexuals, they reasoned, but it would also win the attention of journalists, civic leaders, and political figures whose support would help legitimize homosexuals as a political minority.

The ease with which GAAers found members of the New York City Council willing to introduce legislation to protect homosexual rights confirmed their assessment. Though Carol Greitzer was wary, Theodore Weiss was willing to cosponsor a bill. Eldon Clingan agreed to help in any way he could. And Carter Burden responded to GAA's telephone inquiries with a copy of his proposed legislation to ban housing discrimination of any sort, including that involving sexual orientation. All this occurred before the end of May. Yet, buying time to gather documentation, muster support, and plot a legislative crusade that would have maximum impact, Alliance strategists postponed their push for gay rights legislation until the fall.

Meanwhile, most of the politicos worked at challenging political candidates to speak out about gay rights, and the responsibility for pursuing gay rights legislation devolved to Richard Amato, a Babylon, Long Island, resident who, in the middle and late 1960s, had been president of Suffolk County Young Democrats, a candidate for the county legislature, and a staff worker in Robert Kennedy's Senate campaign. In December 1969, when GAA was organized, Amato was working in the gubernatorial campaign of Nassau County executive Eugene Nickerson. In fact, he was at Nickerson's side when members of the fledgling Alliance questioned him and other Democratic candidates at the Village Independent Democrats meeting. When Arthur Goldberg was ultimately nominated, Amato felt free to investigate the group that had so surprised him by challenging his boss to speak out about gay rights. Learning that Marty Robinson and Jim Owles were unperturbed by his reluctance to go public about his homosexuality, he agreed to help by preparing a report on employment discrimination for submission to the Human Rights Commission.

By advertising in the new local gay newspapers for cases of discrimination, writing for job application forms, and sending openly gay individuals to apply for jobs, Amato gathered evidence that many private firms and governmental agencies refused to employ admitted or obvious homosexuals. In addition, he discovered that firms sometimes employed private investigating agencies to study the sexual habits of job applicants and employees. Amato's report described the work of some of these investigators and presented case studies of individuals who had lost their jobs after checks into police and draft records had uncovered their homosexuality. Yet his concluding paragraph, a poignant commentary on Amato's own situation, acknowledged that the problem was as much the threat of unfair treatment that kept homosexuals fearful and inhibited as the actual denial and loss of jobs: "How many employees now leading double lives . . . can assert their dignity as human beings by lifting the cloud of secrecy around their lives, knowing that such an assertion would result in a cutoff of income and financial ruination?"[1]

Like many, Amato came to GAA convinced that life was difficult for homosexuals but unaware of the extent of actual discrimination. He was taken aback, and drawn more deeply into GAA, by the instances of real abuse he discovered. Toward the end of the summer, Eleanor Holmes Norton echoed William Booth's conclusion offered to MSNY five years earlier by stating that employment discrimination on the basis of sexual preference was a problem worthy of HRC concern, but that it would take legislation to bring the matter under the commission's jurisdiction. Amato agreed to head GAA's Municipal Fair Employment Law Committee.

Upon becoming chairman, Amato announced that his committee would try to persuade the Human Rights Commission to hold public hearings on employment discrimination, "there to confront offending employers and 'pre-employment' investigatory agencies in order to focus public attention on discrimination against gays." In an interview with Donn Teal he elaborated: "Such public attention could prompt the Council to action—with the inside help of councilmen favorable to it."[2]

As his remarks suggest, Amato brought to GAA the views he had developed as a liberal Democrat, and he approached the matter of fair employment legislation more like a homophile leader than a liberationist. As a liberal, Amato saw discrimination as a violation of equal opportunity; he wanted to pursue gay rights legislation to make the public aware of its prejudices and to effect equal opportunity and integration. As liberationists, Robinson, Owles, and Evans saw employment discrimination as an issue with which to establish homosexuals as political minority; they saw legislation as a vehicle for politicizing homosexuals and winning official support. Amato was a seasoned politician, skilled in the traditional give-and-take, comfortable with the time and tact it required, confident that conventional lobbying and public relations would result in legislation and social change. The political reformers were imaginative mobilizers, eager to develop politicizing tactics, excited about using their dealings with public officials as theater, and not at all sure how to balance the politicizing publicity that would come from a legislative crusade with the legitimacy and protections that would come from the actual passage of a gay rights bill.

During the summer, when GAA's political leaders were busy soliciting support from candidates and deterring cultural reformers from diluting political priorities, Amato was left to do what he wished. But in the fall, the push for gay rights legislation took center stage, and conflicts developed because GAAers with different political outlooks wanted different things from the pursuit of legislation.

The first serious clash came shortly after New York state's elections. Amato was at work collecting affidavits from homosexuals who believed they had been discriminated against and trying to persuade Eleanor Holmes Norton that there was material enough to justify HRC hearings. He was also drawing up a bill with Eldon Clingan and sounding out potential supporters for it. The conflict came after *New York Post* reporter Lindsy Van Gelder, in a story about the progress of GAA's pursuit of gay rights legislation, quoted Jim Owles as saying that GAA prided itself on the use of sit-ins, demonstrations, and disruptions, that since "most politicians wouldn't help us if we didn't apply pressure, we'll do all that to the City Council members who don't go along," and that if the HRC failed to hold hearings, "we'll sit in there too."[3] When Norton saw Owles's remarks, she berated Amato. At the next Executive Committee meeting, Amato charged that Owles was out to sabotage GAA's legislative drive and resigned as chairman of his committee.

Ironically, more than other political reformers, Owles was inclined to believe that actual policy changes were as important as the publicity produced by pursuing them. This was evidenced by his tendency to argue for restrained demonstrations and diligent negotiations when others called for provocative challenges and uncompromising demands. At the demonstration in Times Square against police harassment, for example, Owles had insisted on folding up GAA's banner when GLFers led the march down to the headquarters of the sixth precinct in the Village. And after the bloody rioting that followed, he had opposed the Police Power Committee's proposal that GAA henceforth refuse to negotiate with the police. That early, Owles and his supporters were identified as genuine political reformers, while Evans and his followers were perceived as revolutionaries who viewed reformism as a stage necessary to prepare the gay minority for a larger struggle. Evans, trying to attract support for a run against Owles for the presidency of the Alliance, encouraged this distinction.

Owles saw what Evans was doing and realized that his chances for re-election depended on retaining the support of other genuine political reformers without losing any votes from cultural reformers to radical converts like Arthur Bell. Until GAA's leaders had put an end to strictly social affairs and worked to involve all GAAers in political demonstrations, the cultural crowd had been content to leave political matters to the politicos. However, once they were persuaded to turn their attention to political matters, they began to assess them with cultural reformist and radical perspectives. Committed, clear-thinking cultural reformers insisted only that the politicos proceed in ways that encouraged other homosexuals to be openly gay, but those influenced by radical thinking warned that involvement in the political system was inevitably corrupting. They urged the politicos to avoid back-room deals, sellouts, and manipulation.

Unfortunately, demonstrations and other activity staged primarily for public relations met the standards of culturally oriented GAAers, but the types of dealings that the genuine political reformers believed necessary to pass legislation did not. As Amato, Marc Rubin, and other veterans of conventional politics tried to explain, smoothing the way for legislative success called for private meetings where individuals could engage in give-and-take and reach compromise solutions—endeavors that did not necessarily compromise ethical principles or personal integrity. Owles knew as much, but as GAA's elections neared he trumpeted about the need for demands and confrontations in order to retain the support of politicized cultural reformers.

Although Amato had been able to lie low during the summer, he became a lightning rod for criticism in the fall. Cultural reformers complained that he was closeted about his homosexuality; that he chose to live in the suburbs with a lover instead of immersing himself in the gay subculture; that, because he was formal, inexpressive, and "tight," he seemed in no way "gay." Radicals added that Amato was uneasy with transvestites, uninterested in alternate life styles, and enmeshed in The System.

The more the cultural crowd became convinced that Amato was unliberated, the more they tried to make sure that GAA's pursuit of gay rights legislation reflected their values and not his. When Amato reported that Eleanor Holmes Norton had offered to schedule a private meeting between gay political leaders and city councilors, GAA's membership, urged on by cultural leaders, voted "that GAA will only participate in *open* hearings on a Fair Employment bill."[4] When Norton appeared to be trying to avoid having the HRC itself hold hearings, cultural leaders applauded politicos—like Owles—who promised sit-ins and demonstrations to force her hand.

The challenge for the politicos was not just to pursue gay rights legislation in ways that did not displease members with cultural outlooks, but to do so in ways that kept these members enthusiastic about demonstrations. To meet this challenge, the politicos moved to make their strategy of legislative pursuit exceptionally open, principled, and militant.

As a first step, the politicos prepared for GAA's lobbyists to show to those they were lobbying a supplement to Amato's report on employment discrimination that outlined the steps that would be taken to get gay rights legislation. The first item on the list concerned "lobbying efforts in the City Council." Council members who needed to be convinced that it was moral to vote for gay rights legislation "would be," it explained: "One councilman indicated to the G.A.A. over the phone that although he is a civil libertarian and for the bill on ideological grounds, he might nonetheless be forced to vote against the bill because of his 'Jewish constituency' . . . The G.A.A. is enlisting the support of Jewish leaders who will in time educate this particular councilman of the fair-mindedness and true civil libertarian nature of the Jewish community."

The second item on the list proposed to counter the argument that supporting gay rights was political suicide by listing candidates who had spoken out in favor of it and then been elected to office in the fall. Again, information intended to reassure potential supporters was complemented with that intended to goad those who might be unclear about or reluctant to do their moral duty: "The G.A.A. plans to make the issue an even more effective one in the 1971 elections . . . Plans are now underway to unify the gay vote in preparation for exposing those candidates who oppose gay human rights, and to consolidate support behind those who support human rights for homosexuals."

This self-righteous-sounding accounting of traditional political inducements was followed by a description of tactics somewhat less routine. Explaining that the newness of the homosexual rights issue required that people be impressed with its importance, the supplement on strategy pointed out that public hearings were essential and that demonstrations and lobbying would be pursued simultaneously: "Zap actions, which are now a perfected technique of the G.A.A., will continue against offenders in an attempt to pinpoint to the public the frequency and source of discrimination." Asserting that the mayor's failure to become involved gave the lie to deputy mayor Aurelio's assurances that Lindsay "would take action at the appropriate time," the supplement promised that "zap actions and other techniques will be employed against the Mayor until Mr. Lindsay takes definite and positive action." Not even council members were spared the threat of confrontation: "Zap actions will increase in militancy commensurate with developments in the City Council . . . The gay community is impatient for recognition of its human rights, and any delay in or unfavorable action on the Clingan-Burden bill will result in increased militancy in support of corrective action."[5]

If it was somewhat unusual to tell the officeholders one was lobbying just how they were being lobbied, it was even more unconventional to threaten them with protest demonstrations if they failed to respond as desired. In fact, the whole idea of presenting the officials one hoped to influence with a game plan telling them how they were *going* to be influenced departed significantly from established practice. Amato and other politically experienced GAAers recognized this, but they saw that they had to balance strategic with organizational considerations and to proceed in ways that would please their culturally oriented colleagues.

Promising to proceed with openness, principle, and militancy— and outlining on paper a strategy for doing so—were only two of the ways the politicos sought to keep the support of the cultural crowd. Another was to issue "demands" to officials in public and make "requests" in private. Others were to confine organizational discussions of legislative strategy to committee meetings and to place the responsibility for dealing with public officials in the hands of different committees with trusted chairmen.

In line with this last tactic, separate committees were created to handle dealings with state and with local officials, and leaders popular with the membership were put in charge of each. The responsibility for negotiations involving fair employment legislation went to a new Municipal Government Committee headed by Marc Rubin, who had learned the ropes of local politics as president of the Bolivar-Douglass Reform Democratic Club in the East Village and had renewed his contacts recently while representing GAA at the New Democratic Coalition and then managing the Ad Hoc 1970 Elections Committee. Richie Amato was persuaded to resume control of the Municipal Fair Employment Law Committee and to bolster his credibility by concentrating on devising demonstrations that would focus public attention on the employment discrimination issue.

As the formation of a new committee to deal with state officials implied, GAA's involvement in the 1970 elections had opened up opportunities for legislative initiatives in Albany as well as at City Hall. Indeed, although GAA's leaders considered Greenwich Village their political base, they had tried to demonstrate the clout of the gay voting bloc by going to the East Side and publicizing the progay positions of Antonio Olivieri, running as a Democrat for an assembly seat held for fifty-four years by a Republican. After beating the incumbent by seven hundred votes, Olivieri had thanked GAA for its help and acknowledged the support of his gay constituents by joining with Brooklyn assemblyman Stephen Solarz to hold a public hearing on the problems of homosexuals. Early in February 1971, Olivieri, Solarz, and eleven other city-based assemblymen held a press conference to announce that they were introducing bills in the state legislature to proscribe discrimination on the basis of sexual orientation in employment and housing and to repeal the sodomy laws. State senators Roy Goodman and Harrison Goldin had already introduced similar bills.

Although GAA's political leaders instructed the head of the new State Government Committee to work with these state legislators, and although they led GAA into marches and lobbying sessions at the state capitol, they saw that legislative efforts on the city level were a better vehicle for establishing homosexuals as a legitimate political minority and left responsibility for the state legislative push to a Gay Liberation Front in Albany. As a result, local gay rights legislation remained the focus of debate about the style of legislative pursuit most compatible with the quest for gay liberation.

.   .   .

By combining the knowhow of experienced political negotiators like Rubin and Amato with the daring of ingenious political mobilizers like Robinson and Evans, GAA's Executive Committee thought it could accomplish the feat of politicizing homosexuals while passing legislation—the first gay rights legislation in the country. As the Municipal Government Committee courted influential supporters, the Fair Employment Law Committee would carry out publicity-generating demonstrations. While lobbyists worked to win over council members, demonstrators would stir up popular support.

The political sophistication responsible for this two-pronged approach also guided the decision to ask Eldon Clingan to be GAA's chief legislative sponsor. By the end of 1970 councilors Burden, Weiss, and Greitzer had all agreed to introduce bills, but these politicians were secure in their seats and had little need for a new and controversial cause. Clingan had just been elected Manhattan's councilman-at-large on the Liberal Party ticket, and it was judged he would be hungry for an issue with which to build his borough-wide constituency.

Whatever his motivations, Clingan responded to GAA's overtures by moving quickly to draft gay rights legislation. On January 6, 1971, he and Carter Burden held a press conference to announce that they were introducing a bill to extend the protection of New York City's Human Rights Law by adding the words *sexual orientation* to each of its clauses, and that to marshal support for their measure they were organizing a committee of prominent citizens. Thereafter, Clingan taught GAA's lobbyists about council procedures, introduced them to council colleagues, suggested individuals they might ask to be on the citizens' committee, and provided his office as a base for letter-writing, telephoning, and negotiating forays on behalf of "Intro 475," as the bill became known.

Clingan, Rubin, and Amato told lobbyists from the Municipal Government Committee that they had to educate the City Council. The lobbyists tried to do this in meetings with individual councilors by describing unpleasant personal experiences they had had because of their homosexuality and by talking about cases of police harassment and discrimination. The councilors who agreed to see the GAAers tended to be sympathetic about personal problems but doubtful that there were enough institutional abuses to warrant legislation. While members of the Municipal Government Committee responded with copies of Amato's report on employment discrimination, their colleagues on the Fair Employment Law Committee scheduled demonstrations designed to show both that discrimination against homosexuals was a serious problem and that liberated gay life styles were vital and rewarding.

While researching the private investigating agencies used by businesses to identify and exclude homosexuals, Amato had read an article in *Playboy* reporting that during a meeting of the Association of Stock Exchange Brokers, the president of one such agency, Fidelifacts, had explained, "Establishing that someone is a homosexual is often difficult, but I like to go on the rule of thumb that if one looks like a duck, walks like a duck, associates only with ducks, and quacks like a duck, he is probably a duck."[6] To make the public aware of the work of these investigating agencies, sixty-five GAAers armed themselves with little rubber duckies and followed Marty Robinson, dressed as a large white duck, in a spirited picket line in front of the 42nd Street headquarters of Fidelifacts. Jim Owles told the journalists invited to cover the event: "The important thing is to draw the public's attention to the existence of Fidelifacts and other companies like it. We'll need broad support for the passage of the Clingan-Burden Fair Employment Bill, and it is actions like this that will make the public aware of the problems of discrimination that gay people have to deal with."[7] Owles assumed that the ingenuity of the duck motif and the demonstrators' enthusiasm were enough to convey the messages about gay people that the cultural reformers thought it important to send to homosexuals.

Amato's report also maintained that the Household Finance Corporation (HFC) used information from private investigating agencies to deny homosexual applicants loans—an additional dimension of the discrimination issue. On March 1, GAA zap squads distributed leaflets at HFC branch offices and then gathered for a large demonstration at its main headquarters on Park Avenue. While a few angry politicos demanded that HFC executives justify their antihomosexual policies, happy cultural reformers danced in the aisles between desks for the benefit of television cameras.

GAA's political strategists had always prided themselves on the cleverness of their zaps. But their heightened sensitivity to the aspirations of the cultural reformers encouraged them to give special flair to demonstrations promoting the Clingan-Burden Bill. Pete Fisher and Marc Rubin, now lovers, were particularly enthusiastic about showing that homosexuals endowed even their political activities with humor and style. After learning that an article in the *New York Post* on homosexual marriages performed in a local gay church had provoked city clerk Herman Katz to threaten to put an end to the mock ceremonies, Fisher and Rubin decided to highlight this display of official prejudice by holding an "engagement party" at the city clerk's office for two gay male couples (including John Basso, who a year later tried to rob a Brooklyn bank to finance a sex change operation for his lover, an event dramatized in the film *Dog Day Afternoon).* While the hosts of GAA's party distributed coffee and doughnuts to Katz's clerical staff, the couples posed for photographers beside a large wedding cake topped with two little sets of same-sex figurines and the message "Gay Power to Gay Lovers." Pictures of the party appeared in several local newspapers and, later in 1971, were used to introduce the feature on gay liberation that *Life* magazine included in its Year in Review issue.

Although the calculated cleverness of these zaps was a bow to the ambitions of the cultural reformers, the ever-present messages that discrimination against homosexuals was a very real problem and that militant action was necessary to deal with it kept the political agenda clear. "Heavier" demonstrations stressing political points were interspersed with the lighter ones. The "quack-in" at Fidelifacts was followed by a picket line at the board of education, where GAAers presented affidavits attesting to incidents of discrimination in the New York City school system. When Chancellor Harvey Scribner succeeded in defusing the protest by insisting that the board of examiners was responsible for licensing teachers, a sit-in at the board's headquarters followed, and five GAAers were arrested. The arrested five dubbed themselves the "Board of Examiners Cross-Examiners," and Gertrude Unser, chairman of the board, was pilloried in leaflets as "Bedroom Busybody of the Week."

Even as GAA's political leaders led their troops into demonstrations, they continued to negotiate. Early in the spring of 1971, after being told by several members of the council that they would get their bill if the mayor worked for it, Robinson and Owles wrote a letter asking newly sworn Congresswoman Bella Abzug to help them reach Lindsay. Repeating recommendations from the supplement on strategy appended to Amato's study of employment discrimination, they explained that Lindsay could help by making a public statement in support of Intro 475, by issuing an executive order barring discrimination in all city jobs and in all private firms doing business with the city (they pointed out that the 1967 "breakthrough" MSNY took credit for was only a Civil Service Department regulation), and by using his influence to steer Intro 475 through public hearings, out of the General Welfare Committee, and past the full council.

While Robinson and Owles warned Abzug and others that the mayor's continued aloofness might result in events, like rioting, that would cost him support, Marc Rubin worked to reach Lindsay by pointing out that the mayor's support for gay rights legislation would help him politically. In the fall of 1970, when the Police Power Committee had been hell-bent on forcing Lindsay to speak out about police harassment, GAA's contact with the mayor's office had been Barry Gottehrer, Lindsay's liaison for minority groups. Preferring to begin GAA's legislative push with a clean slate, Rubin worked to establish cordial relations with mayoral aide Ronnie Eldridge. He told Eldridge that gay rights was a new item on the liberal agenda and that the mayor, who was talking about running for President, could secure his position as the darling of the liberals by seeing to the passage of Intro 475.

Eldridge was sympathetic, but she pointed out that Lindsay needed to broaden his base of support if he intended to run for President; further, she maintained that the majority leader, not the mayor, was the key to the council. Nevertheless, in May 1971, Eldridge helped produce a letter in which Lindsay lauded Clingan and Burden for their "leadership in bringing this problem to public attention." In June, she set the stage for mayoral assistant Edward Morrison to call for public hearings on gay rights legislation.

By the beginning of June, councilmen Leonard Skolnick and Theodore Weiss had joined the sponsors of Intro 475, and public statements of support had been issued by Eleanor Holmes Norton, City Council president Sanford Garelik, Environmental Protection Agency commissioner Jerome Kretchmar, and Manhattan Borough president Percy Sutton. Two-thirds of the City Council had given visiting GAA lobbyists encouraging responses. But majority leader Thomas Cuite, though courteous to the GAAers who visited his office, showed no signs of giving the sanction or scheduling the hearings that would permit Intro 475 to be reported out of committee.

This inaction disturbed the politicos because Cuite seemed almost invulnerable politically. Having represented a conservative district in Brooklyn for twenty years, Cuite was not ambitious for the support of liberals, rights-conscious voters, or the gay voting bloc. If anything, he seemed to covet the anonymity that protected his monopoly of power. To put pressure on Cuite by threatening his privacy, GAA's politicos decided to make the majority leader the target of the protest activities they planned for the second annual Gay Pride Week.

On the first day of Gay Pride Week II, GAA's leaders led a

candlelight procession to City Hall, where the marchers were addressed by councilor Eldon Clingan. About the letter of congratulation he had received from the mayor Clingan observed: "You know, that letter wasn't written because the people thought it was a nice bill. It was because people from the Gay Activists Alliance kept after the Mayor's office until they finally produced a letter of support from him. Now what we have to do is keep after them and make that support become something very real and tangible."[8] For the next five days, however, the signs carried by the picketers on City Hall Plaza complained of the council majority leader's lack of support. At the end of the week, when police prevented a contingent of GAAers from making their way to Cuite's office, a fracas occurred in which four of GAA's five officers were arrested. Thirty rank-and-file GAAers defied the threat of incarceration and jeered at the police until five more were arrested. Videotapes from the scene were rushed to the Firehouse and shown at a dance being held to commemorate the rioting on Christopher Street that had erupted two years before.

The clash at City Hall did result in a meeting with Cuite, who said only that he would continue to consider GAA's request for hearings. This brought to a boil long-simmering differences over how best to politicize homosexuals. Jim Owles and his supporters argued for continued moderation, while Arthur Evans and his followers retorted that militancy would do more to stir homosexuals.

To some extent, the disagreement was one between genuine political reformers and revolutionaries who saw the pursuit of bread-and-butter reforms simply as a stage. But it also reflected differing assessments of the degree to which homosexuals were ripe for politicization. Owles gauged that most homosexuals thought they managed rather successfully and needed to be seduced into believing that they had anything to gain from becoming involved in politics. Evans, on the contrary, held that most homosexuals harbored repressed rage and that one had to prick gay facades to tap deep-seated anger and trigger political involvement. Writing on the need for angry rhetoric in his manuscript on "The Oppression of Homosexuals," Evans elaborated:

Rhetoric is an important tactical weapon, especially during this first stage of the struggle. The rhetoric of the spokesmen of the vehicle must be carefully planned, making it relevant to the psychology of oppressed homosexuals. Specifically, the best rhetoric to use is that of righteous anger, both in choice of words and in the style of delivery. The reason for the use of angry rhetoric is this: all homosexuals (including those who appear to be doggedly apolitical) have experienced enormous personal rage at their own oppression. In the course of the years, for the sake of "adjustment" to heterosexual mores (passing as straight), this anger has been swallowed and pushed down into the inner soul. There it has festered, and, lacking any political outlet, has turned into guilt and self-hatred. The spokesmen for the vehicle must speak with thunder, bringing this buried anger to the surface and directing [it] against the state and the political powers that control the state.[9]

In the winter and spring of 1971, by engaging simultaneously in clever demonstrations, serious public challenges, and confidential negotiations, GAA bridged the differences not only between political reformers and cultural reformers, but also between politicos favoring moderate tactics and those advocating militancy. But when political prospects turned sour, the political reformers in favor of moderation were challenged by militants bent on provocation, and both were forced to acquiesce to cultural reformers and radicals convinced that changing attitudes was more important than getting a gay rights law. The drive for Intro 475 became ever more volatile.

. . .

Just before daylight on July 18, 1971, four hundred agents of the Federal-State Joint Strike Force Against Organized Crime invaded the premises of nine unlicensed after-hours clubs, most of them catering to homosexuals. Customers were politely asked to leave, but managers and employees were arrested. The next morning, strike force chief Daniel P. Hollman told reporters that the crackdown was intended not to harass homosexuals but to close illegal businesses that were a major source of income for organized crime. *Gay* reported that the reaction of homosexuals was "generally good," quoting the owner of several gay bars on the East Side as saying, "Gay bar owners are stereotyped. Everybody thinks of us as fronts for the Mafia. Most of us who run licensed gay bars are gay, and our money is honest money, raised by us and our gay friends. I say 'right on!' to the cops. The underworld competes unfairly with us, hurts our business, and ruins our reputation."[10]

All the same, the news of the raids produced nothing but anger among members of GAA who were convinced that the police and the Mafia worked hand in hand to bilk hapless homosexuals. Police raided bars, they felt sure, to force the owners to pay bribes to stay open. Police extortion forced bars into the hands of those who could turn to underworld financing in order to make payoffs, and consequently many gay bars were run by unsympathetic characters who charged high prices and invested little in decor and upkeep. These beliefs were only reinforced the following day, when the chief of New York City's police detectives identified one "front man for the Mob" as Mike Umbers, the proprietor of an after-hours bar called Christopher's End and two other Christopher Street establishments known as the Studio Book Shop and Gay Dogs. Two days later, Umbers held a press conference to announce that Christopher's End was reopening as a juice bar. In the words of a sign he posted on the premises: "Open Again—Weirdo Sex—Christopher's End—Now."

What complicated matters was that Umbers presented himself as a benefactor of the gay community. At his press conference, he condemned police harassment of homosexual establishments and contended that he contributed to gay liberation by providing homosexuals with hard-to-get jobs, goods, and places to go after four o'clock in the morning, the legal closing time for local bars: "Some people try to paint me as a gay exploiter. I'm not. I'm a gay catalyst. I try to make things happen and give the gay community things they want and can't get elsewhere. I think I do more for gay liberation in the long run than any of the organizations."[11]

One could not make an issue out of the raids on the after-hours bars without alienating segments of the gay male community, Jim Owles and his supporters were convinced. The Owles camp was all in favor of gay-run sexual and social outlets that were more attractive and "upfront" than Umbers's, but they knew that Syndicate-supported establishments played a key role in providing homosexuals with erotic books, magazines, and movies, with sex toys and sex-enhancing drugs, and with back rooms for late-night cruising and sex. They also believed that the emergence of the gay liberation movement—and the lines of communication that GAA had established with city officials—had brought a flowering of legitimate gay enterprise and a reduction of illegal police behavior. Given the circumstances, Owles and his friends argued that making an issue of the strike force raids might politicize a few homosexuals who were still sensitive about the issue of police harassment, but would also tarnish GAA's reputation by making it look like a defender of the Mafia. On the other hand, demonstrating against Syndicate exploitation might show that GAA was committed to community self-determination, but would antagonize those whose vision of liberation included access to the illicit goods and opportunities made available thanks to the underworld.

Though the moderate camp hesitated to act, their militant associates were convinced that the strike force raids and their aftermath provided an excellent opportunity for demonstrations. Arthur Bell and others contended that a demonstration against Mafia-run bars would not only strike a blow for community self-determination by warning the Syndicate that homosexuals intended to resist exploitation, but also alert habitués of the gay subculture that more humane alternatives, like GAA's cultural events, were available. Arthur Evans and his followers argued that militant action directed at the police would make an impression on homosexuals still skeptical about the need for political activism.

Seeking to placate colleagues and to appeal to homosexuals with different priorities, Owles called a press conference to discuss the problems of Syndicate control and police complicity. In front of reporters, he tried to please everybody. For homosexuals who felt strongly about ending Mafia involvement in gay establishments, Owles stressed that GAA was interested in eliminating exploitation; for those who enjoyed illicit opportunities, he pointed out that homosexuals were "nocturnally inclined" and that the existing laws about bar closing times were discriminatory; for those in favor of promoting gay-run establishments, Owles spoke of using institutions like the unoccupied Women's House of Detention and the vacated sixth precinct headquarters as gay social centers; for those set on militancy, he warned that GAA might have to seize these buildings if the city remained obtuse about "its moral obligation to provide places for gay people."[12]

Although Owles's balancing act was applauded, a group of GAAers infuriated by Umbers's brazenness set out on their own to demonstrate in front of Christopher's End. When some of Umbers's employees threatened to retaliate against GAA, members of this group, at an emergency meeting of the Executive Committee, insisted that GAA meet the challenge with a demonstration. In the excitement, Owles's arguments about the need for caution were overwhelmed by Evans's eloquence about the power of confrontation. That Saturday night, according to plan, more than a thousand people were led from a GAA dance to the front of Christopher's End, where a marcher snatched the sign about "weirdo sex." The crowd moved on to the vacated Charles Street police station, where Owles ripped up the sign and demanded that the city provide gay social centers. The odyssey ended at the new sixth precinct station house, where the smaller crowd still in tow chanted, "The syndicate in blue has got to go."

Before he agreed to these plans, Owles made the militants promise that there would be no attempt to force the police to make arrests. He also arranged for leaflets to be circulated informing homosexuals that GAA was making a scene only at one notorious bar and was not campaigning against bars in general. But the march on Christopher's End was a clear triumph for those who believed that GAA had to be more provocative. Thereafter, the strategy of inspiring people to be open about their homosexuality by enchanting them with the charm and zest of liberated gay activists gave way to efforts to goad homosexuals to come out by charging that closeted lives were unfulfilling and apolitical. The attempt to induce homosexuals to develop political awareness by publicizing their grievances was replaced with a drive to jolt homosexuals into political conscientiousness by demonstrating how essential activism was to freedom.

One sign of this turn to militancy was the resurrection of the Police Power Committee, which had languished as a subcommittee of the Municipal Government Committee during the winter and spring of moderation. A revealing new mandate explained its name change to the Police Action Committee: "With the institution of action against the Mafia/Syndicate operations in the City, GAA is entering into a new phase of Gay Liberation. From July 23rd and 24th, we have started a *hot war* against corruption, oppression, harassment, entrapment, bias, bigotry and procrastination in equality for GAYS in the law enforcement agencies in the country, *not just in New York City!*"

As the stress on countrywide efforts suggested, Evans and other militants were enthusiastic not only about the Police Action Committee but about the National Gay Movement Committee that had been established to help homosexuals in other locales set up groups like GAA. The plan was to have Alliance members from New York share their experience with homosexuals in other parts of the country and to use incidents elsewhere to point up the injustices that made it necessary for Manhattan's homosexuals to band together. It was reported, for example, that police in Bridgeport, Connecticut, were refusing to interfere with gangs of teenagers who were harassing openly gay beachgoers. At the end of July, when a Connecticut gay liberation group called for help, members of GAA–New York (as they began to identify themselves) went to Bridgeport to demonstrate.

But the most dramatic evidence of GAA's new militancy was the decision to protest an incident of police entrapment on Fire Island in early August. Shortly afterward, members of GAA–Long Island, which members of the National Gay Movement Committee had helped form, asked GAA–New York to help rally homosexuals in Suffolk County by holding a demonstration on Fire Island. Owles warned that nothing could do more to alienate New York City homosexuals who made Fire Island their vacation retreat; Evans countered that bold steps were necessary "to prick gay facades." Owles insisted that unpleasant confrontations scared and offended more homosexuals than they enlightened; Evans retorted that dramatic provocation was often a prerequisite for politicization. When Owles threatened to resign if the demonstration on Fire Island were approved, the militants agreed to compromise by having GAA join its Long Island counterpart in a nonviolent picket line in front of the Suffolk County police headquarters at Hauppauge.

On the day of this demonstration, despite complaints from GAA's officers, the police stood frozen while carloads of local teenagers drove by and shouted insults at the picketers. When one of the hecklers flung a sign saying "Queers Suck," a picketer held it up for all to see. A police officer tried to wrestle the sign away, and in the scuffle that followed, one GAAer was roughly arrested and the rest were dispersed with mace.

A week later, two hundred GAAers returned to express their outrage by seizing the office of the Suffolk County district attorney at Riverhead. Their eviction by the police resulted in another bloody fracas. Arthur Evans's response to the bloodshed was quoted in a *New York Post* story, "Homosexuals vs. 'Small Town Fascists' ": "It's going to be a reenactment of the 1960s civil rights movement and we know there will be serious consequence to life and limb."[13]

Although Owles had stayed on the front lines during the hot suburban summer—not least because Evans was rallying support for a second try for the presidency—with the onset of fall he joined those who urged a refocusing of attention on the Clingan-Burden bill. After the early summer meetings with the council's majority leader, there had been promises that the General Welfare Committee would act on Intro 475. But in spite of Marc Rubin's regular telephone calls and visits to City Hall, and despite repeated promises from Saul Sharison, chairman of the General Welfare Committee, no date for hearings was set.

By the beginning of September, Rubin and others were convinced that only demonstrations would bring hearings. Although they were sure that the person responsible for the delay was majority leader Cuite, they resolved to reach him through Sharison, who seemed more vulnerable because he represented a district nearby on the Lower East Side. In the middle of September, GAA's Executive Committee sent a letter to Sharison, Cuite, and Lindsay stating that if a date for hearings was not announced by September 30, "The denial of our rights and needs . . . has moved us to the point where we are willing to take the full power of our anger and frustration into the streets."[14]

When September 30 arrived without word of progress, about a hundred GAAers walked over to Sharison's high-rise apartment building and milled around in the lobby. The demonstrators agreed to leave almost as soon as the police arrived, but they left word that they would be back in greater numbers the following Saturday night if hearings on Intro 475 were left unscheduled.

Saturday night's event was meant to have impact. For by this time, although GAA's membership had leveled off at around three hundred, its weekly dances attracted five times that many. The plan was to stop the dance after midnight, lead hundreds of demonstrators to the foot of Sharison's apartment building, and have a half-dozen GAAers sit in on the floor of the lobby until they were arrested.

As always, the demonstration was meant to be militant but non-violent. Even ardent advocates of provocation like Arthur Evans believed that violence would put an end to GAA's effectiveness. During the summer, GAA's leaders had asked members to attend training sessions on the art of nonviolent demonstrating. The fliers they handed out before each demonstration exhorted, "DON'T provoke, by action or word, any violent actions under any circumstance except in self-defense. (Note: GAA cannot, according to its constitution, provide legal assistance for anyone who knowingly provokes, advocates or instigates any form of violence not in self-defense)." Despite these precautions, the plan for the Sharison protest worried the politicos because it involved recruits from GAA's dance who would lack "zap training" and who would not necessarily be committed to GAA and its policy of nonviolence.

While Marc Rubin was busy organizing the Sharison zap, his lover, Pete Fisher, was working to complete *The Gay Mystique.* After participating in the demonstration, Fisher wrote about it:

The level of tension in the Firehouse rose to unprecedented heights. People were afraid of the demonstration, yet determined to participate in it. As the time approached on Saturday night, our "undercover agents" at the site of the demonstration informed us that police barricades had been set up, paddy wagons were parked along the street, and a busload of TPF—the Tactical Police Force, the city's most brutal cops —had already arrived, armed to the hilt as usual . . .

During earlier discussions with police officials we had come to an agreement that six of us would be allowed to enter the building to verify whether our councilman was present. The TPF were not inclined to honor the agreement . . . When Marc and I attempted to move past the barricades according to plan, the TPF came boiling out, clubs flying . . .

It was the most nightmarish scene I had ever witnessed: long brutal clubs smashing left and right, landing on people's heads, the crowd panicking, pushing first toward the barricades and then falling back. The glare of the TV lights made the whole thing unreal, and doubly frightening.

Dragging one demonstrator off to be arrested, the TPF withdrew behind the barricades: The District Chief for Manhattan South invited Marc and me behind the lines to discuss the situation. He finally permitted six of us to enter the building, where we immediately stated that we would not leave until we had seen our councilman. A half hour later we were arrested by officers from our local precinct . . .

Back at the apartment building, however, the worst was yet to come. The TPF began taunting the crowd, daring them to cross the police lines, insulting them for being homosexuals. When the demonstration was called to a close and the crowd began to disperse, the TPF burst forth from behind the barricades, separated a group of the demonstrators from the mass of the crowd, herded them behind the building away from TV cameras with their clubs, and began to beat them savagely.[15]

Five days later Saul Sharison announced that the General Welfare Committee would hold a public hearing on Intro 475 on October 18. Rubin and Fisher were not sure whether this was the result of the bloody scene at Sharison's apartment building or of their circulation of broadsides revealing that while Sharison received a $5,000 expense account and a $7,000 bonus for chairing it, the General Welfare Committee had not been convened in two years.

Flushed with success, GAA's political leaders failed to see that the steps they had resorted to in order to secure public hearings were destined to prevent them from using those hearings to smooth the way for legislation. Yet their strategy of mounting ever larger and more militant demonstrations had required them to supplement their ranks with radicals who had little interest in policy reforms and who viewed demonstrations as occasions to bolster their sense of identity and community and to challenge the attitudes of those they personally encountered. And the result was an upsurge in behavior of the type that Ralph Hall described in his story of the Sharison zap—an offbeat report that balances the indictment of police behavior in Fisher's account:

At the end of the demo a head pig kept calling for Jim Owles and i said, "what do you need Jim Owles for? he ain't here. speak to us. he's not our boss, etc." Well, he wanted Jim Owles' presence to break the demo up . . . so i started in with this dialogue: "hey! Are you a real strait men? . . . hi, i'm a fag, a faggot, that's right! and you're a pig, right? so you must be one of those heterosexual people, man. dig it brothers . . . faggots . . . look at how strait these pigs are, brothers. don't ya jes think they look so cute—koochi koochi koo little piggies. look at them with their tiny little wooden sticks and cap pistols . . . they ought to be carrying around trees with them, 'cause they'd be able to crack more skulls that way. it takes a real man, brother faggots, to whup a fag . . . 'C'mon beat me up pig . . . (at which point Jim Owles, president of the Gay Activists Alliance of New York City and probably nation by now) comes forward and says to me:

"ralph, you're a provocateur."[16]

. . .

During the public hearing that took place in the middle of October 1971, GAA's political leaders sensed that their strategy for passing Intro 475 was on the brink of success. Although they had been unable to persuade Congresswoman Bella Abzug to testify in person, they had arranged for Eleanor Holmes Norton to speak on behalf of the Lindsay administration. Victor Gotbaum of the Municipal Workers' Union and Dr. Ann Scott of the National Organization for Women delivered endorsements from their organizations. Kate Millett and Fordham's Father Herbert Rogers made moving personal statements of support. GAAers Marc Rubin and Breck Ardery and lesbian activist Barbara Love spoke on behalf of homosexuals.

The members of GAA enlisted to fill the council chamber had been instructed to be on their best behavior, and they sat silently while those who opposed the bill had their turn to speak. City Clerk Herman Katz warned that the passage of Intro 475 would bring gay couples back to his office for marriage licenses. A housewife from Queens expressed fear that homosexual teachers would seduce children. A representative of the Queens Catholic War Veterans Association ranted about legislating immorality. General Welfare Committee member Michael De Marco wondered out loud what would happen if homosexual men were permitted to mix with policemen and firemen required to spend nights at their stations.

The politicos were pleased with the performance, but many of GAA's cultural leaders were not. They complained that Rubin and Ardery, seen for the first time in coats and ties, presented "straight" images and kept to safe arguments. They argued that the restraint shown in the face of insulting and prejudiced remarks was artificial and compromising. They charged that effeminate male homosexuals and transvestites were deliberately kept from view. In their eyes, the discipline adopted to make a favorable impression belied the commitment to genuine self-expression that was the heart of gay liberation.

What the first public hearing did, in fact, was to raise the basic questions about strategy that divided political and cultural leaders: Was it more important to make a favorable political impression or to project distinctive gay models? Was it more strategic to get legislation that would establish homosexuals as a political minority and provide protections that would allow them to be open and political, or to produce theater that would encourage homosexuals to be openly gay and inspire them to demand respect from those they encountered in their day-to-day lives? Before the public hearing, by pursuing a legislative strategy that combined principled negotiations with imaginative demonstrations, GAA's politicos had been able to carry out the official dealings they believed necessary for legislative success without alienating the culturally minded associates they needed for demonstrations. The hearings put dealings between politicos and policymakers on display. The reaction of the cultural crowd was so negative that Marc Rubin, the man who had done more than anyone else to bridge the gap between political and cultural leaders, felt compelled to resign as chairman of the Municipal Government Committee.*

Amato, Owles, and other politicos were more positive about their commitment to passing legislation, but they were forced to accommodate their cultural critics by allowing homosexuals with unconventional life styles to testify at the second day of hearings, scheduled for November 15, and by abandoning their efforts to control the behavior of those in the council chamber. Ethan Geto started the second day of hearings off on a serious political note, reading a strong statement of support from his boss, Bronx Borough president Robert Abrams. Good form came to an end when the next witness, a Bible-carrying nurse from Staten Island, urged those in the audience to read the story of Sodom and Gomorrah and was greeted by a chorus of hisses and boos. Thereafter, despite Sharison's remonstrances, witnesses who spoke in favor of Intro 475 were cheered and those who spoke against it jeered. Passions peaked during the questioning of Amato himself.

Although Amato raised eyebrows by identifying himself as an elected Democratic committeeman from Long Island as well as a

---

*Unlike Amato, Rubin had been able to deal with city officials without losing the support of cultural leaders because, though he taught in the city school system, he was open, warm, and earthy about his sexuality, outspoken about the plight of transvestites, supportive of efforts to build a new gay culture, and visible in every demonstration.

member of GAA, his dramatic coming out was overshadowed by the provocative questioning of councilman Michael De Marco. When Amato began to describe some of the injustices he had discovered when doing his research, De Marco insisted that he was avoiding the central problem: "What if we employ a Mr. Schultz on Monday and Tuesday we get a Miss Schultz? That's the problem. I just saw two people in dresses trying to get into the men's room . . ."

De Marco was referring to Ray "Sylvia" Rivera and another transvestite, who had come to the hearing in full drag. As soon as the councilor spoke, the two screamed that their visit to the men's room had been forced by their ouster from the ladies' room. De Marco urged them to come forward, and they soon joined Arthur Bell, Jim Fouratt, and others who had begun to chant "heterosexual bastards" in the front of the council chamber. De Marco pursued Amato: "Maybe the bill doesn't go far enough for you. Shouldn't it include transvestites?" Amato replied, "Don't divert the issue."[17]

It was not that the questions about transvestites took Amato by surprise. In the fall of 1970, when he began to plan strategy with Eldon Clingan, Amato had guessed that the issue of transvestism would emerge as the biggest obstacle to the passage of legislation banning discrimination on the basis of sexual orientation. He saw that the existence of homosexual transvestites would permit opponents of gay rights to rally support by playing on the popular confusion between homosexuality and transvestism. He knew that the cause of the transvestites would stir up cultural leaders who had strong feelings about the right of sexual self-expression for all. It was to keep people from confusing issues that GAA's legislative strategists tried to keep the crowd in attendance the first day of hearings looking and acting "straight." In a valiant effort to recoup after the scene De Marco precipitated on the second day of hearings, the politicos asked "Bebe" Scarpi, whom they considered the most sensible of GAA's transvestites, to take the stand. Scarpi's presentation was later lauded in GAA's newsletter:

Bebe, a student at Queens College, gave what amounted to a short course on the lifestyle and problems of transvestites with such charm, ready wit and intelligence that even the Councilmen appeared beguiled, although chairman Sharison seemed unable to comprehend the fact that some transvestites were heterosexual. DeMarco wanted to know whether Bebe believed that transvestites would be protected by Intro 475. "Only as a homosexual, not as a transvestite," Bebe explained, adding that perhaps the Councilman would care to introduce legislation protecting the transvestite.[18]

Amato and Scarpi gave similar answers to De Marco's questions. But because Amato was rumored to favor amending the provisions of Intro 475 to exclude cross dressing in order to get it passed, and because he had a reputation for being more interested in the passage of legislation than in personal liberation, critics portrayed his remarks as a sellout of the transvestites and a betrayal of the quest for sexual self-expression. With the discrediting of Amato and the championing of the transvestites, the tide of strategic opinion shifted to militants who argued that provocative confrontations and principled demands were more advisable than public niceness and private compromises.

When De Marco and other members of the General Welfare Committee insisted on hearing testimony from the city's police and fire commissioners, a third day of public hearings was scheduled for mid-December. GAA's strategists were now convinced that Cuite had enlisted De Marco to prevent Intro 475 from being voted out of committee, so they tried to counter the majority leader's opposition by forcing the mayor to become more actively involved. As before, their goal was to pressure Lindsay into issuing an executive order that would ban discrimination in municipal employment, thereby signifying his commitment to Intro 475 and assuaging council members' fears of being responsible for letting homosexuals into the police, fire, and school departments.

Although it put to rest suspicions about back-room deals and sellouts, the return to militancy only partially satisfied GAAers convinced that liberating individuals and promoting community contributed more to gay liberation than official reforms. That the concerns of cultural leaders persisted was apparent in the GAA elections held just before the third day of hearings. A statement circulated by one of the five candidates for president testified: "Actually, all five are agreed on the basic policies of the Alliance and on the *external* tone we have adopted. It is in here—when we are alone with each other—that I think we can do better relating to ourselves and to other members. (The term 'brothers and sisters' has become empty.)" Each candidate vowed to continue the militant pursuit of Intro 475, but there was something of a farewell to GAA's political reformist priorities when Robinson, Owles, and Evans were passed over and Rich Wandel, who promised "laissez faire leadership," was elected.

By the time the third day of hearings arrived, the prospects for anything but militant display were dim. Saul Sharison had announced that he intended to vote in favor of submitting Intro 475 to the full council, but Howard Golden, Matthew Troy, Bertram Gelfand, and Michael De Marco had stated that they were opposed to the bill because it would allow homosexuals to hold jobs as policemen, firemen, and teachers. De Marco told the *New York Post:* "And the kids have so little respect for the police force today. They call them 'pigs.' If we let homosexuals into the police department they would be able to call them 'fags' and 'homos.' "[19] GAA's State and Federal Affairs Committee, under the leadership of Bruce Voeller, had managed to obtain statements in support of gay rights from senators Ted Kennedy and George McGovern, but John Lindsay remained publicly silent and privately distant. Eldon Clingan openly expressed pessimism, telling reporters that "the difficulty of overcoming anti-homosexual prejudice is so great that only vigorous lobbying by Mayor Lindsay and Council Majority Leader Thomas J. Cuite could save the measure."[20] Ads in the gay press called for a "gay-in" at the hearings, saying the bill was "in trouble because there are bigots, hypocrites and phonies who represent you in the City Council." The day before the hearing, two dozen GAAers had returned to Suffolk County to help members of GAA–Long Island present complaints at the County Administration Building about the raid of a local gay bar, and several of them had been badly beaten.

Even once-cool political heads like Robinson and Fisher were tense and emotional as the third day of hearings began on December 17. Right at the outset, when Sharison responded to an outburst of audience disapproval by threatening to adjourn, Robinson, Evans, and others rushed to his desk, raised clenched fists, and shouted, "Justice! Justice! Justice!" and "Bigot! Bigot! Bigot!" The audience joined in and Sharison stammered until Clingan took the microphone and pleaded for an end to demonstrations "that were doing more harm than good."

But the tone was set. Pete Fisher took the stand, read from the

American Declaration of Independence, and explained that "the Council cannot expect us to behave 'like ladies and gentlemen' participating in an abstract philosophical dialogue when we are called 'sinners,' compared to murderers, and the validity of our existence as human beings is threatened."[21] Less civil remarks were made by "Sylvia" Rivera, in a red dress, and by Jim Fouratt, wearing a purple miniskirt over his blue jeans to spoof sex role conventions (a convention-challenging practice known as "gender fuck"). Outbursts from members of the audience punctuated testimony, and the loud demonstration that began when Sharison announced that the hearing was over spilled out onto the streets in front of City Hall. De Marco told reporters later: "How can we have individuals like that teaching our kids? . . . They are just a bunch of freaks the way they are acting."[22]

De Marco expressed almost as much contempt for representatives of the Lindsay administration as he did for homosexuals. During the third day of hearings, when mayoral administrative assistant Marvin Shick read a long statement saying that the mayor and his administration fully supported Intro 475, De Marco charged that Lindsay and his emissary were lying and threatened to delay the committee's vote until the police and fire commissioners made their views known. Sharison instructed Shick to convey this news to the mayor, and just before the day was over, Shick reported that Lindsay was willing to have the commissioners or their representatives give testimony at a future session.

This was the second time that representatives of the mayor promised the council that spokesmen for the police and fire departments would be permitted to present their views, but there continued to be delay. Finally, in mid-January, Shick informed Sharison that Lindsay had reversed his position and decided to continue his policy of having only a single member of his administration speak to the council about matters involving civil rights. Clingan threatened to campaign against Lindsay in the California presidential primary if he failed to live up to his original promise. Rich Wandel warned in his first public statement as GAA's new president, "If this bill fails because of Lindsay, we are going to trash his campaign every time he makes an appearance in California or anywhere else in the nation. There are some 800 organized gay groups in the country."[23]

When a General Welfare Committee vote on Intro 475 was scheduled for January 27 and the mayor showed no signs of becoming more involved, GAA circulated leaflets declaring "TOTAL WAR" until Lindsay agreed to meet with GAA representatives, to permit his police and fire commissioners to testify, and to issue an executive order banning discrimination against homosexuals. The war was to begin on January 25 with a demonstration in front of Radio City Music Hall, where a rally of supporters of Lindsay for President was scheduled.

That evening, just as Lindsay began to speak to the throngs who had paid fifty and one hundred dollars apiece to attend the rally, GAAer Morty Manford, who had climbed in from the fire escape, ran down the aisle to the front of the second mezzanine, handcuffed himself to the railing, and began to scream, "Lindsay is an actor! Lindsay lies on gay civil rights!" On the other side of the mezzanine, "Cora Rivera" followed Manford's example. Activists scattered throughout the audience popped up, joined in the shouting, and set off loud, shrill air horns. Lindsay stopped, then tried to shout through the hubbub that "the gentlemen from the Gay Liberation Front" were only damaging the chances of a bill he supported. The GAAers replied in unison, "Liar! Liar! Liar!" Their conviction that Lindsay cared little about their cause was renewed by the evidence that he was unfamiliar even with the name of their group.

The next morning, GAAer Ron Gold arrived at the grillwork entrance to Lindsay's City Hall office, identified himself as a professor of journalism, and informed the guard that he and his students had come for their appointment with the mayor's press secretary. Permitted to pass, Gold and a female assistant rushed into Lindsay's private office, grappled with surprised staff members, and chained themselves to the mayor's desk. The "students" waiting outside proceeded to manacle themselves to the grillwork and to lecture curious members of the staff and the press about the plight of homosexuals and the need for Intro 475.

That afternoon, forty people arrived at Lindsay's Madison Avenue campaign headquarters and said that they wanted to talk with campaign coordinator Ronnie Eldridge about forming a Lindsay for President group at Queens College. When Eldridge admitted the visitors to her office, they tied themselves to her office furniture, spoke angrily about Lindsay's failure to deliver, and refused to leave until they were arrested.

The next day, five of the fifteen members of the General Welfare

Committee voted in favor of bringing Intro 475 before the full council, seven opposed the resolution, one abstained, and two were absent. Theodore Weiss, the only one of the bill's sponsors who was a member of the committee, told reporters that the mayor's help would probably have done little to save the bill: "Homosexuality is an issue that's deeply tied into people's psyches and some of the councilmen haven't caught up to the realities of life."[24] Disagreeing with Weiss's assessment, Rich Wandel named three councilors whose support the mayor could have swung and promised that until Lindsay committed himself to the drive for gay rights, *"TOTAL WAR"* would continue.

In the wake of the General Welfare Committee's vote, people ranging from opponents such as Councilor Michael De Marco to supporters such as Eldon Clingan, the editors of the *New York Post,* and even officials at MSNY suggested that GAA's disruptive behavior was responsible for the failure to secure gay rights protection. Saul Sharison's comment was typical: "I cannot understand why these people do not understand that their performance and attitude show an irresponsibility towards those who are fighting to make sure that these rights are secured."[25]

The irony of Sharison's remark was that the first American fight for gay rights legislation had originated with the very people he complained about, a handful of individuals who felt so strongly about their right to express homosexual feelings and so convinced that the American political system would protect that right that they had sacrificed security and braved insult and antagonism in order to undertake gay political activity in behalf of all homosexuals.

The value that people like Robinson, Owles, and Evans placed on sexual self-expression was countercultural. Insistent as they were about the need to secure rights and status by developing political influence, they were driven less by philosophical principle than by strong feelings about the naturalness of homosexual behavior and the importance of being true to oneself. So the pioneering political reformers argued that calculated political maneuvering was needed to pass gay rights legislation. And they criticized cultural leaders who contended that it was more important to be honest about their feelings and to challenge the biases of prejudiced public officials. Yet when the legislative campaign they expected to be a political triumph encountered demeaning opposition, only the most controlled politicos were able to refrain from giving in to the strong personal feelings and the countercultural values that were at the root of their activism. There was moving testimony to this in the defense of GAA's behavior that Marty Robinson wrote for the *Village Voice:*

The Stonewall had been sort of a pin prick at our sensibilities as a people. When we gave up the self-denial we had always accepted, when we gave up hiding, when we gave up not expressing ourselves but always suppressing our thoughts and feelings to survive in a hostile world as Gays had done for centuries, we gained a lot more than politics. We gained our emotions. It's hard to explain, but it's like blacks who no longer pretended they were white and who started to enjoy their culture, their speech, their individual expression. Every time the Gays refuse to yield to political and social compromise, every time they rebel at accepting the shit of the system, they can feel superior to their oppressors. To compromise means to threaten self-respect, and this makes the Activists touchy, idealistic, proud. To expect them to be less is almost like asking them to re-embrace guilt.[26]

Indeed, what most of those who criticized the Alliance for behaving in self-defeating ways failed to see was that relatively few of GAA's political leaders believed that passing Intro 475 was the key to protecting gay rights. Most held the early New Left conviction that rights were assured not when public officials were pleased or laws passed, but when those whose rights were at stake developed the awareness and the coherence that enabled them to command political representation and to exercise influence. From the beginning, the pursuit of gay rights legislation was viewed as a vehicle for persuading homosexuals that they had a right to their homosexual feelings and for showing them that they could band together and stage serious political initiatives when that right was threatened. Appropriately, after the first defeat of Intro 475, this too was best explained by Marty Robinson—who just two and a half years before had taken the lead in applying early New Left ideas to the case of homosexuals and inaugurating the reformist thrust of the gay liberation movement:

Civil rights legislation was supposed to be passé. So when GAA undertook Intro 475, it was not advocated as the goal for the movement but as a tactic, a tool toward liberation. It was called anti-closet legislation, to underline how the threat of loss of employment had been used to keep

Gays in silent submission. Intro 475 does have much value in itself, but Gay Liberationists, except for revolutionaries who saw 475 as a way of showing that the system was hopelessly unresponsive, saw Intro 475 as the best way of getting the message to the community: the closet is built in fear, not shame. In that very real sense, Intro 475 never was and never could be defeated. Many Gays came out of the closet for the struggle and many more will join them as that struggle continues.[27]

PART III

THE LESBIAN FEMINIST MOVEMENT

9

Radicalesbians

HOMOSEXUALS WERE NOT the only unrecognized group dramatically affected by the social and political currents of the sixties. Women, too, were greatly influenced by ideas popularized by the civil rights movement and the New Left.

The first to act were women who thought about their lives in the light of liberal civil rights perspectives and who began to feel that America's melting pot was as closed to them as it was to blacks, Jews, and others with unusual ethnic backgrounds. To give citizens born female their share of the American dream, women's rights leaders set out to persuade people that women were every bit as competent as men and to put an end to the discrimination that kept them from being granted equal opportunity and integrated equitably into established institutions. In the early 1960s, these women participated in the Commission on the Status of Women created by President John F. Kennedy and in analogous state commissions. In the fall of 1966, they initiated contemporary feminist political activity by forming the National Organization for Women.

But while some women decided to start a women's rights movement modeled after the civil rights movement, others were spurred to adopt the views and values of the counterculture and to become involved in the New Left. Here, like the homosexuals alongside them, they began to look at their own problems from the cultural radical perspective. In this light, women seemed to lack the opportunities afforded men not merely because of prejudice and discrimination but because of all-pervasive ideas about what women were and could be and about the types of traits and activities most valuable for society. *Sexism* was what these first radical feminists called the stereotyping of the sexes and the devaluation of "feminine" characteristics and behavior. *Radical feminism* was what they called their aspiration to transform America into a society whose absence of sexism would free individuals of both sexes to express themselves naturally and fully and to feel esteemed, whatever they were able to do and to be.

Working with male associates whose sexist attitudes and behavior stood in stark contrast to the radical ideals they espoused hastened this radicalization of women in the Movement. Partly because their male associates refused to acknowledge the contradictions, and partly because the women also applied radical ideas about strategy to their own situation, radical feminists eager to initiate a drive for women's liberation abandoned the New Left. In San Francisco, New York City, and other metropolitan centers, they banded together in small groups to elaborate their analyses of sexism and to help one another learn to live in ways that would trigger a revolution in consciousness. Unlike their sisters in the "rights" rather than the "liberationist" sector of the women's movement, they aspired not to win a place for women in the melting pot but to impress on women that sexist standards and assumptions limited their self-esteem, kept them from being respected for their special qualities, and denied that they could be as competent and professional as men.

Both women's rights leaders and radical feminists worked to attract the support of women, and many who responded to their efforts were lesbians. Most of these lesbians concealed their homosexuality, considering it irrelevant to their feminist activity.

Not all socially conscious lesbians joined women's groups, however; some turned their attention to gay groups. Yet almost all of the lesbians involved in gay political organizations sooner or later realized that their concerns differed from those of their male associates. Lesbian homophile leaders were among the first American women to call for the elimination of discrimination on the basis of sex. Conflicts with male homophile leaders and the need to justify a group separate from ONE, Incorporated, and the Mattachine Society led the leaders of the Daughters of Bilitis to complain in the 1950s just as the founders of the women's rights movement would in the 1960s. From the beginning, moreover, the lesbians in the Gay Liberation

Front were women's liberationists in everything but name. Led by their aspirations for self-realization and social validation to explore how they were oppressed by prevailing standards and attitudes, the first radical lesbians came to grips with sexism right alongside the first radical feminists.

Yet however precociously they appreciated their status as women and their stake in feminism, the lesbians in DOB–New York and in GLF characterized themselves as homosexuals and gay political activists until lesbian émigrés from women's groups persuaded them to attach more significance to their identities as women and to their political callings as feminists. Not until 1970 did lesbian activists in New York come to think of themselves as a special political breed committed to both gay and women's liberation. The efforts that these first lesbian feminists made to build a distinctive lesbian liberation movement—later called the lesbian feminist movement—began with the formation and evolution of Radicalesbians, continued with the politicization of DOB–New York, and were institutionalized with the establishment of Lesbian Feminist Liberation, Inc.

.   .   .

In *Sappho Was a Right-On Woman,* their popular account of the origins of lesbian feminism, Sidney Abbott and Barbara Love trace the creation of Radicalesbians to the efforts of a disaffected member of the National Organization for Women, Rita Mae Brown. According to Abbott and Love, late in 1969, after spending a year and a half trying unsuccessfully to persuade leaders at the national and New York NOW offices to concern themselves with homosexual women, Brown resigned from NOW, went to GLF, and called on lesbians from the gay movement to join lesbians from the women's movement in consciousness-raising groups. Soon afterwards, several of the thirty or so who signed up for the groups met at Brown's apartment and decided to write a paper explaining why the problems of lesbians were of central concern to the women's movement. After that paper, "The Woman-Identified Woman," was circulated in May 1970 at the Second Congress to Unite Women, lesbian gay liberationists and lesbian women's liberationists joined together and formed Radicalesbians.

Like other chroniclers of gay political activity, Abbott and Love explain important developments by discussing charismatic individuals and dramatic events. By focusing more on the ideological evolution and the organizational dynamics responsible for the formation of Radicalesbians, one can see that the emergence of a movement for lesbian feminist liberation was an inevitable consequence of the radical thinking responsible for the formalization of the drive for gay liberation.

Lois Hart's radical conviction that developing liberated life styles was political, for example, made her among the first to perceive that conventional ideas about sex roles, as much as traditional attitudes about sex, kept homosexuals from feeling good about themselves and from relating constructively with peers. The outline of GLF's concerns prepared for *Rat* presented Hart's view that in part gay people were denigrated because they failed to participate in traditional family arrangements: "The socialization process of the society is nothing but a phony morality impressed upon us by church, media, psychiatry, and education which tells us that if we're not married heterosexual producers and pacified workers and soldiers, we are sick degenerate outcasts."[1]

In the statement of GLF aims published in the first issue of *Come Out!* Hart attributed the homosexual's problems to "sex and sex roles which oppress us from infancy."[2] By the winter of 1969–70, when she was invited to discuss the relationship between lesbianism and feminism on the WBAI radio program "Womankind," Hart was ready to argue that the "patterns of domination and submission" characteristic of conventional relationships between men and women were responsible for the oppression, i.e., the thwarting of self-realization, endured by homosexuals as well as by women:

> Male homosexuals and females—they're part of a society that dictates patterns of submission and domination. I mean, that's the hang-up right there. People pick up on models of behavior. It's the root of women's oppression. It's the root of gay oppression. These heterosexual images of male domination and female submission. So you respond in terms of these rules, because people lack alternatives, until you grow to a point where you can throw off these rules and start being yourself . . .
>
> I mean, we're talking about human liberation. And basically, what we're talking about is completely rejecting imposed definitions upon our humanity. I mean, we believe we're endless and infinite, in some kind of

sense, and that we have the right to be ourselves, whatever that might be. It's human liberation, and it's for men and women, regardless of how they turned out, heterosexual and homosexual.[3]

Martha Shelley, who joined Hart on "Womankind," also spoke about human liberation, pointing out that "what we're fighting, in its broadest sense, is a form of racism where, because you are born with a particular color, shape, sex, nationality, or into a family with a particular religious orientation, you are automatically forced into a certain pattern."[4] Like Hart, Shelley recognized that conventional ideas about sex roles prevented individuals of every sexual orientation from expressing themselves as they wished; for her, too, the quest for sexual liberation was inextricably bound up with the quest for sex-role liberation.

In fact, if the articles Shelley wrote for the *Ladder* and *Come Out!* are an accurate measure, she had thought even longer and harder than Hart about the lesbian's stake in women's liberation. In the spring of 1969, not long after she had resigned as president of DOB–New York, Shelley wrote a letter to the *Ladder* which referred to the injustices against women described in the writings of Simone de Beauvoir and Betty Friedan and argued that the lesbian should be proud of herself for refusing to relate to men in traditional ways: "We are a body of women independent of their domination, willing to compete with them on an equal basis—not willing to reduce ourselves to the lowest common denominator so that every living male can feel himself superior to us."[5] For the first issue of *Come Out!,* Shelley elaborated these themes in an article beginning: "Lesbianism is one road to freedom—freedom from oppression by men."[6] On "Womankind," Shelley asserted that lesbianism was a political choice analogous to those made by radical feminists who opted to be separate from men or to have fewer relationships with them. "I think you can see the lesbian in a political sense as unconsciously propelled by whatever hidden motivations—say as a rebel against the accepted mores of society. This is a political decision, even if it happens on an unconscious level."

Agreeing with Shelley, Hart concluded her own remarks on "Womankind" by assessing lesbianism in terms of radical standards: " . . . in living with another woman, and in developing a relationship with another woman . . . I don't have to deal with a lot of my own feelings of oppression as when I'm with a man. I don't have to deal with that part of me that's been trained to respond to men in certain ways and to have certain emotional reactions towards men. It's very clear to me, when I'm with another woman, that I am responsible for myself . . . I see that as a political thing."[7]

In their critique of the way men treated women and their portrayal of avoiding men and associating with women as being liberating and political, Hart and Shelley expressed views that resembled those of radical feminist groups such as Redstockings and The Feminists. What set them apart, at this point, from most radical feminists was the care they took to attribute women's problems to sex-role stereotyping that oppressed both men and women rather than simply to the existence of men. This was partly because they saw themselves as lesbian gay liberationists with special contributions to make to women's liberation, not the other way around, and because they were committed to working with male homosexuals. Not until Hart, Shelley, and other lesbian GLFers became less enchanted with their male colleagues and more enamored of lesbian émigrés from the women's movement was the situation ripe for the emergence of lesbian feminist liberation groups.

Rita Mae Brown's visit to GLF certainly hastened this development. Brown, who has chronicled her early life as a lesbian in the heavily autobiographical novel *Rubyfruit Jungle,* got her first taste of gay politics in the Student Homophile League that Bob Martin organized at Columbia and then extended to New York University, where Brown first met Martha Shelley. Finding that the male homosexuals who dominated SHL had concerns remote from her own and that the gay men exhibited traditional attitudes towards women, Brown moved on to the New York chapter of the National Organization for Women. Yet the NOW leaders in both the New York and national offices were uneasy about Brown's openness as a lesbian and unwilling to have their organization officially take up lesbian concerns. In November 1969, DOB–New York's name was omitted from a press release listing the institutional sponsors of the first Congress to Unite Women, which New York NOW had organized. Soon afterwards, Brown and two lesbian friends resigned, explaining why in a letter they appended to the January 1970 issue of the New York NOW newsletter:

We protest NY NOW's sexist standpoint. The leadership consciously oppresses other women on the question of sexual preference—or in plain words, enormous prejudice is directed against the lesbian. Lesbian is the one word that can cause the Executive Committee a collective heart attack. This issue is dismissed as unimportant, too dangerous to contemplate, divisive or whatever excuse could be dredged up from their repression. The prevailing attitude is, and this is reflected even more on the national level, "Suppose they (notice the word, they) flock to us in droves? How horrible. After all, think of our image." May we remind you that this is a male-oriented image.[8]

It is tempting to argue that Brown's disaffection with the women's movement stemmed from her involvement with women's rights advocates rather than with women's liberationists. The truth is that Brown and other pioneering lesbian feminists found liberationist groups like Redstockings and The Feminists as unsatisfactory as rights groups like NOW.

True, in the radical feminist sector of the women's movement, there was none of NOW's concern with impressing the public and helping women into the mainstream. In New York City, as elsewhere, the fledgling women's liberation movement consisted of small groups of radical feminists who were interested not in winning a place for women in the existing system but in effecting social transformation. Some of these feminists—like many in New York Radical Women, formed in the winter of 1967–68, and its offshoot WITCH, which emerged in the fall of 1968—were attracted to revolutionary as well as radical goals and tactics. Others—like those in Redstockings, another offshoot of New York Radical Women, and The Feminists, the group formed in the fall of 1968 by disillusioned women who followed Ti-Grace Atkinson out of New York NOW when her proposals for a more egalitarian structure were defeated—had perspectives that were more purely cultural radical. These cultural radical feminists approached the task of social transformation by working to understand how sex and sex-role stereotyping and the denigration of so-called feminine traits and behavior kept women from developing their full potential and from feeling fulfilled in their relationships. They wanted to develop liberated life styles and to build exclusively female institutions and communities that would provide a model for future feminist society (usually envisioned as a matriarchy and sometimes spoken of as "Amazon Nation"). Hence, the radical feminists in Redstockings and The Feminists were more willing than their revolutionary counterparts in WITCH to think about how sexism constrained female sexuality, to acknowledge lesbianism as one way of escaping traditional constraints,* and to welcome lesbians into their small groups. Lois Hart joined a Redstockings consciousness-raising group in the fall of 1969. Rita Mae Brown and her friends turned to Redstockings "c-r" groups after resigning from NOW.

Though the welcome that the radical feminists in Redstockings and The Feminists gave lesbians enhanced Hart and Brown's sense that lesbianism had important implications for women's liberation, it was not enough to make them feel they belonged in the women's liberation movement. Among other things, the lesbians who joined Redstockings c-r groups perceived that many women there acted as if they expected the lesbians to be sexual aggressors. When they were not, these women sometimes asked for and engaged in homosexual experiences without feeling that emotional attachments were necessary. This made the lesbians feel that the radical feminists viewed lesbianism not as the basis of a fulfilling way of life for women, but as a preference for a certain kind of sex, a way of escaping oppressive relationships with men, or a dimension of the bisexuality that would become the norm "after the revolution." Indeed, for all their willingness to talk about lesbianism and to consider the concerns of lesbians, the radical feminists seemed far more preoccupied with their relationships with men and far more concerned with issues like contraception, abortion, and child care. These and other perceived slights led lesbian leaders like Hart and Brown to believe that theirs was a cause apart from that of the radical feminists.†

---

*For example, in an article completed in the fall of 1968 called "The Myth of the Vaginal Orgasm," Anne Koedt, who had helped organize both New York Radical Women and The Feminists, argued that women "must discard the 'normal' concepts of sex and create new guidelines which take into account mutual sexual enjoyment." She offered lesbianism as an example: "Lesbian sexuality could make an excellent case, based upon anatomical data, for the irrelevancy of the male organ. Albert Ellis says something to the effect that a man without a penis can make a woman an excellent lover."[9]

†In March 1970, Susan Brownmiller, first an organizer of Redstockings and later a founder of New York Radical Feminists, wrote an article about the women's liberation movement for the New York Times Magazine that took issue with Betty Friedan's charge that " 'the lavender menace' . . . was threatening to warp the image of women's rights." Brownmiller referred to militant lesbians as "a lavender herring, perhaps, but surely no clear and present danger."[10]

Nevertheless, by the end of 1969, a growing number of lesbian GLFers were thinking about their lives in radical feminist terms, and a growing number of lesbian women's liberationists were becoming convinced that neither the women's rights nor the women's liberationist sector of the women's movement cared much about the special concerns of lesbians. When these two breeds of politicized lesbians began to share their perceptions, the rationale for an autonomous lesbian liberation movement emerged.

The main vehicle for this sharing was one of the c-r groups formed in the wake of Brown's visit to GLF. This group brought together leading lesbian GLFers including Hart, her lover Suzanne Bevier, Ellen Bedoz, and Arlene Kisner, and lesbians who had been active in women's rights and radical feminist groups, including Sidney Abbott, Barbara Love, Michela Griffo, and March Hoffman. (Brown and Martha Shelley organized another c-r group, which soon fell apart.) The lesbian gay liberationists shared what they had learned about how conventional standards and attitudes affected thinking about female homosexuality. The lesbian women's liberationists stressed that traditional ideas about sex roles and the sexes inhibited all forms of female self-expression and argued that the fight against sexism required all women to band together to challenge all men. Thus leading lesbian GLFers began to think about the political implications of the problems they were having with their gay male associates.

Of course, long before they met in c-r sessions with lesbians from the women's movement, GLF's lesbian leaders had recognized that their pursuit of liberation was often impeded by the presence of gay male associates. Both radical and cultural reformist men agreed that GLF had to support the women's movement, and many of the men

Three weeks later the Sunday *Times* carried a letter from Lois Hart criticizing Brownmiller and other radical feminists for being callous when it came to lesbians:

Men used to and still do dismiss women's urgent demands for an end to their pain and unjust treatment in just such demeaning and frivolous phrases. The few 'militant lesbians' Miss Brownmiller refers to are women with the incredible courage to acknowledge their sexual preference and to speak up for their human rights. Women who have not thoroughly examined the effects of the male-heterosexual supremacist culture on their own attitudes and psyches have not recognized their own scapegoats and analyzed the implications. They bravely talk about liberating themselves from dehumanizing genital-role definitions, but they employ the same odious treatment in dealing with women who have found a sexual, emotional and spiritual companion in another woman. This constitutes a basic contradiction within women's liberation . . ."[11]

demonstrated their personal commitment to women's liberation by helping with child care so that GLF women could attend feminist events. But at one time or another most of the men expressed reservations about the time and attention given matters important to women at the expense of those said to be important for "all gays." (Michael Brown left GLF after quarreling with Lois Hart about the space in *Come Out!* to be allotted to "women's issues.") And despite frequent reminders, few male GLFers seemed able to eliminate the language (such as use of the term *girl*) and the habits (such as assuming the lesbians would make coffee for meetings) that the lesbians felt reflected sexist assumptions about the status and the jobs appropriate for women.

In her article for *Come Out!* reporting on Rita Mae Brown's visit, Hart described the subtleties of the situation:

Last Sunday Women's Lib came to the Sunday night meeting to organize lesbians and right on time too. "Women's Lib" and "male chauvinism" are terms that are frumiously bandered about among GLFers. It is a source of a lot of tension between the women and men. We know that we are better off than the straights because we can accord each other a certain independence unavailable to a woman and a man entangled sexually, emotionally and financially. Still, the ego-interplay goes on at other levels, and if we see that our liberation lies in the direction of ending alienation among people, then we have to deal with it. We have to end the class distinctions called female and male. To do this women must become conscious of their oppression as women, and men must be aware of how their egos and social advantages have been built on women's assumption of submissive, supportive and secondary roles. Awareness isn't enough. Each of us must create for ourselves an alternative self free of these restrictions, and necessarily women's self-development is a different kind of task than the one that men face. We are in a really tough situation. We want to be able to call each other brother and sister, yet we are still in some ways in the roles of oppressor and oppressed. Women are going to feel anger, and men will feel fear and resentment. Manhood has always meant domination and superiority over women, so if a "man" gives way to a woman his "manhood" is threatened. A Gay man's virility and humanity have been denied by the heterosexual world, and Gay Liberation exists to defeat that lie—so now is this another threat from a supposed ally? If Women's Liberation, the development of the female ego and the abdication of privilege feel like a threat, then that can be only an indication to the particular man how much of his sense of self is bound up in that heterosexual social role called "Masculine." It was beautiful to see how many realized the need to work at this level last Saturday night. Not only women's groups were formed but also male and co-ed groups. If we succeed in working through this one, we will have accomplished what no other movement group has accomplished (or any group that I've heard of). We just might find ourselves a truly nuclear community of that New World we want so much to bring about.[12]

Despite the hope Hart expressed, the more the radical lesbian leaders tried to work with male associates, the more they were reinforced in feeling that the freedom and closeness lesbians could experience in the presence of other lesbians far exceeded the freedom and closeness they could experience among gay men. No matter how hard the men in the *Come Out!* collective and the Aquarius Cell tried to be sensitive, for example, the lesbians in their midst remained uncomfortable. The men talked too loudly to suit the lesbians; they seemed either overly assertive or artificially abashed; and they were always more concerned with making decisions than with making sure that each member of the group felt involved in the decision-making process and comfortable with the outcome.

And the differences in what men and women wanted seemed just as great as the differences in their approach. For example, when it came to dances, the lesbians active in GLF's Aquarius Cell envisioned mellow assemblies in which people could meet one another, engage in conversation, and join in gentle play. The men thought less about helping people get to know one another than about producing an exciting bash. The women wanted the dance hall to be well lighted; the men preferred erotic darkness. The women wanted soft music, love songs sung by women, and slow dancing; the men preferred hard rock and heavy sweating. The women wanted space to "relate"; the men preferred tightly packed crowds.

Indeed, if their working and socializing with gay men gave lesbian leaders the sense that female homosexuals were very different from male homosexuals, their experiences in all-lesbian groups encouraged them to believe that they were much better off working and socializing on their own. The women felt projects undertaken for *Come Out!* and the Aquarius Cell seemed always to proceed more smoothly, to be more rewarding, and to conclude more successfully when they were handled by groups made up solely of women. The weekly Wednesday night sessions of the Women's Caucus, which the lesbians had started in early 1970 when they became convinced that their liberation involved issues of sex as well as sexual orientation, were much more satisfying than GLF's regular mixed-sex meetings. When both men and women were invited to parties, the women inevitably clustered together and "got off" on one another. Their exhilaration reached a peak in April 1970, when they ran an all-women's dance—partly to demonstrate growing feminist awareness, partly to reach out to lesbian radical feminists who refused to attend activities including men, and partly to provide an alternative to the two seedy lesbian bars in the Village (whose owners added insult to injury by refusing to allow lesbian GLFers to post notices or to talk about politics on the premises). An account of the dance in *Rat* glowed:

> The dance was a huge success—we had several hundred women—radical gay women, so-called "bar" lesbians, and women's liberation people. And despite our differences, everyone related to each other. We danced fast, we danced slow, we danced Greek-style, we danced in circles and pairs, we rapped, we were stoned on joy. We were all women, all in love with each other, and we had a tremendous sense of power in our self-sufficiency. Yes, men, not only can we do everything ourselves, but we can enjoy ourselves at it too!![13]

What most led GLF's lesbian leaders to feel that they were best able to pursue liberation apart from gay men was experience. Hart and Bedoz, who more than the others had become interested in radical feminist thinking, were eager to explore the political implications of their experiences, and for this purpose they joined together in a study group with March Hoffman and a woman known as "Barbara XX" from their consciousness-raising group and with Rita Mae Brown and her lover, Cynthia Funk. When the study group decided to elaborate its ideas about the implications of lesbianism for feminism in a paper that could be presented to the second Congress to Unite Women, scheduled by local feminist groups for May 1, its members prepared notes and submitted them to Hoffman, who wrote

"The Woman-Identified Woman." This was the first major exposition of lesbian feminist thinking.*

"The Woman-Identified Woman" began by developing the point —articulated previously in public statements by Shelley and Hart— that because of her homosexuality, the lesbian was more sensitive to the ways that sex and sex-role stereotyping stifled and demeaned women and was more likely to achieve the self-regard, the psychological integration, and the self-actualization possible only for women who saw through sexism. Its first paragraph explained:

What is a lesbian? . . . She is the woman who, often beginning at an extremely early age, acts in accordance with her inner compulsion to be a more complete and more free human being than her society—perhaps then, but certainly later—cares to allow her . . . She may not be fully conscious of the political implications of what for her began as a personal necessity, but on some level she has not been able to accept the limitations and oppression laid on her by the most basic role of her society—the female role . . . To the extent that she cannot expel the heavy socialization that goes with being female, she can never truly find peace with herself. For she is caught somewhere between accepting society's view of her— in which case she cannot accept herself—and coming to understand what this sexist society has done to her and why it is functional and necessary for it to do so. Those of us who work that through find ourselves on the other side of a tortuous journey . . . The perspective gained from that journey, the liberation of self, the inner peace, the real love of self and of all women, is something to be shared with all women—because we are all women.

The "perspective" that the liberated lesbians wanted to share "with all women" had to do with the limits the fear of lesbianism placed on the possibilities for achieving liberation. A first point was that men threatened women with the lesbian label to keep them in the traditional female roles of sex object, wife, child rearer, and home maintainer: "Lesbian is a label invented by the Man to throw at any

*The authorship of "The Woman-Identified Woman" is often mistakenly attributed to Rita Mae Brown, partly because Brown received the by-line when it was reprinted in the August– September issue of the *Ladder,* an error corrected in the October–November issue. The original version of "The Woman-Identified Woman" was signed by the six who belonged to the study group and "other Radical Lesbians."

woman who dares to be his equal, who dares to challenge his prerogatives (including that of all women as part of the exchange medium among men), who dares to assert the primacy of her own needs." In addition to keeping women from expressing themselves fully and freely, the fear of being thought a lesbian was said to prevent them from being intimate with one another and from joining together in a movement and a community strong enough to effect women's liberation:

> Affixing the label Lesbian not only to a woman who aspires to be a person, but also to any situation of real love, real solidarity, real primacy among women is a primary form of divisiveness among women: it is the condition which keeps women within the confines of the feminine role, and it is the debunking/scare term that keeps women from forming any primary attachments, groups, or associations among ourselves . . .

To those clear about the nature of sexism, this might have suggested that women had to rid themselves of the fear of being thought lesbian before they would be free to determine the extent to which they wanted to deviate from traditional female roles and to involve themselves sexually, emotionally, and politically with women. But the radical lesbian feminists responsible for "The Woman-Identified Woman" suggested that sexism was a problem not of culturally perpetuated values and assumptions shared by and limiting to both men and women, but of men—their existence, their undiluted responsibility for prevailing standards and attitudes, their dominating natures and malicious motives, and their universally inhibiting and infecting involvement with women. Thus they inferred that the liberation of women called not for having both men and women change their attitudes about traditional female roles, but for abandoning these roles. They concluded that women who wanted to be liberated had to become lesbian and that women who wanted to be feminist had to avoid all contact with men:

> As the source of self-hate and the lack of real self are rooted in our male-given identity, we must create a new sense of self. As long as we cling to the idea of "being a woman," we will sense some conflict with that incipient self, that sense of I, that sense of a whole person. It is very

difficult to realize and accept that being "feminine" and being a whole person are irreconcilable. Only women can give each other a new sense of self. That identity we have to develop with reference to ourselves, and not in relation to men. This consciousness is the revolutionary force from which all else will follow, for ours is an organic revolution. For this we must be available and supportive to one another, give our commitment and our love, give the emotional support necessary to sustain this movement. Our energies must flow towards our sisters, not backwards toward our oppressors. As long as women's liberation tries to free women without facing the basic heterosexual structure that binds us in one-to-one relationships with our oppressors, tremendous energies will continue to flow into trying to straighten up each particular relationship with a man, how to get better sex, how to turn his head around—into trying to make the "new man" out of him, in the delusion that this will allow us to be the "new woman." This obviously splits our energies and commitments, leaving us unable to be committed to the construction of the new patterns which will liberate us.

In essence, "The Woman-Identified Woman" argued that because lesbians built their lives around women, they were best equipped to develop ways of thinking and acting that were genuinely female and truly self-determined, and that because lesbians were able to live totally apart from men, they were in the best position to form the all-women groups, movement, and communities that were necessary to engender the revolution in consciousness necessary for women's liberation. The final paragraph minced no words in suggesting that radical lesbians were the vanguard of the women's liberation movement and the best hope for social transformation:

It is the primacy of women relating to women, of women creating a new consciousness of and with each other which is at the heart of women's liberation, and the basis for the cultural revolution. Together we must find, reinforce and validate our authentic selves. As we do this, we confirm in each other that struggling incipient sense of pride and strength, the divisive barriers begin to melt, we feel this growing solidarity with our sisters. We see ourselves as prime, find our centers inside of ourselves. We find receding the sense of alienation, of being cut off, of being behind a locked window, of being unable to get out what we know is inside. We feel a realness, feel at last we are coinciding with ourselves. With that real self, with that consciousness, we begin a revolution to end the imposition of all coercive identification, and to achieve maximum autonomy in human expression.[14]

With the sense that they were the vanguard of the women's liberation movement, itself the vanguard of the Movement, members of the study group, accompanied by lesbian GLFers who had yet to identify as feminists, made a dramatic appearance before the overflow crowd of women who gathered for the second Congress to Unite Women on the first weekend in May 1970. On the first night of the Congress, just after the assembly had settled down for a panel discussion, the lights went out. A minute later, when the lights came on again, twenty-five women with T-shirts identifying them as Lavender Menaces were assembled at the front of the stage. Alluding to Betty Friedan, one of them explained: "About a year ago, a media woman made a slur against NOW by saying that they were being run by lavender menaces. She was referring to some officers who were lesbians . . . It got passed around in other parts of the women's movement . . . Lesbians or women who 'seem' to be lesbians were being referred to as lavender menaces or lavender herrings." Another radical lesbian continued: "We have come to tell you that we lesbians are being oppressed outside the movement and inside the movement by a sexist attitude. We want to discuss the lesbian issue with you."[15] Copies of "The Woman-Identified Woman" were distributed to members of the audience.

For the rest of the evening, as their peers held hands and cuddled on the edge of the stage, individual "Menaces" talked about how it felt to be lesbian and invited members of the audience to come forward to tell of their own experiences. A workshop on alternatives in sexuality (which the "Menaces" renamed "workshop in lesbianism") was scheduled for the next day. An all-women's dance was held that evening. The final assembly of the congress voted to adopt the set of resolutions put forward in the name of "The Lavender Menace: Gay Liberation Front Women and Radical Lesbians":

1. Be it resolved that Women's Liberation is a lesbian plot.
2. Resolved that whenever the label lesbian is used against the movement collectively or against women individually, it is to be affirmed, not denied.

3. In all discussions of birth control, homosexuality must be included as a legitimate method of contraception.
4. All sex education curricula must include lesbianism as a valid, legitimate form of sexual expression and love.

At the close of the congress, several radical lesbian leaders announced that they would run c-r groups for women interested in further exploring the significance of lesbianism for feminism. The numbers who signed up encouraged the lesbian GLFers who still saw themselves as gay liberationists to see the women's movement as the place to find fellow travelers. Inviting those who attended the c-r groups to join GLF and to attend the Wednesday night meetings of its Women's Caucus, they argued that by being active in GLF, lesbians could teach gay men about sexism while working simultaneously for gay and women's liberation.

But most of the women who went to the c-r groups wanted nothing to do with activities involving men. They argued that it was a waste of time and energy for lesbians to work with gay men when they had so much to do with women. They contended that it belied the very arguments made in "The Woman-Identified Woman" for lesbians to be involved in any way with the opposite sex. Despite the hopes of the lesbian GLFers, the lesbians from the women's movement they met after the congress—like Brown and other lesbians from the women's movement who had first suggested c-r groups and been active in the study group—insisted on calling themselves "Radical Lesbians," not "Gay Liberation Front Women," so that no one would think they had anything to do with gay men. During May and June, these Radical Lesbians set out to persuade the lesbians still loyal to GLF that a completely independent group was needed for the pursuit of lesbian liberation.

As much as by the arguments of the Radical Lesbians, the Gay Liberation Front Women were won over to the idea of an independent organization by the failure of most of their male associates to acknowledge to their satisfaction that lesbians had distinctive needs and concerns. The male radicals who had formed their own c-r groups to develop nonsexist life styles were willing to acquiesce in all of the steps that the lesbians wanted to take, but most of the male cultural reformers argued that the proliferation of events open only to women and the bonds developing between GLF women and les-

bian women's liberationists hostile to gay men threatened the united
gay community GLF stood for. Indeed, when lesbians in the Aquarius Cell took some of the money the cell had raised for a gay community center to finance an all-women's dance to raise money for lesbian
liberationist activities, Jerry Hoose and his friends were so incensed
that they divided the remaining money into separate accounts for the
men and the women, vowing to prevent future "rip-offs."

It was a measure of how feminist the lesbians had become that,
instead of acknowledging that the cultural reformist males had valid
organizational and strategic reasons for being concerned about the
course of events, they tended to interpret the men's behavior in the
psychological terms suggested by radical feminist perspectives. The
thoughts about the creation of separate treasuries that Ellen Bedoz
published in *Come Out!* were typical:

> It was generally conceded that the Aquarius men acted out of fear—fear
> that the women were so strong and so together that they would make
> unreasonable demands on the men . . .
> We call ourselves a liberation front and acknowledge that liberation
> begins with ourselves. But a frightened man is not a liberated man.
> *Men will have to confront their fears, test them against reality, analyze
> them, discover their source, and place that discovery within a political
> frame of reference.* This can be accomplished through consciousness-
> raising . . .
> Once men begin to discover the politics of their misplaced fears they
> will stop anticipating excessive demands from women and thereby stop
> reacting to women's statements with hostility. This in turn would enable
> the women to drop a defensive posture which has become their armor
> against this unwarranted hostility. Women must feel free to unequivo-
> cally make their needs known. And men must be free to pursue their ends
> unhampered by unrealistic fears and with a clear understanding of the
> political implications of their feelings. Only then can an atmosphere of
> real trust develop so we can honestly relate to each other as sisters and
> brothers.[16]

Believing personal behavior to be the measure of political conviction, Bedoz and others considered the extent to which GLF's men
worked to be mature and supportive in their dealings with lesbians
as an index of their commitment to liberation. And the disappointment the lesbian GLFers felt over the incident of the Aquarius

money turned to disillusionment when a marathon session held to draw up a statement of principles agreeable to both men and women resulted only in more friction and suspicion. Before the end of June, most of the lesbians in GLF agreed that they needed an independent group. The leaflet Bedoz handed out at the June dance financed with the money that the women in the Aquarius Cell had taken announced: "The radical lesbian movement is growing and changing; coalescing would probably be the best word . . . Some 50 women have been meeting informally but regularly as a group (as yet unnamed) for a couple of months; we [have] finally acknowledged our 'groupdom' around awareness of our special interests in the broader Movement . . ."

.   .   .

Because the lesbians, being radical, believed they had to proceed in ways consistent with humane ideals, they spent the whole summer of 1970 working to equip their new group with identity, legitimacy, and resources. At one of their first planning sessions, they decided to call their association Lesbian Liberation rather than Radical Lesbians, fearing that the term *radical* would keep them from attracting lesbians with conventional views. Yet in the end, their desire to have their group embody humane ideals outweighed their ambition to build a successful organization. In the fall, Ellen Bedoz revised her leaflet to announce that the name Radicalesbians had been formally adopted and that building a big organization was less of a priority than developing organizational forms that helped individuals become liberated:

We hope our policy and ideology will assume the shape of our collective needs. We are against hierarchical structures because as women we have experienced firsthand that hierarchy is a fixed status system (those with power and privilege, i.e. men, assume leadership and use it to perpetuate their advantage). We want an organization that encourages growth and fluidity. Therefore, we do not have "leaders." We experiment with forms that promote the participation of everyone in decision-making and actions. Some of these are consensus (sense of the meeting) instead of the vote, the lot system of assigning responsibilities, and a preference for meeting and rapping *with* small groups of women, rather than speaking *at* them in auditoriums and lecture halls. The quality of our exchanges with women is more important to us than reaching large numbers with stale rhetoric. We believe that we must live by revolutionary forms while we struggle against sexism, racism, and imperialism; that part of the revolution is process, not goal. Small action-oriented collectives seem to be the direction in which we are headed.[17]

What Bedoz did not acknowledge was that the radical preoccupation with working in new ways had alienated most of the lesbians responsible for the beginnings of lesbian feminism, even before Radicalesbians, nicknamed RL, was formalized. Among the first to go were intellectual recruits from the women's movement such as Sidney Abbott, Barbara Love, and March Hoffman. Abbott, a Smith alumna, was completing a master's in urban planning at Columbia when she met Rita Mae Brown and was asked to join in the consciousness-raising group of lesbians from the gay and women's liberation movements. Barbara Love, Abbott's lover, was working at CBS and completing a book on women in the media. Their friend March Hoffman, a graduate of Vassar and Columbia and a veteran of The Feminists, was continuing her research on feminism and psychology.

Abbott was put off at the beginning by the way the organizers of Radicalesbians treated Kate Millett, a professor at Barnard whom she had become acquainted with at meetings of Columbia's Women's Liberation Group. In April 1970, knowing that Millett, in her capacity as educational chairman of New York NOW, was planning to address the Congress to Unite Women, Abbott had disclosed that she was lesbian and warned her friend of the impending Lavender Menace demonstration. Much to Abbott's surprise, Millett confided that she too was lesbian. During the congress, by saying that it was necessary for the women's movement to embrace lesbians, and by helping Abbott prepare the resolutions that were adopted on the final day, Millett took a big step toward acknowledging her sexual orientation publicly. Abbott was so impressed that she invited Millett to attend the first organizational meeting of lesbians eager to form an independent lesbian liberation group.

When Millett arrived at the meeting, a few days after the *New York Times* carried an announcement of the forthcoming publication of her *Sexual Politics,* she was greeted by an unsigned flier condemning her for violating radical ideals by promoting herself at the expense of her sisters and by permitting the "pig media" to perpetrate elitism and competition by making stars of privileged individuals. Insisting that the charges were unfair, Abbott succeeded in persuading most of those in attendance to destroy their copies of the leaflet, but she could not persuade its author to identify herself. (Most believed it the work of Rita Mae Brown and Martha Shelley, who frequently argued that in order to avoid being co-opted radicals should publish only in alternative journals like *Rat* and *Come Out!*) Neither Millett nor Abbott attended subsequent organizing sessions—Millett because she was hurt and frightened, Abbott because she was away for the summer. By the fall, avoiding the established media had become a tenet of Radicalesbian operating procedure.

The reception given Millett made Abbott suspicious not only of Brown and Shelley but also of Hart, Bedoz, Kisner, and other lesbian GLFers who, unlike Brown and Shelley, belonged to the consciousness-raising group that Abbott, Love, and Hoffman had joined at the beginning of 1970. At the first meeting of this c-r group, Abbott and Love recognized that the lesbian GLFers had countercultural views and values that made their own seem very traditional. With each passing week they felt greater pressure to adopt the nontraditional ways of thinking and acting that the radicals equated with liberation. Before the end of the summer, when they agreed to write an essay on the origins of lesbian feminism for Vivian Gornick's anthology on women's liberation, Abbott and Love had come to believe that pursuing lesbian liberation was a matter not of persuading lesbians to abandon conventional professional, social, and political aspirations, but of changing conventional mores so that they could be both open about their homosexuality and true to their femininity without sacrificing their opportunity to compete for conventional rewards. Contact with the views of the radicals had transformed Abbott and Love into the first of a breed of lesbian feminist reformers.

Indeed, that autumn, Barbara Love felt so alienated by RL's radicalism that she decided to resurrect GLF's Women's Caucus. To distinguish "GLF Women" from Radicalesbians, she wrote a statement for *Come Out!* outlining lesbian feminist positions that would later be regarded as distinctively reformist. Seeing that those in RL, in their eagerness to exemplify innovative, woman-identified ways, hesitated to include lesbians with conventional outlooks and women uncertain about their lesbian identities, Love began her statement by pointing out that "GLF women welcome all women." Personal experience had shown Love that RL's aspiration to embody new ways of thinking and acting put strong pressures on members to abandon traditional pastimes and to participate in consciousness-raising that encouraged conformity. GLF's Women's Caucus was to be different: "In meetings and activities we maintain a flexible way of doing things to encompass our sisters of different social, economic, racial, religious, and political interests, and to permit individual freedom in actions and activities, both inside and outside of GLF." The members of Radicalesbians vowed to seed a new culture by transforming their own lives. "GLF Women," according to Love, "are dedicated to changing attitudes, institutions, and laws that oppress lesbians . . . We work for a common understanding among all people that lesbianism is . . . a valid life style." Radical dreams led RL members to disavow cooperative efforts even with gay liberationists and straight feminists. Reformist ambitions made GLF Women more accommodating: "As homosexuals, we work with our gay brothers to fight oppression based on society's exclusion of individuals who love members of the same sex. As women, we work with Women's Liberation to fight the oppression of all women."[18]

Pioneering lesbian feminist reformers like Love were not the only women to be alienated by RL's radicalism. Rita Mae Brown and Martha Shelley, whose revolutionary outlooks became more pronounced as they began to write for Robin Morgan and others on the staff of *Rat,* agreed with the radical critique of sexism. But they insisted that dealing with economic, political, and racial matters was equally important. And they expressed skepticism that individuals could revolutionize conciousness just by thinking and living in innovative ways. Brown, who derided the proponents of alternative life styles as "touchie-feelies," charged that the psychological approach to social change advocated by Lois "Loving" Hart was naively sentimental and middle class. Hart and her friends responded that Brown was caustic, cerebral, and cold because she was male-identified and hence unliberated.

Unlike the radicals, Brown and Shelley advocated hard-headed theorizing, tightly structured organization, and practical political action on problems involving class and race as well as sex and sexual orientation. Both urged their associates to consider violence as a tool for challenging the system and fomenting revolution. Both portrayed lesbians as the vanguard of a revolutionary movement that had to include straight women, the economically exploited, and Third

World peoples. Both were disillusioned enough to turn their attention to other projects, including their own writing careers, upon learning that distraught members of Radicalesbians had agreed to help the "pigs" after one of their number, Lydia French, was found murdered.

Radicalesbian regulars were unfazed by Brown and Shelley's defection, not least because they considered them loners who limited their organizational involvement to periodic appearances at meetings during which they made standard revolutionary pitches. More bothersome to those in RL were the internal squabbles they had as they worked to translate radical ideals into practice. For despite all the avowals that RL would provide each of its members with affirmation and intimacy, and despite all the time taken and procedural innovations devised for this purpose, many in Radicalesbians complained that they felt unfulfilled and alienated, and more and more members, disenchanted and exhausted, dropped out.

What shared ideals and carefully wrought procedures could not overcome were the very real differences among RL members. From the beginning, for example, Hart's clear-sightedness and charisma made her the leader of a group committed to eliminating leadership. Moreover, the natural affinity that existed among Hart and her lover Suzanne Bevier, Bedoz and her high school friend Arlene Kisner, and Ellen Broidy and her lover Linda Rhodes—all attractive, well educated, professionally experienced, and self-confident—made them a powerful clique in an association committed to the abolition of powerful cliques.

Partly because they were younger, physically smaller, and shyer, and partly because they were less clear in their thinking and newer to Movement politics, Fran Winant and "Judy Grepperd" felt particularly overwhelmed and excluded by the "Big Six." They were hurt because they had not been invited to participate in the writing of "The Woman-Identified Woman" and in the planning of the Lavender Menace demonstration, and they felt used because they were enlisted at the last minute to appear as Lavender Menaces. Didn't this, Winant and Grepperd asked, belie the radical goal of making each individual feel significant by undertaking all projects collectively? Weren't the Big Six behaving in ways that were male-identified?

Questions such as those raised by Winant and Grepperd made the de facto leaders of Radicalesbians wonder if it was possible for them to be themselves without making their organizational associates feel overwhelmed and excluded. And they were just as unclear about how to deal with the regular arrival of newcomers who were unexposed to radical thinking, inexperienced politically and organizationally, unacquainted with veteran activists, and uncomfortable in the new environment. On the one hand, the radical leaders wanted to instruct their sisters, to impress them with the beauty of woman-identified ways, and to push them to develop the self-assurance and the skills that would guarantee them a place in the liberated lesbian vanguard. On the other hand, convinced that their primary duty was to abide by liberationist ideals, they were inclined to satisfy their own needs and wants without being directive and demanding, to let others assume responsibilities and experience growth in their own ways and at their own rates, and to avoid perpetuating their group simply for the sake of perpetuating their group.

By the fall of 1970, Hart, Bedoz, Kisner, and the other lesbian GLFers responsible for organizing Radicalesbians had ceased to believe that lesbian liberation could be effectively pursued in formal groups of any size. Radical ambitions called first for each individual to concentrate on her own self-realization and to be involved with others only when this enhanced personal growth. Experience showed that individual differences, diverse histories, and changing circumstances made it difficult for individuals to feel enriched and affirmed in any but small self-selected groups. The only feasible moral course seemed to be for all individuals to live their own lives according to liberationist ideals: learning in their own ways how to express themselves fully and freely; growing at their own rates; striving to deal with others more intimately and supportively in personal relationships and informal groups; joining in organized political activity only when it felt right; and affecting others in the course of their daily lives in ways that were, for all involved, respectful of individual differences and personal autonomy.

Late in December 1970, a group of Radicalesbian veterans went to Vermont to write a paper on the construction of "lesbian nation" and "decided to live it instead." In the spring of 1971, anticipating the migrations to the countryside made later by many radical lesbian feminists, Hart and her friends set out to buy some land and settle a rural commune. A photograph of them adorns the cover of *Amazon Expedition,* the first published anthology of lesbian feminist writing.

To some extent, the first lesbian liberationists felt that they had to go off on their own to live liberated lives because their involvement in organized political activity had been so intense for so long. Hart and Bevier, for example, lived in a large loftlike space which they made over themselves, drove a van, and were continually housing and helping people who dropped by to talk politics or to work on projects. During the first half of 1969, they were heavily involved in Alternate U. Continuing that association while helping to organize the Gay Liberation Front, they raised a GLF banner at the headquarters of the Alternate U contingent when they went with it to Woodstock in the summer of 1969. And as their interest in radical feminism grew, Hart and Bevier also turned their attention to women's liberation. Arlene Kisner's appointment book records that in January 1970, she, Hart, and others met for the first time with Robin Morgan to talk about setting up a women's center. Rita Mae Brown remembers that late in the spring of 1970, she and her lover and Hart and hers met with Ti-Grace Atkinson to discuss relationships between lesbianism and feminism. Jill Johnston describes how Hart worked to transform her into a lesbian feminist in the collection of articles and journal entries she published as *Lesbian Nation.* That book begins with the radical encomium: "Every important revolutionary movement produces its fearless catalysts prodding pushing proving challenging irritating power-tripping seducing all new comers and incurring much wrath on their own heads in this crucial sacrificial action and personal upheaval moving toward liberation with dramatic confrontation with others. lois hart is one of these."[19]

Though they were less involved with prominent feminist leaders, the women who became senior Radicalesbians after the departure of the Big Six devoted much of their lives to politics. Sensitive to the way that leadership asserted itself informally and determined to worry less about their own self-expression than about seeing that their peers felt fulfilled and affirmed, Fran Winant and Judy Grepperd worked to make each of the lesbians who attended RL meetings feel that she had an equal voice in decisions and a respectable role in activities. This attempt to perfect what they called radical feminist collectivism (something Grepperd experienced in the small radical feminist publishing collective she belonged to) took interminable hours of discussion at formal meetings and countless more in private sessions with individuals and in small groups. What time and energy remained went into efforts to allocate justly the jobs involved in running dances; to select representatives equitably to handle speaking engagements; to divide the responsibility fairly for responding to letters; and to prepare an article on lesbian health care collectively (accomplished by having individuals interview one another and then edit the manuscript in turn). Because process was more important than product, devising ways of doing things that included everyone and making sure that everyone felt good about everything that was done took precedence over coming up with ideas for new projects or seeing that they were carried out efficiently and effectively.

Yet for all their efforts to have their smaller and more intimate version of Radicalesbians embody radical ideals, even Winant and Grepperd ended up doubting whether liberation could be effectively realized in formal associations. Much as they tried to be self-effacing at RL meetings, they found that they were drawn into being assertive because they had knowledge and experience. Members with less aptitude and interest asked, expected, or left the veterans with no choice but to take the lead.

For that matter, despite all that was accomplished within Radicalesbians, Winant and Grepperd's hope that their group would be seen as a model of egalitarian collectivism was dashed when women who had dropped out or who failed to attend meetings identified themselves—or were identified—as Radicalesbians when they acted on their own. Martha Shelley proclaimed herself a radical lesbian (understood as Radicalesbian) in August 1970 when she stormed the stage at the first NOW-sponsored Women's Strike Day rally to demand that straight feminists support their lesbian sisters, and then again in September, when she helped organize a sit-in in Weinstein Hall to protest New York University's discrimination against the surrounding gay community. Ann Sanchez was identified as a Radicalesbian in December when, in the presence of a reporter from *Time*, she challenged Kate Millett to acknowledge that she was a lesbian at a public forum on the gay and women's liberation movements at Columbia. Sidney Abbott identified herself as a radical lesbian when she and Barbara Love organized a press conference of prominent feminist leaders to protest a subsequent story in *Time* that suggested that Millett had discredited herself as a spokeswoman for the women's movement by publicly acknowledging that she was bisexual.

Each of these events made Winant and Grepperd despair of seeing genuine collectivism become the hallmark of lesbian liberation. But none was more disheartening than when Ellen Broidy and members of her privately organized consciousness-raising group appeared at the second Christopher Street Liberation Day March wearing T-shirts emblazoned with what they said was the flag of "lesbian nation." To those who were presiding over the final disintegration of Radicalesbians, the fact that the colors were worn by some—but not all—was dramatic proof that the lesbian nation they had envisioned was not to be.

10

The Disintegration of
DOB–New York

IF RADICAL LESBIAN LEADERS rapidly became disillusioned, others refused to give up on pursuing lesbian liberation in formal associations. Late in the fall of 1970, Sidney Abbott and Barbara Love invited the most prominent lesbians they knew to join in a consciousness-raising group that would promote the reformist variety of lesbian feminism they believed in. During the next year, members of this so-called supergroup formed about a dozen replicas, all of which were duly termed supergroups. Simultaneously, thanks to the ambitions of Ruth Simpson, the Daughters of Bilitis in New York joined in activities sponsored by the gay and women's liberation movements. Yet DOB–New York remained something of a militant homophile–women's rights hybrid until the spring of 1971, when a coalition of lesbians with reformist and radical lesbian feminist outlooks ousted Simpson and her followers and made DOB the locus of a second concerted effort to institutionalize lesbian feminism.

The seeds of these metamorphoses in DOB–New York's identity were sown by the Stonewall Riots. Because so many said that the raid on the Stonewall warranted a political response from homosexuals, and because Martha Shelley made the case personally to DOB leaders Jeanne Perry and Eleanor Krane, DOB–New York joined MSNY in cosponsoring a vigil in Washington Square. Yet Shelley was the only lesbian whom Perry and Krane could enlist to speak at the vigil on DOB's behalf. And before the summer was out, fearing that the activities of self-styled gay liberationists would threaten DOB–New York's status as a legitimate support group for lesbians and as a reliable repository of information about female homosexuality, Perry and Krane followed the lead of Dick Leitsch and tried to keep their distance from liberationist efforts. By the end of 1969, all that remained of the Stonewall stimulus was a renewed interest in exposing rank-and-file DOBers to the thinking of homophile militants; a willingness to join in legal and negotiating initiatives with MSNY moderates (early in 1970, DOBers joined Mattachine officials in a discussion of fair employment legislation with newly elected councilman Eldon Clingan); and a greater receptiveness to those who questioned DOB–New York's role as a group committed solely to lesbian-centered education, social activities, and services. This receptiveness grew as Perry and Krane encouraged new young leaders to take charge.

DOB–New York's continued conservatism was partly an unintended upshot of visits to DOB meetings by radical lesbians eager to lead the Daughters into the gay liberation movement. With words and example, the lesbian GLFers hoped to help their more traditional sisters see how convention constrained their self-expression and inhibited their personal relations. The impression they made on lesbians with conventional views and values was satirized in a letter one conservative member wrote to the *Ladder:*

> Nowadays in New York we have lots and lots of Lesbians who belong to the now generation and look just like any other hippie and who in fact rather seldom sleep with girls. I went to a DOB meeting the other night and there was this new style Lesbian from GLF who we can call Lois Hart who talked quite a lot and here is what she said and I quote exactly because I actually wrote it down, "We've got to find out where everybody's head is at, we've got to get our thing together and like wow really be beautiful and relate to each other and be real in a meaningful way."[1]

Undaunted by such reactions, Hart and other radical lesbians continued their visits to DOB through the winter and spring of 1970. By then they were saying that the lesbian's capacity to develop truly woman-identified life styles suited her for a position in the vanguard of the women's movement. The implied invitation to see themselves as radical lesbian feminists left most DOBers as cold as the challenge to become radical gay liberationists. In fact, in April 1970—partly at

Kay Tobin's urging that they join the wave of political activism spearheaded by the Gay Activists Alliance—a majority in DOB–New York voted to abandon the group's long-standing policy of limiting all events to women and to sponsor periodic meetings with gay men. That summer, when copies of a new version of a brochure called "What Is DOB?" arrived from the national offices, the New Yorkers complained that the brochure suggested that DOB was a feminist group that happened to include lesbians rather than a lesbian group concerned also about women's rights.

Those in charge of DOB–New York wanted the tone of the promotional brochure to be just right because they were beginning to feel that they had to compete for the loyalties of local lesbians not just with GLF and Radicalesbians but with the less unconventional Gay Activists Alliance. Largely to attract new members and boost attendance, early in the summer of 1970 program director Ruth Simpson began to ask prominent feminists to address membership meetings.

To a late June meeting Simpson invited Ti-Grace Atkinson, who, though now ousted from The Feminists, retained her reputation as a leading radical feminist theoretician. Atkinson used the occasion to argue that lesbians had an essential role in women's liberation. Her argument, not nearly so well developed but similar in thrust to that presented a month earlier in "The Woman-Identified Woman," was summarized in its most memorable line: "Feminism is the theory; lesbianism is the practice." The DOB–New Yorkers were flattered by the tribute paid them by so renowned a straight feminist but horrified when a group of radical lesbians in the audience, seeking to raise consciousness about the need to live, as well as talk about, woman-identified life styles, challenged Atkinson to practice what she preached. The incident led Atkinson to change her mind about joining DOBers at the first Christopher Street Liberation Day march, but it did not deter her from supporting DOB–New York by enrolling as a member.

The leaders of DOB–New York continued to identify with the gay movement, but Atkinson's interest encouraged them to ask other prominent feminists to talk to them. To the sixth biannual conference of the Daughters of Bilitis, run in July 1970 by the New York chapter (and boycotted by the ultrafeminist national officers), they invited Carolyn Bird, author of *Born Female;* Minda Bikman and Mickey Zacuto, members of the New York Radical Feminists; and

Del Martin and Phyllis Lyon, by then more involved in NOW than in DOB. At August membership meetings, the DOB–New Yorkers heard lawyer, civil rights activist, and feminist Florynce Kennedy, who argued that being lesbian was like being black, and Kate Millett, more exuberant about having participated in the Liberation Day march than soured by the way she had been greeted by the organizers of Radicalesbians. As she had done after the Lavender Menace demonstration, Millett acknowledged her lesbianism publicly: "I wanted to be here, in a surreptitious way, for a long time—but I was too chicken." (An account of Millett's talk in DOB–New York's September newsletter—mailed out the same week Millett was first featured in *Time*, in a cover story that made no mention of her homosexuality—said simply, "Hearing Kate Millett had more therapeutic value than twenty sessions with a shrink.")[2] In the fall, DOB–New York welcomed Phyllis Chesler—who suggested that lesbian relationships were a valid alternative for women who felt confined in heterosexual arrangements—and Ivy Bottini and Jackie Ceballos, president and public relations director, respectively, of New York NOW. Bottini and Ceballos argued that the women's movement needed lesbians but that it was not strategic for NOW to jeopardize reforms benefiting all women by championing homosexual causes officially.*

If the words of the famous feminists were a call to activism, the decision of the sixth biannual convention to dissolve DOB's national structure provided local lesbians excited about making DOB–New York more political with an opportunity to redefine their chapter. After receiving an invitation to appear on a local television talk show,

*There was a division of opinion on this matter among New York NOW leaders that showed three weeks later, when New York NOW sponsored a panel discussion on the topic "Is Lesbianism a Feminist Issue?" The panelists, some of them closeted lesbian members of NOW, included Dr. Barbara Sang, Dolores Alexander, Ivy Bottini, Vivian Gornick, Sidney Abbott, Barbara Love, and Kate Millett, and they overwhelmingly favored NOW's championing lesbian concerns. Millett contended that the women's movement had "been carried on the backs of Lesbians for about five years" and that "Lesbians did a lot of the work for abortion and child care centers 'while trying not to look like dykes,' and now it's time for the movement to do something for Lesbians."[3]

With the approach of NOW–New York's annual elections, the lesbian issue became the focus of controversy between liberal and conservative leaders in the national and New York offices. Relying largely on information obtained from former New York NOW president Ivy Bottini, today an acknowledged lesbian, Abbott and Love report in *Sappho Was a Right-On Woman* that the conservatives, led by Betty Friedan, made a dramatic effort to keep lesbians from being elected or reelected to office and that their "purge" succeeded partly because of the support it received from closeted lesbian NOW members Jeanne Perry and Eleanor Krane.[4]

DOB–New York's president, reluctant to go public, resigned, and Ruth Simpson, who agreed to make the television appearance, was selected as acting chief. Soon afterward, Simpson helped Tina Mandel and her lover Alma Routsong (the "Isabel Miller" who wrote *Patience and Sarah*) protest a talk at the William Alanson White Institute by two psychologists who characterized lesbians as "cannibals, vampires, and utopia seekers." Subsequently, in addition to DOB–New York's regular bimonthly membership meetings, the activists scheduled planning sessions to discuss how DOB could be more political. Ellen Povill and her lover Eileen Webb found the sessions so exciting that they abandoned GLF Women in order to help Simpson and the others transform DOB–New York.

Still, the number of DOB–New Yorkers who believed political activity important remained small until an incident in the beginning of October. Two police officers unexpectedly barged into a planning session at the Corduroy Club, the headquarters of a gay male social group from which DOB–New York sublet space, and asked to see the certificate of occupancy that entitled the group to use the premises. Ruth Simpson complained that the visit was unwarranted harassment and refused to cooperate. The police threatened to arrest her. After Povill telephoned DOB–New York's lawyer, who told the officers about the group's arrangement with the Corduroy Club and instructed Simpson to comply with their request for her driver's license, the police were content to hand over a summons ordering the DOB president to appear in court a few weeks later.

Just before the police arrived, a majority of the planning session had voted not to have DOB–New York accept GAA's invitation to participate in joint demonstrations. Once the police left, the vote was reversed. During the next week, a demonstration was planned to show support for Simpson when she appeared in court. GAA was asked to participate, and DOB–New York submitted to the Homosexual Community Council a list of "demands" it wanted issued to public officials. In an editorial in the November newsletter, Alma Routsong explained why DOB–New York had become politicized:

> D.O.B. since its beginning has been a quiet social and educational organization. It gives a protected first step toward fellowship and self-acceptance. It is a home and family for lesbians. Most of us don't want it to be anything else. We are not marchers and chanters and demanders.

So what are we doing in the streets and courthouses? Why are we issuing demands and allying ourselves with other groups to get the strength to back up our demands?

Because:

· If the police can interrupt our meetings we can no longer feel like a safe first step for the shy and hidden.

· If the police can make our officers waste time and thoughts on legal problems, the quality of our meetings declines.

· If we have to pay legal fees to protect ourselves from whimsical, random charges, our treasury is depleted.

· If our officers have to miss work to go back and back to court, no one will be willing to accept an office . . .

We have the powers Flo Kennedy told us about: voting power, dollar power, and body power.

We must use them concertedly now.[5]

· · ·

Routsong portrayed the politicization of DOB–New York as a fait accompli, but the October events were simply the beginning of six months of contention about whether and how DOB–New York should contribute to gay political activity. Most of the participants in the disputes that took place remember them as emotional personality clashes. From a broader perspective, it is clear that personal frictions were rooted in different political outlooks and organizational ambitions and that conflict was the process through which those in DOB–New York came to grips with lesbian feminism.

The first disagreement arose between newly inspired proponents of political activism like Simpson, Mandel, and Routsong and veterans convinced that DOB–New York should not abandon its moderate homophile character. The veterans began to make their pitch shortly after Simpson and her supporters on the Executive Committee voted to require that members who wanted to run for president and vice-president in the upcoming organizational elections be willing to appear in court. This was taken to mean that members who wanted to be officers had to use their real names publicly. It provoked the incumbent vice-president, a professional woman who was reluctant to be open, and others fearful that the Simpson regime would do away with DOB–New York's long-standing role as a lesbian support group to announce that they would secede and form a new group to continue DOB's traditional social and service endeavors.

Told that these disaffected women spent most of their time discussing refreshments for their meetings, Simpson and her followers nicknamed them "the bagels."

With the threatened membership loss posed by the organizing efforts of these defectors, Simpson redoubled her efforts to give DOB–New York a reputation for activity and versatility. To show that the Daughters could play a role in feminist as well as gay political affairs, she attended the press conference of prominent feminist leaders held to protest *Time* magazine's attempt to discredit Kate Millett as a feminist leader after she had spoken publicly of her lesbianism. To make it clear that political involvement did not preclude social events and services, with help from Webb and from Povill, who had been elected vice-president, Simpson arranged to have DOB–New York housed in a large loft on Prince Street in Soho. The new headquarters was billed as an all-purpose Lesbian Center.

Enlisted to speak at the opening of the center were Florynce Kennedy and Ti-Grace Atkinson. Atkinson used the occasion to expand on ideas about the tactical significance of lesbianism for the women's movement that she had elaborated in an essay on the *New York Times* op-ed page. Atkinson had argued in the *Times* that by virtue of their total commitment to women, lesbians were the "shock troops" of women in the struggle against men. She suggested that women committed to women in all but sexual ways could be called "political lesbians," while women married to or otherwise intimately involved with men were "collaborators with the enemy." In her expanded version of this argument at the Lesbian Center opening, Atkinson contended that lesbians occupied a "criminal" or "buffer" zone between the male and female classes and that the male ruling class's treatment of lesbians was a tool for keeping the entire female class subservient. She argued that once members of the lesbian "buffer" class and of the "pro-rebellion" female class recognized that society's treatment of lesbianism was intended to perpetuate the bondage of women, they would band together and acknowledge that women totally committed to women (sexually or not) were the vanguard of the feminist revolution. To downplay the distinction between "real lesbians" and "political lesbians," Atkinson concluded, "I'm enormously less interested in whom you sleep with than I am in with whom you're prepared to die."[6]

Once DOB–New York was installed in its new center, political activity proliferated. Atkinson coordinated a weekly Feminist Workshop to train "real lesbians" for their positions in the feminist vanguard. Povill presided over an Action Committee formed to handle DOB–New York's participation in gay political actions, including GAA zaps held to publicize the Clingan-Burden gay rights bill and planning meetings for the second annual Liberation Day march. At the beginning of March 1971, at Simpson's urging, participants in one of DOB–New York's planning sessions voted to contribute $350 a month to support Human Rights for Women, a feminist group in Washington, D.C., established to challenge discriminatory laws and policies in the courts. A few days later, members of the Action Committee went to Central Presbyterian Church to protest the showing of a film they felt contained a biased portrait of lesbianism. In mid-March, a DOB–New York contingent traveled to Albany to participate in a rally for the progay legislation that had been introduced in the state legislature. Toward the end of the month, members of the Feminist Workshop accompanied Ti-Grace Atkinson to Washington, D.C., where she gave a speech at Catholic University critical of the Roman Catholic Church's stands on abortion, birth control, and sexuality. Back in Manhattan, Simpson, Povill, and Webb organized a picket line and press conference at St. Patrick's Cathedral to publicize their support for Atkinson, who had been slapped during her speech by Mrs. Brent Bozell, wife of the editor of *Triumph* magazine and sister of James and William Buckley.

Simpson, Povill, and Webb believed they were leading DOB–New York in the right political directions, but others were not so sure. On the one hand, there was the grumbling from members who felt that it was a waste of time and energy for lesbians to join in political crusades championed by gay men. Like so many DOBers before them, they maintained that the issues raised by sodomy, solicitation, and other practices associated with the gay male subculture were of relatively little consequence to lesbians, who had problems with rights and status primarily because they were women. On the other hand, there were the complaints of members who objected that the time and resources allotted to the efforts of straight feminists were misplaced. Straight women were as prejudiced about homosexuality as everyone else, these critics said; and despite the welcome extended by the prominent feminist leaders who addressed DOB–New York meetings, this was painfully obvious from New York NOW's efforts to purge lesbians from its official ranks.

The reservations of those critical of DOB's involvement with straight feminists were reinforced by the fear that Simpson's fascination with Ti-Grace Atkinson, as well as her willingness to contribute so much money to enterprises like Human Rights for Women, would lead to a neglect of lesbians' distinctive needs as homosexual women —particularly their need for activities to build up lesbian pride and a supportive lesbian community. Tina Mandel was stunned to discover that Simpson had gone through each copy of the January newsletter and inked out a sarcastic allusion to the militant tenor of Atkinson's remarks at the opening of the Lesbian Center. Alma Routsong, the newsletter editor, was blamed for the sarcasm, and Simpson replaced her with Eileen Webb. Mandel also saw evidence of misplaced priorities in the flood of superficial feminist rhetoric that filled the newsletter after Webb took over. One of Webb's first products began: "Hello, Darlings. Feeling Oppressed?! . . . Let's raise our voices and fists in protest! Power to Women! Power to Lesbians! . . . Get your life in order! Know your enemy!"[7]

Routsong was equally offended by her successor's rhetoric. It also disturbed her that Simpson seemed to have lost interest in getting DOB–New York legally incorporated and in drawing up by-laws that would assure the rank and file a chance to participate in organizational affairs. Agreeing with Mandel that Simpson, Povill, and Webb had become progressively more headstrong and misguided, Routsong helped her organize a small group to talk about making their complaints heard and to groom leaders who might succeed the ruling clique. They called their group The Caucus.

At meetings of The Caucus Simpson's critics clarified their sentiments about what best served the interests of lesbians into a reformist variety of lesbian feminism. Their efforts were guided by the views that Mandel and Routsong carried to Caucus meetings from the consciousness-raising supergroup that Sidney Abbott and Barbara Love had organized—a group that included Kate Millett (who wrote about it in *Flying*), Ivy Bottini, and other influential lesbians purged from New York NOW. Most of the members of supergroup #1 agreed that it was necessary to challenge both the sexism and the homophobia* that kept openly lesbian women from being accorded representation and respect in established institutions. They believed this was best done by bringing lesbians together in a movement dedicated to developing and promoting fulfilling lesbian feminist life styles and community (they regarded the latter as particularly important because lesbians lacked the elaborate web of subcultural patterns and institutions that gave gay men some support). Mandel and Routsong came away convinced that instead of joining in initiatives sponsored by gay and women's liberationists, DOB–New York should concentrate on activities that brought lesbians together to explore their lesbian feelings and their womanhood and to make these the bases of liberated life styles, activities, institutions, and communities.†

Though vague about exactly what "liberated" meant, Mandel, Routsong, and other Caucus members accepted the radical lesbian feminist assumption that homosexual women, as women with the ability to be totally intimate with other women, had quintessentially female sensibilities, and that these could be developed into modes of thinking and acting that would permit each individual to express herself fully and freely without making anyone else feel dismissed or belittled. In the light of this assumption, they criticized Simpson, Povill, and Webb not only because they failed to give priority to forms (such as participatory democracy) and activities (such as small group discussions) in which lesbians could develop their special sensibilities, but also because they seemed to betray lesbian feminist ideals by being self-righteous, insensitive, and domineering.

While those in The Caucus worked out reformist lesbian feminist positions, rank-and-file DOBers in Atkinson's Feminist Workshop evolved radical lesbian feminist viewpoints. When they were asked

---

*According to the leaders of GAA, *homophobia* was a word used to refer to the irrational fear and loathing of homosexuals, coined by psychologist George Weinberg, one of the first mental health professionals to appreciate gay liberationist thinking. The term became popular after Weinberg used it in *Society and the Healthy Homosexual,* published in 1972.

†In contrast, the self-help and social activities favored by DOB–New Yorkers with moderate homophile ambitions were intended to help lesbians deal with the problems they had relating to straights, to help lesbians measure up better to conventional ideas about how women were supposed to look and act, and thereby to help them fit more skillfully into the mainstream. In the early 1960s, Barbara Gittings and Kay Tobin used to parody the *Ladder*'s moderate homophile orientation by saying that its motto should be "up the ladder, into skirts, and into society."

to serve as bodyguards during Atkinson's public appearances, these DOBers began to feel that the feminist ideal of individual parity was being violated. (They appear in the photograph of Atkinson's arrival for her speech at Catholic University in *Amazon Odyssey,* a collection of Atkinson's writings.) To members of the workshop, including Ann Sanchez and Lyn Kupferman, who was close to Tina Mandel, it seemed that Atkinson, lacking institutional affiliation after her ouster from The Feminists, was trying to make DOB–New York her new base, and that Simpson, enamored of Atkinson and impressed by her celebrity, was allowing DOB–New York to be used.

The suspicions of the Feminist Workshop members festered until the end of April, when Sanchez announced that she mistrusted Simpson's motives. Alarmed, Atkinson suspended meetings of the workshop and informed Simpson, who, upon investigating, also found out about The Caucus. Seeing a threatening cabal, Simpson made known her discoveries by criticizing Mandel, Routsong, and others in a three-page letter printed at the head of the May newsletter. Simpson listed the complaints of her critics, defended her actions in each case, and called for a special meeting on May 6 "to confront our own pathology."[8]

To prepare for the expected confrontation at the May 6 meeting, members of The Caucus and of the Feminist Workshop prepared statements separately and then worked out tactics together to make sure Simpson would not be able to prevent her critics from having their say. Both dissident groups felt that Simpson had overreacted when she discovered their disaffection and that this confirmed that she lacked the self-assurance and capacity for trust that were the hallmarks of liberation. The statement by Caucus members stressed that Simpson's "power-tripping" and paranoia interfered with the participatory democracy necessary to help others achieve liberation: "We have been oppressed for too long by those who make all our choices for us. And here at DOB we see another attempt to take our choices from us. Shall we be creators of, and consenters to, our own oppression?" The critique from disillusioned members of the Feminist Workshop, more radical feminist in its language, contended that Simpson's intolerance of criticism prevented the evolution of "communal pride and purpose" and that DOB–New York's "hierarchical structure" had to be replaced:

The hierarchical structure that D.O.B. has is a male-identified trip. In our patriarchal society we are taught to look up to one person as our leader—first in the family in the form of "Father." This we transfer to society when we grow older as we elect and look up to "Presidents." The family maintains patriarchy and male supremacy. D.O.B. is modeling itself after this system of hierarchies. How can any woman call herself a feminist if she believes in this hierarchical structure? . . . When existing conflicts become irreconcilable within the established political framework, the rational, intelligent course *is not* simply to choose a side, ready to fight to the bitter end, but for *all* sides to redesign the political framework so that the existing conflicts can be reconciled. *All* sisters should collectively decide what the objectives are that they wish to obtain, and then *we can all* mold the parts into the form that is most conducive to those objectives. The framework that we must strive for is one in which Lesbians can disagree without feeling compelled to seek the destruction of their opponents. We must strive for an organization that will be for *all* Lesbians, where there will be room for *all* . . .

Radical feminist idealism notwithstanding, instead of a thoughtful assessment of Simpson's stewardship in the light of lesbian feminist principles, the May 6 meeting turned into an angry confrontation between supporters and critics of the existing regime. To ensure support for their challenge to the leadership, members of The Caucus and the workshop had invited unaffiliated radical lesbians and members of Radicalesbians and GLF Women, which was now independent and renamed Gay Women's Liberation Front (GWLF). RL and GWLF members were angry because they believed that Simpson was violating feminist principles of sympathy and sisterhood by refusing to let their own groups meet in the Lesbian Center and by denying entrance to DOB–New York events to sisters who could not afford admission fees. These radicals, caring less about revamping DOB–New York than about jolting Simpson and her supporters into liberated consciousness, denounced her loudly and emotionally. The chaos reached a climax when one of Simpson's supporters picked up a chair and started to fight with Deni Covello, who had reinvolved herself in gay political activity by taking charge of GWLF. During the uproar, Simpson, Povill, and Webb walked out. At the following week's monthly membership meeting, with Ti-Grace Atkinson in the back of the hall to lend support, Simpson declared that there was a conspiracy afoot to take over DOB and that she and her officers had decided to resign.

At the time, Simpson showed no awareness that her critics had political outlooks and organizational concerns that differed from her own. (Despite her involvement with GAA and with Atkinson, Simpson's convictions remained more militant homophile and women's rights than gay and women's liberationist in character.) Even in *From the Closet to the Courts,* the heavily autobiographical book she wrote afterward, she fails to acknowledge that the women who drove her from the presidency had legitimate disagreements with her about goals and strategy. In fact, by claiming in her book that those who put an end to her regime were simply "outside disruptors," Simpson indicates that she never grasped early lesbian feminist ideas about the priority of internal consciousness-raising and collective process. What those familiar with these ideas would recognize as efforts to devise alternative forms and procedures to promote validated self-expression and healthy social relationships, Simpson describes as "signs of impending disruption by 'pseudo-militants' ":

> What are some of the early symptoms? When a structured organization finds itself spending a lot of time discussing whether the chairs should be arranged in a circle or not; whether 'homosexual' isn't really a 'sexist' word, so why don't we call ourselves 'dykes'; whether non-members shouldn't be allowed to vote on administrative and other issues in order to avoid an 'elitist' structure . . . When time and energy are wasted discussing with the pseudo-militants whether members of the group should or should not be interviewed by the 'pig, capitalistic press,' and when these same 'militants' start meeting with other members outside the organization—often with the ultra-conservative faction which believes the group is moving too fast politically—watch out![9]

. . .

After Simpson and her associates walked out, the fifty or so lesbians remaining chose a parliamentarian, elected Tina Mandel and Ann Sanchez interim cochairwomen, and appointed temporary collectives to be responsible for dances and the newsletter. It was agreed that subsequent meetings would be spent developing policies and projects and hammering out a constitution that reflected lesbian feminist ideals. At the next meeting, the membership resolved to

make DOB–New York's facilities available to GWLF and Radicalesbians, to sponsor a Lesbian School of study groups and classes in
crafts and skills, and to create a legal collective that would consult
with lawyers about incorporating DOB–New York and handling the
notice of eviction that Simpson had received but kept secret until
after she resigned. (DOB's landlord wanted to convert his building
into condominiums.)

The new lesbian feminist constitution was ready by midsummer.
Among other things, it stipulated that DOB–New York be run by
three cochairwomen, two agenda cochairwomen, three treasurers,
and a host of collectives; that the three cochairwomen use their real
names; that membership dues be scaled according to income; that
members of Radicalesbians and GWLF would also be members of
DOB; that members work in at least one collective; that admission
to membership and events not be denied those who could not afford
to pay; and that all major decisions be ratified by a consensus of those
who attended membership meetings.

With the adoption of the constitution, hopes reached a peak, but
by the fall of 1971, DOB–New York was all but dissolved. Irreconcilable disagreements divided the very lesbians who had agreed that their
group had to be operated according to lesbian feminist principles if
it was going to survive. For in working to make DOB–New York a
lesbian feminist group, lesbian feminist reformers were alienated by
radicals, and the radicals, like Radicalesbians before them, had to
face the basic contradictions in their political and organizational
aspirations.

During the spring of 1971, the differences between the views of the
reformers in The Caucus and those of the radicals inside and outside
the Feminist Workshop appeared less important than the ambition
they shared to help lesbians develop liberated life styles and supportive community. This ambition gave rise to a common interest in
consciousness-raising self-help and social activities and in procedures
and membership requirements that would maximize individual participation.* Yet as soon as the reformers and the radicals began to

---

*Radical and reformist lesbian feminists were also united by their desire to protect DOB–
New York from lesbian feminists with revolutionary outlooks, particularly those who belonged
to the Socialist Workers Party (SWP). The radicals were incensed when the SWP prevented
them from adding the issue of "sexual self-determination" to the program of the national
conference on abortion sponsored at Columbia by the Women's National Abortion Coalition

work together, they disagreed over how to define liberated self-expression and social support and how much maintaining an organization mattered in the quest for lesbian liberation.

Reformers wanted to help lesbians feel good about expressing themselves as they wished. They viewed enterprises like study, crafts, and c-r groups as vehicles for bringing lesbians together to explore their lesbian and feminine natures in the company of other personable and attractive homosexual women. They believed that this would give them the self-confidence and the sense of support they needed to express themselves fully and freely and to enjoy rich and rewarding relationships.

Radical lesbian feminists, like radical gay and women's liberationists, were much more ambitious. They believed lesbians should develop liberated ways of thinking and acting with an eye to pioneering a revolution in consciousness. Because they assumed that these liberated ways of thinking and acting had to be new and "female" rather than conventional and "male," they worked to define "woman-identified" ways of living and working. The radicals insisted that it was woman-identified to concentrate attention on individuals professing to be unhappy or unskilled, and they criticized as "male-identified" overly self-centered, ambitious, and accomplished peers. This criticism provoked the reformers to object that lesbian feminist liberation did not require all to express themselves with the same competence in the same ways at the same time. A letter in the September issue of the newsletter cried out:

> Did a sister have an idea, take some action, *do* something? Tear her down, ridicule her, destroy her!
>
> Is she bright, ambitious, skilled? Outshout her, scream and swear, mock her!
>
> These are the rules—in Connecticut,* at DOB, at the Women's Interart Center—by which some women are effectively destroying the movement.
>
> I am desperate about what we are doing to ourselves in the name of equality and community. Must we reduce ourselves to the lowest com-

in July 1971. They detailed their grievances in an article called "SWP Infiltration" in the August issue of DOB–New York's newsletter.

*In August 1971, a group of gay women from New Haven sponsored a conference of eastern "Lesbian Feminists" to determine "what we believe" and "what we demand." This was the first large eastern convocation of lesbians who considered themselves hybrid gay and women's liberationists. It helped popularize the label *lesbian feminist* for these activists.

mon denominator in order to be sisters? Women have never had power and confidence; the only way we learned to fight was by tearing others down rather than by building ourselves up. Our egos, our ambition, our creativity have been systematically repressed by society—but we cannot be destroyed unless we do it ourselves.

Do we have so little faith in each other that any sign of strength, independence, or initiative by one of us must be seen as a threat by the others? Recognizing real accomplishment or superior skills in one sister is not a condemnation of the others; it is a triumph for all of us and a lead we can follow. More than one person can excel, but none of us will ever crawl out of this mire if we do not stop clawing at our strongest sisters. The sister who begins to learn to assert herself and exercise her full personhood must be encouraged—not ridiculed by her sisters as she is by men.

We need our leaders.[10]

While some of the reformers worried about the costs to individual lesbians of radical efforts to assure that all were progressing in the "right" ways at the same pace, others found the threat to organizational survival more worrisome. Alma Routsong responded to the letter pleading for respect for individual success with the reassurance, in her own letter, that

> we're learning, painfully, to be responsible for ourselves and each other and our sisters, and not sit passively and silently while some wise mama takes care of all that for us . . .
>
> There are weaknesses and strengths in our new structure.
>
> So far, we have seen mostly the weaknesses—the cumbersome collectives whose work can be interrupted and delayed by anyone who wants to drop in, the long Thursday meetings where it takes twenty minutes to decide to buy a garbage can and hours to discuss whether it is proper for DOB women to appear on commercial TV.
>
> The strengths are being developed: *dozens* of women now know how to put out a newsletter, run a dance, talk to lawyers, keep accounts, speak in public, answer mail, welcome timid newcomers, teach a skill. Maybe someday we'll even learn how to draw up an agenda and chair a meeting —and you can be sure no one will let up on us until we do.[11]

Unlike Mandel and other reformers, who were driven to withdraw from DOB by the quarreling, Routsong was willing to endure unpleasantness and inefficiency in order to promote individual growth. What she found harder to countenance were the challenges from radicals who believed that the need to develop woman-identified ways of thinking and acting eliminated the need to ensure DOB–New York's survival through practical steps. Routsong was annoyed by how little the radicals appreciated the efforts Mandel made—clearing every little step with the membership in order to remain faithful to the principle of collectivism—to obtain the services of a feminist lawyer and to speed DOB–New York's incorporation. And she was pained when the radicals talked heatedly but vaguely of sit-ins and resistance when she and others warned that DOB–New York would disintegrate unless it found a headquarters to replace its Prince Street loft. (When put on the spot, the radicals argued that DOB was more a state of consciousness than an institution and was therefore destined to persist no matter what happened to its physical plant.)

Because the radicals refused to take seriously the matter of house-hunting, the reformers jumped at the first opportunity they saw to install DOB–New York in a new home—an invitation to rent space for a nominal fee in GAA's Firehouse. This idea met with the objections of radicals eager to separate themselves completely from men.* One of the first to identify herself as a separatist was cochairwoman Rose Jordan, who argued that GAA, being male-identified, should compensate for its sexism by permitting DOB–New York to use the Firehouse for nothing.

Instead of renting space in the Firehouse, the separatists suggested

---

*As in Radicalesbians, the radical lesbian feminist DOBers who wanted to have no dealings whatsoever with men tended to believe that sexist behavior stemmed from the existence of men rather than from culturally perpetuated values and assumptions about sex roles and the sexes shared by and limiting to both men and women. In response to the objections to moving to the Firehouse voiced by lesbian separatists, for example, radical Pat Maxwell (whose views did become more separatist later) countered:

Sexism, as I understand it, is an institution of our oppressors which puts down any individual who doesn't wish to be confined to proper sex defined roles—male and female. Even though these roles seemed to be based on the defamation of women, I have seen men who refused to play the male role put down as frequently as women who refuse to play the female role. I would like to note that gay men are put down violently, not because I wish to promote oppression competition, but to point out more clearly that gay men are oppressed for somewhat the same reason that autonomous women are, and by the same male chauvinism . . .

When I read a sister's comments that it wasn't up to the lesbians to help raise their gay brother's consciousness, I wondered out loud, "Who then is it up to?" . . . I can see that it is up to you, gay brother, to commit yourself to raising your consciousness; but I can see that it is up to me to help. It is also up to you to raise my consciousness about my own sexism. We are all in this together.[12]

leasing a vacant storefront on First Street in the East Village. Reformers like Routsong saw that this locale was less familiar and less friendly than the neighborhood around the Firehouse, which was just around the corner from DOB's Lesbian Center, but they went along because they felt that some official home was better than none.

The Daughters moved into their new headquarters at the beginning of October and scheduled a dance for Saturday the tenth to celebrate. That night, a squad of uniformed officers from the ninth precinct barged into the dance, searched the premises, and arrested Alma Routsong and Rose Jordan for selling beer without a license —over their protests that DOB–New York was a nonprofit organization and that such groups customarily provided beer to guests who made donations. When Routsong and Jordan were taken to the station, a score of women followed to demonstrate outside. Others called GAA's officers and asked them to use their contacts in the mayor's office to have the women released. Soon afterward, a group of GAAers who had been celebrating Jim Owles's birthday when the call from DOB came joined the impromptu demonstration in front of the ninth precinct. Some time later, mayoral aides Ronnie Eldridge and Carl Irish arrived and arranged for Routsong and Jordan to be freed.

Instead of clearing the way for DOB–New York to re-establish itself, this raid and its aftermath exacerbated existing divisions. Frightened by the episode with the police, the reformers felt it all the more important to incorporate DOB–New York and to avoid behavior, such as serving alcohol at dances, that might be used as an excuse to close down the organization. Routsong was particularly anxious because she had lied in telling the police that DOB–New York was a legally incorporated nonprofit organization: it had lost that status when the national DOB was dissolved in the summer of 1970. But the radicals were enraged at the dramatic new instance of oppression, and they insisted that it was useless to try to accommodate rather than to defy the system. Indeed, angry that GAA's leaders had turned to City Hall and resentful at what they considered GAA's attempts to take credit for saving DOB, the radicals found new cause to object to any dealings with gay men; the reformers, in contrast, were thankful for GAA's support, and they were now doubly convinced that it was necessary for lesbians to cooperate politically with gay men.

Because action required consensus, disagreement meant paralysis. The lack of activity, in addition to the fear of further harassment, led to a suspension of DOB events and to the demise of the newsletter. By the middle of December 1971, when Rose Jordan and the group of radicals who persisted in identifying themselves as DOBers sponsored a forum to discuss the future of the lesbian movement, DOB–New York's reputation as an exciting place for lesbians had already been overtaken by GAA's Women's Subcommittee. This was the seed that slowly but surely flowered into Lesbian Feminist Liberation, Incorporated, the group that was to pick up where DOB–New York left off in trying to institutionalize the drive for lesbian feminist liberation.

11

Lesbian Feminist
Liberation, Inc.

BY THE WINTER of 1971–72, the first radical lesbian groups were reduced to small coteries centered around political veterans with strong personalities. Fran Winant and Judy Grepperd spoke for the half-dozen friends who continued to identify themselves as Radical-esbians. Deni Covello led the group of twelve women known as Gay Women's Liberation Front. Rose Jordan claimed title to DOB–New York by retaining access to its bank account. For lesbians interested in other organized ways of exploring the political implications of their sexuality and of associating with lesbians in situations other than bars or private circles, the opportunities were limited. There were transient study and consciousness-raising groups maintained by unaffiliated radical lesbians and radical feminists, there were about fifteen supergroups started by members of Abbott and Love's original one,* and there was the Women's Subcommittee run under the auspices of GAA's Community Relations Committee. During 1972 and 1973, the Women's Subcommittee became first a full committee, called the Lesbian Liberation Committee, and then an independent organization, Lesbian Feminist Liberation, Inc. (LFL). The story of LFL is in many ways the story of how lesbian feminist reformism was refined and institutionalized in New York City.

---

*In the spring of 1972, the members of supergroup #2 invited all of the lesbians involved in supergroups to a convention, where it was proposed that they establish a lesbian feminist organization to replace DOB–New York. Most of those in attendance opposed the idea for fear that the radical lesbians would do to any new organization what they had done to DOB.

Paradoxically, GAA's Women's Subcommittee was started by lesbians who aspired to transform lesbians into gay liberationists rather than lesbian feminists. Chief among these was Nathalie Rockhill, a Smith graduate who worked in publishing and lived in the Village. Rockhill was one of the handful of lesbians GAA had managed to attract during 1970, and she was named "chairman" of its Community Relations Committee in 1971. That May, after GAA's political leaders accommodated cultural leaders by agreeing to sponsor self-help groups, Rockhill, her lover, and a bisexual woman whose husband was also in GAA organized a "talk group" to "find ways to make GAA more relevant to women." When neither the women's talk group nor the dance it sponsored in June attracted more than a half-dozen women, Rockhill proposed to create a subcommittee of her Community Relations Committee that would work to build bridges between GAA and lesbians.

Early in the summer, Dinah Robertson began attending meetings of the women's talk group, and after a long summer vacation, she agreed to try to boost the membership of what was by then the Women's Subcommittee by running a lesbian film festival. The programs—movies with lesbian themes plus a film of the second Christopher Street Liberation Day march and a videotape of a panel of lesbians who that fall appeared on "The David Susskind Show"— were held on eight consecutive Sunday afternoons in November and December. Discussions and refreshments followed the screenings.

By the end of 1971, the programs of this "International Lesbian Film Festival" were attracting as many as a hundred and fifty women. The dozen or so who actually belonged to GAA were spurred to ask that their subcommittee be graduated to full committee status. After being elected vice-president in the December elections, Rockhill persuaded the Executive Committee and the membership to approve the establishment of a Lesbian Liberation Committee (LLC) with Dinah Robertson as its "chair." (By this time, in response to complaints, terms like *chairman* had been replaced in GAA's constitution and official parlance by nonsexist terms like *chair*.)

LLC did not come into being without opposition. Pointing out that Rockhill and Cora Rivera were the only members of the Women's Subcommittee who participated in political activities and almost the only ones who attended general meetings, political reformist leaders expressed doubts as to whether establishing a separate unit for women was the best way to get lesbians to become gay liberationists. Jim Owles warned that the caucusing of lesbians in GLF had been the first step in that group's dismemberment and suggested that providing lesbians with a place to meet apart from gay men might well make them less rather than more involved with GAA. Rockhill responded that few lesbians took part in gay political activity and in GAA because few felt affected by issues such as police harassment and gay rights or cared about politics; indeed, few felt they belonged to a "gay community" made up of both male and female homosexuals. The first step toward politicizing lesbians, she argued, was to give them the time and the space they needed to strengthen their gay identities and gain the sense that they belonged to a distinctive community.

Because her arguments struck a responsive chord in cultural reformers, Rockhill won approval for her proposals. Like the late 1971 election of Rich Wandel instead of Owles, Robinson, or Evans to GAA's presidency, the establishment of the Lesbian Liberation Committee was a sign that cultural leaders were reshaping GAA according to their own priorities.

Wandel provided the laissez-faire leadership that the cultural crowd thought necessary for their identity and community-building activities. The leaders of LLC used this freedom to continue their Sunday afternoon programs and to schedule lesbian dances, theater events, and cabarets. During the third annual Christopher Street Liberation Day march and Gay Pride Week at the end of June 1972, LLCers joined their radical sisters at the head of the march and staffed a "lesbian booth" at the street fair afterward; that summer, they held biweekly picnics in Central Park.

Wandel believed his style of leadership would ensure harmony. ("Many long for a charismatic leader of Gay Liberation; I prefer simply to work out my own freedom and to work with others in facilitating the freedom of my brothers and sisters.")[1] But the lack of centralized authority that characterized his presidency, coupled with the influx of radicals and street people attracted by the new tenor of his administration and the comforts of the Firehouse, resulted in disorder and then conflict. For Dinah Robertson and her lover Nancy Johnson, the problems began when the men in charge of GAA's entertainments grew careless about seeing that the movie equipment and the kitchen facilities were ready for LLC's Sunday afternoon programs. Their annoyance turned to anger when several male GAAers ignored requests that the lesbians be permitted privacy and tried to attend LLC programs or to use the Firehouse on Sunday afternoons. Because Wandel had so little control, Robertson and Johnson could only quarrel with individual interlopers and complain about carelessness at general membership meetings.

Neither course nurtured loyalty to GAA or good feelings about gay brothers. GAA's membership meetings—which seemed filled with large, loud men, most of them totally absorbed in one another —had never appealed much to the handful of LLCers who ventured to attend. With Wandel's laissez-faire leadership and the influx of radicals and street queens, the meetings seemed to become even more raunchy and raucous. Few men welcomed the lesbians or encouraged them to speak. When the leadership of LLC complained, some men made insulting remarks about "oversensitivity" and "bitchiness," while others offered sympathy and promised help but lacked the influence to change things. The more often they attended membership meetings, the more the lesbians felt dismissed.

At the beginning, Robertson, Johnson, and others attributed their unpleasant experiences to bad manners on the part of the gay men they were forced to deal with. But with exposure to lesbian feminist and radical feminist ideas, they began to see the rudeness as evidence of sexism—of the attitude that women and their concerns mattered less than men and theirs. Some women in GAA came to this feminist perspective by participating in lesbian feminist consciousness-raising groups (Robertson and Johnson belonged to supergroups #4 and #5); others from reading things like the arguments for "dyke separatism" that began to fill Jill Johnston's columns in the *Village Voice;* and still others from listening to lesbian feminists at LLC programs.

Robertson was particularly moved to consider feminist perspectives when in March 1972, just before one of LLC's Sunday afternoon programs, Fran Winant and another Radicalesbian tacked a petition of protest over the cutout photograph of a nude woman that artist John Button had included in the large collage he had erected in the Firehouse. The petition charged that the picture of the woman was sexist. The Radicalesbians were quick to explain that photographs of sexy nude women taken by and for men contributed to the devaluation of all women by perpetuating the idea that women were sex objects, that they existed mainly to provide sexual satisfaction for men. The Radicalesbian challenge stirred Robertson and other members of LLC to talk about the meaning of sexism. The difficulty they had convincing their male associates that the rendering of the woman in the mural was sexist and that the photographic cutout should be removed bolstered their feeling that gay men were insensitive to the cultural problems lesbians faced as women—indeed, that gay men, consciously or unconsciously, perpetuated these cultural problems.

The charge that the mural was sexist gave Robertson mixed feelings. In explaining these feelings, she says that most in LLC found it easier to recognize that they were kept from expressing themselves as gay people than to realize that they were oppressed as women. In the first place, she recalls, most LLCers found disapproval of their homosexuality, though it often went unarticulated and rarely led to sanctions, more obvious and anxiety-producing than the subtle stereotyping and devaluation that was the heart of sexism. Second, she adds, most LLCers avoided conventional domestic arrangements with men and therefore did not experience directly the constraints associated with traditional female roles; thus it was harder for them to see that sex-role stereotyping was oppressive.

In addition, according to Robertson, most LLCers had had unpleasant experiences involving fearful heterosexual women and believed that many of their problems as homosexuals stemmed from the prejudices of straight women. Thus, even as they learned about sexism, they continued to believe that they had more in common with gay men than with straight women and more of a stake in gay groups than in feminist groups. More than a year was to pass before the majority in LLC were persuaded that women's liberation was as essential to their well-being as gay liberation, and that their interests would best be served by the distinctive political cause that embraced both concerns—lesbian feminist liberation.

.   .   .

More instrumental than anyone else in persuading LLCers to think of themselves as lesbian feminists was Jean O'Leary. O'Leary had realized that she was homosexual in a convent in Cleveland; after reading an article in *Cosmopolitan* saying that Greenwich Village was a haven for lesbians, she left the convent and enrolled in a graduate program in educational curriculum and organizational development at Yeshiva University. When she moved to New York City in the summer of 1971, she shared an apartment with a male friend from Cleveland—who, she discovered, had also migrated to New York City to find other gay people. Soon afterward, she and her roommate began to attend meetings of Gay Activists of Brooklyn (GAB),one of the borough-based groups organized by GAA's Community Relations Committee. Getting to know Nath Rockhill at GAB led O'Leary to the Women's Subcommittee and then to LLC.

Early in the summer of 1972, at Dinah Robertson's request, O'Leary agreed to represent LLC at planning sessions for the third annual August 26 Women's Strike Day march. There she met B.J. Michaelson, a lesbian member of New York Radical Feminists, who became her lover. Selected over Rose Jordan to speak for lesbians at the Strike Day rally, O'Leary began reading radical feminist literature and discussing radical feminist ideas with B.J. and her friends.

By the end of the summer, O'Leary was convinced that lesbians were oppressed as much because of their sex as because of their homosexuality. During the fall, her sense that lesbian liberation called for both gay and women's liberation was reinforced by the arguments she read in the newly published *Sappho Is a Right-On Woman.* O'Leary found inspirational models in lesbians such as Liza Chan, who just then was organizing Lesbian Activists at Barnard instead of joining Gay People at Columbia, and in some lesbians in Detroit who broke away from the local gay liberation group that winter to form a lesbian liberation group. She was impressed also by the number of lesbians in radical feminist groups who were beginning to come out and to insist that their straight sisters deal with their homophobia.

Even as O'Leary struggled to show LLCers the urgency of dealing with the oppression they suffered as women, events dramatized how difficult it was to do this while they were working out of GAA. GAA was constitutionally defined as a one-issue organization, and most of its male members balked at taking initiatives on "women's issues" such as abortion and child care.

Nor did the men have particular sympathy for the professional injustice reportedly endured by women. This was underscored during the summer of 1972. Male leaders of GAA refused to pay the full amount of a fee requested for by feminist lawyer Emily Goodman, who had been retained to represent Morty Manford and other GA-Aers assaulted in April during a demonstration at a journalists' club called the Inner Circle. Goodman enlisted feminist lawyer Florynce Kennedy to help her collect her fee, and feminists and lesbian feminists alike pushed members of LLC to endorse Goodman's claim. (Martha Shelley threatened to stop advertising LLC events on her WBAI radio show, "Lesbian Nation," if the committee did not support Goodman.) Although LLC eventually voted to ask GAA to accede to Goodman's request, the anguish of choosing between feminist and gay liberationist antagonists showed them the dilemma of being "politically correct" as feminists while working in a group dominated by gay men.

Just as disturbing as these constraints on LLC's freedom were circumstances that seemed to interfere with LLC's efforts to help lesbians develop the unity they needed to be vital and visible as a community. Even members of LLC indifferent to feminist causes and leaders felt that lesbians, being different from gay men,* needed time and space to develop the identity, political awareness, and skills that would allow them to contribute significantly to the gay liberation movement. All agreed that it was necessary to limit LLC meetings and activities to women. When male GAAers persisted in showing up at the Firehouse on Sundays and in stumbling into LLC functions, several women proposed asking GAA's membership to ex-

---

*More specifically than anything else, a set of questions prepared by the LLCers appointed to write a statement about lesbians for GAA's Agit-Prop Committee listed the ways the situation of lesbians was thought to differ from that of male homosexuals:

1.Do Lesbians need and/or deserve more recognition? Is the word *homosexual* used by or interpreted by many people as referring only to men? Have fewer studies of Lesbians been made than of gay men? If so, why?

2.Why are there so few women's bars as compared to men's bars?

3.Are fewer Lesbians than gay men working in the gay movement? If so, why?
Possible answers:

1.There are fewer gay women than gay men in the American society; the proportion of women to men reflects the distribution in society.

2.Many gay women have a strong commitment to feminism and have divided their energies between the gay movement and the women's movement. Some prefer to work in organizations exclusively composed of women.

3.Women are not as political as men—not socialized to assert themselves politically . . .

6.Do gay men and gay women have different life styles? Do they love differently? Do Lesbians invest themselves more emotionally in their love relationships than gay men do? Do they have longer relationships? Are they more monogamous? More dependent? More gentle and affectionate?

clude men from LLC events, perhaps even to ban them from the building on the days LLC activities were scheduled. They discovered that most male GAAers believed such steps would violate the liberationist principles enshrined in GAA's constitution. This reinforced the belief that gay men were no more sensitive to the needs of lesbians than to those of women in general. Alienated from gay male associates and yet unwilling to cast their lot with straight feminists, more and more LLCers concluded that lesbians had to organize on their own to battle male sexism on the one hand and general homophobia on the other.

Jean O'Leary's belief in the need for an independent group to fight the two-front battle came to a head in December 1972, when newly elected GAA president Bruce Voeller tried to exercise his constitutional prerogative of being present when committees elected their chairs (a right Wandel had let slide). At an LLC meeting on December 11, O'Leary, who promised to lead LLC into feminist as well as gay activities, won a closely contested election for the position of chair over Doris London, who maintained that LLC had to concentrate on gay liberation and that lesbians had to work in concert with gay men. The following Thursday, at a general membership meeting, Voeller expressed chagrin that LLC had held its election without his being there and urged a rerun. This provoked O'Leary to complain that Voeller's attitude showed typical male insensitivity to the lesbian's need for autonomy, the type of insensitivity that made it impossible for lesbians to develop a voice of their own in an organization in which men predominated.

At the time, few LLCers jumped at the idea of transforming LLC into an independent lesbian feminist group. The actual minutes of the December 18 meeting make plain that most in attendance expressed reservations about being able to keep such a group afloat; many expressed fear that leading LLC out of GAA would result in the demise of the one institutional center of lesbian liberationist activity left in New York City. Instead, the LLCers proposed to work to make male activists more conscious of their sexism, to help them understand why LLC events had to be limited to women, and to persuade them to change GAA's charter so that it would be constitutional to have "separatist" events and to deal with feminist issues.

O'Leary responded that spending time and energy trying to influence men was precisely what kept women from marshaling the necessary resources to take care of themselves, and that asking the membership for constitutional changes might result in a bitter floor fight that would keep GAA from renting space to the independent lesbian feminist group LLC might become. She argued that it would be better for LLC to prepare a position paper elucidating lesbian feminist principles and outlining the rationale for an independent lesbian feminist group—a statement that could be used to rally lesbians as well as to educate gay men.

At the beginning of LLC's January 8 meeting, Ginny Vida, who had succeeded Robertson as LLC's chair the previous summer and Rockhill as GAA's vice-president that winter, reviewed the reasons that those persuaded by O'Leary's arguments at the previous meeting had cited for having LLC become an independent group:

1. To become independent women
2. A need for separatist events
3. Need to act on Feminist Issues
4. To promote our growth as an Org.
5. Not to be subsidized by men[2]

Doris London, Trish Brumbaugh, and others expressed fears that lesbians who wanted to continue working in GAA would be criticized once the new group was formed, but O'Leary assured them that individual choice would be respected and that the new group would "be in the middle of both Gay and Feminist issues." When some LLCers continued to be skeptical, it was decided to delay a formal vote on the split until a paper outlining the purposes of the new group was completed.

At the following week's LLC meeting, thirty-six participants broke up into small groups and then reassembled to make a master list of projects that the proposed lesbian feminist group could pursue. The same approach was used the week after in an attempt to come up with generalizations about goals and operating procedures that could be incorporated into a position paper. When the small-group approach to this second project proved unworkable, a committee to write the position paper was selected by lot. After a week's work, members of this Structure Committee reported that they had come up with a sentence summarizing the proposed lesbian feminist mission: "We, _____, dedicate ourselves to promoting our identities as

Lesbians and combating sexism as it manifests itself in heterosexual chauvinism and male supremacy."

. . .

Three months later, members of the Structure Committee put the finishing touches on the preamble to the constitution of Lesbian Feminist Liberation. The sentence that the committee had come up with to summarize its mission stood as the preamble's first paragraph. The second paragraph described the limited (to the dimensions of sex and sexual orientation) but open-ended vision of self-expression that the reformers intended to champion:

> We as Lesbian feminists assert the right of every woman to be a self-defined individual. We declare the necessity for all women to discover and use the potentials and resources which exist in themselves and each other. We assert the right of every woman to express herself with her body, intellect and emotions as the complete human being that society has discouraged her from being. We assert the right of every woman to express her sexuality in any way she chooses as an affirmation of her individuality. We declare our intention to confront and disarm the attitudes and institutions that attempt to limit these rights.

The third paragraph specified that lesbian liberation, because it involved female as well as homosexual self-expression, required careful attention to women's liberation. This paragraph ended with a statement of the reformist conviction that lesbian feminists could force society to allow them to express themselves fully and freely by banding together in an explicitly lesbian feminist movement and by encouraging female homosexuals to develop distinctively lesbian feminist issues, institutions, life styles, and communities. In addition, it took characteristically reformist note of the need to avoid separatism by promising to work in concert with both gay men and straight women:

> As Lesbian feminists the focus of all our thoughts and actions centers on our identities as Lesbian women. Now we must dedicate our energies primarily to discovering ourselves and our special causes, and, acting as our own spokeswomen, to promoting ourselves everywhere, at all times, as Lesbian women. To this end, it is crucial that we function as an organization distinct from both the gay and feminist movements, unique

unto ourselves, yet making coalitions with groups on gay and feminist issues specifically as they relate to our Lesbian identities.

The ideas about goals and strategy elaborated in the preamble had lengthy intellectual roots. The format of portraying various dimensions of self-expression as rights, of identifying "attitudes and institutions" as obstacles to the realization of these rights, and of promising to "confront and disarm" these obstacles was borrowed from the elaboration of reformist gay liberationist ideals in the preamble to GAA's constitution. The premium placed on self-actualization linked the reformist lesbian feminist vision of liberation to that of radical lesbian feminists, of reformist and radical gay and women's liberationists, of the radical sector of the New Left, and—the original source of this vision—of the counterculture. From the same political and philosophical lineage stemmed the conviction that the system inhibited self-realization and that by bringing oppressed individuals together, encouraging them to be themselves, and forcing people to acknowledge the ways in which they led their lives, the group could challenge and dispel stifling and demeaning standards and assumptions.

Though they knew that the roots of their ambitions reached back to the political and social movements of the 1960s, the authors of the preamble were more affected by the specific experiences that had shaped their views. The neglect and abuse they felt they suffered at the hands of their gay male associates were probably the most immediate cause of the LLCers' belief that the lesbian's major problem was status—often manifesting itself in the feelings of insignificance and inferiority that followed dealings with male homosexuals who presented themselves as "colleagues." That so many male GAAers failed to respect LLC's desire to limit its activities to women seemed one very tangible sign of the lack of status accorded lesbians. The scant mention given Abbott and Love's *Sappho* and Martin and Lyon's *Lesbian/Woman* in a survey of "Homosexual Literature" that Martin Duberman prepared for the *New York Times Book Review* at the end of 1972 was another. The letter of protest that Ginny Vida and Jean O'Leary dispatched to the *Times* explained: "What Duberman's article does, as does our society in general, is to focus on men while ignoring the existence of women and the importance of their contributions."[3]

Of course, gay men were not the only ones who made the lesbians feel that they were accorded little recognition and respect. Late in 1972, at the urging of GAA strategists who thought that the lesbians might be able to command the attention they wanted by joining in gay liberationist demonstrations, a group of male and female GAAers went to a straight singles dance bar, paired off with partners of the same sex, and—hoping to demonstrate that discrimination was a problem affecting homosexuals of both sexes—waited for the management to oust all of them. When the manager ejected the men and ignored the women, the lesbians concluded that he either failed to realize that they were lesbians or did not consider the activities of female homosexuals very important.

The sense that they were just not deemed very important grew when, after GAA's officers complained about Jack Paar's use of derogatory terms like *fairy* on his show, Paar invited a group from GAA to express their grievances on the air—and then objected when the GAAers insisted that their delegation include a lesbian. According to Vida's analysis of the situation, which also cited several similar incidents, "The media's reluctance to include lesbians in gay programs is not surprising in view of the fact that women are seen as less important and therefore less newsworthy than men."[4] Experience did more than anything else to help the founders of LFL see, as they noted in their preamble, that "our liberation as gay people would leave us still oppressed as women" and that "our primary strength is in feminism."

Yet the talk of feminism in the preamble was not a pledge of fealty to the women's movement or an assertion that LFL's members viewed themselves simply as feminists. Such a move was avoided partly in deference to the members of LLC who enjoyed being with gay men and who believed it important for lesbians to continue to contribute to the gay liberation movement. Then, too, it reflected the fact that many in LLC continued to believe that homophobic straight women were their major oppressors and that the women's movement was relatively uninterested in the lesbian's concerns as a homosexual.* LLC leaders also believed that a lesbian group identified simply

*On her own working draft of the preamble to LFL's constitution, Jean O'Leary summarized the strategic assessments that led the founders to feel that LFL had to be something more than a feminist group by itemizing the major concerns of reform-oriented feminists and noting alongside them related lesbian concerns left unaddressed:

as feminist would have little appeal to the masses of lesbians who also felt loyal to gay men and the gay movement or who shared reservations about straight women and the women's movement.*

The authors of LFL's preamble made sure to specify that their group was for "Lesbians" and not just (as DOB officially specified) for "women," yet they did not refrain from suggesting that lesbians were in the best position to discover "the potentials and resources" that existed in all women, and therefore to be in the forefront of the women's movement. This idea originated with the thinking of the radical lesbians who had incubated lesbian feminism in their consciousness-raising and study groups and developed and promoted it in Radicalesbians and DOB–New York. By 1972, these radical lesbian feminists, reluctant "to contaminate" their efforts to create a feminist utopia by associating with either straight women or gay men, identified themselves as "dyke separatists." The arguments made by dyke separatists, by radical lesbian feminists in general, and

Legal Abort.—Legal Sex
Equal Pay, Equal Work—Can't Keep Jobs
Child Care Centers—Can't Keep Children
Equal Sharing Household Chores—Can't Live Together Openly

*That these personal, organizational, and strategic considerations were what kept the founders of LFL from casting their lot with straight feminists is evidenced in the fact that by 1973 most feminist leaders and organizations *had* taken steps to show that they were willing to welcome lesbians and to champion their concerns. The mass press conference held to demonstrate support for Kate Millett after *Time* questioned her credibility as a feminist spokeswoman was a dramatic first step in this direction. A few months before, at NOW's 1970 national convention, a resolution in support of lesbianism was withdrawn because members of the national office thought it was too controversial. But NOW's 1971 national conference voted, under the rubric of Resolution 128, "That NOW recognizes the double oppression of women who are lesbians"; "that a woman's right to her own person includes the right to define and express her own sexuality, and to choose her own lifestyle"; and "that NOW acknowledge[s] the oppression of lesbians as a legitimate concern of feminism."[5] Even before NOW acted, organizers of the National Women's Political Caucus, formed in the summer of 1971, said that they cared about lesbians and their concerns. By the winter of 1973, when the NOW national convention resolved that "NOW actively introduce and support civil rights legislation to end discrimination based on sexual orientation . . . in areas such as—but not limited to—housing, employment, finance, child custody and public accommodations," Betty Friedan, perhaps the best-known founder of NOW, was the only major leader in the women's movement who continued publicly to oppose lesbian involvement (probably because she was one of the few to retain a women's rights rather than a women's liberationist outlook).[6]

Early in 1973, Friedan wrote a memoir for the *New York Times Magazine* in which she identified "the disruptors of the women's movement" as "the ones continually trying to push lesbianism or hatred of men."[7] A few days after the article appeared, officers of organizations including National and New York NOW, the National and Manhattan Women's Political Caucus, *Ms.* magazine, and GAA's Lesbian Liberation Committee held a press conference at the Overseas Press Club to rebut Friedan's charges and to affirm that lesbians were welcome in the women's movement.

by lesbian radical feminists—both at LLC meetings and at feminist conferences such as the "Feminist/Lesbian Dialogue" held at Columbia in December 1972—encouraged the founders of LFL to consider themselves the vanguard of the women's liberation movement.

At the same time, exposure to the ideas of the radicals did as much as anything else to lead the founders of Lesbian Feminist Liberation to cast their organization in a distinctly reformist mold. Nath Rockhill had first despaired of the radical resolve to re-create society back in December 1970, when she stumbled into a Radicalesbians meeting and found they were debating whether it was "correct" for lesbians to "relate" to New Year's Eve—said to be an artifact of "the male-dominated culture"—by attending the New Year's Eve Dance sponsored by a coalition put together by GLF Women and DOB–New York. (Rockhill remembers being embarrassed about not understanding what the radicals meant by "relate.") Ginny Vida, an editor of children's textbooks at Macmillan who had acknowledged that she was lesbian after witnessing the Lavender Menace demonstration, had been alienated both by the antiestablishment assumptions she encountered at the ensuing consciousness-raising sessions and by the chaos that accompanied the refusal to use traditional operating procedures at Radicalesbian meetings. Not until the next summer, when she attended a meeting of GAA's Women's Subcommittee, had Vida begun to believe that there was a place for people like her in gay political activity. Personal experiences such as those of Rockhill and Vida—plus the negative impressions made at LLC events by dyke separatists who ignored rules and "trashed" lesbians who "related to" men and had conventional views—encouraged the founders to commit LFL to operating procedures that were characteristically reformist. Notably, the preamble specified that LFL intended "to create a climate in which women of diverse political and social backgrounds can function comfortably together, each one reaching her own place at her own time." The preamble also indicated that LFL was determined to balance its use of modes of operation that would maximize individual participation and intra-group solidarity with its need for structures that would preclude the informal domination of a moralistic few.

The creation of LFL was guided not only by ideas popularized by radical lesbian feminists, gay liberationists, women's liberationists, and members of the Movement—ideas its founders assessed and adapted in the light of their own experiences—but also by careful thinking about the feasibility of forming an independent organization. Like their thinking about goals and strategy, the attention LFL's founders paid organizational considerations was stimulated partly by the example of their gay political predecessors. Those in charge of LLC blamed not only the short, rocky lives of GLF and Radicalesbians but the disintegration of DOB–New York on the idealism and naiveté of radical lesbian feminists. In fact, Rockhill, Vida, and others who initially cautioned against secession argued that once outside GAA's institutional umbrella, their group would be vulnerable to dyke separatists and radical lesbian feminists bent on challenging everything that was at all conventional. Even those more confident about their ability to control and exclude the radicals were afraid that it would be difficult, once they were on their own, to secure and manage facilities, to attract resources, to enlist members, and to preserve harmony. Some candidly expressed fear that in the absence of male targets, lesbians would vent their hostilities on one another, especially because there would be offices and other opportunities to vie for. Concern was such that almost from the beginning, O'Leary and others eager to make LLC an independent group spent as much time arguing that the plan was organizationally feasible as they did insisting that it was politically desirable.

Right at the start, O'Leary acknowledged the importance of organizational considerations by coupling her proposal that LLC secede with the suggestion that it rent space from GAA and continue to meet in the Firehouse. Indeed, she maintained that withdrawing from GAA precipitously or fighting for the right to hold separatist events would jeopardize the chance that GAA would make space available on favorable terms. The Structure Committee showed its awareness of organizational concerns by talking not only about the aims and operating procedures appropriate for a lesbian group that was feminist but also about how effectively to structure, finance, and house such a group.

O'Leary's graduate work in organizational development helped make her sensitive to these institutional considerations. In the essay she submitted for her candidacy examination at Yeshiva late in 1972, she wrote about the challenge of making LLC a "more humanistic alternative" to "traditional forms of hierarchical organization." Her essay confirms that disillusionment with radical innovations as well as reformist ambitions led the LFLers to endow their group with explicit structure. The essay begins by summarizing the sentiments of Rockhill, Vida, and others who had been put off by radical "structurelessness":

> In order to find viable alternatives to existing organizational structures, we have to acknowledge that structure "per se" is not inherently oppressive. Any group of people of whatever nature that comes together for any length of time for any purpose will inevitably structure itself in some fashion. The structure may be flexible; it may vary over time; it may evenly or unevenly distribute tasks, power and resources over the members of the group. *But* it will be formed regardless of the abilities, personalities or intentions of the people involved. The very fact that we are individuals with different talents, predispositions, and backgrounds makes this inevitable. . . . For everyone to have the opportunity to be involved in the group and participate in the activities, our structure must be *explicit,* not implicit, or assumed. The rules of decision-making must be open and available to everyone, and this can happen only if they are formalized. Informal structure forms the basis for elitism.

O'Leary then argued that the reformist ambition to influence existing institutions required the division of labor, the assignment of responsibility, and the establishment of coordinating authority that constituted organizational structure:

> It has often happened that within the movement, many groups generate much motion and few results. If we are to be more than a *communications* link or educational group, we must have the means for specific follow-ups to our actions. We can learn much from G.A.A. in this regard . . .
>
> The more unstructured a group is, the less control it has over the directions in which it develops and the political actions in which it engages. This does not mean that its ideas do not spread. Given a certain amount of interest by the media and the "appropriateness" of social conditions, the ideas will still be diffused widely. *But* diffusion of ideas does not mean they are implemented, it only means they are talked about (which is a start). Insofar as they can be applied individually, they will be acted on; insofar as they require coordinated political power to be implemented, they will not be . . . After our goals are clear to us, we should be able to develop those forms of organization best suited to our

healthy functioning. Hopefully, we will not imitate the traditional forms of organization. But neither must we reject them all.[8]

Like O'Leary, members of the Structure Committee worked to design forms and operating procedures that would reflect feminist ideals yet avoid unrealistic extremes. To prevent a single powerful leader from being able to ignore or to dominate the rank and file, they divided the chief executive's job into the offices of Spokeswoman (responsible for LFL's external relations) and Internal Coordinator (responsible for managing intraorganizational affairs); they limited terms of office to six months, subject at any time to votes of no confidence by the membership; and they vested final responsibility for executive and committee actions in weekly membership meetings. To convey the message that duties commonly devalued were important, they replaced the office of secretary with that of "scribe."

Yet aside from the extra limits placed on officeholders and the use of new terminology, LFL's constitution was markedly like GAA's, not least because of the contributions of Nath Rockhill, who agreed to help the Structure Committee and later joined LFL's Political Committee even though she regretted LLC's decision to secede. Rockhill remembers a good deal of talk about feminist principles but little sense of what these called for other than the participatory democracy embodied in GAA. Indeed, like the architects of GAA, the designers of LFL prepared both their preamble and their by-laws hoping to win the approval and support of those they judged to be the majority of the community: homosexual women ready to be proud and open about their identities as lesbians and active in efforts to build a lesbian feminist cultural and political community, but unwilling to embrace the personal, social, organizational, and political extremes advocated by their radical sisters.

.   .   .

By the end of March 1973, when the Structure Committee was ready to announce its proposals, the Lesbian Liberation Committee was flooded with newcomers who expressed reservations about the feasibility of establishing an independent lesbian feminist group. To accommodate the new members, LLC's leaders created committees on politics and legal affairs, public relations, program, fund-raising, and membership. To reassure those unclear about how an independent lesbian group would operate, they pointed out that LLC's subcommittees could be transferred intact to LFL.

The anxieties of the leaders were rekindled by the qualms of the newcomers, but their courage was renewed by the lesbians from feminist groups (particularly the then well-established New York Radical Feminists) who promised to transfer their allegiance once LLC was out from under the aegis of GAA and who maintained that they were only the first of the feminists who, turning to woman-identified life styles, would be ready to join a lesbian feminist movement. This vision of new resources gave members of the Structure Committee the enthusiasm to preside over a series of general meetings at which the by-laws they had drawn up were discussed and amended, the constitution ratified, and a contract to rent space in the Firehouse approved. All this was accomplished by mid-May. Once LFL's birth was official, the lesbians who wanted to continue working in GAA decided not to perpetuate LLC but to participate in GAA's project-oriented committees and general membership meetings.

While members of the Structure Committee pushed foot-dragging peers to polish and ratify LFL's constitution, Jean O'Leary got new feminist spirit from reading Jill Johnston's just-released *Lesbian Nation* and from attending a large lesbian feminist conference in Los Angeles with prominent New York NOW leader Jan Crawford. *Lesbian Nation,* subtitled "The Feminist Solution," chronicled Johnston's conversion to lesbian feminism and discussed the radical lesbian feminist strategy of transforming society by developing and disseminating woman-identified consciousness. The conference in Los Angeles was attended by 1500 lesbians from all over the country. The keynote speaker, Robin Morgan, defended her right to speak as a lesbian though she was married and a mother and derided GAA's attempt to use "women to give GAA a good front—which women, by the way, are finally getting wise to, and leaving."[9]

Returning from California in time to run for the office of spokeswoman, O'Leary elaborated an ambitious program of lesbian feminist goals in her campaign speech to the thirty or so lesbians who showed up for the elections. In the notes for her speech she itemized the movement-building priorities that marked her ambitions as liberationist:

· Build Strong Base of L/F in N.Y.
· Reach out to ALL Lesbian Women—Bars, Offices
· NATIONWIDE MOVEMENT (within the next two years connect W. Coast)

The movement-building tactics she noted were "Educational— write, write, write, speak, speak, speak." Yet where the radical strategy she had recently been exposed to called only for conscious- ness-raising efforts that would enlighten the ever-growing numbers of women who were ready to embrace woman-identified ways, O'Leary spoke also of reforming institutions: "Start on the institu- tions and [do] not be afraid to demand." Indeed, for all of O'Leary's radical sentiments in her campaign speech, her con- tinued commitment to reformist ambitions was demonstrated in her promise to unite lesbians of every kind, reaching them through the established media, so that they could use their influence to win a place in existing institutions.

Although O'Leary rejected the radical idea that lesbians could do their political duty simply by banding together and learning how to live in liberated ways, she recognized that it would take study and discussion to clarify what the lesbians' problems were and to figure out how to address them. In fact, after promising to have LFL proceed in every direction she could think of, she acknowledged, according to her notes, that "it's going to take every one of us exploring the insides of our guts for a basis for future direction . . . From here on in we'll be talking about Lesbian Politics."

Of course, discussions of the goals and tactics that would define "lesbian politics" had begun six months before, when O'Leary pro- posed transforming LLC into an independent lesbian feminist group and skeptics like Nath Rockhill responded by asking what an inde- pendent lesbian group could do that LLC could not. A consensus had evolved that society's sexist and homophobic attitudes prevented lesbians from feeling good about themselves and happy with one another. To change this situation it seemed necessary to create a community of openly lesbian women who were so manifestly happy, powerful, and successful that people would be forced to modify their assumptions about lesbianism and about womanhood.

Most of the first reformers among lesbian feminists were inclined to model their activities after the self-help, social, and artistic enterprises developed by cultural reformers in gay and women's liberationist circles. But others believed that their aims were more effectively pursued by capturing the attention of the established media through activities involving the political system. Following the example of the cultural crowd in GAA who used political activities for consciousness-raising purposes, and of the politicos who argued that it was necessary to encourage political involvement, O'Leary and other reformers wanted to develop distinctly lesbian issues that would generate publicity focusing on lesbians and provide an occasion for all-lesbian demonstrations.

The challenge, of course, was to come up with the issues. Gay rights legislation pertained as much to male as to female homosexuals and was already associated with GAA. Women's rights legislation pertained as much to heterosexual as to homosexual women and was already associated with the women's movement. During the winter and spring of 1973, to focus attention specifically on the problems of lesbians and on how lesbian liberationists were trying to resolve them, the leaders of LLC complained about an episode of a television program, "The Bold Ones," that portrayed lesbians unsympathetically. They also tried to make an issue out of Dinah Robertson's having lost her job at the Women's Club after she appeared on a "David Susskind Show" featuring lesbian couples. Yet "The Bold Ones" episode warranted little more than a letter of protest, and Robertson's case could not be portrayed as a dramatic instance of discrimination because, when her superiors at the Women's Club expressed concern about her Susskind appearance, Robertson had resigned rather than be fired.

Unable to find specific grievances with sole bearing on the lot of lesbians (even the issue of child custody seemed to involve homosexual men, as Bruce Voeller's battle with his former wife over his right to visit his three children demonstrated), lesbian feminist reformers seized on every opportunity to bring lesbians into the public eye. Promoting their group and stressing that it was an independent lesbian feminist organization was one form of publicity. Devising and publicizing distinctly lesbian social and cultural events was another. Few of these events, however, were newsworthy enough to merit media attention. Indeed, because there seemed no other way to attract attention, LFL strategists agreed to begin their publicity drive by making lesbians visible participants in the events of the fourth annual Gay Pride Week and Christopher Street Liberation Day in June 1973.

The proposal that LFL participate alongside gay men in commemorating the Stonewall Riots provoked a predictably heated debate—particularly when the organizers of the CSLD march refused to let lesbians lead the march. To get the exposure they thought necessary, LFL strategists urged lesbians to walk together at the end of the march and to participate in a Lesbian Pride Week running concurrently with Gay Pride Week. Yet controversy flared anew when LFL's leaders learned that the CSLD organizing committee planned to have a pair of female impersonators appear in the entertainment planned to follow the march. (For the first time the CSLD planning committee was composed of unaffiliated gay liberationists with great affection for the gay subculture and a desire to make CSLD more a celebration of gay community than a political demonstration. The march was to start at Central Park and end with festive entertainment in Washington Square in the Village.)

The subject of male transvestism had first come up in LFL that spring, when a female impersonator performed at a cabaret at the Firehouse. To most of the lesbians—many of them only just exposed to the feminist argument that male ideals of how women should look and act impeded women's natural self-expression—the spectacle of men caricaturing female ways of dressing and acting seemed inappropriate. Some likened male transvestites to the black-faced vaudevillians who personified (and, they argued, perpetuated) racist assumptions about blacks. Some suggested that male transvestism was a dramatic manifestation of the general propensity of gay men to think of themselves as "girls," to refer to each other with feminine pronouns and with names like "Mary," and to develop stereotypically feminine gestures and mannerisms—behavior said to stem from self-hate and to reflect and reinforce the contempt for women characteristic of society in general. Transvestites, these lesbian feminists argued, were simply another breed of men determined to keep women down by telling them how they should look and act.* Lesbian

*Almost as spirited as the discussions of male transvestism at LLC and LFL meetings, and equally significant for the belief of early lesbian feminists that female homosexuals were very different from male homosexuals, were the debates over the interest in sado-masochism and in sex with homosexually inclined teenagers shown by some gay male GAAers and generally defended by other gay men.

feminists less taken with radical feminist ideas challenged these points of view, arguing that women who liked to wear male attire such as shirts, jeans, and loafers were also transvestites in their way and that male transvestism was a legitimate, even heroic form of self-expression that defied sex roles. The consensus was that male cross dressing, though a suspect style of liberated behavior, was acceptable, but that female impersonation, thought to demean women and perpetuate sexism for the sake of showmanship and profit, was not.

Learning of the plan to include female impersonators in the post-march program, O'Leary threatened to have LFL withdraw from the events. When the planners stood their ground, citing the need to represent all segments of the gay subculture in the entertainment, O'Leary asked for permission to make a speech presenting lesbian feminist objections. The planners, anxious to avoid divisive political speeches, denied the request.

Undeterred, LFL leaders prepared a statement outlining their objections to female impersonation. On the day of the march, they distributed their position paper to those assembled in Washington Square for the post-march program: "We support the right of every person to dress in the way that she or he wishes," it read, "but we are opposed to the exploitation of women by men for entertainment or profit . . . What we object to today is another instance in which men laughing with one another, at what *they* present as women, are telling us who they think we are."

In the middle of the program, after Ray "Sylvia" Rivera walked onstage and made a speech complaining that the middle-class crowd cared nothing about the harassment and arrests of street queens, O'Leary grabbed the microphone and spoke further about why lesbian feminists found female impersonation offensive. While O'Leary talked, a man who was beautifully coifed, heavily made up, and dressed in a stunning red suit appeared behind her. When the microphone was free, he introduced himself as Lee Brewster and explained that he had organized a group called Queens Liberation to advance the interests of traditional drag queens. His voice rising, Brewster declared that the "drags" had started the gay liberation movement by rioting in front of the Stonewall and that they were not about to let "these bitches" and the men who sympathized with them oust transvestites from their own movement.

As Brewster spoke, the lesbians, clustered together in the crowded audience, began to jeer. Knots of transvestites screamed back at them. And gay men in the middle squirmed at the prospect of having to take sides. Vito Russo, the emcee, swears that only the sudden appearance of Bette Midler averted outright violence. Having followed what was happening on the radio in her Greenwich Village apartment, Midler had rushed to Washington Square, burst on stage, and begun to sing "Friends."

Midler's appearance may have prevented the festivities from ending in chaos, but it did not prevent a new round of debate about loyalties at the LFL meetings that followed. This time, prodded by what they saw as gay male support for male transvestites and female impersonators and by renewed conviction that gay male liberation had little to do with the women's issues at the heart of the lesbian's cause, most of the women agreed that their agenda would be most effectively pursued independently of gay men. Nath Rockhill, Meryl Friedman, and other members of the Political Committee who wanted to continue working for gay rights legislation on LFL's behalf were told to go ahead, but few members responded to their pleas for help and most resolved to devote themselves to projects that did not involve male homosexuals.

Toward the end of July, two members of the Political Committee with strong feminist views proposed a demonstration to protest the sexism they had seen in the anthropological section of the American Museum of Natural History. During a trip to the museum, the two reported, they had discovered that the labels on exhibits were filled with terms like *man* and *mankind*, and this, they felt, reflected the lack of societal status accorded women. In addition, there were no exhibits showing women's contributions to civilization and no women on the museum's anthropological staff. The Political Committee decided to stage a demonstration on the last day of Women's Liberty Action Week, which had replaced the annual Women's Strike March, it was said, because influential straight feminists feared that lesbians had taken over its planning.

On Sunday, August 26, almost two hundred women gathered at the main entrance of the museum, circulated leaflets itemizing their grievances, and marched, to the music of the Victoria Woodhull Feminist Marching Band, around an eight-foot-high plaster of paris dinosaur, specially constructed and painted lavender to attract attention. A picture of the lavender dinosaur and news of the demonstration were featured in the next day's *Daily News*. Meetings between LFL representatives and museum officials were scheduled for the beginning of September. The LFLers who identified strongly with the women's movement were pleased, but those who felt it important for the lesbian cause to be distinguished from that of women in general were left complaining that the issues raised by the demonstration were more feminist than lesbian.

Members of LFL who identified primarily with the gay rather than the women's movement were even more disturbed by the anti-male tone of Jean O'Leary's speech at a feminist rally in Battery Park during Women's Liberty Action Week. The reservations expressed by LFLers concerned to protect relations with gay men alienated those from feminist groups whom LFL's growing feminist tone had attracted. LFL leaders eager to devise actions that would embrace both dimensions of lesbian concerns wondered where to turn next.

Late in September, Ginny Vida happened upon an advertisement in the *Village Voice* for a film about "tortured lesbian relationships." After she and Media Committee chairwoman Judy Burns saw and reported on the film, members of the Media Committee decided to demonstrate against its "constant portrayal of lesbians as mere extensions of male sexual fantasies" and to "offer positive images of ourselves." On October 15 and 16, a dozen from LFL stationed themselves in front of the theater at Lincoln Center, where Rainer Fassbinder's *The Bitter Tears of Petra Von Kant* was being shown as part of the New York Film Festival. Their flier explained:

> *The Bitter Tears of Petra Von Kant* is a *man's* sado-masochistic vision of the universality of dominant/submissive power relationships, acted out by six *women* . . . Such use of women only reinforces sex role stereotyping, and gives women no independent image of themselves . . .
>
> We also protest the fact that the "Lesbian" theme was played up in the *advertising* of "Petra Von Kant." Lesbians have been ignored by the media for years. Now that the media have suddenly discovered that there is a market for Lesbian culture, the label is used indiscriminately to attract lesbians and sensation-seekers alike. The relationships in this film are primarily sado-masochistic (a term which the press does not yet use freely) and are not interchangeable. The relationships in the film do not typify Lesbian relationships, any more than they do heterosexual ones.

We demand to see ourselves in films and in all media portrayed as we know ourselves to be.

Though it was later judged to have been more directly concerned with lesbianism than with the lavender dinosaur demonstration, the picketing at Lincoln Center left LFL leaders doubting whether their undertaking had done much to serve lesbian feminist goals. In the first place, since the film was really about sado-masochism and only incidentally about lesbianism, it was a poor vehicle for showing that the communications media portrayed lesbians in stereotypical terms. In the second place, to make an issue of the way the media portrayed lesbians, it was necessary for LFL's objections to be widely publicized, whereas the dozen who showed up to picket at Lincoln Center neither attracted reporters nor drew much attention from passersby.

Instead of feeling that demonstrations over portrayals of lesbians in the media could spotlight objectionable stereotypes and counter them with an image of self-confident and attractive lesbians, the LFL leaders were left feeling, after the picketing at Lincoln Center, that it was extremely difficult to develop distinctly lesbian concerns as public issues. Apparently, most people believed lesbianism nonexistent, rare, or, in any event, socially and politically insignificant. That it received so little attention from the media assured there would be few opportunities to make an issue of how lesbians were popularly portrayed. Even when there were opportunities, it would be difficult to get press coverage of lesbian grievances against the media and other opinion-shaping institutions. In turn, because there would be so few incidences of publicity, persuading lesbians themselves that they had serious grievances would be a challenge, and it would be all but impossible to overcome the fears and the lack of enthusiasm for politics that kept most lesbians from joining organized political efforts.

In light of these difficulties, it seemed that the quest for recognition and respect was best served by having lesbians take the lead in initiatives pertaining to homosexuals or to women in general and, when gay male and straight feminist insensitivity to their special need for visibility arose, to make an issue of it. Thus, during 1973 and 1974, LFLers who joined in efforts to pass gay rights legislation insisted that lesbian participation be highlighted at meetings and press conferences. They asked that the phrase "lesbians and gay men" (with "lesbians" placed first) be used in public statements and official literature and that lesbians be given places at the head of marches and demonstrations. Similarly, LFLers who visited feminist groups and participated in conferences and demonstrations sponsored by the women's movement insisted that they be acknowledged as lesbian feminists rather than simply as feminists.

Others in LFL responded to the challenge of making lesbians visible by focusing less on issues and actions than on self-help, social, and cultural events. This preference for consciousness-raising activities was especially strong among LFLers interested in feminism, who were beginning to echo the radical argument that preoccupation with issues and actions reflected male-identified rather than feminist conceptions of politics. These LFLers contended that protest demonstrations, with their aggressive tone, manifested characteristically male attitudes and behavior. They suggested, in fact, that the whole idea of trying to manipulate the system was a conventional male approach to social and political change. Instead of emulating male models, they wanted LFLers to spend their time trying to understand what it meant to be lesbian, talking and writing about their lives, and sponsoring discussion groups, social programs, and cultural events that would bring lesbians together and help them feel good about being lesbian. Thanks to the prodding of these LFLers, besides its usual programs, LFL sponsored the first Lesbian Feminist Olympics, sent speakers to local radio talk shows, and met with the editors of *Ms.* magazine to urge that they publish articles on lesbianism.

Some who believed it necessary to proceed in truly feminist ways contended that it was all right for LFLers to deal with established institutions as long as they retained their self-assurance and sensitivity. But others began to make the radical argument that true feminism meant abandoning all conventional ways. These LFLers disapproved not only of giving attention to issues, actions, and established institutions, but of following organizational forms and operating procedures that were "male-devised" and hence "elitist." Among other things, they objected to the use of Robert's rules of order, to requests for dues and admission fees, to the routine way in which LFL was legally incorporated, and to efforts to promote and raise funds "for the organization."

Discussions of what was and was not truly feminist had occurred throughout the long process of LFL's emergence, but in the fall of 1973, for the first time, LFL's reformist leaders were all but paralyzed by radical criticism of their ambitions. Jean O'Leary's behavior became the focus of contention.

In many ways, O'Leary had set herself up for the challenge by espousing radical positions in her speeches and then behaving like a reformer. For example, in her talk before the feminist conclave in Battery Park at the end of Women's Liberty Action Week, O'Leary publicly disassociated herself from the goal of "reforming a society with gay males who know no other way of fighting our shared oppression than to attack the system through tired and ineffectual male politics." In the weeks that followed, she seemed to go back on her words, joining with GAA and MSNY leaders in pressing for the passage of gay rights legislation, meeting with mayoral candidates, and requesting that the New York chapter of the American Psychiatric Association ask the national convention to eliminate the classification "homosexuality" from its list of mental disorders.

At Battery Park, O'Leary expressed the radical conviction that it was necessary to avoid traditional modes of operating politically:

> To the extent that the male principle is carried over in any form to the women's movement, we must be rid of it. From our personal relationships we can extract principles which when adapted on another level (an organizational level) could mean the elimination of hierarchy—of the creation of stars or leaders who are then in danger of being destroyed by the movement that created them. By doing away with the concept of Big People and Little People.

In practice, because her office as LFL's spokeswoman and her belief in the need to promote both lesbian visibility and LFL led her unfailingly into the spotlight, O'Leary was the "star" and her friends were the "Big People."

At Battery Park, O'Leary joined in the radical call for innovative, woman-identified life styles:

> We all have been socialized to some extent by the soap operas, movies, commercials, text books, popular music (cock rock) to believe the lie of Romantic Love—that it is something to be sought after. By romantic love, I'm not talking about true, exciting, growth producing love. I'm

talking about something created by men and synonymous with prick power. Words I associate with it are conquest, pain, loss of self, destruction, and short-termed. The same people who promote it promote war, competition, and the concept that there must be a winner and a loser. To the extent that we carry over any of this destructive excess baggage into Lesbian relationships we must be rid of it.[10]

But in practice, during 1973, O'Leary had affairs with three attractive women as well as a host of shorter relationships and "one night stands." A graffito on the wall of the women's bathroom in the Firehouse attested to radical reservations about the ex-nun: "Sister Mary Macho Is a Priest in Drag," it read. Critics, many of them LFLers who felt spurned or used, called O'Leary's approach to personal relationships male-identified and unliberated.

Not coincidentally, given the radical belief that personal behavior was the touchstone of political integrity, the leader who most denounced O'Leary for her transgressions was Lin Farley, a former Radicalesbian whose affair with O'Leary had soured shortly after it began in the fall of 1973. The feud between O'Leary and her supporters and Farley and hers rapidly paralyzed LFL and drove most of those determined to pursue reformist lesbian feminist enterprises elsewhere. Those loyal to the gay liberation movement (like Nath Rockhill and Meryl Friedman) resolved to work for the passage of gay rights legislation independently and with the newly formed National Gay Task Force. Those who objected to the extremes of the radicals but identified strongly with the women's movement (like Judy Burns and Noreen Harnick) formed informal consciousness-raising and study groups and thought and wrote about the meaning of lesbianism on their own.

During 1974, among those who stayed in LFL and fought over its lesbian feminist orientation, the reformers demonstrated greater support than the radicals. In January, Nancy Fish was elected over Lin Farley's friend Liz Wallace to succeed O'Leary as spokeswoman. In June, Ginny Vida ran against Farley herself—and was elected to succeed Fish after Farley dropped out of the race to take a job at Cornell. Yet even then, the belief that LFL had to proceed without violating feminist principles—combined with the difficulty of developing uniquely lesbian issues and mustering enthusiasm for conventional political and organizational activities—kept the group inward-looking. Self-help, social, and public relations enterprises continued, with the goal of building identity and developing community, but direct efforts to affect political and cultural institutions were limited to joining in the actions initiated by gay and women's liberation groups.

PART IV

THE EXPLOSION OF THINGS GAY

12

Liberationist Politics and the Spread of Gay Life

THIS HAS BEEN a story of American society in the middle of the twentieth century. On one level, it is an analysis of three gay political movements that have improved life for homosexuals and touched off an explosion of things gay. On another level, it is an account of fundamental social, cultural, and political trends and basic organizational dynamics that have transformed modern American society.

Like so many of America's significant stories, this one begins with the ideals of individual liberty and equal opportunity that led the founders of the United States to establish a republic. Since then, the effort to extend these ideals within the republic and around the world has been a major theme in American history. During the first half of the twentieth century, this theme was highlighted in public consciousness by the efforts of liberal civil rights leaders to bring individuals with foreign backgrounds, unpopular religions, and dark skins into the American melting pot. Early in the 1950s, the idea that minorities could work to eliminate the prejudice and discrimination that kept them out of the mainstream prompted homosexuals to form voluntary associations to secure rights and status for "sexual variants." The efforts of these first politically active homosexuals, as they were carried forward by groups like the Mattachine Society and the Daughters of Bilitis, constituted the homophile initiative.

But even as homophile leaders worked to help homosexuals become acculturated and integrated, America nurtured social and political movements that would inspire very different ambitions in a new generation of homosexuals. The social movement was the drive for fuller and freer self-expression and more humane social interaction that began in the 1950s, when "bohemians" criticized and abandoned traditional mores; it flowered during the 1960s into a counterculture, as growing numbers of young people joined the quest for more fulfilling and humanistic ways of life by experimenting with forbidden drugs, mystical religions, unconventional relationships, and unusual living and working arrangements. The political movement was the New Left, which was begun in the early 1960s by the leaders of SNCC and SDS, who set out to force existing institutions to grant equal opportunity to members of disadvantaged groups by organizing these minorities into powerful blocs. As more and more people were persuaded that America's capitalistic system was hopelessly racist, elitist, imperialistic, and inhumane, the New Left became a broad-based drive for social transformation.

When those with countercultural views and values were politicized by the New Left, and when New Left leaders embraced countercultural perspectives, there emerged a new set of ideas about political goals and tactics and a new generation of political activists with bold new visions for American society. Some of these activists were homosexuals whose vision of the future included sexual liberation: these were the gay liberationists who organized the Gay Liberation Front and the Gay Activists Alliance and thereby established the gay liberation movement. Some were women who hoped for the elimination of stifling sex roles: these were the radical feminists who initiated the women's liberation movement. Others were lesbians sensitive to the need for both sexual and sex-role liberation: they banded together in Radicalesbians, DOB–New York, and Lesbian Feminist Liberation, and set in motion the lesbian feminist movement. The liberationist politics practiced by members of the gay, women's, and lesbian liberation movements transformed the face of America by legitimizing and encouraging the spread of lesbian and gay life.

· · ·

At the end of 1973, most of the major gay leaders in New York City agreed that things had never been better; at the same time, they complained that things had never been worse. On the one hand, more than had seemed possible at the outset, homosexuals had been politicized and mobilized, the support of political leaders and public officials had been elicited, and gay activity of every kind was more prominent. On the other hand, GLF, RL, and DOB–New York had disintegrated and MSNY, GAA, and LFL were on the verge of collapse. Many from these pioneering gay groups had indeed gone on to form new organizations, including the National Gay Task Force, the first gay group with a national purview and a paid professional staff. Still, arguments among activists continued to paralyze organizations and to divide coalitions; the mortality rate among new groups was high; and no one quite understood why the gay movement seemed to be forever growing while gay organizations were always struggling to survive.

This book has shown that the men and women who formed and ran trend-setting gay groups in New York City tried to pursue the aims suggested by their gay political outlooks in ways that would cultivate the identity, legitimacy, and resources needed to sustain their organizations. Its analysis has suggested that gay leaders ran into problems when the directions suggested by their political outlooks ran counter to the self-interest of their organizations. One can conclude that just as basic sets of ideas about gay political activity and organizational maintenance were rooted in contemporary political and social currents, so the fate of the first gay groups in New York City—and hence the course of gay political activity there and elsewhere—was determined, ultimately, not only by the degree of coherence between organizational and political ambitions, but by the extent of compatibility between political and organizational perspectives and underlying social and political conditions.

. . .

The problem with the homophile initiatives shaped by liberal civil rights assumptions was that they did little to crystallize issues and attract sources of support that might have permitted gay political organizations to thrive. Because the homophile message said that sexual orientation was inconsequential and that homosexuals were in important respects like heterosexuals, it did little to stir people with homosexual feelings to acknowledge and to value their sexuality. Because homophile tactics (including picket lines staged by men and women instructed to look straight) reinforced the conviction that the way society defined respectability was important, they discouraged homosexuals from compromising themselves by associating with enterprises concerned with behavior commonly perceived as illicit, unhealthy, and immoral. Indeed, since the homophile goal was to promote acculturation and integration, homophile leaders refrained from encouraging homosexuals to consider how they differed from heterosexuals and to develop the sense of having a distinctive place in society to protect and promote. Paradoxically, the nature of the gay political goals and tactics inspired by liberal assumptions was precisely what precluded the growth of organizations strong enough to achieve homophile ambitions.

The circumstances that kept gay political organizations few and weak began to change when growing numbers of people abandoned liberal assumptions for the existential perspectives of the counterculture. Those in the counterculture rejected the conventional view that respectability—as evidenced by material goods, social position, professional status, power, self-control, and conformity—was desirable. They cherished instead emotional, sensual, spiritual, aesthetic, experiential, spontaneous, and individualistic modes of self-expression, which they felt traditional standards and attitudes discouraged. Homosexuals with countercultural perspectives were led to value their sexuality, to deem gay modes of self-expression and interaction distinctive and fulfilling, to consider it important to express themselves openly and be intimate with and affirming of their own kind, and to believe that those who adopted gay life styles and joined together in gay community had an important place in the pluralistic "Age of Aquarius." The emergence both of an environment in which conventional views and values were challenged and of a population of homosexuals enthusiastic about gay life (something permitted in part by the decline of police harassment that resulted from the Mattachine's mid-sixties militancy) prepared the way for the emergence of gay groups with liberationist orientations.

Homosexuals with the countercultural belief that they should be free to express themselves and to socialize with one another as they wished caused the disorderly protest that followed the police raid on the Stonewall Inn in June 1969. But homosexuals with cultural radical New Left convictions took the initiative of forming the Gay Liberation Front. Because these radical homosexuals rejected traditional standards of behavior and celebrated unconventional ways, they had no compunctions about glorifying their sexual orientations publicly or about reveling in gay life styles. Because they believed that the approval their group needed had to come from those also seeking liberation, whom they represented, and not from members of the Establishment, whom they vowed to enlighten or to overwhelm, they felt no need to equivocate about the health or morality of homosexual behavior. In a few short months, GLF drew dozens, then hundreds, not only because its radical founders promised to help homosexuals make their sexuality the basis of distinctive and fulfilling life styles and supportive community—what those with countercultural views and values desired above all—but also because they presented the exploration of appealing sexual and social pastimes as a matter of moral and political necessity.

The radical founders of GLF trumpeted about the importance of self-realization and social diversity, but they rapidly betrayed these countercultural ideals by objecting to the personal, political, and organizational preferences exhibited by many of their peers. GLF began to lose sizable segments of its membership when homosexuals who had evolved reformist and revolutionary gay political outlooks became convinced that radical dogmatism threatened their own ambitions. The political reformers who left to form the Gay Activists Alliance felt that their efforts in GLF to develop and exercise political influence had been hindered by radical objections to any involvement with the political system and to traditional operating procedures. The revolutionaries who seceded as the Red Butterfly were angered by radical impatience with Marxist exegesis and by the radicals' unwillingness to agree that activists seeking to retain influence with socialist groups and carry on Marxist propagandizing sometimes had to hide their sexual orientations. GLFers with cultural reformist outlooks joined the others in feeling alienated by the radical tendency to equate liberation with the abandonment of traditional gay pastimes, the avoidance of conventional aspirations and established institutions, and the embrace of styles of thinking and acting declared "woman-identified."

Although the radicals' condemnation of political and personal modes others found moral and fulfilling contradicted fundamental countercultural and radical ideals, the organizational disintegration they set in motion did not. To the radicals, building and preserving organizations mattered less than encouraging others to see how conventional standards and attitudes inhibited their opportunities for growth and support and to learn how to think and act in ways that would undermine oppressive mores and engender a countercultural society.

Not coincidentally, most of the radicals active in establishing GLF went their separate ways soon after GLF was formed. Early in 1970, several who felt misunderstood and left out because of their age as well as their sexuality formed a cell, later an independent association, called Gay Youth. A half-dozen GLFers who were spurred to seek respect for their race as well as their sexuality organized a Third World Gay Caucus, later the autonomous Third World Gay Liberation. Lesbian GLFers who came to believe that they were deprived of empathy and acknowledgement as much because they were women as because they were homosexual formalized the quest for lesbian feminist liberation by organizing Radicalesbians. Radical males who felt that conventional male roles kept them from expressing themselves fully and freely and from communicating intimately with others joined in living collectives intended to help them escape their sexist conditioning.* And effeminate male radicals who felt that the widespread devaluation of traits and behavior presumed feminine made them outcasts even among other radical males withdrew into groups of their own and resolved to battle against sexism as "effeminists." In short, GLF splintered not because its radical leaders failed to equip it properly, but because their zeal to be and to make others liberated induced them to alienate GLFers with differing political priorities and personal preferences and then to disperse into groups better able to advance their own liberation.

Even more than in GLF, the contradiction between radical aspirations and formal organizations showed up in relatively homogenous groups like Radicalesbians. Radical lesbians from GLF and from radical feminist groups banded together in Radicalesbians because they felt that in all-female groups they could pursue liberation better.

*Most of these radical males equated an escape from sexist conditioning with the abandonment of traditional male or male-identified ways, but a few argued that liberation could include experimenting with "butch" styles and roles in the spirit of playfulness or adventure as long as others, particularly those who were not butch, were not belittled. At least one of those who made this argument was involved in the beginnings of the Eulenspiegel Society, an organization formed to promote the liberation of people, gay and straight, who enjoyed sado-masochistic sexual and social behavior.

Yet they brought to RL the assumption that certain traits (such as intuitiveness) and certain behaviors (such as deferring to the wishes of others) were inherently female while others (such as rationality and aggressiveness) were characteristically male. Efforts to "correct" lesbians who exhibited male-identified traits and behavior alienated those who felt that liberation meant expressing oneself as one was inclined to express oneself.

Had those in Radicalesbians—and the radical male GLFers who followed their lead—clearly realized that the idea of self-realization, as cherished by the counterculture, called not for forcing individuals to express themselves in the same ways, but for permitting each individual to grow in whatever ways were natural and satisfying, there might have been less ambition to equate liberation with specific traits and behaviors and fewer attempts to challenge individuals who failed to manifest them. As it was, any inclination the radicals had to welcome diversity was overwhelmed by the conviction that conventional ways were reactionary and that liberation had to be defined substantively so that others could be shown the route to a revolution in consciousness. The resulting dogmatism and captiousness was reinforced by the radicals' failure to understand the countercultural ideal of supportive community.

To those with countercultural perspectives, communities were supportive when they affirmed that each individual's self-expression was valid, however unusual its manifestation, as long as it was accompanied by respect for the self-expression of others. Moreover, diversity *per se* was championed because it seemed to permit each person a greater range of experience and to give society at large a better shot at successful social adaptation and evolution. With regard to sexuality, the countercultural ideal called for a community in which individuals would be confident and comfortable with their own sexual interests and respectful of other varieties of sexual self-expression. With regard to gender and sex roles, the countercultural ideal called for a community in which both men and women would be free to express themselves in ways that were conventionally considered exclusively either masculine or feminine. The countercultural ideal was seen as the only vision of community compatible with the fact that different people had different endowments and interests, that different individuals set out to grow at different times and with varying degrees of skill and dedication, and that self-discovery and self-realization proceeded at different rates and produced different results in different individuals.

The organizers of Radicalesbians set out to realize this ideal community by bringing lesbians together and encouraging them to help each other learn how to express themselves fully and freely. But instead of perceiving that supportive community called for each Radicalesbian to encourage all others to express themselves as they wished, the radicals tended to equate liberation with the adoption of "female" traits and behaviors, to goad peers to think and act in ways that were truly woman-identified, and to ostracize those who failed to accept and meet these standards. This alienated lesbians inclined to behave in ways termed male-identified. It troubled those who saw that acceptance of individual differences had to be the touchstone of supportive community. And it forced even those Radicalesbians who took the lead in identifying, personifying, and urging their peers to embrace woman-identified ways to wrestle with the difficult questions that confronted all radicals who felt that being supportive meant more than genuinely acknowledging all modes of self-expression and interaction but those which intentionally belittled others: How much was any given radical obliged to restrain her own self-expression to allow others in her presence to feel good and to grow? To what extent and with how much assertion, aggressiveness, and manipulation was it appropriate to force others to grow in ways for which they lacked inclination or ability? What was one's obligation to those who maintained they felt incompetent, unloved, or unfulfilled, especially when they appeared, in fact, to be untalented, unlikable, or congenitally dissatisfied?

Their thirst for growth and support frustrated because they could not answer these and similar difficult questions, most of the Radicalesbians soon went their own ways. Those attracted to Marxist views developed revolutionary lesbian feminist analyses and activities. Those who believed not only that liberation meant expressing oneself and relating to others as one wished, but that it did not preclude developing traits and aspirations that most radicals called male-identified, turned their attention to associations like Abbott and Love's informal supergroups and the Daughters of Bilitis, where they evolved a reformist variety of lesbian feminism. Most of those who retained radical outlooks resolved to live independently in ways they found fulfilling and to join together when and where they wished in small, informal, task-oriented groups. Enterprises run by gay women proliferated.

.   .   .

By spurring homosexuals to follow the varied and changing paths that served their quests for self-realization and support, radical thinking encouraged diaspora; by concentrating on the homosexual dimensions of self-expression and affirmation, its reformist derivative promoted coalescence. The political reformist founders of GAA wanted to help homosexuals to feel comfortable expressing their sexual feelings and enjoying the company of other homosexuals. The way to achieve this, they thought, was to organize homosexuals into a bloc so active and influential that politicians and public officials would have to respond to it by acknowledging that homosexuals had rights and status, thereby encouraging others to grant recognition, respect, and representation to people who were openly gay and to their life styles and institutions. By focusing on whether government officials were willing to confirm publicly that homosexuals had rights, GAA strategists gave concrete form to the issue of whether society accorded recognition and respect to homoerotic sensibilities. By challenging politicians and public officials to speak out about gay rights, the GAAers captured the attention of the media and conveyed the impression that there *was* a legitimate gay minority. Because their efforts to politicize and mobilize homosexuals served also to build the organization that claimed to be the political mouthpiece of local homosexuals, GAA rapidly became the most powerful gay group in New York City.

Like the founders of GLF, the founders of GAA ran into problems not because they failed to maintain their group but because their very success attracted large numbers of members with incompatible ideas about pursuing gay liberation. As noted earlier, homosexuals with countercultural views and values were the easiest to persuade that it was worth flouting conventional standards and assumptions and risking the loss of social status, professional advancement, material reward, family, and friends in order to integrate one's sexuality into one's personal, social, and professional life. Countercultural homosexuals who enjoyed political strategy and public affairs and who derived satisfaction from the decision-making and administration involved in running organizations found activities involving political figures and political groups an effective way of integrating their sexual and professional interests and of finding comradeship. But those who lacked the interest and the disposition found politics and organizational responsibilities like fund-raising, personnel management, and plant maintenance incompatible with their countercultural impulse to find more self-expressive and satisfying pursuits. So some of those attracted to GAA found it fulfilling to join in the political and organizational activities championed by GAA's political reformist founders, but most preferred social, self-help, and cultural events. These GAAers were slowly but surely drawn to the cultural reformist argument that gay liberation was best served when the lives of individual homosexuals showed such security and fulfillment that the lives would themselves refute traditional misconceptions about what it meant to be homosexual.

As the politicos realized that those stirred to be proud and open about their homosexuality would not automatically view political activism as the key to gay liberation, they tried both to politicize members with cultural interests and to make political activities more appealing. On the one hand, they used dances and other social events to make speeches and to distribute leaflets stressing that homosexuals had to protest official interference with any segment of the gay subculture in order to prevent the repression of all gay activity. On the other hand, they portrayed political demonstrations as opportunities for participants to affirm their gay identity and community and to raise the consciousness of homosexual and heterosexual bystanders. Yet this attempt to appeal to the cultural crowd engendered even more skepticism about conventional political and organizational enterprises. Before GAA was a year and a half old, the politicos had to accommodate cultural leaders by making their pursuit of gay rights legislation exceptionally open, principled, and militant; by identifying GAA as a cultural as well as a political organization; by establishing committees to sponsor self-help, social, artistic, and educational activities; and by leasing the Firehouse to provide space for these culture-building efforts.

With the institutionalization of efforts to build a distinctive gay culture, contradictions between the needs of politically and culturally oriented gay organizations grew even more apparent. To preserve GAA's reputation as the political representative of the local gay community and to attract support from political leaders and homosexuals interested in politics, the politicos believed it necessary to raise serious political issues, to stage demonstrations with the sobriety and fervor befitting homosexuals with substantial griev-ances, to sustain mature rapport with established political figures, and to abide by the laws and contractual obligations necessary to maintain GAA's headquarters. (Of course, by the summer of 1971, politicos whose revolutionary ambitions led them to stress the utility of heated demonstrations and provocative confrontations ceased to share the last two of these concerns.) But cultural leaders wanted to establish GAA's reputation as a center for avant-garde sexual, sen-sual, and sex-role experimentation and to attract homosexuals inter-ested in developing liberated gay life styles and a distinctive gay culture. The more the politicos complained that their efforts were being compromised and diluted by the convention-challenging be-havior of members and by the energy invested in cultural activities, the more cultural leaders responded that their activities were in and of themselves political and that traditional political and organiza-tional endeavors fostered traits and behavior that were neither gay nor liberated. Frustrated and alienated, some politicos resolved to pursue political reformist enterprises in specialized committees. Some left GAA and abandoned gay politics altogether. Others, like Jim Owles and his friends, organized gay groups concerned exclu-sively with conventional politics—the Gay Democratic Club, Gays for Bella, the Gay Caucus of the Village Independent Democrats, and the Gay Political Union (which evolved into the "Study Group" of gay politicians and public officials, some "out," some closeted, that has worked effectively behind the scenes to advance gay political interests in New York City).

With the displacement of the politicos, and with the election late in 1971 of a president willing to run GAA in the laissez-faire manner that seemed compatible with the sensibilities of cultural leaders, GAA became a proliferating collection of self-governing committees. Then the obstacles to harmony were the challenges to cultural re-formers made by radicals, many of them veterans of the defunct GLF, and by newcomers with revolutionary perspectives—mostly from the Socialist Workers Party, newly committed to the strategy of having its members infiltrate gay political organizations. Reform-ers eager to reach out to traditional homosexuals with new interest in openness and community encountered radical and revolutionary objections that homosexuals involved in the Establishment or enamored with "unliberated" subcultural pursuits such as sado-masochism were less worthy of attention than those oppressed for their involvement in cross dressing, prostitution, and sex with teenagers, and those doubly oppressed because, besides being homosexual, they were poor, Third World, underage, or female. Reformers willing to abide by state laws and city codes and to accommodate public officials so as to keep GAA housed in its spacious physical plant encountered objections that "government intrusion" and "red tape" had to be resisted in order to undermine "the system." Reformers who argued that through traditional institutions like professional associations and the media, they could simultaneously enlighten heterosexuals and reach homosexuals were told that it was necessary to avoid the Establishment and to work through alternative institutions to keep from being co-opted.

The more GAA's cultural reformers felt interfered with by radicals and revolutionaries and deprived of peer-group support, the more they followed the lead of the political reformers and withdrew. Some decided to pursue the missions they valued under the auspices of GAA committees but to avoid general membership meetings and to disassociate from GAA as a whole. Some left GAA, planning simply to be openly gay and enthusiastic about the gay subculture in their daily lives—strengthened by their belief that this, in and of itself, was political. Some sought enhanced integration and affirmation by striving to combine their homosexual and their professional interests by joining with other openly gay professionals in projects that would further cultural reformist aims. During 1972, GAAers interested in therapy (including Dr. Charles Silverstein, who later became founding editor of the *Journal of Homosexuality* and coauthor, with Edmund White, of *The Joy of Gay Sex*) formed supportive gay counseling centers like Identity House. Some of their associates moved on to organize community service institutions like Liberation House, the Gay Switchboard, and the Gay Men's Health Clinic. Doric Wilson, a GAAer interested in making his love for drama the basis of a contribution to gay culture, took the lead in organizing a gay arts collective, The Other Side of Silence. A group of scholars, many of whom had first been exposed to gay political activity in GAA, organized the Gay Academic Union, an association of graduate students and faculty members interested in research and political issues involving homosexuality.

Late in the fall of 1972, at the urging of a number of political and cultural reformist veterans who agreed that only strong leadership would keep GAA from disintegrating, Bruce Voeller ran for president. For most of 1972, Voeller had managed GAA's State and Federal Affairs Committee during off hours from his job as an associate professor of biology at Rockefeller University. After being elected, he showed his professional expertise by insisting on the need to clarify GAA's priorities, to reduce and restrain its autonomous committees, to protect its physical plant by paying taxes and enforcing regulations about such activities as drug sales, and to increase efficiency by limiting the number of matters that required debate and a vote by the membership. Furthermore, although he continued to participate enthusiastically in political demonstrations and cultural events, Voeller wanted to use the growing recognition of homosexuals as a legitimate minority to enlist the help of important civic and political leaders, of prestigious mental health professionals (such as certain leaders of the American Psychiatric Association), and of established figures in the media (such as certain editors at the *New York Times*).

His supporters on GAA's Lesbian Liberation Committee had helped Voeller to overcome the opposition of radicals and revolutionaries who mistrusted his strategic and organizational ambitions, but when the new president tried to reestablish control over that committee, LLCers charged that he was insensitive to lesbians' need to manage their own affairs and to deal with their distinctive dual concerns. Late in the spring of 1973, at the urging of Jean O'Leary, GAA's Lesbian Liberation Committee became the autonomous Lesbian Feminist Liberation, Inc.

Like the leaders of GAA, the reform-oriented heads of LFL were challenged and alienated by radicals. Lesbian feminist reformers eager to mobilize and politicize a broad cross-section of lesbians by treating established institutions in ways that would generate publicity and by building a large, resourceful organization were criticized by radicals who argued that it was more important for members to develop innovative, woman-identified life styles and for leaders to pursue strategic and organizational objectives in distinctly feminist ways. Because woman-identified life styles were equated not with the development of traits and pursuits that individual women found natural and fulfilling but with the avoidance of male-identified characteristics and aspirations, leaders who were considered overly intellectual, calculating, conventionally ambitious, and comfortable in established institutions were criticized. Because lesbian feminist ways of operating were said to entail more than allowing each woman to contribute as she wished in the ways that she wanted, everything from efforts to get LFL's name in the newspapers to the use of Robert's rules was declaimed as male-identified and hence inappropriate.

The more those in LFL debated what it meant for individuals and organizations to operate in woman-identified ways, and the more particular leaders were rebuked, the more debates became angry and emotional. LFLers who felt that the infighting betrayed basic feminist ideals withdrew with the idea that they could best pursue liberation by working to develop woman-identified life styles on their own and by finding support in smaller, more directed groups of compatible peers. (Doris London and a group of LFLers interested in the media formed Lesbians Organized for Video Experience—LOVE. Joan Nestle and others who attended LFL events established the Lesbian Herstory Archive.) LFLers eager to pursue lesbian feminist aims by dealing with established institutions with the backing of a large and resourceful organization turned their attention to the newly formed National Gay Task Force.

Having encountered the same kinds of challenges that frustrated and estranged the lesbian feminist reformers in charge of LFL, Bruce Voeller and his close associates in GAA had become convinced by the fall of 1973 that the only way they could avoid the paralyzing interference of members with radical and revolutionary convictions was to reorganize GAA so that it was run by a board of directors, a salaried staff, and a membership that met monthly to consider general policy. When the radicals and revolutionaries insisted that such plans were reactionary, Voeller and his supporters resigned. A few days later they announced that they were forming a group called Gay Action. After recognizing that their ambitions were national rather than local in scope, and after they enlisted as chairman of their prospective board Dr. Howard J. Brown (the former Lindsay administration health services administrator whose public acknowledgement of his homosexuality was reported on the front page of the

New York Times in October 1973), they changed the group's name to the National Gay Task Force (NGTF). By the end of 1973, only dwindling factions of warring radicals and revolutionaries remained in GAA.

Though it is often attributed to the ambitions of particular leaders and to circumstances they encountered, the disintegration of both the radical and the reformist groups responsible for the birth of the gay and lesbian liberation movements was ultimately produced by a fundamental tension between liberationist gay political perspectives and the imperatives of organization. The pursuit of gay and lesbian feminist liberation—like the quest for liberation generally—was a political incarnation of personal aspirations characteristic of the counterculture.

The basic aim of liberationist gay political activity was to force society to accommodate openly gay people by encouraging homosexuals to express their feelings fully and freely. For homosexuals interested in public affairs and group dynamics and with the disposition and background it took to work effectively in and with traditional institutions, involvement in gay political and organizational activity helped fulfill the quest for self-realization and solidarity as homosexuals, leaving them free to develop other dimensions of their lives elsewhere. But for those without the interest or ability to think and act with the necessary calculation, discipline, and formality, and for those who fulfilled these dimensions of their lives elsewhere and mainly sought the opportunity to explore their homoerotic and emotional selves, having to constrain personal wishes in order to conduct political and organizational business frustrated the very desires that had led them to gay and lesbian liberation groups in the first place. So gay and lesbian liberationists interested in politics and organizations lost patience with peers more concerned with feelings and relationships as rapidly as those peers lost patience with them. And liberationists of every disposition participated in political organizations only as long as their involvement remained satisfying and validating—and not for very long at the expense of the fulfillment that came from the personal dimensions of their lives.

In short, by defining self-actualization and social validation as the touchstones of liberation, and by making it a matter of moral principle and political consequence to attain these, the first gay and lesbian liberationists discouraged homosexuals from enduring conventional political and organizational activity that was constraining and encouraged them to indulge in more pleasant pastimes and to move on to more satisfying institutions. As a result, the lives of the first gay and lesbian liberation groups were short, but the proliferation of other types of gay and lesbian activity was swift.

.   .   .

Developments in New York City frequently affect other parts of the country. Things tend to happen first and very dramatically in New York, and what happens there is extensively publicized. The Manhattan media make pacesetters of New Yorkers by reporting on their activities and by publishing and distributing their books, magazines, and journals. The avant-garde in the city can attract visitors, expose them to new developments, and count on their carrying away tales of what they have seen and heard.

This is why it was the emergence of gay liberationist political activity in New York City that triggered the explosion of gay life nationwide that made the seventies in America so remarkable. Although countercultural homosexuals and feminist lesbians in Los Angeles and San Francisco established gay groups with liberationist orientations in the 1960s, gay and lesbian liberationists in New York City elaborated and publicized the ideologies, set the examples, and offered the help that encouraged people all across the country and in Canada and Western Europe to organize homosexuals during the 1970s. By the end of 1973, GAA's National Gay Movement Committee, which from its base in the Firehouse dispatched "firemen" to help homosexuals elsewhere organize replicas of GAA, had the names of some 1100 gay groups in its records.

Even as the heads of GAA traveled around the countryside pushing political and cultural reformism, the founders of the National Gay Task Force sought to set a new example for homosexuals. Cognizant both of the success that GAA and its neighbors had had in establishing homosexuals as a legitimate political and cultural minority and of their failure to maintain a strong organization and to fashion a unified local movement, the organizers of the Task Force wanted to synthesize the old homophile and the reformist gay and lesbian liberationist approaches into a new hybrid with broader appeal. Thus, in addition to asking that gay men and lesbians be recognized and respected for the ways in which they were distinctive,

NGTF would ask that homosexuals be acknowledged and rewarded for the ways in which they were as competent and ethical as straights. In addition to securing the right to enjoy gay and lesbian life styles and to develop from their subcultures distinctive institutions and communities, NGTF would seek for homosexuals the right to be treated equitably and, without having to be wholly acculturated, to be integrated. In addition to staging initiatives that would politicize and mobilize homosexuals, NGTF would take advantage of the status of homosexuals as a recognized bloc to command responses from the Establishment that, by further changing popular attitudes about homosexuality and providing protections for homosexual rights, would encourage more and more gay people to come out and to become political. The organizers of NGTF had left successful careers in academia, journalism, publishing, and the social services to become involved in gay political activity, and they wanted to be recognized and respected for their general personal and professional competence as well as for their special sexual and emotional gifts. They believed that by having their organization press for recognition of the ways in which homosexuals resembled heterosexuals, as well as those in which they were different, they could win the support of other gay professionals, whose skill and status would help convey the message that homosexuals were as well-adjusted, competent, and ethical as heterosexuals even though they had special ways of fulfilling themselves sexually and emotionally.

The first evidence that the time was ripe for this hybrid new approach came in the variety of veteran activists that the founders attracted to the Task Force, the structure of which they modeled after that of the American Civil Liberties Union. Carrying the homophile banner to NGTF's board of directors were Barbara Gittings and Frank Kameny. Bearing the reformist gay liberationist colors were Pete Fisher, Marc Rubin, and "Bebe" Scarpi. Bringing the reformist lesbian feminist standard were Sidney Abbott, Barbara Love, Ginny Vida, and Meryl Friedman. Presenting themselves as gay professionals were board members Martin Duberman, Distinguished Professor of History at Lehman College in the City University of New York; Joseph Norton, professor of education at the State University of New York in Albany; and David Rothenberg, executive director of the Fortune Society, an organization concerned with reforming the criminal justice system. Howard Brown, then a professor of public administration at New York University, agreed to be chairperson of the board. Bruce Voeller, abandoning all thought of returning to academia, assumed the post of executive director. Ron Gold, formerly a reporter for *Variety,* volunteered to be communications director. Nath Rockhill assumed the position of national coordinator and later became legislative director in addition.

By the end of 1974, NGTF had 2500 members, including individuals from each of the fifty states and from over a dozen foreign countries. These included openly gay mental health and social welfare professionals, such as Walter Lear, deputy commissioner of health in Pennsylvania; openly gay athletes, such as pro football star Dave Kopay; and openly gay members of the armed forces, such as Air Force sergeant Leonard Matlovich, who early in the fall of 1975 was featured in a *Time* magazine cover story.

Almost as soon as the Task Force was ensconced in its small Fifth Avenue offices, events provided new evidence that the approach synthesized by its founders was destined for success. In December 1973, as Ron Gold completed the negotiations that he and a committee including Drs. Charles Silverstein and Henry Messer had begun under the auspices of GAA, the board of trustees of the American Psychiatric Association (APA) voted to remove homosexuality from its list of mental disorders. The following April, in a referendum instigated by dissenting psychiatrists, a majority of the APA voted to uphold the action of the trustees.

During 1974, NGTF orchestrated successful national campaigns to protest the biased portrayals of homosexuals in scheduled episodes of television programs on ABC and NBC. Sponsors in some locales canceled their support for the episodes. Six local stations refused to carry them, and some stations gave local gay groups air time to express their objections. With the help of the American Civil Liberties Union, NGTF prepared legal challenges involving the rights of lesbian mothers and gay fathers, the rights of homosexuals in the armed forces, and the constitutionality of state government restrictions on consensual adult sex—including the case of *Doe* v. *The Commonwealth of Virginia,* which was appealed all the way to the United States Supreme Court where a majority of the justices voted not to rule on it.

During the spring of 1975, NGTF worked closely with Bella Abzug's office to introduce, with twenty-four congressional cosponsors, a bill that would amend the 1964 and 1968 Civil Rights Acts to prohibit discrimination based on "affectional or sexual preference." Before the end of the year, in many cases with the help of NGTF-provided information on legislation and lobbying and NGTF-secured statements of support from national associations—such as the National Organization for Women, the YWCA, the American Bar Association, the American Civil Liberties Union, the National Education Association, the American Federation of Teachers, the National Council of Churches, and the Federation of Priests Councils—gay groups had succeeded in having gay rights ordinances passed in over twenty-five cities and counties. The largest were San Francisco, Washington, D.C., Seattle, Detroit, Minneapolis, St. Paul, San Jose, Columbus, Austin, and Portland, Oregon.

As in New York, gay and lesbian liberation groups in these and other cities around the country had given birth to a host of more specialized groups; to identifiably gay and lesbian populations, businesses, and neighborhoods; and to organizations that combined approaches in order to deal with the problems that still confronted them. Like the New Yorkers who were their inspiration, gay and lesbian liberationists in other locales succeeded in giving gay life legitimacy because they used strategies of liberationist politics to stir homosexuals to think positively about themselves and their peers, to unite politically and socially, and thereby to force the communities in which they lived to accord them recognition and (though these were not always protected) rights. Slower to come was what gay leaders of every political outlook had pursued in their different ways from the beginning: respect.

EPILOGUE

TEN YEARS AGO one could walk down Christopher Street in Greenwich Village and find a family crowd. In the summer of 1969, when Marty Robinson, insisting that that crowd had always included a disproportionate number of homosexuals, persuaded a half-dozen of his friends to join him in a "protest hangout" to claim Christopher Street as gay turf, only a few hippies paid him any notice.

Things are very different in 1980. The full length of Christopher Street is now populated by homosexuals. Businesses run by gay people line both sides of the street. Craig Rodwell's Oscar Wilde Memorial Bookshop has moved from its original location to a spot just a few hundred yards from the site of the Stonewall Riots. The pornographic bookstore further down now bears a lambda.

Lesbians, as always, are much less visible than gay men. Some women mingle in the traffic on Christopher Street, usually in androgynous-looking pairs that make their very masculine neighbors look all the more traditionally macho. A lesbian bookshop stands not far away from the Oscar Wilde, beside a host of successful small businesses run by women. But the defining ambience of the Village, as of most gay ghettos, is male homosexual; lesbians there as elsewhere cluster together in their own friendship groups, social clubs, and apartment buildings.

The homosexuals are not alone in Greenwich Village. Still visible in its population, though much less present on the erotic avenue Christopher Street has become, are the bohemian artists and intellectuals and sympathetic heterosexuals who made homosexuals welcome if inhibited in their midst long before the beginnings of gay political activity. There are also the ethnic businesspeople who count on gays for patronage, teenagers and tourists, straight women who "get off" on the freedom and intimacy they feel with gay men, avant-garde old people, and straight couples who find the gay life style and its institutions chic. Here and there one sees a drag queen, but most of these now feel more comfortable in other parts of the city.

Gay life in every form has also spread well beyond the Village. The National Gay Task Force, more professional than ever, has been joined by groups of homosexuals championing every variety of sexual liberation and making every type of political demand. Gay bars, discos, restaurants, bathhouses, sex shows, porn shops, novelty stores, art galleries, and hustling bars, as well as homoerotic books, newspapers, and magazines and gay clothing styles, now abound everywhere. So many sections of the city have been populated densely by gay men and by lesbians that *gayification* may be a more appropriate term than *gentrification* for the renaissances taking place in some local neighborhoods. Openly gay people are so visible all over the city and within the Establishment that almost everyone knows at least one. Whether they have any idea what that person does sexually is another question.

It is hard to deny that in the last ten years there has been a dramatic growth of gay activity in New York City. It is easy to see the same pattern of change in Boston, Washington, D.C., Atlanta, Miami, Houston, Los Angeles, San Francisco, Seattle, Denver, and Chicago—indeed, in most every sizable American city and in many resort areas (Fire Island, Provincetown, Key West, Laguna Beach, Russian River). Moreover, gay life in America has become a refuge for homosexuals from countries all over the world, where they are much less free to be gay; and American gay political activity has been the model for politically active homosexuals in Canada, England, Australia, Israel, and many countries on the Continent. For people interested in contemporary political and social change and in the relationships between them, it is hard to think of a development more worthy of attention than the recent explosion of things gay.

The liberationist politics that triggered this explosion seem to have set in motion an ever-accelerating process: as gay people come out and become politicized, regardless of how they are treated and whether they win or lose individual battles, other homosexuals fol-

low their example, join together, and force the surrounding society
to accommodate them. If this process has changed at all from the
days of the first gay and lesbian liberationists, it is in the number of
affluent, professional, and socially prominent homosexuals who have
taken part, and in their demand that liberationist goals include respect for the ways in which homosexuals are like heterosexuals, as
well as respect for the ways in which they are different.

They are different most precisely in their affinity for members of
their own sex and in their eagerness to explore that affinity. Just as
feminist lesbians have taken it upon themselves to discover the meaning of liberation alongside and for the benefit of all women, so gay
men, though often much less self-consciously, have been led by their
desire for liberation to investigate the distinctive pulls and rhythms
of male sexuality and of traditional male roles. For the society at
large, the intense sexuality of the gay male's homoerotic explorations
is more threatening than the less obvious explorations of the lesbians,
and that sexuality is a source of continued dispute and division
between gay men and lesbians themselves. The challenge for future
historians will be to see how the different trends apparent in the gay
male and lesbian subcultures have furthered and frustrated, for those
involved as well as for the rest of society, the countercultural ideals
of self-realization, supportive community, and, above all, respect for
diversity.

In many ways, like the boisterous and well-publicized gay political
activity of the early 1970s, the counterculture seems to have disappeared. Yet as countercultural values have been diffused, among
straights as well as gays, gay life has won acceptance, and the proliferation of gay subcultures is perhaps the most dramatic evidence
today that the counterculture thrives.

By the end of the decade, members of the sixties' and early seventies' counterculture had learned much from their thinking and their
experimenting and their struggling to be free. They had discovered
that the countercultural life involved more than just experiencing the
erotic or the mystical side of life. They had learned that they had to
be responsible for themselves emotionally and financially if they were
to allow others the opportunity to grow that they prized for themselves. They had seen in the reality of a tightened economy that they
had to adapt and thrive as well as their more conventional peers if

they were to prove that their humanistic new ways could stay the course. And they had recognized that they most effectively won converts to their ways of thinking and living when they showed that they could play The System's game as well as anyone, drawing on the strength they gained from enjoying their senses and their sexuality, from involving themselves genuinely and openly with others, from pondering life and its meaning, and from struggling to lead sensibly ethical lives.

Indeed, many who remained true to countercultural ideals even as they abandoned early countercultural styles found that they enjoyed something of a competitive pride in succeeding by traditional standards while also expressing themselves in ways foreign to their less avant-garde contemporaries. They took pride in doing things that society admired and rewarded without abandoning varieties of self-expression that society forbade. They enjoyed feeling that they had unusual integrity and experience as well as status and material success. And they believed that this made them especially good neighbors, unusually conscientious citizens, and particularly noteworthy contributors to the American experiment—for if the truth be known, many of them also realized that they loved the America that they had criticized, challenged, and changed so successfully.

The goal of politicized members of the counterculture was never really to get all Americans to wear blue jeans—though by the end of the seventies that had nearly happened, and Americans had elected a President who wore jeans to the Oval Office. It was not to encourage everyone to smoke marijuana—though in 1979 federal officials estimated that the marijuana trade was a multibillion-dollar industry. Nor was the goal to make everyone promiscuous sexually —though by the end of the decade, the degree of attention given every form of sexual expression at every level of society surpassed what even the most ardent proponents of sexual liberation had dreamed possible ten years before. What liberationists of every type basically set out to do was to persuade people that expressing themselves as they wished and respecting others who did the same was the only ethical way to live. They successfully demonstrated that it was possible for individuals to express their feelings openly without losing the respect of everyone around them.

Some of the protagonists in the history presented in these pages are still involved in gay political activity. All but the one or two who remain closeted are enjoying lives that were inconceivable before gay liberation.

The man who called himself Donald Webster Cory is a professor of sociology in a prominent New York City university, using his real name. Since the middle of the 1960s he has written a host of books and articles critical of the gay political activity his first book helped spark. In contrast, Henry Hay is thrilled that so much of what he dreamed of doing in the early 1950s is now being done. Hay and his lover now live in New Mexico; they are the older gay male couple in the film *Word Is Out.* Tony Segura is also delighted that so much has happened so much sooner than he dreamed possible. He is involved in gay political activity in Richmond, Virginia, where he remains in the job that he left New York and MSNY to take. Al de Dion and Curtis Dewees still live in Brooklyn. Barbara Gittings and Kay Tobin remain in Philadelphia. Remembering her own painful early search for information, Gittings for years has produced and circulated a gay bibliography under the auspices of a Task Force on Gay Liberation she organized in the American Library Association. She has also served on the Governor's Council for Sexual Minorities in Pennsylvania.

Craig Rodwell is still behind the counter at the Oscar Wilde Memorial Bookshop, which he started when he left MSNY in 1967. Randy Wicker left MSNY to manufacture and sell political buttons, and the profits from his button business are now reinvested in the antique shop he runs at the end of Christopher Street. Meredith Grey and Shirley Willer have for some years managed a rock shop in Key West, where they settled after leaving DOB in 1968. Dick Leitsch, still with his lover but no longer living in Madolin Cervantes's apartment, was at last check editing a guide to gay life in Manhattan. Jeanne Perry, now only friends with Eleanor Krane, emerged from gay political retirement to help form the Gay Women's Alternative, which picked up where DOB left off in providing social and support activities for lesbians in New York City. Frank Kameny's militant homophile aspirations have been abundantly realized: a member of the District of Columbia's Human Rights Commission, he helped persuade the United States Civil Service Commission to drop provisions excluding homosexuals from federal employment.

Most of the radicals responsible for the beginnings of the gay liberation movement were "burned out" by the intensity of their early efforts to devise truly fulfilling lives for themselves while helping others to do the same, and few are involved in political groups. Michael Brown now works as a carpenter on Cape Cod. Pete Wilson, still exploring the gay male subculture and still friendly with Charles Pitts, now an avowed boy lover on WBAI, has made the Libertarian Party the focus of his political activity. Jim Fouratt manages a rock disco in Manhattan. Steve Dansky and John Knoebel continue to promote faggot effeminism. Allen Young now lives in an octagonal house he built himself in western Massachusetts; he and Karla Jay, whom he met in GLF, have edited several lesbian and gay anthologies. Lois Hart for a long time has been living quietly with a lover in Brooklyn. A few years ago, she re-emerged to help organize a local group called the Committee of Lesbian and Gay Male Socialists, one of the many organizations that have worked to synthesize the radical and revolutionary gay and lesbian feminist positions that at the turn of the decade were so distinct and divisive. John Lauritsen, of the revolutionary GLFers, remains the most prominent in local gay politics; his writings include a book about gay political activity in Germany and England during the early part of this century. John O'Brien has moved to Los Angeles.

As might be expected, many of the original gay liberationist reformers have made places for themselves in the gay community they worked so hard to build. Jerry Hoose now lives on Christopher Street and still enjoys the abundant subcultural pleasures that surround him. For the last few years Bob Kohler has managed a gay bathhouse in the East Village. Marty Robinson, who dropped out of gay political activity after the first defeat of Intro 475, lives with his lover in his family's home in Brooklyn. Jim Owles remains active in efforts to get the New York City Council to pass gay rights legislation, sobered by his ten years of trying. Ray "Sylvia" Rivera tells friends that he is now a "housewife" in the suburbs. Richie Amato still lives with his lover in the suburbs. Pete Fisher and Marc Rubin are still together and still writing; Rubin and Meryl Friedman, also a teacher, took the lead in organizing the city's Gay Teachers Association. Arthur Evans lives, works, and remains politically and philosophically active in San Francisco; he recently published a book on witchcraft and the gay counterculture. Arthur Bell is a columnist for the *Village Voice.* After resigning as co-executive director of the National Gay Task Force, Bruce Voeller took to the lecture circuit for a series of debates with California state senator John Briggs, an admirer of Anita Bryant who sponsored an antigay proposition that the voters of California defeated by a margin of three to two in the fall of 1978. Voeller is now executive director of the Mariposa Foundation, which has raised controversy by proposing to install a sculpture celebrating gay liberation in Christopher Park.

Rita Mae Brown's writing career has flourished with the publication of a third successful novel; she is currently working to sell a screenplay based on the first, *Rubyfruit Jungle.* Martha Shelley has continued her writing in a lesbian publishing collective in Oakland. March Hoffman, now Artemis March, has for the last few years pursued her interest in relationships between lesbianism and feminism at Radcliffe's Bunting Institute, a center for women's studies affiliated with Harvard University. Sidney Abbott and Barbara Love, now just friends, remain visible in both the gay and the women's movements. Ellen Bedoz and Arlene Kisner, still close friends, live in lofts in Manhattan. Fran Winant and Judy Grepperd, still lovers, publish Winant's songs and poems under the imprint of their Violet Press. Ruth Simpson now lives with Ellen Povill. Alma Routsong continues to write. Tina Mandel is a successful lesbian feminist therapist.

Dinah Robertson and Nancy Johnson run a feminist graphics business. Nath Rockhill is a lawyer with the Equal Employment Opportunity Commission and treasurer of Lambda Legal Defense and Education, Inc. Until recently, Ginny Vida and Judy Burns worked for the National Gay Task Force. Jean O'Leary, for five years co-executive director of the National Gay Task Force, has been perhaps the most visible lesbian in national politics: she was elected a delegate to the 1976 Democratic National Convention; appointed by President Carter to the National Commission on the Observance of International Women's Year (IWY) and to the National Advisory Committee for Women, established in the wake of the IWY-sponsored National Women's Conference held in Houston in the fall of 1977; appointed by Ed Koch to the Mayor's Commission on the Status of Women in New York City; and elected an alternate delegate to the 1980 Democratic National Convention, where she was one of 77 openly gay delegates and alternates.

At the National Women's Conference in Houston, admitting that "we have all made mistakes and we have all learned," Betty Friedan agreed it was time for the women's movement to make lesbian issues an official concern; the conference itself adopted a resolution calling for the repeal of laws restricting private sexual behavior among consenting adults and the passage of gay rights protections, especially in cases of child custody and visitation. Kate Millett, whose efforts to make the concerns of lesbians a feminist issue began in 1970, has continued to write about her life as a lesbian and a feminist; early in 1979 she made headlines by going to Iran to lend support to Iranian women agitating for liberation. Ti-Grace Atkinson, though still friendly with Ruth Simpson, has dropped from sight. Robin Morgan, Kenneth Pitchford, and even their son Blake now write for *Ms.* magazine.

All of these individuals—and the hundreds of others just as committed to gay political activity who made them leaders—enjoy lives that are dramatic proof that their efforts were successful.

NOTES
INDEX

NOTES

Chapter One

[1] Donald Webster Cory, *The Homosexual in America: A Subjective Approach* (New York: Greenberg, 1951), p. xiv. This account of Cory's personal history is based both on material in *The Homosexual in America* and on interviews with Cory and those who knew him in the fifties.

[2] Ibid., p. xvi.

[3] Ibid., p. 99.

[4] Ibid., pp. 13–14.

[5] Ibid., pp. 227–28.

[6] Ibid., p. 14.

[7] The account of early gay organizing activity in this chapter is based on documents and histories in Marvin Cutler (pseud.), ed., *Homosexuals Today: A Handbook of Organizations and Publications* (Los Angeles: ONE, Incorporated, 1956); on contemporary interviews with and memoirs by early gay organizational entrepreneurs in all parts of the country; on interviews with early gay organizational leaders in New York City about their predecessors and peers inside and outside New York City; and on documents from the files of the Mattachine Society of New York, now housed at the Church of the Beloved Disciple in New York City. Information about the Chicago-based Society for Human Rights, evidently the first gay political group formed in the United States, can be found in Jonathan Katz, *Gay American History* (New York: Crowell, 1976), pp. 385–93, 632–33. Information about early gay political organizations in Europe can be found in John Lauritsen and David Thorstad, *The Early Homosexual Rights Movement, 1864–1935* (New York: Times Change Press, 1974). A detailed account of early gay organizing on the west coast appears in the series of articles by John D'Emilio that appeared under the title "Dreams Deferred" in *The Body Politic,* beginning in November 1978.

[8]Katz, *Gay American History,* p. 409.

[9]Ibid., pp. 406–20; Cutler, *Homosexuals Today,* pp. 32–39.

[10]Cutler, *Homosexuals Today,* pp. 13–14; Katz, *Gay American History,* p. 412.

[11]Cutler, *Homosexuals Today,* p. 72.

[12]Ibid., p. 30.

[13]Katz, *Gay American History,* p. 416.

[14]Ibid., p. 417.

[15]Cutler, *Homosexuals Today,* p. 44.

[16]Letter from Gonzalo (Tony) Segura, Jr., to Dwight Huggins, September 4, 1956; MSNY files. Here and elsewhere, minor misspellings and typographical errors in quoted documents have been corrected.

[17]Letter from Hal Call to Dwight Huggins, Sam Morford, Tony Segura, et al., August 30, 1956; appended to Segura's letter to Huggins in MSNY files.

[18]A dramatic, if partisan, depiction of the circumstances that kept homosexuals fearful and inhibited appears in Donald Webster Cory's *The Homosexual in America.* Other accounts of what it was like to be homosexual in the 1950s and early 1960s are found in Ann Aldrich, *We Walk Alone* (New York: Fawcett, 1955); Jess Stearn, *The Sixth Man* (New York: Doubleday, 1961) and *The Grapevine* (New York: Doubleday, 1964); R.E.L. Masters, *The Homosexual Revolution* (New York: Julian Press, 1962); and J.D. Mercer, *They Walk in the Shadow* (New York: Comet Press, 1959).

[19]"Daughters of Bilitis Chapter Formed in New York," *New York Mattachine Newsletter,* October 1958, p. 6.

[20]Del Martin and Phyllis Lyon, *Lesbian/Woman* (New York: Bantam, 1972), pp. 238–39.

[21]Katz, *Gay American History,* p. 428ff.

[22]Ibid., pp. 426–27.

[23]Donald Webster Cory, *The Homosexual in America,* 2nd ed. (New York: Castle Books, 1960), pp. xx–xxiii.

[24]*Newsletter of the Mattachine Society, Inc., of New York* 7 (May 1962): 2. (N.B. Different issues of the New York Mattachine newsletter bear slightly different names and many lack volume numbers; hence citations to different editions vary and volume numbers are sometimes omitted from them.)

Chapter Two

[1]Kay Tobin and Randy Wicker, *The Gay Crusaders* (New York: Paperback Library, 1972), p. 94. This book contains accurate biographical sketches not only of Frank Kameny, but of Barbara Gittings, Del Martin, Phyllis Lyon, and other important early homophile and gay liberation leaders.

[2]Kameny's speech at the New York Mattachine's one hundredth public meeting was reprinted as "Civil Liberties: A Progress Report," in the *New York Mattachine Newsletter* 10 (January 1965): 7–22.

[3]"Live and Let Live, Part III," *Realist* 38 (October 1962): 11.

[4]William J. Helmer, "New York's 'Middle-Class' Homosexuals," *Harper's,* March 1963, p. 42.

[5]Letter from J.C. Hodges to Richard A. Inman, January 27, 1965; MSNY files.

[6]The campaign statements of candidates for election to MSNY offices in the spring of 1965, like many other documents referred to or quoted in the text, are in the files of the Mattachine Society of New York.

[7]"We're on the Move Now," *Eastern Mattachine Magazine* 10 (June 1965): 2.

[8]Information about the characteristics of participants in the public-toilet sex scene can be found in Laud Humphreys, *Tearoom Trade: Impersonal Sex in Public Places* (Chicago: Aldine, 1970).

[9]"Entrapment, Inc.," *New York Post,* March 7, 1966.

[10]"Meeting on Village Cleanup," *New York Mattachine Newsletter* 11 (April 1966): 1–2.

[11]"Garelik Urges Public to Report Police Trapping of Homosexuals," *New York Times,* April 2, 1966, p. 1.

[12]"Entrapment, Inc.," *New York Post,* April 5, 1966.

[13]For a more specific account of Mafia involvement in New York City's gay bars, see Charles Grutzner, "Mafia Buys Clubs for Homosexuals," *New York Times,* November 30, 1967, pp. 1, 50.

[14]Lucy Komisar's humorous account of MSNY's sip-in, "Three Homosexuals in Search of a Drink," appeared in the *Village Voice,* May 5, 1966.

[15]Charles Grutzner, "S.L.A. Won't Act Against Bars Refusing Service to Deviates," *New York Times,* April 26, 1966, p. 55.

[16]"New York City Hiring Policy," *Mattachine Society, Inc., of New York Newsletter* 12 (January–February 1967): 1.

[17]Letter from Dick Leitsch to Henry Wiesbauer, November 15, 1966; MSNY files.

[18]"MSNY Endeavors," *New York Mattachine Newsletter,* October–November 1967, p. 10. When persuasion proved fruitless in this case, MSNY worked with the New York Civil Liberties Union to stage a successful legal challenge.

Chapter Three

[1]Minutes, DOB–New York, June 1965. Copies of these minutes and the ones cited below are contained in the files of the New York Mattachine.

[2]Minutes, DOB–New York, August 1965.

[3]Willer's speech was printed under the title "What Concrete Steps Can Be Taken to Further the Homophile Movement?" in *Ladder* 11 (November 1966): 17–20.

[4]Del Martin and Phyllis Lyon, *Lesbian/Woman* (New York: Bantam, 1972), p. 249. The conservatism of DOB's national leaders is described in more detail in a thesis on homophile groups in San Francisco. See Roxanna Thayer Sweet, "Political and Social Action in Homophile Organizations" (D. Crim. dissertation, University of California, Berkeley, 1968).

[5]Letter from Meredith Grey to Jonathan Katz, August 23, 1974; Katz's personal files.

[6]Willer, "What Concrete Steps," pp. 17–18.

[7]Letter from Foster Gunnison to Bob Martin, March 2, 1967; MSNY files.

[8]Foster Gunnison, "An Open Letter to All Homophile Organizations," October 15, 1968; MSNY files.

[9]Del Martin, "The Lesbian's Majority Status," *Ladder* 11 (June 1967): 23–24.

[10]"Readers Respond," *Ladder* 11 (August 1967): 20.

[11]"Readers Respond," *Ladder* 11 (July 1967): 27.

[12]"S.E.W.," "Women Who Marry Women," *Newsletter,* DOB–New York, December 1966, p. 3.

[13]"Marion G.," "A Look At *Look,*" *Newsletter,* DOB–New York, March 1967, p. 2.

[14]"DOB Hosts Regional Conference," *Newsletter,* DOB–New York, May 1967, p. 2.

[15]"A Message from the New President," *Newsletter,* DOB–New York, November 1968, p. 2.

[16]Letter from Dick Leitsch to John Marshall, September 7, 1965; MSNY files.

[17]Carbon copy of a letter from Dick Leitsch to Frank Kameny, December 6, 1965; MSNY files. The analysis that follows is based on various drafts and carbon copies of the letters that Leitsch wrote to Kameny, all contained in MSNY files.

[18]Leitsch's account of the UCC conference. This document is only one of many in MSNY files detailing Leitsch's reservations about the ideas advanced by the militant leaders of other eastern homophile groups.

[19]Ibid.

[20]Letter from Dick Leitsch to Frank Kameny, June 19, 1968.

[21]Leitsch to Kameny, June 28, 1968.

[22]Kameny to Leitsch, June 19, 1968.

[23]Leitsch to Kameny, June 19, 1968.

[24]Leitsch to Kameny, June 27, 1968.

[25]*New York Hymnal* 1 (February 1968): 1.

[26]*New York Hymnal* 1 (April 1968): 2.

[27]*New York Hymnal* 1 (August–September 1968): 1.

[28]Ralph W. Weltge, ed., *The Same Sex* (Philadelphia: United Church of Christ–Pilgrim Press, 1969), pp. 143–45.

[29]"Readers Respond," *Ladder* 13 (August–September 1969): 47.

[30]"March Topic: 'Homosexual or Gay?'," *New York Mattachine Newsletter,* March 1962, p. 2.

Chapter Four

[1]Lucian Truscott IV, "Gay Power Comes to Sheridan Square," *Village Voice,* July 3, 1969, pp. 1, 18.

[2]"Queen Power: Fags Against Police in Stonewall Bust," *Rat,* July 1969, p. 2.

[3]*New York Hymnal* 1 (February 1968): 2.

[4]Truscott, "Gay Power Comes to Sheridan Square," p. 18.

[5]Ronnie Di Brienza, "Stonewall Incident," *East Village Other,* July 1969, p. 2.

[6]Tom Burke, "The New Homosexual," *Esquire* 72 (December 1969): 316–18.

[7]Charles A. Reich, *The Greening of America* (New York: Bantam, 1971), pp. 238–39.

[8]Kirkpatrick Sale, *SDS* (New York: Vintage, 1974); see especially pp. 39, 98–101, 203–04, 317–19, 344–52.

[9]Edward J. Bacciocco, *The New Left in America* (Stanford, Calif.: Hoover Institution Press, 1974), pp. 212–13.

[10]Reich, *Greening,* p. 2. Reich explains how the cultural radical strategy for social transformation was supposed to work in his chapter "Revolution by Consciousness," pp. 322–78.

[11]Ibid., p. 241.

[12]"Gay Revolution Comes Out," *Rat,* August 12–26, 1969, p. 7.

[13]Lois Hart, "GLF News," *Come Out* 2 (January 10, 1970): 16. (Because there were only nine issues of *Come Out!,* they are easily identified by number. Issues number 2 and 3 lacked an exclamation point in the title.)

[14]These and other references to the thoughts and actions of gay and lesbian liberationists are based on lengthy, unstructured interviews with the individuals involved and on writings and documents they offered as evidence of their views and activities. The words of interview subjects, though quoted on the basis of notes taken during interviews, are not footnoted.

[15]See Sale, *SDS,* especially pp. 95–115; and Bacciocco, *The New Left,* especially pp. 29–86, 101–02, 201–02, 227–30.

Chapter Five

[1]Kirkpatrick Sale, *SDS* (New York: Vintage, 1974), pp. 318–19.

[2]"Gay Revolution Comes Out," *Rat,* August 12–26, 1969, p. 7.

[3]*Come Out!* 1 (November 14, 1969): 1.

[4]Ibid., p. 2.

[5]Charles Reich, *The Greening of America* (New York: Bantam, 1971), pp. 276, 279.

[6]Lois Hart, "Community Center," *Come Out!* 1 (November 14, 1969): 15.

[7]Leo Louis Martello, "A Positive Image for the Homosexual," *Come Out!* 1 (November 14, 1969): 16.

[8]Jim Fouratt, "Word Thoughts," *Come Out* 2 (January 10, 1970): 15.

[9]Marty Stephan, "Bitch: Summer's Not Forever," *Come Out!* 1 (November 14, 1969): 12.

[10]Leo Louis Martello, "Gay Power Is Pay Power," *Gay Power,* undated, p. 8.

[11]Mike Brown, "Michael Tallman," and Leo Louis Martello, "The Summer of Gay Power and the *Village Voice* Exposed," *Come Out!* 1 (November 14, 1969): 11.

[12]Donn Teal, *The Gay Militants* (New York: Stein and Day, 1971), p. 98.

[13]Austin Wade and Madolin Cervantes, "Report to the Board of MSNY Delegates to ERCHO," undated letter in MSNY files, p. 6.

[14]Letter from Foster Gunnison, Jr. to Bob Kohler, December 21, 1969; personal files of Craig Rodwell, New York City.

[15]Lois Hart, "GLF News," *Come Out* 2 (January 10, 1970): 16.

[16]Minutes of the Eastern Regional Conference of Homophile Organizations, November 1–2 (Session 6); MSNY files.

[17]Hart, "GLF News," p. 16.

[18]*Playboy* 17 (May 1970): 236–37.

[19]*Playboy* 17 (August 1970): 47.

[20]Steve Dansky, "Hey Man," *Come Out!* 4 (June–July 1970): 6.

[21]GLF Men's Collective, "Five Notes on Collective Living," *Come Out!* 7 (December–January 1971): 7.

[22]Allan Warshawsky and Ellen Bedoz, "G.L.F. and the Movement," *Come Out* 2 (January 10, 1970): 4–5.

[23]Carl Wittman, "A Gay Manifesto, with Red Butterfly Discussion," pamphlet prepared by the Red Butterfly, undated. Wittman's manifesto was originally published as "Refugees from Amerika: A Gay Manifesto," *San Francisco Free Press,* December 22–January 7, 1970.

[24]Warshawsky and Bedoz, "G.L.F. and the Movement," pp. 4–5.

[25]Hart, "Community Center," p. 15.

[26]Jerry Rubin, *Do It!* (New York: Ballantine, 1970), p. 129.

[27]Lois Hart, "Some News and a Whole Lot'a Opinion by the Frumious Bandersnatch," *Come Out* 3 (April–May 1970): 3.

[28]Hart, "GLF News," p. 16.

[29]Lois Hart, "Bandersnatch's Again," *Come Out!* 4 (June–July 1970): 17.

[30]"News," *Come Out!* 4 (June–July 1970): 5.

[31]Huey Newton, "A Letter from Huey to the Revolutionary Brothers and Sisters about the Women's Liberation and Gay Liberation Movements," *Black Panther,* August 21, 1970, p. 5.

[32]"Gay People Help Plan New World," *Gay Flames* 2 (September 11, 1970): 1.

[33]"Gay Man in Philadelphia," *Come Out!* 7 (December–January 1971): 15.

[34]For a more complete account of GLF's participation in the first session of the Revolutionary People's Constitutional Convention see Teal, *Gay Militants,* pp. 169–78.

[35]Allen Young, "Out of the Closets, Into the Streets," in Karla Jay and Allen Young, eds., *Out of the Closets: Voices of Gay Liberation* (New York: Douglas Books, 1972), p. 22.

[36]Allen Young, "The Cuban Revolution and Gay Liberation," in Jay and Young, p. 216.

[37]Young, "Out of the Closets," pp. 23–24.

Chapter Six

[1]Arthur Bell, *Dancing the Gay Lib Blues* (New York: Simon and Schuster, 1971), pp. 16–17.

[2]Donn Teal, *The Gay Militants* (New York: Stein and Day, 1971), pp. 105–07.

[3]Eldridge Cleaver, *Soul on Ice* (New York: McGraw-Hill–Ramparts, 1968), p. 110.

[4]"Marchi or Procaccino: Jail or Asylum," *Come Out!* 1 (November 14, 1969): 4.

[5]Teal, *Gay Militants,* p. 106.

[6]*Come Out!* 1 (November 14, 1969): 5.

[7]Ibid., p. 3.

[8]Ralph Hall, "Gay Liberation News," *Gay Power,* December 1969, p. 2.

[9]Teal, *Gay Militants,* pp. 105–06.

[10]The preamble to GAA's constitution is reprinted in Teal, *Gay Militants,* pp. 126–27.

[11]Kay Tobin and Randy Wicker, *The Gay Crusaders* (New York: Paperback Library, 1972), p. 196. Accurate biographical sketches of Robinson and Owles are also included in *The Gay Crusaders.*

[12]Arthur Evans, "The Oppression of Homosexuals," unpublished manuscript, undated, Chapter 4, pp. 16–18.

[13]Bell, *Gay Lib Blues,* p. 31.

[14]Sandra Vaughn, "Lindsay & Homosexuals: An Edited Encounter," *Village Voice,* April 23, 1970, p. 8; Bell, *Gay Lib Blues,* pp. 53–56.

[15]Teal, *Gay Militants,* pp. 141–42.

[16]Bell, *Gay Lib Blues,* p. 59.

[17]Teal, *Gay Militants,* p. 141.

[18]Arthur Irving (pseud. of Arthur Bell), "Zapping with Carol: Hello Bella," *Gay Power,* undated, p. 4. Bell used many of the accounts that he wrote for his column in *Gay Power* in *Dancing the Gay Lib Blues.* The story of the Greitzer zap appears there on pp. 69–73.

[19]Kay Tobin, "GAA Confronts Goldberg, Blumenthal," *Gay,* June 29, 1970, p. 1. See also Teal, *Gay Militants,* pp. 145–47.

[20]Teal, *Gay Militants,* pp. 252–53.

[21]Stuart Byron, "Gay News and the *Times:* An Indelicate Balance," *Village Voice,* April 1, 1971, pp. 13, 14, 38.

Chapter Seven

[1]Arthur Bell, *Dancing the Gay Lib Blues* (New York: Simon and Schuster, 1971), p. 50.

[2]Minutes of the Eastern Regional Conference of Homophile Organizations, November 1–2, 1969; MSNY files.

[3]Letter from Frank Kameny to Craig Rodwell, July 11, 1969; Rodwell's files.

[4]Austin Wade and Madolin Cervantes, "Report to the Board of MSNY from Delegates to ERCHO," undated letter in MSNY files, p. 7.

[5]"Reactions," *New York Mattachine Newsletter,* May 1970, p. 8.

[6]Lacey Fosburgh, "Thousands of Homosexuals Hold a Protest Rally in Central Park," *New York Times,* June 29, 1970, pp. 1, 20.

[7]Lacey Fosburgh, "The 'Gay' People Demand Their Rights," *New York Times,* July 5, 1970, p. 12.

[8]When Owles repeated his views during a debate about legal initiatives later in the summer, they were captured on Donn Teal's tape recorder. See Donn Teal, *The Gay Militants* (New York: Stein and Day, 1971), p. 229.

[9]Bell, *Gay Lib Blues,* p. 87.

[10]Minutes of Gay Activists Alliance meeting, July 16, 1970; copies of these and other minutes are in the personal files of ex-secretary Arnie Kantrowitz.

[11]In the published version of his autobiography Kantrowitz deals more briefly with the clash between "political people" and "social people." See Arnie Kantrowitz, *Under the Rainbow* (New York: William Morrow, 1977), p. 168.

[12]Minutes, GAA meeting, August 27, 1970.

[13]Minutes, GAA meeting, August 13, 1970.

[14]Minutes, GAA meeting, May 28, 1970.

[15]Bell, *Gay Lib Blues,* p. 98.

[16]Minutes, GAA meeting, September 3, 1970.

[17]Morty Manford and Arthur Evans, "The Theory and Practice of Confrontation Tactics: Part 2, the Political Function of Zaps," *Gay,* February 26, 1973, p. 17. See also Teal, *Gay Militants,* pp. 248–49.

[18]Minutes, GAA meeting, September 24, 1970.

[19]Letter from Peter Fisher to WINS Radio, September 18, 1970; Fisher-Rubin files.

[20]Joseph Epstein, "Homo/Hetero: The Struggle for Sexual Identity," *Harper's* 241 (September 1970): 51.

[21]Kay Tobin and Randy Wicker, *The Gay Crusaders* (New York: Paperback Library, 1972), p. 193.

[22]Teal, *Gay Militants,* p. 267.

[23]Minutes, GAA meetings, August 27 and September 3, 1970.

[24]Letter from Peter Fisher to Willie Morris, September 14, 1970; Fisher-Rubin files.

[25]Teal, *Gay Militants,* pp. 267–69.

[26]Bell, *Gay Lib Blues,* p. 134.

[27]Letter from Merle Miller to Willie Morris, October 27, 1970; Fisher-Rubin files.

[28]Teal, *Gay Militants,* p. 271; Bell, *Gay Lib Blues,* p. 165.

[29]Letter from Marc Rubin to Arthur Bell, April 23, 1971; Fisher-Rubin files.

[30]Peter Fisher, "Reflections on Reflections," unpublished seminar paper, 1971; Fisher-Rubin files.

[31]Ibid.

[32]"Cultivating Gay Culture," *Gay Activist* 1 (May 1971): 7.

[33]"GAA Finds a Home," *Gay Activist* 1 (May 1971): 8–9.

[34]"Agitprop," *Gay Activist* 1 (September 1971): p. 4.

Chapter Eight

[1]"Employment Discrimination Against Homosexuals," a report presented by the Gay Activists Alliance to the New York City Commission on Human Rights, July 14, 1970, p. 12.

[2]Donn Teal, *The Gay Militants* (New York: Stein and Day, 1971), p. 236.

[3]Lindsy Van Gelder, " 'Gay Bill of Rights' Makes Progress," *New York Post,* November 5, 1970, p. 16.

[4]Minutes, GAA meeting, October 8, 1970.

[5]"Employment Discrimination Against Homosexuals," Supplement #1,

a report presented by the Gay Activists Alliance to the New York City Commission on Human Rights, February 3, 1971, pp. 13, 15, 16.

[6]Alan Westin, "The Career Killers," *Playboy* 17 (June 1970): 233; quoted in "Employment Discrimination Against Homosexuals," p. 2.

[7]Peter Fisher, "Fidelifacts: Sex-Snooping Agency Draws Gay Fire," *Gay*, February 15, 1971, p. 3. See also Peter Fisher, *The Gay Mystique* (New York: Stein and Day, 1972), pp. 145–47.

[8]Peter Hadley, "City Councilman Addresses a Candlelight Rally," *Gay*, August 2, 1971, pp. 1, 18.

[9]Arthur Evans, "The Oppression of Homosexuals," unpublished manuscript, undated, Chapter 4, p. 20.

[10]"Federal, State Cops Hit Unlicensed Clubs," *Gay*, August 16, 1971, p. 16.

[11]"Mike Umbers, Back Room Czar, Arrested Again," *Gay*, October 25, 1971, p. 6. See also Arthur Bell, "Christopher's Emperor," *Village Voice*, July 22, 1971, pp. 3, 66.

[12]Anthony Burton, "Gay Group May Grab Gals Jail," *New York Daily News*, July 23, 1971, p. 16.

[13]Barbara Trecker, "Homosexuals vs. 'Small Town Fascists,' " *New York Post*, August 25, 1971, p. 26.

[14]A copy of this letter was printed in the *Gay Activist* 1 (October 1971): 4–5.

[15]Fisher, *The Gay Mystique*, pp. 162–63.

[16]Ralph Hall, "Ralph, Your [sic] a Provocateur," *Faggot*, undated mimeographed pamphlet; personal files of Ralph Hall.

[17]Leo Skir, "Equal Rights Hearings Continue: 'I Should Have Worn My Maidenform Bra!'," *Gay*, December 20, 1971, p. 6. See also "Intro 475 Hearings Begin," *Gay Activist* 1 (November 1971): 1, 8, 9, 11; Alfonso Narvaez, "City Aide Backs Homosexual Bill," *New York Times*, October 19, 1971, p. 39; Arthur Bell, "Gay Job Hearings: Palatable for Mom?," *Village Voice*, October 28, 1971, p. 38; Edward Ranzal, "Homosexual Bill Argued in Council," *New York Times*, November 16, 1971, p. 49; "Unruly Hearing Fails to Move Intro 475," *Advocate*, December 18, 1971, p. 3.

[18]Phil Katz, "Intro 475: Round 2," *Gay Activist* 1 (December 1971): 18.

[19]Joe Nicholson, Jr., "Gay-In Set for Council Rights Hearings," *New York Post*, December 17, 1971, p. 13.

[20]Ibid.

[21]"Intro 475—Round 3: Is It Up to Lindsay?" *Gay Activist* 1 (February 1972): 8.

[22]Guy Charles, "N.Y. Hearing Fuss Perils Rights Bill," *Advocate*, January 19, 1972, p. 8. See also Leo Skir, "The Hearings on Intro 475: Part III," *Gay*, January 24, 1972, pp. 1, 4; and Edward Ranzal, "Council Presses

Lindsay on Issue," *New York Times,* December 18, 1971, p. 23.

[23]"Intro 475 May Dog Lindsay Campaign," *Advocate,* February 2, 1972, pp. 1, 8.

[24]"Defeat of the 'Anti-Closet' Bill," *Village Voice,* February 3, 1972, p. 38.

[25]Guy Charles, "N.Y. Hearing Fuss," p. 8.

[26]Marty Robinson, "Trashing of Intro 475: The Closet of Fear," *Village Voice,* February 17, 1972, p. 18.

[27]Ibid.

Chapter Nine

[1]"Gay Revolution Comes Out," *Rat,* August 12–26, 1969, p. 7.

[2]*Come Out!* 1 (November 14, 1969): 1.

[3]A transcript of the "Womankind" program on lesbianism and feminism appears in Leslie B. Tanner, *Voices from Women's Liberation* (New York: New American Library–Mentor, 1970), pp. 349–61.

[4]Ibid.

[5]"Readers Respond," *Ladder* 13 (April–May 1969): 43.

[6]Martha Shelley, "Stepin Fetchit Woman," *Come Out!* 1 (November 14, 1969): 7.

[7]Tanner, *Voices,* pp. 350–51.

[8]*Newsletter,* New York NOW, January 1970.

[9]Anne Koedt, "The Myth of the Vaginal Orgasm," in Anne Koedt, Ellen Levine, Anita Rapone, eds., *Radical Feminism* (New York: Quadrangle Books, 1973), pp. 198–207.

[10]Susan Brownmiller, "Sisterhood Is Powerful!," *New York Times Magazine,* March 15, 1970, p. 140.

[11]*New York Times Magazine,* April 5, 1970, pp. 39, 136.

[12]Lois Hart, "Some News and a Whole Lot'a Opinion by the Frumious Bandersnatch," *Come Out* 3 (April–May 1970): 3.

[13]"pigmafiapigmafiapigmafia," *Rat,* April 17, 1970, unnumbered page.

[14]Quoted here and above is the version of "The Woman-Identified Woman" that appeared in *Ladder* 14 (August–September 1970): 6–8.

[15]These quotes come from an account of the Lavender Menace demonstration that a lesbian GLFer wrote for *Gay Power* 17; it was reprinted a few years later in *Majority Report,* June 27, 1974, p. 11. Other accounts of the demonstration appeared in *Rat,* May 8–21, 1970, p. 12; and in *Come Out!* 4 (June–July 1970): 14–15.

[16]Ellen Bedoz, "Afraid of What?," *Come Out!* 5 (September–October 1970): 7.

[17]"Radicalesbians," *Come Out!* 7 (December 1970): 10.

[18]"GLF Women," *Come Out!* 7 (December 1970): 10.

[19]Jill Johnston, *Lesbian Nation* (New York: Simon and Schuster, 1973), pp. 98–99.

Chapter Ten

[1]"Readers Respond," *Ladder* 15 (October–November 1970): 45–46.

[2]"Kate Millett, Kate Millett, Kate Millett, Kate," *Newsletter,* DOB–New York, September 1970, pp. 1, 3.

[3]"Lesbians Tell National Organization for Women How It Is," *Newsletter,* DOB–New York, December 1970, p. 3.

[4]Sidney Abbott and Barbara Love, *Sappho Was a Right-On Woman* (New York: Stein and Day, 1973), pp. 119–31.

[5]"Editorial: Back to the Closet?," *Newsletter,* DOB–New York, November 1970, p. 2.

[6]The texts of Atkinson's essays appear in a collection of her writings published as *Amazon Odyssey* (New York: Links, 1974), pp. 131–89.

[7]*Lesbian Letter,* DOB–New York, March 1971, p. 1.

[8]*Lesbian Letter,* DOB–New York, May 1971, p. 3.

[9]Ruth Simpson, *From the Closet to the Courts* (New York: Viking, 1976), pp. 153–54.

[10]*Lesbian Newsletter,* DOB–New York, September 1971, p. 3. (Like MSNY's newsletter, DOB–New York's newsletter was given different names in different issues.)

[11]Ibid., p. 2.

[12]Letter to the editor, *Gay Activist* 1 (November 1971): 6.

Chapter Eleven

[1]Rich Wandel, "What Is This Thing Called 'Leadership'?," *Gay,* December 25, 1972, p. 10.

[2]Notes, LLC meeting, January 8, 1973; Karol Lightner files.

[3]"N.Y. Times Book Review Neglects Lesbian Literature," *Lesbian Activist,* March 1973, unnumbered page.

[4]Ginny Vida, "TV Anti-Lesbianism up to Paar," *Majority Report,* August 1973, p. 3.

[5]*NOW Acts* 4 (Fall 1971): 1.

[6]"NOW Passes Lesbian Rights Resolution," *Lesbian Activist,* March 1973, unnumbered page.

[7]Betty Friedan, "Up from the Kitchen Floor," *New York Times Magazine,* March 4, 1973, pp. 31, 35.

[8]"Certifying Exam," Jean O'Leary, undated, unpublished manuscript; O'Leary files.

[9]Morgan's speech, "Lesbianism and Feminism: Synonyms or Contradictions?," was printed in pamphlet form and circulated by KNOW, Inc., of Pittsburgh, Pa.

[10]Jean O'Leary, "Lesbian Feminism—The Building of a New Society"; O'Leary files. Reprinted in *Lesbian Feminist* 1 (October 1973): 3, 10–13.

INDEX

Abbott, Sidney, 231, 237, 248–49, 254, 259n, 285, 323, 332; and "super-group," 256, 264, 275, 314

ABC (American Broadcasting Company), 324; ABC-TV, 114

Abortion, 28, 236, 259n, 263, 280, 287n; national conference on, 269n

Abrams, Robert, 218

Abzug, Bella, 157, 181, 206, 217, 324

Acculturation/assimilation, 3, 9, 20, 307; acculturation defined, 4; and integration, 64–65, 110, 198, 309

Advocate (gay newspaper), 152, 153

Alcoholic Beverage Law (New York), 38, 40

Alexander, Dolores, 259n

Alpert, Richard, 87

Alternate University ("Alternate U"), 81–82, 87, 91, 119, 253

Amato, Richard, 196–206 *passim,* 218–20, 331

Amazon Expedition (anthology), 253

"Amazon Nation," 236

Amazon Odyssey (Atkinson), 265–66

American Bar Association, 325

American Civil Liberties Union, 323, 324, 325. *See also* New York Civil Liberties Union

American Communist Party, 8. *See also* Communism

American Dream, The (Myrdal), 6

American Federation of Teachers, 325

American Library Association, 330

American Museum of Natural History, 297

American Psychiatric Association (APA), x, 301, 319, 324

American Psychological Association, 13

"America's Peace Poll" (antiwar petition), 8

Aquarius (GLF) Cell. *See* GLF

Ardery, Breck, 217

Army, U.S.: policies toward homosexuals, 22, 23, 28, 32

Assimilation. *See* Acculturation/assimilation

Association of Stock Exchange Brokers, 204

Atkinson, Ti-Grace, 56, 235, 253, 258, 262–68 *passim,* 333

Aurelio, Richard, 155–56, 201

Baba, Meher, 81

Bacciocco, Edward, 85

"Bachelors Anonymous," 8

Ballard, Ron, 82, 88, 89, 139

Bar(s), gay, 121, 168; police harassment and closings of, x, 35–36, 38, 41, 42, 45, 71–74, 115, 139, 153–54, 177, 179, 209–12, 221 (*see also* Stonewall Inn); underworld/Mafia/"Syndicate"/ control of, 36, 38, 73, 74–75, 79, 140, 167, 209–12, 339n13; legitimization of, 39, 59, 74, 75, 150; lesbian, 52, 240; closing-time laws and, 211. *See also*